BLACK WOMEN OF THE HARLEM RENAISSANCE ERA

BLACK WOMEN OF THE HARLEM RENAISSANCE ERA

Edited by
Lean'tin L. Bracks
Jessie Carney Smith

ROWMAN & LITTLEFIELD

Lanham • Boulder • New York • London

Published by Rowman & Littlefield
A wholly owned subsidary of The Rowman & Littlefield Publishing Group, Inc.
4501 Forbes Boulevard, Suite 200, Lanham, Maryland 20706
www.rowman.com

16 Carlisle Street, London W1D 3BT, United Kingdom

British Library Cataloguing in Publication Information Available

Library of Congress Cataloging-in-Publication Data
Black Women of the Harlem Renaissance Era / edited by Lean'tin L. Bracks,
Jessie Carney Smith.
     pages cm
  Includes bibliographical references and index.
  ISBN 978-0-8108-8542-4 (cloth : alk. paper) — ISBN 978-0-8108-8543-1 (ebook)
1. American literature—African American authors—Encyclopedias. 2. African American
women authors—Biography. 3. Harlem Renaissance—Encyclopedias. 4. African American
women artists—Biography. 5. African American arts—20th century. 6. African Americans in
literature—Encyclopedias. 7. Harlem (New York, N.Y.)—Intellectual life—20th century—
Encyclopedias. I. Bracks, Lean'tin L., editor. II. Smith, Jessie Carney, 1930- editor.
  PS153.N5B557 2014
  810.9'928708996073—dc23
                                                                    2014016465
  ISBN 978-0-8108-9502-7 (pbk : alk. paper)

Printed in the United States of America

To the black women of the Harlem Renaissance Era
and the women who supported their vision.

CONTENTS

PREFACE

The "other side" has not been represented by one who "lives there." And not many can more sensibly realize and more accurately tell the weight and the fret of the "long, dull pain" than the open-eyed but hitherto voiceless black woman of America.

—Anna Julia Cooper, 1856–1964

One of the goals of every scholar is to produce works that add to and enhance the understanding and discussion of a time period, event, or idea. One of the ways that we have chosen to address this goal in this text is to reclaim the life stories and legacies of individuals who have contributed to the progress and humanizing of the United States. It is the era that includes the Harlem Renaissance and the often unrealized or limited exploration of black women's lives that are revealed in this text. Researching black women of the Harlem Renaissance era serves to enhance the cultural and political involvement of a people who, by 1919, had only been established on paper as citizens for fifty-four years. There was much work to be done by black Americans to remove and destroy systematic racism and disrespect, as well as change hearts and attitudes. Although the Harlem Renaissance primarily focuses on a literary and artistic awakening as achieved through opportunity and access, it also speaks to the determination of women to change and transform their lives and the quality of life for their families, and express their own desires to be full partners in every way. Women of this era did not limit themselves to one aspect of transformation, but they challenged and redefined many aspects of society.

When one speaks of a renaissance person, a vision of a multitalented, educated activist and role model comes to mind, but seldom does that vision include women. Women during this period were multitasking in spheres beyond the home and impacting families and communities both within and outside of the black community.

As renaissance women, they operated in multiple spheres of change, while opening the door of possibilities for others. Black women found opportunities to work outside the home or take on roles that may have previously only been held by men, or they took to the streets to challenge systems, racism, and discrimination. The contributions of these women can be accessed in this text alphabetically or through their talents and various roles, from activists and entertainers to anthropologists and writers and much more. In researching the era, we also found it important to recognize the lives of white women who aided black women in creating change.

Those interested in the Harlem Renaissance era and the role of black women in society at this juncture in American and African American political, social, and economic history, and those with an interest in the ingenuity and determination of the human spirit, will find this text an interesting, informative, and affirming view of this time period, which extended from 1919 to 1940. Whether the reader is familiar with the significant figures of the time period, one who browses through the alphabetical listing for names unfamiliar yet intriguing, or one who is seeking names in various categories as presented by the appendix, there is much to know and learn about all aspects of this era, which is inclusive of such artists and creators as sculptor Meta Warrick Fuller, textile designer Lois Mailou Jones, and composer Florence Smith Price. Biographies include entrepreneur Lillian Harris Dean, orchestra leader Marie Lucas, playwright Eulalie Spence, and sociologist Elizabeth Ross Haynes. The life stories of the women of the Harlem Renaissance era are told in such a way as to inspire further exploration of these important figures both individually and collectively and actualize their legacies by reclaiming a compilation of stories about lives well lived.

By casting our net widely, we embraced several white women who helped a number of black women along their way and became renaissance luminaries. For the financial support that these women provided, their work in founding black organizations, or their influence with publishers to recognize the work of black renaissance women, they are recognized as patrons of the era. Thus, we include in our alphabetical list such women of means as Charlotte Osgood Mason, affectionately known as "Godmother" (a term that Mason encouraged her beneficiaries to use); Mary White Ovington, a cofounder of the National Association for the Advancement of Colored People; and Annie Nathan Meyer, founder of Barnard College.

We chose an easy arrangement of the book, beginning with the preface and continuing through the chronology, introduction, entrants, sources, index, and a listing of editors and contributors. While we preferred to include numerous illustrations, we were required to limit the size of our work. Hence, there are some images of women of the Harlem Renaissance era. Our restrictions further led us to limit the length of the entries, yet we were tempted to say much more about these fascinating women. The cross-references will guide the reader to names by which an entrant may also be recognized.

As a result of our efforts, this work also offers new ways to view the Harlem Renaissance and a means to further acknowledge the people and forces that made the time such a pivotal period in the early twentieth century. The more one recognizes and shares the stories, the more the cultural breadth and depth of perseverance, ingenuity, and belief in the inner voice—verses worldly exclusion—is revealed. Women of the Harlem Renaissance era immersed themselves in the changing times, while engaging the worst and enjoying the best that this time had to offer.

In our efforts to create a thought-provoking, illuminating, and engaging text, we would like to thank our writers for researching, writing entries, and helping to make this work possible. It is appropriate that we thank Aisha M. Johnson, special collections librarian at the John Hope and Aurelia E. Franklin Library at Fisk University, for scanning a carefully selected group of photographs. We are also grateful to Bobby Bracks, an accomplished artist, for photographing a rare and original work, and all others who contributed their time, enthusiasm, and encouragement to this project.

> She sang of their sorrows; she sang of their hopes; she gave them relief by singing of love, or faith, or God. She personified the needs of the people of her day. And incidentally, she made a million dollars.
>
> —Ethel Waters, 1896–1977

CHRONOLOGY

Note: There were numerous firsts during this period, but the focus of this section is to shed light on the political contributions that often go unnoted, as well as key events and statistics reflective of the times and cultural moments and practices.

1919

Jessie Redmond Fauset, literary editor for *Crisis* magazine, has an immeasurable impact on the opportunities and exposure of African American artists through her work.

Madam C. J. Walker (Sarah Breedlove), renowned black female millionaire and black hair product business woman, dies of a stroke at fifty-one.

Red Summer (a name given to a period of race riots) erupts in Charleston, South Carolina; Longview, Texas; Washington, D.C.; Chicago, Illinois; Kansas City, Kansas; Kansas City, Missouri; and other American cities. Altogether, twenty-five riots erupt. Most are initiated by whites who attack black soldiers and other blacks in fear of competition for jobs and housing.

1920

The Nineteenth Amendment is passed. Black women in the North have some access to voting, while black women in the South are prevented from partaking in the voting process by the same violent and terrorizing measures used to disenfranchise black men in the South.

Thirty-eight percent of black women are wage earners.

1920s

In Harlem, 96.5 percent of black women are employed as houseworkers/maids and laundresses. Department stores bar black women from being employed as salespeople and clerical workers, while many companies bar them as employees entirely.

Semblances of slave markets are created in white neighborhoods in New York, Philadelphia, and Chicago, where black women gather and white women come to bargain for day workers or hire for other domestic jobs.

1920

Mamie Smith records "You Can't Keep a Good Man Down" on the Okeh label in New York City and becomes the first black woman to record a song.

1921

The first Africa American women to receive Ph.D. degrees are Georgiana Simpson, from the University of Chicago; Sadie Tanner Mossell Alexander, from the University of Pennsylvania; and Eva Dykes, from Radcliff.

Florence Mills, the first black female headliner on Broadway, joins the Harlem production of *Shuffle Along*, a musical by Noble Sissle and Eubie Blake. The production runs for 504 performances and also launches the careers of Josephine Baker and Caterina Jarboro.

1922

The Dyer Antilynching Bill, supported by African American Club women, passes the House, 230 votes to 119, but is killed by a filibuster in the Senate. Fifty-one blacks are lynched that year.

1923

The Cotton Club, owned by mobster Owney Madden, caters only to white patrons. The servers and entertainers are all black. Female entertainers are subjected to the "paper bag" test and hired only if they are lighter in complexion than a paper bag.

1924

Mary McLeod Bethune is named president of the National Association of Colored Women's Clubs. She serves until 1928.

Ora Washington begins her career in tennis and ultimately wins seven consecutive titles in the American Tennis Association. Her extraordinary record lasts until 1937.

The only female member of the United Negro Improvement Association to Liberia is Henrietta Vinton Davis.

1927

Eleven women are lynched between 1918 and 1927, three of them pregnant.

1928

Majorie Stewart Joyner (1896–1994) is one of the first black women to receive a patent. Her product is a hair waving machine.

1929

The stock market crashes and the Great Depression begins.

1930

Four out of every ten graduates in the black community are women.

1932

Tom-Tom, the first opera produced by a black woman, Shirley Graham McCanns (the second wife of W. E. B. Du Bois), opens in October. The production is staged and performed by an all-black cast and premiers in Cleveland, Ohio.

1933

Billie Holiday makes her first recording, *Your Mother's Son-in-Law*, with the Benny Goodman Orchestra.

1935

The National Council of Negro Women is founded in New York City. Mary McLeod Bethune becomes the first president.

1935

Riot erupts in Harlem in response to unemployment and racism.

1937

"Torchy Brown in Dixie to Harlem" is the first black female character in a comic strip. She deals with issues of racism, bigotry, and sexism, while being smart, young, independent, and attractive.

1938

The first black female legislator, Crystal Bird Fauset, is elected to the Pennsylvania legislature.

Rosetta Tharpe receives national acclaim as she performs a gospel revival at the famed Cotton Club nightclub in Harlem, New York.

1939

Hattie McDaniel receives an Oscar for Best Supporting Actress for playing Mammy, a servant, in the film *Gone with the Wind*.

Marian Anderson sings at the Lincoln Memorial for a crowd of 75,000 after she is denied permission to sing at Constitution Hall by the Daughters of the American Revolution, only because she was black.

1940

The Selective Service Act is passed. The act is amended to include African American nurses but fails to address the issue of discrimination.

Sixty percent of all black women in the labor force are still employed in domestic service.

INTRODUCTION

The Harlem Renaissance Era, 1919–1940

The Harlem Renaissance is considered one of the premier literary periods for the creative and intellectual blossoming of African American expression. The goal of this period was to reject the overall stereotypes regarding African Americans and confront the racist, social, political, and economic ideas that denied citizenship and access to the "American Dream." The study of the Harlem Renaissance period has encompassed years as early as 1914 to 1919 through 1930 to 1945. It was set in motion by social and political changes in the nation and the vision of African American scholars and intellectuals, while being supported by promoters and mentors, black and white.

The majority of the recognized literary and artistic contributors to this period were black males, but black women, motivated yet limited by the expectations of societal roles, were also key players. Some records of women's contributions during the early twentieth century attest to their success, as shown in the 1916 publication *Who's Who in Colored America*, which is comprised of 131 men and only 8 women, with 124 of the men and all of the women of mixed blood. Women's acknowledged participation in the Harlem Renaissance from an artistic perspective has been explored since that time, but only a portion of the broader picture has been presented that shows women's roles in the transformation of individual and community concerns within black America.

To fully realize the breadth of these contributions and struggles in the years that include the Harlem Renaissance, it is important to research the era that encompasses the full scope of influences from 1919, with the Great Migration and the Red Summer, to 1940, and the last vestiges of opportunities after the Great Depression and before World War II. These dates, which encompass the Harlem Renaissance, allow the investigation of contributions by black women in the areas of education, activism, entertainment, entrepreneurship, literary and creative areas, and professional roles, as well as supporters of these endeavors. It is also important to acknowledge the role of white women, who, in pursuing their own place in American society, sought to render aid, creativity, and support in fostering the creative energies of this period.

AFTER RECONSTRUCTION TO THE END OF WORLD WAR I: 1877–1918

After the legal end of the institution of slavery with the Thirteenth Amendment in 1865, Radical Reconstruction, beginning in 1867, became the governmental tool for transforming the South and repositioning freed slaves within this new national identity. The new generation of black Americans took full advantage of the reconstructed South in political, social, and economic arenas. Women, in particular, who had been key participants in the abolitionist movement, expanded their roles during Reconstruction to include leadership, administrative, and political involvement. As the government-supported Reconstruction ended in 1877, black Americans in both the South and North were presented with a legal sense of citizenship with the Fourteenth Amendment (1868), along with the Fifteenth Amendment (1870), which gave black men the right to vote.

The late nineteenth and early twentieth centuries brought economic and political opportunities to immigrants and other groups, but, by 1900, most blacks had become legally disenfranchised and were confronted with violence and murder on a daily basis. In truth, black men and women were faced with the reality that racist- and gender-based stereotypes remained fundamental in the national consciousness. With a shift in group dynamics in the North and a heightened sense of group potential, even in the throes of segregation, in the South, black women engaged in a sphere of "autonomy, consumption, mobility, and performance" that had previously been inconsistent or inappropriate for the roles designated for them (Lindsey 2010, 176). They rejected the perceptions established by stereotypical roles and the "occupational and familial responsibilities [that sought] to dictate the boundaries of their lives" (Lindsey 2010, 176). Black women, in seeking their identity, also envisioned their roles as integral to the community, while at the same time not determined by obligation or economics.

With potential access to political power through the vote for women, black women intensified their efforts to confront negative factors in every aspect of their lives. Their roles within and beyond the church became even more crucial, as family and faith were the defense against a segregated, violent, and hypocritical American legal and social system. White women who often rejected blacks as equal participants in the struggle for rights had many who "broke ranks" and offered aid, new perspectives, and creative opportunities during the twentieth century.

Women's active role in missionary societies, auxiliaries, and national conventions became the foundation for the women's club movement. By 1917, the black women's club movement, which represented more than 50,000 primarily middle-class black women, supported the ideas of home and family, but also self-awareness and reform. As the century progressed, black women continued to champion their own inclusion regarding women's suffrage, challenge industry and unions regarding equal pay and employment, and take on more leadership roles in religious and community organizations. They also confronted such social atrocities as lynching and terrorism by white supremacist groups and organized and promoted education and opportunities for black women and black Americans.

Black women recognized particularly through the suffrage movement that their participation in the vote could help ensure community well-being and thus familial progress and safety. The vote was the only way to secure their voice to obtain economic opportunities, since most were in menial jobs that were part of a growing movement of unionization to secure equal pay. The organization House of Ruth declared that because black women were primarily wage earners, they needed the vote for protection. This was combined with the fact that black male voters had been terrorized and tortured to eliminate their vote. With the end of World War I in 1918, and the return of white males to the work force, by 1919, black men and women had to struggle for employment of any kind to make a decent living.

Although not aligning with the white suffrage movement until 1916, it was apparent to black women that their rights as voters were not fully supported. White suffragists had made alliances with racist thinkers that would have resulted in the exclusion of black women's voices. In 1918, a bill was introduced by white Southerners, including Congressman John Williams from Mississippi, that would allow only white women to vote. Black women strategically campaigned, marched, protested, and subsequently blocked support of the bill and similar amendments. With the passage of women's right to vote with the Nineteenth Amendment in 1920, black women clearly saw their contributions in the national suffrage movement stained by racial and gender stereotypes that were pervasive in the American perspective. Their resistance to staying in their socially assigned place encouraged an activism that promised to "lift others as they climbed."

Black women created coalitions and organizations that openly challenged national and community issues and sought to influence and change economic and social decisions. They continued to break both racial and gender barriers and enter professional and skill-based careers. Many were attending college, and some, for example, Mary McLeod Bethune, even started their own schools. Although breaking new ground, most black women were still relegated to domestic and menial jobs (Giddings 1984, 74–77). Since the abolition of slavery was only a little more than fifty years in the past at that time, black women continued to draw on generations of cultural ingenuity that had sustained their very existences in the face of physical and mental attack. Black Americans took every opportunity to be educated and become economically self-sufficient and politically active.

A NEW ERA: 1919

By 1919, black women had made enormous progress in industry and other economic ventures and were a key presence in areas both North and South due to opportunities created during World War I. Many found employment in venues other than as domestic workers. With the end of World War I, there was a siege of violence, riots, murder, and terrorism imposed on black Americans as a response to black servicemen and women returning from the conflict. Often still wearing their uniforms, those returning were met with torment and lynching as their open claim to their rights and citizenship enflamed whites who had been accustomed to more "accommodating" blacks. This clash resulted in the Red Summer of 1919, with riots and violence that erupted in more than twenty-five American cities. This attitude of racial hate also resulted in the termination of opportunities in the work place and areas outside the domestic sphere.

In response to this violence, the economic downturn, and the continuing absence of equality, black women became more active in finding ways to uplift the race and redefine their own image while dealing with the decrease in manufacturing and professional jobs. Domestic service, which was a key part of black peoples' legacy of struggle, once again became almost the singular source of employment. "Light-skinned blacks were able to use their social capital or skin privilege to find jobs, sometimes by 'passing' for white, but when their race was discovered, they often were demoted or dismissed" (Dorman 2010, 84). Overall, in spite of economic challenges, racial pride was encouraged and promoted by the community, which, although segregated, was determined to affect change with regard to equality and citizenship.

Black women were bound by racism and further defined and limited by over-sexualized gender stereotypes and perceived limited intellectual abilities. As they became more of a presence in the work force, family and women's place in the home were impacted by their evolving identity. Many black women were marrying later and having fewer children, and the issue of their sexuality was a key focus, particularly in how it related to the "Cult of True Womanhood," a Western Christian perspective of the role of women in society (Giddings 1984, 137). This concept required submission and dependence, while the survival of the black woman and her family and community required participation, leadership, and independence.

The national reform movement, which advocated and offered birth control for all women, challenged the narrowness of women's lives and further impacted the roles of women. By 1918, the Women's Political Association of Harlem, New York, offered the first open lectures to black women regarding birth control, along with many other organizations and groups who would later follow their lead. In spite of this, the debate in the black community was waged regarding birth control as impacting community survival, racism, and sexual exploitation. As women sought ownership of their bodies and opportunities to enrich their minds, others challenged this as race suicide and an attack on the traditional roles of women, as voiced by such antifeminist figures as Kelly Miller, dean of Howard University (Hine, Hine, and Harrold 2003, 129). It took until almost the 1930s for this reform movement to secure a prominent place in the black community and be operated by the black community.

Black women maintained their roles as activists and advocates, a reflection of African cultural traditions in defiance of masculine Western Christianity and culture, and encouraged a feminist perspective and the idea of the New Negro premise of "self-respect and self-dependence" (Locke 2004, 985). Middle-class women promoted women's voices in the home and the work force through such organizations as the National Association of Colored Women, which, by the mid-1920s, had nearly 200,000 members. As more and more women had to work low-paying and largely domestic jobs, much of their individual gains were secondary to the need to resist poverty.

THE HARLEM RENAISSANCE

Harlem was the destination of many black Americans who migrated from the South, West, and Southwest seeking safety, opportunities, and positive change, while participating in the exhilaration and cultural celebration that was promised them by black newspapers, letters, and word of mouth. Well into the 1920s and 1930s, blacks migrated in hopes of better economic opportunities and the realization of their dreams. Although Harlem is seen as the urban center of black creativity, it served as a destination more so than the singular source of creativity. Urban cities and many communities in various locations in the North, like Harlem and Washington, D.C., were thriving literary creative centers, but this burgeoning of energy was also seen in cities and communities in states in the South, West, and Southwest, for instance, Texas, Oklahoma, California, Missouri, Kansas, Nebraska, Washington, and New Mexico, as well as other communities (Glasrud and Wintz 2012, 8). Research regarding the Harlem Renaissance has established it as a national phenomenon that served as a model and template for this cultural explosion.

Although other areas, through a centralized community effort to challenge artistic stereotypes, sought to recreate the energy that drew many to the Harlem section of New York City, Harlem had a unique combination of factors. With a network of white supporters, black publications, and intellectual promotion through the presence of the headquarters for some of the largest black political organizations in the nation, Harlem became the ultimate place of opportunity for creativity and the possibility of recognition, as well as extended opportunities to create.

During the Harlem Renaissance era, black women were seen "more in terms of their femininity, which broke racist and sexist stereotypes of the past, than from a feminist perspective that assumedly reflected a perspective of aggressiveness and male-hating" (Giddings 1984, 183). In the midst of this, black women redefined their roles as uneducated and submissive individuals and transformed themselves into partners in the struggle for equal rights and justice. A sense of pride regarding the black woman was presented in major black periodicals of the time, including *Crisis*, *Opportunity*, and particularly the January 1924 issue of *Messenger*, which announces its goal to "show in pictures, as well as writing, Negro women who are unique, accomplished, beautiful, intelligent, industrious, talented, and successful" (Giddings 1984, 185).

In religion, the role of "mothers" in the church and their ability to act within a degree of autonomy and independence while sharing power to some degree reflects on the "precolonial social philosophies of West Africa, which do not support sexual oppression" (Gilkes 2001, 61). Many black women became popular in the realm of music and theater. Singers and dancers like Florence Mills thrilled their audiences in such Harlem productions as *Dixie to Broadway* and *Blackbirds*, while others, for example, Adeliade Hall, who also danced in *Blackbirds*, later opened their own nightclubs in London and Paris. In Omaha, vocalists the likes of Anna Mae Winburn, who gained prominence as director of the female band International Sweethearts of Rhythm, and mezzo-soprano Lena Louisa Johnson, from Tacoma, Washington, who starred in *Ethiopia at the Bar of Justice* in 1927, came to the forefront (Glasrud and Wintz 2012, 218). Such writers as Zanzye H. Hill, who studied law at the University of Nebraska at Lincoln and became the institution's first black female law school graduate, wrote poetry reflective of Harlem Renaissance themes, poems that were published in the Alpha Kappa Alpha publication *Ivy Leaf* in 1928 (Glasrud and Wintz 2012, 135). Poets like Anne Spencer, Mae Cowdery, and Effie Lee Newsome found outlets for their work in other well-known black journals and compilations, including Alain Locke's book *The New Negro* (1925). And premier writers the likes of Zora Neale Hurston, Jessie Redmon Fauset, and Nella Larsen were widely known and received acclaim, as they served as examples of the full potential of women's creativity.

Artistic expression by black women covered the gamut of creativity, from painting and sculpting to theater and dance. Although the period focused on the validation of the black genius and the ability to create art as the highest form of human endeavor, black women were not only key players in these movements, they were confronting barriers in all aspects of American society and changing how they were perceived as citizens and partners.

THE GREAT DEPRESSION: 1935–1940

As a result of the stock market crash of 1929 and other negative impacts on the national economy, opportunities and economic progress that blacks had made diminished and almost entirely disappeared with the Great Depression of 1935. As early as 1931, job opportunities for black women had decreased by 25 percent in every major city with a sizeable black population. Many found themselves fighting for survival on levels of poverty akin to the days of slavery. The depression had a devastating effect on black women who were concentrated in domestic service in the North, as many families who had previously been employers of blacks coming to the North were no longer able to support hires. For those who were able to find work, the pay was barely enough and few other options existed.

Black women's survival during the Depression also required self-sufficiency and hard work, as well as collective ingenuity and women helping women. Many resorted to catching and selling fish, selling wares grown in their gardens, and selling baked goods or whatever it took to survive. Many of these entrepreneurial ventures kept families alive. Black women's response to this economic crisis was to become more proactive in women helping women and become contributors to organizations that supported economic and social equality. Their efforts went beyond continued participation in club organizations. They were extraordinary in their support of such community organizations as the National Association for the Advancement of Colored People; the Harlem Housewives Cooperative; the Women's Day Workers in Harlem; the Federation of Negro Women in the twin cities of St. Paul and Minneapolis, which promoted the development of political and social ideas of the New Negro; and the Detroit Housewives' League, which, by 1934, had 10,000 members.

From the 1930s to 1940s, many who made up the Harlem Renaissance as an artistic movement based in Harlem had departed to other cities, as a lack of publishing opportunities and interest by white benefactors and audiences in black creativity had diminished. Unemployment and discrimination against blacks was fueled by racism and supported by segregation. As a result of black women's organizations and civil rights organizations, marches and protests were orchestrated on local and national fronts for fair and equal pay. This direct action and the entrance of the United States into World War II opened employment opportunities and intensified the movement by the black community to receive equal opportunity based on citizenship rights and not the exploitation of workers due to the needs of war or other exploitive situations reminiscent of slavery.

In spite of these advances and reversals, black women had clear goals in meeting the ongoing challenges in the United States. They chose to focus on such political and economic issues as antilynching laws and unionization to secure safety and economic equality, pursue creative ventures to change the intellectual and creative myths of inferiority regarding race and gender, and support and create clubs and organizations that actively challenged inequality and injustice and promoted racial uplift. Their activism was also religious, social, and community based. Having the ancestral legacy of resistance and agitation that helped to orchestrate the ultimate ending of slavery provided black women with the spiritual fortitude to survive and thrive in the changing times of the twentieth century. Black women made their presence known during the Harlem Renaissance era, which encompasses the Great Migration, the Red Summer, the Harlem Renaissance, and the Great Depression, through involvement as artists, entrepreneurs, writers, poets, educators, activists, journalists, organizers, entertainers, religious leaders, and contributors in all aspects of American society.

BIBLIOGRAPHY

Bennett, Lerone, Jr. *Before the Mayflower*. Chicago: Johnson Publishing, 2003.

Dorman, Jacob S., "Back to Harlem: Abstracts and Everyday Labor during the Harlem Renaissance." In Jeffrey O. Ogbar, ed. *The Harlem Renaissance Revisited: Politics, Arts, and Letters*, 74–92. Baltimore, MD: John Hopkins University Press, 2010.

Franklin, John Hope, and Evelyn Brooks Higginbotham. *From Slavery to Freedom*, 9th ed. New York: McGraw-Hill, 2011.

Giddings, Paula. *When and Where I Enter*. New York: Bantam, 1984.

Gilkes, Cheryl Townsend. *If It Wasn't for the Women . . . : Black Women's Experience and Womanist Culture in Church and Community*. Maryknoll, NY: Orbis, 2001.

Glasrud, Bruce A., and Cary D. Wintz. *The Harlem Renaissance in the American West*. New York: Routledge, 2012.

Gordon, Linda. *Woman's Body, Woman's Right: Birth Control in America*. New York: Penguin, 1990.

Guy-Sheftall, Beverly, ed. *Words of Fire: An Anthology of African American Feminist Thought*. New York: New Press, 1995.

Hine, Darlene Clark, William C. Hine, and Stanley Harrold. *The African American Odyssey*, vol. 2. Upper Saddle, NJ: Prentice Hall, 2003.

Honey, Maureen, ed. *Shadowed Dreams: Women's Poetry of the Harlem Renaissance*. New Brunswick, NJ: Rutgers University Press, 1989.

Kaplan, Carla. *Miss Anne in Harlem: The White Women of the Black Renaissance*. New York: HarperCollins, 2013.

Lewis, Jone Johnson. "African American History and Women Timeline, 1920–1929." *About.com Women's History*. Available online at http://womenshistory.about.com/od/aframwomentimeline/a/aaw1920_time.htm.

Lindsey, Treva B. "Configuring Modernities: New Negro Womanhood in the Nation's Capital, 1890–1940." *Duke University Libraries Electronic Theses and Dissertations*, 2010. Available online at www.dukespace.lib.duke.edu/dspace/handle/10161/2409.

Locke, Alain. "The New Negro." In Henry Louis Gates Jr. and Nellie Y. McKay, eds., *Norton Anthology of African American Literature*, 2nd ed., 984–93. New York: W. W. Norton & Co., 2004.

Ross, Loretta J. "African American Women and Abortion." In Rickie Solinger, ed., *Abortion Wars: A Half-Century of Struggle, 1950–2000*, 161–208. Berkeley: University of California Press, 1998.

Wall, Cheryl. *Women of the Harlem Renaissance*. Bloomington: Indiana University Press, 1995.

Wilkerson, Isabel. *The Warmth of Other Suns*. New York: Vintage, 2010.

Wintz, Carl. *Black Culture and the Harlem Renaissance*. Houston, TX: Rice University Press, 1988.

A

ADAMS, ELIZABETH LAURA
(February 9, 1909–September 9, 1982) Writer

Elizabeth Laura Adams was among the first African American women whose writing has become a key part of Catholic literary works. As writers of the Harlem Renaissance era found ways to express themselves and define and discover their place, Adams chose to explore her spiritual life as a "young colored woman" who saw Catholicism as her spiritual goal. Her audience, although primarily white, saw a different perspective through her religious musings. Her autobiography of her spiritual awakening offers a journey toward peace and spirituality that culminates in her conversion to Catholicism. Her experiences as an African American who found a religious home in the Catholic church remains one of the key recommended readings for this faith. Adams's writing, which began in the late 1920s and 1930s after her father's death, focuses on her religious musing, for example, the work "The Finding of a Soul," published in 1930, and other earlier poems and writings.

Born February 9, 1909, in Santa Barbara, California, Adams became an only child with the death of her infant brother. Her family, which was Methodist, strongly encouraged Adams's commitment to her faith, but she feared the conversion, which, for church members, consisted of shouts and screams of frenzied emotions. Forbidden to pursue Catholicism primarily by her father, it was after his death in 1924 that Adams sought out the Catholic experience. When she graduated from high school, her mother gave her permission to convert.

Adams had always had an interest in art, music, and literature, thanks to her mother's influence, and she submitted poems and essays to both literary and religious publications. She published "The Finding of a Soul" in 1930, and received a moderate degree of popularity for her work inclusive of the award she received from the *Morning Star* and the favorable review for her poem "Consecration." Unfortunately, the literary club that favored her poem refused to publish it when they discovered she was a black woman. Racism was continually part of Adams's life, from being denied communion to not being allowed to attend a Catholic school. Her mother, who operated from accommodating views, as espoused by Booker T. Washington, taught Adams to dismiss the anger of racism and pray for the offender.

In her journey for peace regarding racism and spiritual fulfillment, Adams decided to write about her personal journey in an essay series entitled "There Must Be a God . . . Somewhere: A True Story of a Convert's Search for God," printed in 1941, in *Torch*, a national Catholic magazine. As a result of its success, she published the compiled work as *Dark Symphony* in 1942, which serves as her most important work. This autobiography not only details the importance of poetry and music in her life, but it is structured thematically to address many topics. Even though Adams acknowledges that dismissing racism, as she was taught, may not have been the best solution and that faith does not eradicate evil, she still concludes her journey with the sense that through faith comes peace and salvation.

Dark Symphony, Adams's most important work, reached a broad audience. The Catholic church embraced her autobiography, while many blacks saw her passive and patient response to racism as submissive and accommodating. Supported by the Catholic church, the book was reprinted for readers in Great Britain and Italy and printed in Dutch. As a seminal text in the Catholic religious tradition and an importation inclusion to conversion narratives found in American and African American traditions, her book continued to be recommended well into 1959 in the *National Catholic Almanac*. Although the success of the book sustained Adams and allowed her to care for herself and mother for more than ten years, Adams had to take on other jobs as a result of poor health for them both. She took positions as a secretary, domestic worker, and maid to sustain her family. Adams continued to live in Santa Barbara for the remainder of her life.—LEAN'TIN L. BRACKS

ALIX, MAE [MAY OR LIZA]
(August 31, 1902–?) Blues, cabaret, and jazz vocalist

During the 1920s and 1930s, Mae Alix was known as the "Queen of the Nightclubs." Because of her popularity, several entertainers, including famed jazz and blues singer, Alberta Hunter, used the pseudonym May Alix or Mae Alix on recordings.

The real Mae Alix was born in Chicago. She began performing as a teenager in local cabarets and night spots after winning a talent contest. Her voice and stage charisma were recognized by bandleader Jimmie Noone, who was headlining at Chicago's Apex Club. With Noone, she performed and recorded several songs, including "Ain't Misbehavin." She was also billed as the "Queen of the Splits" because of the inclusion of running splits in her act.

Alix's Chicago venues included the DeLuxe 400 Lounge, Club DeLisa, and the Sunset Club. Her fame spread to Harlem, Los Angeles, and Parisian night spots. She is remembered for catching the attention of the greatest jazz musician of any era—Louis Armstrong. With his Hot Five band, they recorded "Big Butter and Egg Man" on November 16, 1926, which became Armstrong's first chart hit. Alix also worked with bandleaders Luis Russell, Carroll Dickerson, Ollie Powers, and Duke Ellington. Her marriage to pianist and songwriter Warley Asher ended in divorce. She retired from the business in 1941.—GLORIA HAMILTON

ANDERSON, HALLIE
(January 5, 1885–November 9, 1927) Dance orchestra conductor

Dance orchestra conductor Hallie Anderson turned her talents to directing theater bands during the Harlem Renaissance era. She was one of the young black women who were musical pacesetters for all-male, all-female, and mixed-gender groups. When she was with an orchestra, however, Anderson was always wielding the baton.

Anderson was born in Lynchburg, Virginia, and, while still a child, she and her family moved to New York City. There she studied music in three settings, with a private teacher, in the public schools, and at New York German Conservatory of Music. Early in the twentieth century, Anderson formed and led dance orchestras. She also gave concerts with the New Amsterdam Musical Association Band. Her 100-piece orchestra was different for that period, for it was integrated by gender and race. She handled her own business matters for her orchestras and advertised her work in the New York Age, offering an "orchestra for any occasion." Beginning in 1905, and extending for many years, Anderson promoted an Annual Reception and Ball. She directed a five-piece male orchestra at the Lafayette Theater in 1914, and, in the late 1910s and early 1920s, she was organist at Harlem's Douglas Theatre. She was again seen playing at the Lafayette in 1919, when she led a "lady band." Large dance orchestras fell out of vogue, prompting her to take her talents elsewhere. She then directed theater bands. During the 1920s, Anderson directed theater orchestras in Philadelphia. She died in New York City.—JESSIE CARNEY SMITH

ANDERSON, MARIAN
(February 27, 1897–April 8, 1993) Contralto, concert singer, opera singer

Marian Anderson was born in 1897, to John Anderson, an employee at the Reading Terminal Market, and Anna, a former teacher, in Philadelphia, Pennsylvania. She was the oldest of three daughters: Marian (1897), Alyse [Alice] (1900), and Ethel (1902); they were all musically talented. It was Marian for whom music was a passion. Throughout her life, she devoted her time and energy to honing her craft in spite of the limitations of race and poverty, which were rife in her career.

Anderson's career began when she was six years old, and she became a member of the junior choir at Union Baptist Church. Her musical career reflects the individualism and struggles against racism of the Harlem Renaissance. Her repertoire emphasizes the awareness of and need to keep alive the history of her people. She is recognized as the first black American opera singer, the foremother of later black opera performers, singing for the inauguration of presidents Dwight D. Eisenhower (1957) and John F. Kennedy (1961), and for the miles covered and number of performances during her transcontinental tours.

Like many musicians, Anderson's talents blossomed in the church; she was a natural contralto, sang soprano, and was capable of singing other parts in the choir.

Marian Anderson

In the church she performed duets and solos. She was supported by both the church and her family. Her father purchased a piano for her when she was six but was unable to pay for lessons. The girls taught themselves to play, and later Marian also taught herself to play the violin. At the age of thirteen, she joined the senior choir and began visiting and performing at other churches and gained increasing recognition. Anderson was encouraged to enroll in a music school in Philadelphia, but she was denied admission because of her race. During her senior year in high school, she was heard by Giuseppe Boghetti and offered lessons, but she initially could not afford the cost of instruction. Due to her financial constraints and performing successes, her study was financed by a variety of financial endeavors. Among these were performing at social gatherings, a special collection at Union Baptist, and benefits. The Philadelphia Choral Society's benefit concert garnered $500. Consequently, Anderson was able to study for varying periods of time under Emma Azalia Hackley, Mary Saunders Patterson, Giuseppe Boghetti, and Agnes Relfsnyder and expand her repertoire. In 1919, she sang to a crowd of thousands at the National Baptist Convention, U.S.A. Inc., in Atlantic City. William "Billy" King, her accompanist, became her manager and booked a concert for her on April 23, 1924, at New York City's Town Hall, which proved unsuccessful.

In spite of the Town Hall performance, Anderson's exposure, achievements, and earning power increased. She entered a contest sponsored by Philadelphia's Philharmonic Society and won, the first time a black person had done so. In 1925, she won a competition sponsored by Lewisohn Stadium in which there were 300 entries. Her prize was an appearance with the New York Philharmonics at Lewisohn Stadium. As a result, Anderson got a new manager, Arthur Johnson, a top concert manager, who put her under contract in 1926. She toured the eastern and southern United States. On December 30, 1926, Anderson performed a solo recital at Carnegie Hall that was a success; however, most of her performances were limited to black audiences. Like so many other black artists, she found Europe to be more receptive of her talents. She gained a scholarship thorough the National Association of Negro Musicians to study in Europe.

Anderson's European studies allowed her a brief stay in England and thus began her numerous trips across the Atlantic to study and perform. On September 16, 1930, she made her European debut at London's Wigmore Hall and later appeared at a Promenade Concert. She worked for a brief time and studied with Amanda Aldridge, renowned musician and daughter of the great African American Shakespearean actor Ira Aldridge. Following a lackluster period in Europe, Anderson returned to the United States, but, after a 1931 concert, she returned to Europe on a Julius Rosenwald scholarship to study in Germany. Her debut concert in Berlin attracted the attention of Rule Rasmussen and Helmer Enwall, managers who arranged a Scandinavian Tour; Enwall later became her manager for additional tours throughout Europe. Anderson returned to the United States and then to Europe in 1933, again through the Rosenwald Fund. During this time she sang before King Gustav in Stockholm; King Christian in Copenhagen; and John Sibelius, a Finnish composer who dedicated his song "Solitude" to her. She traveled throughout Europe, performing more than 100 concerts. In 1935, Anderson performed in Paris, Brussels, Geneva, and Vienna, ending her trip in Salzburg, at an international festival called the Mozarteum. It was following this performance that Sol Hurok, a manager, made a contract with her for U.S. concerts. She returned to the United States and performed on December 2, 1935, for the second time at New York City's Town Hall, and was a great success; she gave two concerts at Carnegie Hall and then toured the United States from coast to coast. She toured Europe again and Latin America through 1938, giving approximately 70 concerts per year.

By this time, Anderson was internationally known and received; however, the racial barriers that had confronted her during her career still permeated American society. In 1939, Hurok attempted to rent Constitutional Hall in Washington, D.C., for a concert, but the Daughters of the American Revolution (DAR), owners of the venue, denied her access because of her race. First Lady Eleanor Roosevelt immediately resigned her membership in the DAR; Walter White of the National Association for the Advancement of Colored People encouraged Harold Ickes, secretary of the interior, to arrange a free concert on the steps of the Lincoln Memorial on Easter Sunday, April 9. Anderson sang before 75,000 people, and millions listened on the radio; several weeks later, she gave a private concert at the White House, where Franklin D. Roosevelt was entertaining George VI and Queen Elizabeth of England. She appeared at Constitution Hall in several charity concerts during World War II.

In 1943, Anderson married Orpheus H. Fisher, a Delaware architect, and they lived on Maruianna Farm in Connecticut. In 1952, she made her television debut on the *Ed Sullivan Show*. In January 1955, Anderson performed as Ulrica in Verdi's *Un Ballo in Maschera* at the Metropolitan Opera House and was the first black American singer at the Met. In 1957, she traveled as a goodwill ambassador sponsored by the U.S. State Department and the American National Theater and Academy, performing twenty-four concerts in twelve weeks; this led to the filming of *The Lady from Philadelphia* for the CBS Television Network. In 1956, Anderson wrote *My Lord, What a Morning*, her autobiography. Her farewell performance took place on April 19, 1965, at New York's Carnegie Hall.

During her career and posthumously, Anderson received numerous awards and recognitions. Among them were the Spingarn Medal (1939); the Bok Award for an outstanding Philadelphia citizen (1941); the American Medal of Freedom, presented by President Lyndon Johnson (1963); and the National Medal of Arts, presented by President Ronald Reagan (1986). The U.S. Treasury also coined a half-ounce gold commemorative medal with her likeness (1980). In July 1992, Anderson moved to Portland, Oregon, to live with her nephew, conductor James DePriest. She died of heart failure.—HELEN R. HOUSTON

ANDREWS, REGINA M. ANDERSON
[URSALA OR URSULA TRELLING, HENRY SIMONS]

(May 21, 1901–February 5, 1993) Librarian, civic leader, playwright, arts patron, community activist

During the most productive years of the Harlem Renaissance, Regina M. Anderson Andrews became a highly visible figure by providing an intellectual center for the active young artists of that period at the library where she worked, as a participant in the cultural movement, and by making her apartment a social haven for artists.

Andrews, who had a multicultural background, was born in Chicago, on May 21, 1901, to William Grant Anderson, a New York attorney, and Margaret Simons Andrews. She was educated at Wilberforce University in Ohio, the University of Chicago, and City College of New York, and she received her degree in library science from Columbia University Library School. In 1926, she married lawyer and New York assemblyman William T. Andrews and had one daughter.

Before her marriage, Andrews, Ethel Ray Nance, and Louella Tucker shared an apartment on Sugar Hill, one of Harlem's most upscale residential areas. Their 580 Nicholas Avenue address became a place to meet the new cultural figures who came on the scene. It functioned as a literary salon and an intelligence outpost to identify new artists. Andrews and Nance then alerted the National Urban League's executive director of research, Charles S. Johnson, who was often called the "godfather of the Harlem Renaissance," of the new talent. Andrews also persuaded her supervisor, Ernestine Rose, of the 125th Street Branch of the New York Public Library (later renamed the Schomburg Center for Research in Black Culture), to set up a place in the basement to give the emerging artists a forum for presenting their talents. Andrews and Nance also helped instigate the formation of the Civic Club, which became a launching pad for the young and unknown artists, including Countee Cullen, Langston Hughes, and Jean Toomer, and a chance for them to meet W. E. B. Du Bois, Alain Locke, James Weldon Johnson, Carl Van Doren, and others who were in a position to help their careers.

As library assistant at the 135th Street Branch, Anderson was associated with Du Bois's Krigwa Players and advocated serious black drama. After the group disbanded in February 1929, Andrews, Dorothy Petersen, and several community leaders, including Jessie Redmon Fauset, Harold Jackman, and Ira De A. Reid, established the Negro Experimental Theater. The group relocated and also produced a number of plays, including several by Andrews and one of her first and later highly successful, *Jacob's Ladder*, performed in 1931. It also attracted Broadway star Rose McClendon, who gave expert direction. Andrews's other plays, written under the pseudonym Ursala or Ursula Trelling, included *The Man Who Passed, Matilda, and Underground*. She also used the pen name Henry Simons.

Andrews became the second vice president of the National Council of Women and National Urban League representative to the U.S. Commission for the United Nations Educational, Scientific, and Cultural Organization. She also worked with the State Commission for Human Rights. The Musical Arts Group Award and Community Heroine Award were given to her in recognition of her work. Before her retirement from the 135th Street Branch library, she became the first African American supervising librarian in the New York Public Library system and later moved to the Washington Heights Branch of the system. Andrews died in the New York City suburb Ossining.—JESSIE CARNEY SMITH

ARMSTRONG, LILLIAN "LIL" HARDING
(February 3, 1898–August 27, 1971) Musician, composer

One of America's great early jazz pianists, Lillian "Lil" Harding Armstrong spent fifty years in a successful musical career centered in Chicago and New York, and became the first woman to enter the jazz field. Beginning in the 1920s, she played with some of the great jazz musicians of that period, as well as such accomplished singers as the blues great Alberta Hunter. For many years, Armstrong organized and led her own band.

The Memphis-born Armstrong was the daughter of Dempsey Harding; nothing is said of her father. She took piano and organ lessons while still a child and was also pianist and organist at a church and school. She began her higher education at Fisk University in Nashville, and later studied at the Chicago College of Music and New York College of Music. After leaving Fisk in 1917, she joined her family in Chicago and started her professional career at Jones's Music Store, where she plugged songs and established contacts with important musicians. This led to her first major band experience, in 1918, with the Original New Orleans Creole Jazz Band, which played in swinging New Orleans style at the De Luxe Café. Armstrong joined a King Oliver-led band and, for six months in 1921, traveled to San Francisco with Oliver's Creole Jazz Band. By the summer of 1922, she had returned to her position in Chicago, with Oliver's original band. Then she met Louis Armstrong, who joined the band that year; their courtship led to marriage in 1924.

Lil, who recognized Louis Armstrong's talent and ability, had a marked influence on his life. She encouraged him to leave Oliver and join Fletcher Henderson and his band at the Roseland Ballroom in New York. She helped him become a better music reader and receive featured billing. She then organized her own band, the Dreamland Syncopators, performed at the Dreamland, and promoted Louis Armstrong as the "World's Greatest Trumpet Player." Between 1925 and 1929, Lil appeared on many of Louis's Hot Five and Hot Seven recordings, led some Hot Five dates as Lil's Hot Shots, and joined recordings with the group Butterbeans and Susie, Alberta Hunter, and the Red Onion Jazz Babies. She became productive as a composer of jazz songs and wrote many of them without her husband's assistance.

The Armstrongs returned to Chicago, and, in 1926, Lil's job at the Dreamland ended. She led all-female and all-male bands in the Midwest during the mid-1930s, at times appearing as Mrs. Louis Armstrong and Her Orchestra. Back in New York from 1936 to 1940, she had regular radio broadcasts and was soloist in the revue *Shuffle Along* (1933). She recorded on the Decca label under the name Lil Harding. Her compositions included "My Hi-De-Ho Man," "Born to Swing," and "Let's Get Happy Together." The Armstrongs divorced in 1938, and Lil continued with diverse and successful experiences.

In the 1940s, Lil returned to Chicago and held long engagements at local clubs, made several tours, became a soloist in Paris, lived in London for a while, and returned to Chicago in the late 1950s. Her recordings continued, and she participated in the telecast *Chicago and All That Jazz* and NBC's *DuPont Show of the Week*. She suffered a fatal heart attack on August 27, 1971, while performing at a memorial concert for Louis Armstrong held in Chicago.—JESSIE CARNEY SMITH

AUSTIN, LOVIE [CORA CALHOUN]
(September 19, 1887–July 10, 1972) Pianist, jazz singer, composer

Lovie Austin helped to enrich the lives of black female musicians of the Harlem Renaissance era with her own performances and compositions, as well as by working with such legendary figures as Gertrude "Ma" Rainey, Alberta Hunter, and Bessie Smith. In 1923, her combo, the Blue Serenaders, accompanied blues singer Gertrude "Ma" Rainey in her first recordings. Austin wrote "Graveyard Blues" for Bessie Smith and helped Alberta Hunter, who began to transcribe and copyright her early blues compositions.

Austin was born Cora Calhoun in Chattanooga, Tennessee, in 1887, and she died in Chicago in 1972. Her parents are unknown, and she may have been raised by her grandmother. Austin studied music theory and piano at Roger Williams University in Nashville, and later attended Knoxville College, both black institutions. She was married briefly to a movie house operator in Detroit, and later married a vaudeville performer named Austin, of the team Austin and Delaney. Some sources say that her second husband was Tommy Ladnier of the vaudeville circuit. Austin worked the vaudeville circuit and began to tour with the circuit in 1912. She later traveled with Irving Miller's *Blue Babies* revue. She managed, composed, arranged, and directed her own musical shows, including *Sunflower Girls* and *The Lovie Austin Revue*, a popular attraction at Club Alabam in New York City.

Austin was one of the first female pianists to accompany early blues singers, including Ida Cox, Gertrude "Ma" Rainey, and Ethel Waters, and she made her first recording in 1923, with Cox. Her collaborating instrumentalists included Louis Armstrong and Edward "Kid" Ory. Austin composed and arranged music for race records of the mid- and late 1920s. For twenty years, she arranged vaudeville improvised music for Chicago's Old Monogram Theater, where many leading black performers appeared. When her playing style fell out of vogue, Austin became a security inspector at a naval defense plant during World War II. She later worked at a dance school in Chicago and recorded for Capitol Records in 1946 and Riverside

Records in 1961. She retired in 1962, and died ten years later. A revived interest in women in jazz came in the 1970s and spurred renewed fascination with Austin's musical contributions.—JESSIE CARNEY SMITH

AYER, GERTRUDE ELISE JOHNSON MCDOUGALD
(October 11, 1884 or 1885–June 10, 1971) Educator, essayist, writer, activist

A multitalented contributor to the educational community during the Harlem Renaissance, Gertrude Elise Johnson McDougald Ayer took a stand that some women only dared to consider: racial and gender inequality. Her various writings, published in *Crisis* and *Opportunity* magazines, enabled her to make her views widely known. Despite her work, she was never considered part of the mainstream of the Harlem Renaissance.

Born on October 11, 1884, (or 1885), in New York City, Ayer was the daughter of Peter Augustus Johnson, who, among a variety of achievements, was a founder of the National Urban League. He also founded McDonough Memorial Hospital and was the third black American to practice medicine in New York City. Ayer's mother, Mary Elizabeth Whittle Johnson, was English and an expert in fine needle work. Ayer studied at Hunter College, City College of New York, New York University, and Columbia University, but she never obtained a college degree. She became a teacher at Public School 11 in Manhattan in 1905, and remained there until 1911, when she resigned and married Cornelius W. McDougald. They had two children. McDougald Sr. was the initial counsel for Marcus Garvey, a journalist, activist, and organizational founder who was tried for mail fraud in 1923. In 1928, she remarried, this time to A. V. Ayer, a medical doctor and district health officer in Harlem; he died in 1976.

Ayer remained active in areas of her professional interests and spent some time working with the New York Urban League. Beginning 1915, she was assistant industrial secretary and attracted the interest of the Women's Trade Union. The YMCA gave her financial support to conduct a survey entitled "New Day for the Colored Woman Worker," which examined the work of black women in New York. Ayer later headed the Woman's Department of the U.S. Labor Department Employment Bureau and became a counselor at Henry Street Settlement. In 1918, following the request of the Board of Education for New York Public Schools, Ayer initiated the counseling program for the local schools. She was a school administrator from 1924 to 1927, when she served as assistant principal of Public School 89 in Manhattan. She continued to speak and write about black women and employment, and she examined the stratification of these women in the job market and the discrimination that they encountered. Her article "The Task of Negro Womanhood," published in Alain Locke's *The New Negro* (1925), is an account of groups of women in the leisure class, business and the professions, and trades and industry.

In 1936, Ayer became the first African American woman to have a full-time principalship in New York City's public schools. She became principal of Public School 119 in 1945, and remained there until 1954, when she retired. Expressing her teaching philosophy, she said that education should combine academic and practical learning. While lacking a college degree, she believed that those with degrees may know their subject matter but do not necessarily know how to teach.

Ayer was active in numerous organizations, including the New York chapter of the Workers' Defense League, National Council of Women in Administration, Advisory Committee of the Hope Day Nursery and Neighborhood Children's Center, and Ladies Auxiliary of Lincoln University. She was also a honorary member of the Alpha Kappa Alpha sorority.

During the Harlem Renaissance era, she published numerous pieces in *Opportunity*, *Crisis*, and Alain Locke's *The New Negro* (including the aforementioned article). Her articles also include "Social Progress" and "The Schools and the Vocational Life of Negroes." Ayer's works, as well as her beauty, were enduring. German American artist Winold Reiss captured her in a pastel reproduced in the March 1925 issue of *Survey Graphic* entitled "Harlem: Mecca of the New Negro."—JESSIE CARNEY SMITH

B

BAKER, JOSEPHINE

(June 3, 1906–April 12, 1975) Singer, dancer, entertainer

Josephine Baker brought the creativity characteristic of the Harlem Renaissance to theatrical shows in France in the 1920s. She became world-famous, a greatly admired woman, a highly paid entertainer, and a trendsetter. She was also a prominent performer in the newly developing technology of phonograph records and motion pictures in the 1920s and 1930s.

Born Freda Josephine MacDonald on June 3, 1906, in St. Louis, Missouri, Baker was the child of Carrie MacDonald and Eddie Carson, who were not married. Carrie aspired to be a professional dancer but performed domestic work to support her family. Eddie was a musician who played the drums. Josephine was the first of four children born to Carrie. Eddie deserted the family when Josephine was young. Carrie married Arthur Martin, who was unable to earn enough to support the family. Lacking adequate food and money for rent, moving their residence often, the family's home life was unpleasant, and due to Arthur's violent temper and Carrie's moodiness, also unpredictable. To combat poverty, at just eight years of age, Carrie required Josephine to go live and work for white families. She was treated badly by her first family and better by the next. Josephine's early experiences led her to be wary of others and develop a sense of self-reliance.

Josephine quit school at the age of twelve. At thirteen, she fled from home, found a restaurant job to support herself, and, with the written permission from her mother, in December 1919, married an older man, Willie Wells, whom she divorced a short time later. She became interested in musical shows and theater, and joined a street band that, shortly thereafter, became part of a traveling group performing as the Dixie Fliers, starring Clara Smith. The group's engagements, arranged by the

Theater Owners' Booking Association, involved unpleasant and demanding working and living conditions.

In September 1921, when the tour reached Philadelphia, Josephine met and married William H. Baker and decided to keep his name, but not him, for the rest of her life. She would later have romantic liaisons of varying durations with numerous different men. She remained legally married to Baker until 1936, when she obtained a divorce.

In 1921, Baker auditioned for a New York show, *Shuffle Along*, produced by the successful team Sissle and Blake, but she was turned down due to her immaturity of age—she was not yet sixteen—and required to work in the theaters of New York. She worked in the road company assisting with costumes. Observant and talented, Baker learned the show's dance routines and, when a substitute was needed for a regular performer, was available. She subsequently became a regular line dancer, usually at the end. A traditional routine had developed in which the last line dancer pretended to be incompetent, forgetting dance steps and being out of rhythm, for example. Then, when the chorus line performed the encore, the last dancer would not only be accurate, but she would excel in some manner to conclude the show. Baker became a "crowd pleaser" noted for her comic antics and dancing skill.

After the road show concluded, Baker was accepted for Sissle and Blake's new show in 1924, *Chocolate Dandies*, which ran until May 1925. Baker then performed at the Plantation Club in New York, where she came to the attention of Caroline Dudley, a wealthy white woman who was organizing an "authentic Negro show" to perform in Paris. Baker accepted Dudley's offer to be in the show. Baker was originally not the star of the show, but a Frenchman, Paul Colin, increased her importance by emphasizing Baker's role for a poster advertising the show, *La Revue Nègre*, which opened in October 1925.

To increase the audience's interest, Baker was persuaded to perform one dance seminude, which became known as *Danse Sauvage*, creating a sensation with the audience and considerable notice, both positive and negative, in newspaper reviews. Some critics did not comprehend the uniqueness of African American dance styles, whereas they fascinated others. After the Paris show ended in December 1925, *La Revue Nègre* was scheduled to perform in Berlin and then Russia; however, Baker had accepted an offer to perform at the Folies Bergère and, after appearing in a Berlin engagement, she declined to continue on, bringing an end to the tour. Returning to Paris, she starred in *La Folie Du Jour*, attracting considerable notice for a seminude costume of artificial bananas and rhinestones around her waist and erotically provocative movements. Baker performed in the show from 1926 to 1927. Widespread acclaim cemented her status as a talented and creative world-famous entertainer.

Of her many romantic relationships, the one most significant to furthering her career was her ten-year (1926–1936) relationship with Giuseppe Abatino, also called "Pepito," who served as her business manager in Europe and was also her lover. When Baker was threatened with a lawsuit, she placed her financial assets in Abatino's name. He was conscientious in handling her finances and assisted Baker in sharpening her skills and improving her stage and public persona. He insisted that she undergo intensive training with a voice coach, who was able to develop her singing voice to be outstanding.

In December 1926, Baker and Abatino cooperated in opening a nightclub in her name, "Chez Joséphine," on the Rue Fontaine in Paris. This was a cabaret that would attract admirers who would pay to watch Baker sing and dance from late night until dawn. Her regular presence was the main attraction. She also opened clubs for periods of time during her trips to Berlin and New York.

Baker embarked on a world tour to European and Scandinavian countries in 1928, and South America in 1929. Her performances received a mixed reception of praise and criticism. She returned to Paris in 1930, with a stronger, more mature singing voice. Her performances eliminated the comic parts and emphasized singing and dancing.

Upon her return to Paris in 1930, Baker performed in the show *Paris Qui Remue* at the Casino de Paris, a venue that was considered more prestigious than the Folies Bergère. This show featured the song "J'ai Deux Amours," or "I Have Two Loves, My Country and Paris," which became her signature song, being sung at all her future performances. Pepito arranged for Baker to study ballet with George Balanchine, which enabled her to perform a ballet in the 1931 show *La Joie de Paris* at the Casino de Paris. Baker's popularity was enhanced as she developed the ability to sing in six languages: English, French, German, Spanish, Portuguese, and Hebrew. Baker was also honored by being named queen of the Exposition Coloniale Internationale in 1931.

Although Baker appeared in a little-noticed silent film, *La Sirène des Tropiques*, in 1927, she pioneered as the first African American female to have a lead role in a major motion picture, *Zouzou*, in 1934. She followed that with two other significant films, *Princesse Tam Tam* in 1935, and *Fausse Alerte* in 1940. These films were met with positive acclaim in Europe but received little notice in the United States. Baker also made phonograph recordings on the Oden Record label in the 1920s and 1930s, and with Columbia Records in the 1930s. In the fall of 1934, she was a success in the lead role in Offenbach's operetta *La Créole*.

In 1935, Baker and Pepito traveled to New York City, where she spent several months preparing to perform the lead role in the *Ziegfeld Follies* of January 1936. Unfortunately, reviews of her performance were extremely negative, and, after several performances, her contract was cancelled by mutual consent and she was replaced in the show. Baker stayed in New York and had more success in a nightclub engagement, while Pepito returned home, dying before Baker's return. Pepito's will returned to Baker the property and financial assets she had entrusted to him.

Baker returned to France in 1936, starring in *En Super Folies* at the Folies Bergère. In November 1937, she married Jean Lion, an industrialist, and became a French citizen. She divorced Lion in 1941. She married Jo Bouillon, an orchestra conductor, in May 1947, and divorced him in 1968.

During World War II, Baker gave full support to France, her adopted country. She was recruited by the French Resistance to be a spy, report conversations of

Japanese and Italian diplomats, smuggle secret messages, and, in 1941, entertain troops in North Africa. For her efforts, she received the Medal of Resistance in 1946, as well as France's highest honor, the Legion d'Honneur, in 1961.

Baker subsequently continued to perform in Paris and on tour. In 1948 and again in 1951, she had successful and warmly received tours of the United States. In the 1950s, Baker pushed to end racial segregation, successfully integrating audiences in Miami Beach and a hotel in Las Vegas. She also supported the Civil Rights Movement in the United States, speaking briefly at the August 1963 March on Washington and, in October 1963, giving a fund-raising concert for civil rights organizations. Beginning in the 1950s, Baker attempted to demonstrate the ideal of human cooperation and mutual respect by adopting twelve children of different nationalities to show that her "Rainbow Tribe" could live in harmony. She eventually needed the assistance of Princess Grace of Monaco to provide the initial payment for a home for her children.

Baker continued to perform, with a well-received appearance in New York's Carnegie Hall in 1973, and a one-woman show, *Joséphine*, at the Monte Carlo Casino in 1974. She also appeared in Paris in April 1975. After fifty years as an acclaimed performer, Baker died.—DE WITT S. DYKES JR.

BALDWIN, RUTH S.
(1863–1934) Philanthropist

Ruth Standish Baldwin was a white philanthropist and social activist who, during the Harlem Renaissance era, sought to impact in a positive manner the lives of "colored" (or black) people in the United States. As cofounder of the Urban League, this was one of the highlights of the organization and its causes that she supported.

Baldwin was born in 1863, in Springfield, Massachusetts, to a New England family that believed in service to others. After graduating from Smith College, Ruth Standish married William Henry Baldwin Jr. on October 30, 1889. Her husband, also deeply committed to the poor, the disadvantaged, and the immigrant, was an active participant in civic groups and had ties to the Negro community. He was also president of the Long Island Railroad. The two worked together until his death in 1905. Baldwin dedicated herself to continuing their work in such organizations as the Committee for Improving the Industrial Conditions of Negroes in New York and the National League for the Protection of Colored Women, which provided aid and protection for women migrating to the North.

On September 29, 1910, Baldwin called together representatives from various groups, as well as leaders both black and white, to discuss urban and economic conditions for Negroes. As a result of this conference, in less than a year, she and cofounder George Edmund Haynes, a Fisk University graduate and the first Negro to earn a Ph.D. from Columbia University, founded the Committee on Urban Conditions among Negroes (CUCAN). Less than a year later, the Committee for Improving the Industrial Conditions of Negroes in New York, established in 1906, and the National League for the Protection of Colored Women, established in 1905, merged with CUCAN. CUCAN and the combined groups were subsequently named the National League on Urban Conditions among Negroes (NLUCAN). Haynes served as executive secretary of NLUCAN from 1910 to 1918, and Baldwin served as president of the Board of Trustees from 1913 to 1915. The organization shortened its name to the National Urban League in 1920.

Baldwin dedicated her life to the service of the poor and disadvantaged, and the health and welfare of black migrants. She continued the work that she and her husband found a common interest in, and those she served saw her not as patronizing, but as someone who offered not charity, but opportunity, to take advantage of what the country had to offer. Baldwin died in New York City.—LEAN'TIN L. BRACKS

BEASLEY, DELILAH LEONTIUM
(September 9, 1871–August 18, 1934) Historian, journalist

Although Delilah Leontium Beasley was best known as a pioneer historian in California, her major work, *The Negro Trail Blazers of California* (1919), helped destroy negative stereotypes of blacks and supported black achievement—two issues that the Harlem Renaissance also addressed. Her regular columns in the *Oakland Tribune* further condemned derogatory racial designations and demanded that writers capitalize the word *Negro*.

The eldest of five children, Beasley was born in Cincinnati, Ohio, to Daniel Beasley, an engineer, and Margaret (Heines) Beasley, a homemaker. The Beasley children's background was enriched by the father's favorable view of education. When she was only twelve years old, she published the first of her writings in the *Cleveland Gazette*. Her column "Mosaics," published in the Sunday edition of the *Cincinnati Enquirer* when she was only fifteen years old, made her the first African American woman to be regularly published in a mainstream newspaper.

The death of both parents when Beasley was in her mid-teens was a temporary blow to her emerging career as a journalist. To support herself, she worked as a domestic laborer for a white judge named Hagan and traveled with his family to Elmhurst, Illinois. She found the work undesirable and soon moved to Chicago to become a masseuse. As she sought a comfortable place in life, Beasley moved often. She studied hydrotherapy and massage in Springfield, Ohio, and diagnosis at a Buffalo sanitarium in New York, and then moved to Michigan to become head masseuse at a family resort.

Beasley maintained a near obsession for writing about African Americans, and in 1910, when in her early forties, she was offered a post in Berkeley, California, as nurse and physical therapist. For eight years she concentrated on the history of her race; devoured black newspapers in the Bancroft Library at the University of California, Berkeley; and traveled the state to conduct oral testimonies from California's black pioneers. In 1915, she began a series of articles published in the *Oakland Tribune* protesting the controversial film *The Birth of a Nation*, by D. W. Griffith, culminating in a nationwide boycott of the racist film. In 1919, she published a local history, *The Negro Trail Blazers of California*, which remains a valuable source for information on African Americans in California. Although early reviews were unfavorable, the work clearly broke virgin ground in documenting notable black

California figures of early times. Beasley's writings continued in the 1920s, with the beginning of a regular column in the *Oakland Tribune* in 1923.

Beasley was active in matters dealing with women's rights; for example, she was the only black female member of the 1925 National Convention of Women Voters held in Richmond, Virginia, and she worked with the League of Nations Association, the League of Women Voters, and other organizations on civil rights and world peace matters. She was also a participant in the National Association of Colored Women and a founding member of the Oakland branch of the National Urban League.

Beasley spent her lifetime dealing with her own heart problems and other health issues, which led to her death.—JESSIE CARNEY SMITH

BEAVERS, LOUISE [LOUISE ELLEN BEAVERS]
(March 8, 1902–October 26, 1962) Entertainer

In an era when black characters in predominantly white productions were often reduced to roles with no names and little to no lines, Louise Ellen Beavers made history with her performance as Delilah in the 1934 film *Imitation of Life*. Early forms of entertainment in the United States were plagued with gross misrepresentations of black people. Traveling vaudeville shows and the theater depicted black people as a race that was greatly inferior to white people, who were depicted as a civilized and refined race. The film industry adopted the same racial stereotypes of black people used in earlier forms of entertainment. Although Beavers's character Delilah continues this tragic tradition of inferiority, Delilah's central role in the plot cannot be denied. Beavers appeared in several films prior to 1934, but her roles were minor and some not credited. The height of Beavers's career came during the middle of the Great Depression and the waning years of the Harlem Renaissance.

Beavers was born on March 8, 1902, in Cincinnati, Ohio, to Ernestine Monroe Beavers and William M. Beavers. Ten years later, in 1912, the family moved to Pasadena, California, where Beavers graduated from Pasadena High School. This proximal location to Los Angeles proved beneficial, as it positioned her close to the movie industry. Beavers worked as a maid for actress Leatrice Joy. Her moment of discovery is disputed. Some hold that she was discovered after performing with the Lady Minstrels at the Loew's State Theater in Los Angeles, while others contend that it was her performance at the Philharmonic Auditorium in Los Angeles that led to her discovery by casting agent Charles Butler. He recommended her for the 1927 Universal Studios production of *Uncle Tom's Cabin*. Harriet Beecher Stowe's novel saw much adaptation on film during the early half of the twentieth century. Beavers played the role of cook. She held deep reservations about the portrayal of blacks on film as wild savages but made peace with the more refined but still inferior role of maid that was popular during the Harlem Renaissance and Great Depression era of Hollywood big studio productions.

Carrying a pleasant and inviting demeanor on and off the stage and having a heavy, round figure, Beavers became the quintessential maid in early Hollywood films. She was sought after by Hollywood executives whose films needed her distinctive touch to manifest the idea of a domestic. Coming from Ohio and then moving to California did not expose Beavers to the southern dialect that she often used. Aside from her employment by Leatrice Joy, she had no experience as a maid or cook. Beavers had to study and develop the talent necessary for the roles she played. She took pleasure in reading a wide variety of subjects and keeping up with the current events of her day. Although not a socialite, she enjoyed symphonic concerts at the Hollywood Bowl amphitheater in California. Beavers's love for symphony and orchestral music was cultivated in her by her mother, who died the same year as the completion of *Imitation of Life*. Her love of music dated back to her church involvement growing up. As an adult, Beavers followed Christian Science.

Despite the limited opportunities for blacks in Hollywood, Beavers demanded respect. She insisted that the black press not be excluded from a special press-only showing of the film. She also publicly expressed support for the *Chicago Defender* and its founder, Robert S. Abbott. The black press received Beavers's roles with a dichotomy of opinions. They were proud to see a black person play such a significant role in Hollywood but disappointed that this role was so degrading to black people. Beavers requested that the word *nigger* be removed from the script of *Imitation of Life* in a scene with Delilah's daughter Peola. This scene did not make the final cut. Actress Fredi Washington plays the older Peola. During the Harlem Renaissance, Washington acted in *Shuffle Along*, *Black Boy*, and *Emperor Jones*, among other films. Washington's brother-in-law was famed Harlem politician Adam Clayton Powell Jr.

Beavers married twice. Her first marriage, in 1936, was to Robert Clark of New York, who also was her manager. Beavers's second marriage was to Leroy Moore. Neither marriage resulted in children. Throughout the early years of the Harlem Renaissance, Beavers appeared in more than 200 films. Her roles increased in importance with such films as *Coquette* (1929), *She Done Him Wrong* (1933), *Forty-Second Street* (1933), *What Price Hollywood?* (1932), and *Bombshell* (1933). She stepped out of the role of maid in some films. She also acted in all-black cast films, including *Dark Manhattan* (1937) and *One Dark Night* (1939).

Beavers continued acting after the Harlem Renaissance, eventually moving to a newer form of media, television. She died in Los Angeles, due to health problems attributed to diabetes.—SARAH-ANNE LEVERETTE

BENNETT, GWENDOLYN

(July 8, 1902–May 1981) Poet, short story writer, artist, editor, educator

Gwendolyn Bennett is known as a poet and artist of the Harlem Renaissance, but she is also remembered for her work as assistant editor of *Opportunity* magazine and her work with the Federal Writers' Project. Her poetry and art appeared in *Opportunity* and *Crisis* magazines during the 1920s. Two of her most famous poems, "To a Dark Girl" and "Heritage," invite pride in the culture and express the beauty of African Americans; this sense of cultural esteem is prominent in most of Bennett's poetry and reflective of the spirit of the Harlem Renaissance. Another of her frequently anthologized poems, "Hatred," published during the same period, reflects the all-consuming and captivating nature of a universally understood feeling.

Bennett's turbulent beginnings may well have influenced her career as an artist and a writer. Born in Giddings, Texas, her father, Joshua Robin Bennett, was a teacher and an attorney. Her mother, Maime Bennett, taught at the local African American elementary school. By the time Gwendolyn was four years old, her family had moved from Texas to Washington, D.C. Soon thereafter, her parents separated. Maime was given custody of her daughter. Dissatisfied, Joshua took his daughter and moved her from one city to another, evading the law and his former wife. He eventually established a home with his daughter and new wife, Marshall Neil Briscoll, in Harrisburg, Pennsylvania. Marshall worked as a teacher, and Joshua did janitorial work to support his family. He studied and passed the bar examination and began working as an attorney when he moved his family to Brooklyn, New York.

In Brooklyn, Gwendolyn attended an integrated school and became the first black member of the literary and drama societies. When she graduated from high school in 1921, the Harlem Renaissance was just beginning to take shape. Bennett enrolled at Columbia University, but because of the hostility shown to her at the school, she soon transferred to Pratt Institute. She graduated from Pratt in 1924. During this period, Bennett enjoyed the successful display of her art work, illustrating the covers of *Opportunity* and *Crisis*. Her art work featured positive imagines of African Americans and is reflective of the celebration of black culture that characterized the Harlem Renaissance. After graduation, she taught briefly at Howard University in Washington, D.C. In 1925, she was awarded a scholarship to study art in Paris. There she came into contact with artists, black and white, from the United States and Europe. Bennett studied at the Académie Colarosis, Académie Julian, and École de Pantheon, as well as at the Sorbonne. She returned to Harlem in 1926.

Upon her return, Bennett began working as editor of *Opportunity*, one of the few vehicles for black artists to present their work. She wrote a literary gossip column, "Ebony Flute," and also served on the editorial board for *Fire!*, a magazine that published only one promising issue, featuring young black artists; however, she soon returned to Howard University to continue teaching, where she met her future husband, Alfred Joseph Jackson, a student at Howard's medical school. Despite the fact that he was older, relationships between faculty and students were against the school's regulations. Bennett resigned her position soon after her courtship with Jackson began. The two were married on April 14, 1928. After a brief separation, during which Bennett taught at Tennessee A&I College (now Tennessee State University), Bennett joined her husband in Eustis, Florida, where he established his medical practice. The couple had difficulties in Florida, and after Jackson passed the New York medical examination, they moved to Long Island, New York. Jackson later died in 1936.

After returning to New York, Bennett earned a teaching degree from Columbia University and worked toward a graduate degree at New York University. In 1935, she helped found the Harlem Artists' Guild. This organization was directed by artist Aaron Douglas and assisted black artists in gaining support from the Works Progress Administration. From 1935 to 1941, Bennett worked with the Federal Art Project and became director of the Harlem Art Center in 1937. In 1941, her success was met with resistance, as she was investigated as a Communist sympathizer. She established the Jefferson School for Democracy and the George Washington Carver School, but these efforts were undermined by her alleged Communist affiliations. She married Richard Crosscup in 1940, and moved to Kutztown, Pennsylvania. Bennett died a year after her husband's death.—REBECCA S. DIXON

BENTLEY, GLADYS
(August 12, 1907–January 18, 1960) Entertainer

Gladys Bentley was a talented, flamboyant, and popular blues singer who entertained audiences from the Harlem Renaissance years of the 1920s to the 1950s. She was a "butch" who dressed in a top hat and tails and flirted with women in the audience. Her act attracted many Harlem Renaissance participants and patrons, as well as numerous members of the prominent white community.

Bentley was born in 1907, and raised in Philadelphia, Pennsylvania. She was a muscular and masculine girl. She started cross-dressing in elementary school and was sent home more than once for wearing boys' clothes. By the time she reached adolescence, she knew that her attraction to women made her different from other girls during a time when gays and lesbians were seen as social deviants. Most states had laws that criminalized same-sex relationships. Gay men and lesbians hid their sexual orientations and gathered in settings outside of mainstream society.

When she was sixteen, Bentley left Pennsylvania and moved to New York City. In the 1920s, New York City was the incubator for a new African American literary, musical, and intellectual cultural scene that became known as the Harlem Renaissance. Harlem became the center for jazz, literature, and the fine arts. Wealthy whites frequented Harlem nightclubs, where Duke Ellington, Fats Waller, Cab Calloway, Bessie Smith, and Ethel Waters performed. In New York, Bentley could be an open lesbian without the risk of harassment or ridicule.

A big, gregarious woman who weighed at least 250 pounds, Bentley seemed larger than life. She was a talented piano player who sang in a raspy, growling voice. She began her career performing at rent parties and buffet flats. The flats were private apartments that operated after nightclubs closed, offering alcohol, dancing, prostitutes, gambling, and rooms to which couples could go.

Bentley moved on to performing in speakeasies and nightclubs. She eventually became the headline performer at a gay speakeasy, the Clam House, and later at the Ubangi Club. Bentley's performances were bawdy and risqué. She transformed popular songs with her own raunchy lyrics and flaunted her sexual orientation and made it part of her performances.

Bentley's performances could be so lascivious that the clubs in which she performed were sometimes raided by vice squads. Her fame grew in the 1930s. Characters based on her appeared in novels, including Carl Van Vechten's *Parties*, Clement Woods's *Deep River*, and Blair Niles's *Strange Brother*. In his autobiography *The Big Sea*, Langston Hughes describes the energy and attraction of Bentley's performances.

The affluent whites who frequented Harlem nightclubs in the 1920s loved Bentley and paid for private performances. Carl Van Vechten became a patron and hired her to entertain at one of his parties. Many celebrities visited the nightclubs in which Bentley performed. Cary Grant, Mary Astor, Bruce Cabot, Franchot Tone, Harold Jackman, Eslanda Robeson, J. P. Morgan, and the Prince of Wales were among the celebrities who enjoyed her performances. One observer described Bentley as a person who blurred the boundaries between male and female, homosexual and heterosexual, wealthy and working class.

Harlem's nightlife began to decline after the repeal of Prohibition and arrival of the Great Depression. In 1937, Bentley moved to Los Angeles to live with her mother. During the World War II era of the 1940s, many women frequented Bentley's shows at Joquins' El Rancho in Los Angeles and Mona's, a popular San Francisco nightclub known for lesbian entertainment.

In the 1950s, the congressional hearings targeted Communists and homosexuals. Bentley, who had always been open about her sexuality, worried about persecution. She started wearing dresses and sanitizing her act. In 1952, she married Charles Roberts, a cook who was sixteen years her junior. The couple eventually divorced. Bentley joined the Temple of Love in Christ and became a devout churchgoer.

Bentley wrote an article for *Ebony* magazine in 1952 describing her return to heterosexuality through the use of hormone treatments. In May 1958, Bentley appeared on a television show, *Groucho Marx's You Bet Your Life*, wearing flowers and a dress. Some observers suspected that these were subterfuges used to deflect attention during the McCarthy era. Bentley died during a 1960 flu epidemic at the age of fifty-two. She was a talented entertainer who was open about her sexual orientation at a time when doing so took tremendous courage.—LELAND WARE

BETHUNE, MARY MCLEOD
(July 10, 1875–May 18, 1955) Educator, scholar, political leader, clubwoman, entrepreneur

Mary McLeod Bethune rose from a life of poverty and discrimination in the South to become an influential example for many leaders and a nurturer of numerous ideas central to the Harlem Renaissance. By the beginning of the Harlem Renaissance, she was already a well-known and respected educator. Forty-three years old at the end of World War I, she had been a school president for thirteen years. She founded Daytona Normal and Industrial School for Negro Girls in 1904. The school merged with the Cookman Institute of Jacksonville, Florida, in 1923, and later became Bethune-Cookman University.

Born July 10, 1875, in Sumter County, South Carolina, Bethune was the fifteenth of seventeen children of Samuel McLeod and Patsy McIntosh McLeod, both former slaves. Bethune related that after she was ridiculed by a white child for looking at a book that she could not read, she was instilled with a desire to learn and rejoiced when she got the opportunity to attend the Presbyterian mission school in Maysville, South Carolina. She then attended Scotia Seminary in Concord, North Carolina. After graduating in 1893, she journeyed to Chicago to Moody Bible Institute in hopes of becoming a missionary in Africa. In 1895, Bethune completed

Mary McLeod Bethune

the program at Moody but was turned down when she applied to the mission board to go to Africa.

In Chicago, Bethune ministered to the poor and needy and sang while she traveled with the Moody choir. This work convinced Bethune that she should continue her missionary work in the United States. She moved to Augusta, Georgia, and worked as an instructor at Haines Institute. There she worked with Lucy Laney from 1895 to 1896. While teaching in Sumter County, Bethune met and married another teacher, Albertus Bethune. Together they had one son, Albert. The family then journeyed to Florida, where she worked at Palatka Mission School from 1899 to 1903, before founding her own school with only $1.50, a rented cottage, and a lot of faith and determination. From the school's beginning, churches stepped in to support the work.

Bethune studied the work of Booker T. Washington at Tuskegee Institute and the operations of other schools, and became adept at developing her school into an efficient operation. She was an engrossing and charismatic public speaker who captivated audiences throughout the United States. Bethune's diplomatic skills were legendary. Her work began to gain national attention, leading U.S. presidents Calvin Coolidge and Herbert Hoover to confer with her on matters relating to child welfare.

Because she was nationally prominent, Bethune was able to influence and mentor some of the leaders of the Harlem Renaissance. One of the great patrons of the period was A'Lelia Walker, the daughter of millionaire hair product mogul Madam C. J. Walker. When A'Lelia died in 1931, Bethune was invited to give the eulogy at the invitation-only funeral of 1,100 people. Harlem minister Adam Clayton Powell Sr. presided, and poet Langston Hughes read a poem he had composed for the occasion. Soon after the funeral, Hughes expressed his admiration for Bethune's oratory ability in a letter to fellow Harlem Renaissance poet Arna Bontemps. Hughes and Bethune struck up a friendship that same year.

Despite the nuances that presented challenges in the racial politics of the era, Bethune's steadfastness in her convictions appealed to many Harlem Renaissance intellectuals. Bethune played an important role in shaping the political ideas and activities of numerous Harlem Renaissance leaders. Hughes was among those

Harlem Renaissance thinkers inspired by her. Hughes, a poet, an intellectual, and himself a social activist during the black cultural movement, teetered between overtly and covertly asserting his political ideals during the course of his career. As white hysteria and objections to Communism grew and Harlem Renaissance artists and other black figures like Paul Roberson claimed the political ideology as their own, the U.S. Congress's Special Committee on Un-American Activities targeted Hughes as a Communist. Hughes never claimed to be a Communist and looked to Bethune for guidance.

Like Hughes and other Harlem Renaissance figures, Bethune was slandered and defamed for alleged Communist ties during the 1940s. Despite the political antagonism, Bethune exemplified to Hughes a person of unwavering resilience, which encouraged him to continue his work. Reflected in her own life, she believed public discourse and the exchange of political ideas to be imperative, a fact that influenced her strong recommendations for Hughes to begin his poetry tours. Hughes followed Bethune's suggestions and humanized the voice behind his craft through his domestic and international travels. Hughes, Bethune, and other prominent blacks, for instance, A. Phillip Randolph, even collaborated on a publication that criticized segregation.

Bethune not only personally counseled blacks during the Harlem Renaissance, her school, Bethune-Cookman College, became an avenue for the cultural movement to expand. In January 1934, Zora Neale Hurston founded the school of dramatic arts at the institution. Bethune was president of the school during Hurston's short tenure. Later, in 1956, Hurston went on to receive a prestigious award from Bethune-Cookman in recognition of her accomplishments. Bethune also inspired other Harlem Renaissance members, for example, Gertrude Elise Johnson McDougald Ayer, a literary critic of black women in American culture. Ayer believed that Bethune's leadership of the National Association of Colored Women would help to amend some racial disparities for African American women.

Racial tolerance was central to Bethune's worldview, and because of her interracialist philosophy, she achieved many accomplishments, including stabilizing her school, opening a hospital, and even creating elementary and high schools. In 1923, however, Bethune passed another big milestone by merging her all-female institution with the all-male Cookman College to create Bethune-Cookman College. In light of the unification of the two schools, the Methodist Episcopal Church, to which she belonged, had to take over the institution because of persisting financial troubles. Nevertheless, Bethune supported the merger and takeover because she wanted the school to remain private and not be taken over by the state. Even with immense support from the Methodist Episcopal Church, Bethune maintained control of the school's affairs. She also led the institution to become one of the first accredited black colleges.

Bethune embarked on another journey in her life's mission of securing political peace and prosperity for all Americans, especially her black counterparts. After organizing the National Council of Negro Women in 1935, the following year, Bethune's political esteem reached another height when President Franklin D.

Roosevelt appointed her director of minority affairs for his National Youth Administration. Serving in this role provided her with the opportunity to become the first African American to serve as director of a federal agency; she also lobbied for other blacks to assume high-level governmental positions.

Bethune's affinity for blacks exemplified that she was a race woman. Her mother claimed ancestry from African royalty. Carter G. Woodson, known as the "Father of Black History," was Bethune's contemporary. Woodson received his doctorate from Harvard University in 1912. He founded the Association for the Study of Negro Life and History in 1909, the *Journal of Negro History* in 1916, Negro History Week in 1926, and the *Negro History Bulletin* in 1937. Bethune partnered with Woodson, serving continuously as president of his association from 1936 to 1951. She published in the *Journal of Negro History*, wrote a weekly column for the *Chicago Defender* newspaper, and wrote many other articles and editorials. She won the coveted Spingarn Medal from the National Association for the Advancement of Colored People (NAACP) in 1935, and the Haitian Medal of Honor in 1952. She traveled to Liberia in 1952, as the U.S. representative for the inauguration of President William V. S. Tubman. At various times, Bethune held vice presidencies in the NAACP, the National Urban League, the Commission on Interracial Cooperation, Central Life Insurance Company, and numerous other organizations or businesses. She was cited several times with honorary degrees and awards. She also served as a consultant to the San Francisco Conference to draw up the United Nations Charter in 1945, and was the only African American woman present.

Bethune portrayed her commitment to uplifting the black community in her selfless acts of helping her fellow African Americans attain political power; however, evidence of her longtime belief in government's ability to assist in changing the plight of blacks was also depicted in her work as minority affairs director. Although criticized by such African American leaders as W. E. B. Du Bois for leading a racially segregated organization, Bethune maintained her position that New Deal programs were more beneficial than harmful for blacks—even if categorized and dispersed in racially separate terms. Full integration was a primary political goal of Bethune, but she insisted that mere interracial cooperation, like her close relationship with First Lady Eleanor Roosevelt and other whites, was a pragmatic way to achieve racial equality. Bethune also broke with the African American tradition of Republican affiliation and publically committed herself to the Democratic Party.

In addition to her notable political presence, Bethune was an astute scholar and writer. She fulfilled a leading role in the Harlem Renaissance. Her college also served as an epicenter of learning, while expanding the scope of the movement. Bethune advised and inspired members of the Harlem Renaissance until her death in 1955.—DEBRA NEWMAN HAM AND CHERYL E. MANGO-AMBROSE

BLANKS, BIRLEANNA
(February 18, 1889–August 12, 1968) Entertainer, singer

From vaudeville to stage performer and singer, Birleanna Blanks was able to carve out a highly successful stage and musical career in the early part of the Harlem

Renaissance era. With a mixed heritage of Native American and African American lineage, she was a positive example for mixed-race women and all women of color. Blanks was born on February 18, 1889, in Iowa, to a Native American mother and African American father. After completing her education, Blanks and her sister Arsceola established a vaudeville act. The sister's act, which toured nationwide, later added Leonard Harper, who also became Arsceola's husband. Birleanna later married baseball player Chesley Cunningham.

In 1919, Blanks made her stage debut in the musical comedy *Over The Top*, written by African American playwright Billy King. The production was performed at the Lafayette Theater in Harlem, New York, which played to all black audiences, and it was one of the first theaters to allow integrated seating. Blanks's career flourished while at the Lafayette, and she performed in additional works by King, including *Exploits in Africa* in 1919, and *A New American* in 1920, as well as *A Trip Round the World* and *Derby Day in Dixie*, both in 1921. After traveling throughout the United States and performing with other groups, for example, the Panama Amusement Company and the Harlem Production Company, Blanks became a member of the singing group Three Dixie Songbirds in 1923 and performed with Amanda Randolph and Hilda Perlina. She remained with the group from 1925 to 1926, as they performed in the production of *Lucky Sambo*. She also made a name for herself by recording the song "Mason Dixon Blues" and other songs with the Fletcher Henderson Orchestra for Paramount Records.

Although Blanks left the music industry for other opportunities after 1928, she had established herself as a successful female entertainer. She died of cancer at the Florence Nightingale Home in New York City.—LEAN'TIN L. BRACKS

BONNER, MARITA ODETTE [MARIETA BONNER; MARITA OCCOMY]
(June 16, 1899–December 6, 1971) Writer, playwright

Despite never living in Harlem and rarely visiting New York, Marita Odette Bonner has a firm place among the writers and within the literary movement of the Harlem Renaissance. Her critique of masculinity, discussion of the constraints of femininity, and keen understanding of social change won her much praise. Her landmark essay "On Being Young—a Woman—and Colored" is considered a major work in African American literature. Its analysis challenged the racial, gender, and class dynamics of Harlem. One of her mentors was Georgia Douglas Johnson, whose weekly salon on S Street in Washington, D.C., was a celebrated intellectual haven for such writers as Langston Hughes, Jean Toomer, Alain Locke, and Willis Richardson. This relationship proved fruitful for Bonner, who won numerous writing awards in the 1920s.

Bonner was born on June 16, 1899, in Brookline, Massachusetts, to Joseph and Mary Anne Bonner. After excelling academically at Brookline High School, she entered Radcliffe College. She majored in English and comparative literature, while becoming fluent in German. Her literary foundation was laid during the writing seminar of Charles T. Copeland.

After graduation in 1922, Bonner began teaching at Bluefield Colored Institute in Bluefield, West Virginia. She then moved to Armstrong High, the first manual training school for blacks in the city. In 1924, she moved to Washington, D.C., to teach high school. It was here that she met Georgia Douglas Johnson and began the most productive period of her writing career. *The Pot Maker* (1927), *The Purple Flower* (1928), and *Exit: An Illusion* (1929) were among the works that yielded her widespread recognition as an important African American writer.

Bonner moved to Chicago in 1930, when she married accountant William Occomy. While she taught high school and raised three children, she continued to publish under her married name, producing the *Frye Street* collection of short stories, set against the backdrop of urban multiethnic life in Chicago. She published her last short story in 1941, deciding to focus on teaching at the Phillips High School in Chicago. From 1950 to 1963, she taught at the Doolittle School, which served educationally deprived children. Bonner died in 1971, from injuries sustained from an apartment fire. For years after her death, her work went unnoticed, but in 1987, a posthumous edition of her complete work was published under the title *Frye Street and Environs*. The volume also contains previously unpublished work that had been preserved by her daughter.—MYRON T. STRONG

BOOZE, MARY CORDELIA MONTGOMERY
(1877–c. 1948) Civic leader, activist, clubwoman

Mary Cordelia Montgomery Booze was known during the Harlem Renaissance era as a clubwoman and activist in the Mississippi Republican Party, as well as an ardent supporter of equitable public service to black people in her home state. She was born at Brierfield (Davis Bend), Mississippi, in 1877, to former slaves Isaiah T. and Martha Robb Montgomery. After high school, she completed two years of college at Straight University, a university that was incorporated in 1869, and located in New Orleans, Louisiana. Booze was employed as a bookkeeper for her father and an instructor at Mound Bayou Normal Institute. In 1901, she married businessman Eugene P. Booze and had two children.

In nineteenth-century Mississippi, where many blacks earned a living by sharecropping and working on plantations, Booze's grandfather was a plantation owner and cotton producer who became Mississippi's first black to hold an office. Her father was a town builder, businessman, and state Republican leader. After losing the plantation, the family moved to Mound Bayou, Mississippi, an all-black colony founded by her father, who echoed his friend Booker T. Washington's philosophy of self-help and racial solidarity.

In 1924, at the Republican National Convention, Booze became the first black woman to be elected and subsequently represented the state of Mississippi for many years. Her political activism continued with the "Black and Tan" Republican Party, which referred to the skin colors of the new Republicans. Although this party was preferable to the foundation of a "Lily White Party," it was dissolved in 1956 by President Dwight D. Eisenhower.

Booze relocated from Mound Bayou to New York City after her husband was murdered in 1939. She remained with the Republican National Committee until her death in 1948.—SHARON D. BROOKS

BOOZER, THELMA BERLACK
(September 26, 1906–March 6, 2001) Journalist, feminist, administrator, trendsetter

Thelma Berlack Boozer

Thelma Berlack Boozer became a professional writer during the Harlem Renaissance years. She was born on September 26, 1906, in Ocala, Florida. In 1920, her family moved to New York. She attended Theodore Roosevelt High School in the Bronx, graduating as valedictorian of her class. She then attended New York University, graduating magna cum laude with a bachelor's degree in commercial science in 1924, and a master's degree in journalism in 1931.

Boozer exercised her journalism skills with a number of organizations, some of which included working as a professional journalist for the *Pittsburgh Courier* and a journalist with the *New York Amsterdam News* from 1926 to 1942. She also wrote a newspaper column, "The Feminist Viewpoint," in 1949. A trailblazer, she broke new ground as one of the first females in her day to use her maiden and married surname in her writings. Boozer held many notable positions during her accomplished career, including chief of the New York City Office of Civil Defense, director of public relations at Harlem Hospital, and director of the Greater New York Alumni Division of the United Negro College Fund. In addition, she was active in numerous organizations that supported Martin Luther King Jr.'s nonviolent Civil Rights Movement and provided monetary support and letters of encouragement.

Boozer was married to James C. Boozer for fifty-eight years; she had two daughters, Barbara and Thelma. She died in New York.—MARSHA M. PRICE

BOWLES, EVA DEL VAKIA
(January 24, 1875–June 14, 1943) Organization worker

Work as a leader in the Young Women's Christian Association (YWCA) from 1917 to 1932, years that embraced the Harlem Renaissance, enabled Eva del Vakia Bowles to bring about racial cooperation in the various communities where her efforts took her. She employed some of black America's leading women to lecture or serve in facilities in New York City and elsewhere. Women of achievement who aided in her work include Crystal Bird (Faucet), Ruth Anna Fisher, Josephine Pinyon, Ionia Whipper, and Cordella A. Winn. Bowles opposed an all-black YWCA as much as she opposed a program where all decisions were made by white leaders. She was also the first salaried black YWCA secretary in the United States.

Born in Albany, Athens County, Ohio, to John Hawkes Bowles and Mary Jane (Porter) Bowles, Bowles came from a distinguished and well-educated family. John was the first black school principal in Marietta, Ohio, and he became one of Ohio's first black railway postal clerks. Her paternal grandfather, Baptist minister John Randolph Bowles, was chaplain of the renowned all-black 55th Massachusetts Infantry Regiment during the Civil War. Bowles followed the family's commitment to education and attended Ohio State and Columbia universities.

While teaching in Virginia, Bowles met Addie Waites Hunton, whose husband William was secretary for the Young Men's Christian Association in New York City. Hunton recommended Bowles as director of a project for black women sponsored by the YWCA in New York. This marked her initiation into YWCA work and enabled her to address heavy wartime emigration of blacks to the North, problems of urban black women, and various issues that black women faced. After years of successful leadership, Bowles became disillusioned with the organization, charging that its reorganization would prevent blacks from participating in policy-making decisions, and she resigned her post. She then became an executive of the National Colored Merchants Association. Bowles died in Richmond, Virginia, and is buried in Columbus, Ohio.—JESSIE CARNEY SMITH

BOWMAN [BRADFORD], LAURA
(October 3, 1881–March 29, 1957) Actress, singer, teacher

Laura Bowman was born Laura Bradford in Quincy, Illinois, and raised in Cincinnati, Ohio. Her mother was Dutch and her father multiracial. Church provided Bowman with the opportunity to discover her passions for singing and acting. In 1902, she landed her first role with the Williams and Walker Company's *In Dahomey*. After the company disbanded, Bowman and her second husband, Pete Hampton, formed Darktown Entertainer. In the first decade of the 1900s, the duo toured heavily in the United States, Russia, and Europe. Bowman married four times; her first—and brief—marriage was to Henry Ward Bowman, at the age of sixteen. Widowed after her second and third marriages, she married LeRoi Antoine, who survived.

Bowman shined on the stage, on film, and on radio during the crux of the Harlem Renaissance; she also taught drama. Already an established performer, she joined the Lafayette Players in 1916. She secured roles in *The Wolf*, *The Conspiracy*, and *The Price*, among several other plays, often receiving positive reviews. Bowman met her third husband, Sidney Kirkpatrick, while with the company. Although they would return, the couple left the Lafayette Players and eventually joined the Ethiopian Art Players in 1923. Before that, they performed in Indianapolis as the Hawaiian Duet. Five years later, Bowman formed the National Arts School to teach aspiring actors. Her first of several appearances on Broadway was in *Sentinels* in 1931.

Bowman's film career began in the 1920s, in Oscar Micheaux's *The Brute*. Other films from the 1930s and 1940s include *Drums of Voodoo, Son of Ingagi*, and *The Notorious Elinor Lee*. Radio proved to be another successful medium for her. During the 1930s, she appeared on *The New Penny Show, Stella Dallas*, and *Pretty Kitty Kelly*, to name just a few. Bowman never left the theater, even while teaching and doing film and radio.—SARAH-ANNE LEVERETTE

BRIGHT, NELLIE RATHBONE
(March 28, 1898–February 7, 1977) Teacher, writer

In response to the intellectual flourishing of the Harlem Renaissance, Nellie Rathbone Bright cofounded the magazine *Black Opals* to provide a platform for publication and encouragement of black writers in Philadelphia in the 1920s. This, along with her thirty-year commitment to education, played a key role in the uplifting of black children in Philadelphia.

Bright was born on March 28, 1898, in Savannah, Georgia, where she spent the early years of her childhood. Her father, a native of St. Thomas and the first black Episcopal priest in Savannah, accepted an appointment in Philadelphia in 1911. It is here that Bright received most of her education. From elementary school in the public school system to earning her bachelor's degree in English from the University of Pennsylvania in 1923, Bright pursued her interests in teaching, writing, and the arts by attending Berkshire School of Arts in Berkshire Hills, Massachusetts, and doing research at the Sorbonne and Oxford.

As a teacher in Philadelphia, Bright, when cofounding *Black Opals* in the 1920s, saw the publication as an opportunity to encourage other writers. She also contributed to the magazine by writing about literature, education, black history, and other important matters of the day. In 1935, Bright earned the position of principal, which she held until 1952, and she then became director of the Board of Education until 1959. In her commitment to education and uplift, she also served as a member of more than fifteen civic boards that advocated nonviolence, racial tolerance, and civil rights.

Bright's advocacy and service continued into her later years, and she received numerous awards for her work. On June 10, 1972, she was awarded a certificate from the Pennsylvania Society for the Abolition of Slavery. Her literary interest also remained strong, as she coauthored the children's book, *America: Red, White, Black, Yellow*, focusing on social history, in 1970.—LEAN'TIN L. BRACKS

BROWN [SCOTT], ADA
(May 1, 1890–March 31, 1950) Singer, actor

Singer and actor Ada Brown was a Harlem Renaissance blues attraction during the 1920s and 1930s. She sang on both the East Coast and West Coast, made a number of recordings, and toured with musical revue teams. Her 1928 recording, which included "Panama Limited Blues" and "Tia Juana Man," earned her the title "Queen of the Blues." She performed at the Lafayette Theater in *Plantation Days* (1927), *Bandannaland* (1928), and *Tan Town Tamales* (1930). Her voice and persona landed her in the all-black cast in the Broadway musical *Brown Buddies*, with tap-dancer Bill "Bojangles" Robinson. The show opened on Broadway in October 1930, for 113 performances.

Born Ada Scott, in Kansas City, Kansas, Scott later took the name Ada Brown. Some sources say that she was born in Junction City, Kansas, in 1889. She came from a musical family and began piano lessons at an early age, soon singing in the local church choir. She developed a "full, rich, and mellow voice" that led her to singing in clubs in Paris and Berlin as a teenager. By 1910, she was singing in Chicago's Pekin Theater. After a colorful and successful early career, in 1936, Brown was an incorporator of the Negro Actors' Guild of America. Later in the decade, she sang with the Fletcher Henderson Orchestra in Chicago, and, in 1943, she sang "That Ain't Right" with Fats Waller in the film *Story Weather*.

Brown left the stage and performances in 1945, and returned to her hometown. She died there and is buried in Westlawn Cemetery.—JESSIE CARNEY SMITH

BROWN, CHARLOTTE EUGENIA HAWKINS [LOTTIE HAWKINS]
(June 11, 1883–January 11, 1961) Educator, school founder, civic leader

Charlotte Eugenia Hawkins Brown

Although not a central participant in the Harlem Renaissance, Charlotte Eugenia Hawkins Brown joined other leaders of the renaissance period who worked for interracial harmony, civil rights, and the promotion of racial pride. In 1919, she founded the Commission on Interracial Cooperation to help further one of her causes. Through Palmer Memorial Institute, which she founded in North Carolina to provide preparatory education for black youth, her work in education was aimed at uplifting young black girls. Via the North Carolina State Federation of Negro Women's Clubs, Brown's influence as a leader in many worthwhile causes impacted black women from North Carolina to New York and elsewhere.

Born Lottie Hawkins on June 11, 1883, in Henderson, North Carolina, Charlotte Hawkins Brown, as she became internationally known, was the daughter of Caroline Frances Hawkins and Edmund H. Height, a brick mason. Her grandmother, Rebecca Hawkins, was a favored slave on a local plantation owned by the descendants of her white father. After Caroline remarried, she relocated to Cambridge, Massachusetts, in 1888, with her daughter, son, and members of her extended family. Lottie's talent for leadership and oratory was demonstrated when she was twelve years old and organized a Sunday school at Union Baptist Church in Cambridge. She was chosen orator for a church activity, and by the time she was ready to graduate from Cambridge English High and Latin School, Lottie met Alice Freeman

Palmer, former president of Wellesley College, who would have a lasting influence on her life. She also changed her name from Lottie to Charlotte.

Palmer voluntarily paid Brown's expenses to State Normal School in Salem, Massachusetts. At the beginning of her second year, Brown met with a representative of the American Missionary Association (AMA) and accepted an offer to return to North Carolina and operate an AMA school. She later received credit for her work in North Carolina and was awarded a diploma from State Normal School. Brown set up class in a one-room shack called Bethany Institute in the Sedalia community, located about six miles east of Greensboro, and began schooling fifteen students. After the AMA decided to close its small schools at the end of the year, she solicited money from northern philanthropists, returned to Sedalia, and opened Palmer Memorial Institute on October 10, 1902, naming the school in honor of her friend and benefactor, Alice Freeman Palmer.

Brown continued her intellectual development during summers by studying at Simmons College, Temple University, and Harvard University. In June 1911, she married Edward S. Brown, whom she met at Harvard. He taught in Brown's school for five years, until they divorced. Palmer thrived, occupied 300 acres, and became a preparatory school. It provided high school and junior college-level training, and had a student body represented by the children of many black elite. The school underwent expansions and submitted to two fires, yet the facility continued to function and graduated its first accredited high-school class in 1922. Palmer had a far-reaching reputation for its excellent music program. The Sedalia Singers often performed at the White House, Boston's Symphony Hall, and elsewhere, and the group enjoyed the support of the local white and black communities.

The national leadership ability of Brown was in full swing by the 1920s. She worked in support of black people throughout the United States who were bitterly opposed to racial discrimination and even filed suit to fight Jim Crow laws in the South. In 1926, she was inducted into the North Carolina Board of Education's Hall of Fame. Through her work with the North Carolina State Federation of Negro Women's Clubs, Brown established the Efland Home for Wayward Girls and led the publication of *Negro Braille Magazine*. She was president of the North Carolina Teachers Association from 1935 to 1937, and was successful in improving the educational facilities for blacks and black teachers' salaries. She continued to achieve and was in demand as a lecturer and speaker at college commencements. In 1940, she was named to the North Carolina Council of Defense; she held other appointments as well. Brown's published works include *Mammy: An Appeal to the Heart of the South* (1919) and *The Correct Thing to Do, Say, and Wear* (1941), for which she became known as the "First Lady of Social Graces." Brown retired from her post in 1952 and, after a lingering illness, died in Greensboro.—JESSIE CARNEY SMITH

BROWN, HALLIE QUINN
(March 10, 1845?–September 16, 1949) Educator, civil rights leader, elocutionist, writer, clubwoman

The multitalented Hallie Quinn Brown was widely respected in many areas, particularly as an elocutionist, public speaker, and public performer. She wrote several books, including those relevant to the Harlem Renaissance: *Our Women: Past, Present, and Future* (1925); *Homespun Heroines and Women of Distinction* (1926); and *Pen and Pictures of Pioneers at Wilberforce* (1937). These works, published during the Harlem Renaissance years, showcase the lives of black women, many of whom were contributors to that cultural and literary period. Her works, particularly *Homespun Heroines and Women of Distinction*, became classics in women's studies.

Born in Pittsburgh, Pennsylvania, Brown was one of six children of Thomas Arthur Brown, a riverboat steward and express agent, and Frances Jane Scroggins, advisor to students at Wilberforce University. Both parents were born into slavery and became active on the Underground Railroad. The family relocated to Chatham, Ontario, Canada, around 1864, and returned to the United States around 1870. They settled in Wilberforce, Ohio, where Hallie and her younger brother enrolled in the historically black Wilberforce University, which was founded and operated by the African Methodist Episcopal Church. In 1873, Brown graduated from Wilberforce with a bachelor of science degree. The university honored her later on with two honorary degrees, a M.S. in 1890, and a LL.D. in 1936.

Brown moved to the South shortly after completing her undergraduate education and taught literary skills to black children and adults in Yazoo, Mississippi, and Columbia, South Carolina. From 1875 to 1877, she taught at Allen University and served as the school's dean. She returned to Ohio in 1887, and, for four years, taught in Dayton's public schools. Educator Booker T. Washington then hired her as lady principal of Tuskegee Institute (later University) in Alabama, a position she retained from 1892 to 1893; she returned to her alma mater in 1893, as professor of elocution. Her extensive travels, however, delayed her acceptance of the post until 1906. Brown's summer enrollment in elocution training at the Chautauqua Lecture School ended in 1886, upon her graduation.

Brown joined Wilberforce Grand Concert Company, later known as Stewart Concert Company, and traveled with the group to raise money for the school. After being largely unsuccessful, the group disbanded in 1887, and she traveled extensively throughout the United States and abroad as lecturer, elocutionist, and fund-raiser for Wilberforce. Brown toured Europe between 1894 and 1899, and gave recitations on black life in the United States, black songs, folklore, and temperance. When she returned to Wilberforce and full-time teaching, she also became a pioneering force behind the formation of the black women's club movement and a cofounder of the Colored Women's League of Washington, D.C. Two years later, in 1895, the league joined the Women's Era Club of Boston to become the National Federation of Afro-American Women, later renamed the National Association of Colored Women. From 1920 to 1924, Brown was national president of the organization and then honorary president until her death in 1949, when she was nearly 100 years old.—JESSIE CARNEY SMITH

BROWN, IDA G.

(1900–?) Singer, entertainer

Ida G. Brown was a singer and entertainer possibly born in New Orleans, Louisiana, around 1900. Although sources do not list her full impact on the music industry, she is known to have recorded two blues songs with the Prion Orchestra of New Orleans in February 1924. The songs "Jail House Blues" and "Kiss Me Sweet" were also recorded and released by other singers, including Bessie Smith. The Piron Orchestra, which, at the time, was one of the most notable African American dance orchestras in New Orleans, on their second visit to New York City, broadcast on station WJZ and identified Brown as part of the group. Ida "Baby Blues" Brown, as she was referred to in the music industry, is said to have gotten the nickname "Baby Blues" from her time as a performer in the Lafayette Theater in New Orleans.—LEAN'TIN L. BRACKS

BROWN, LILLYN [LILLIAN]

(April 24, 1885–June 8, 1969) Actress, jazz and blues singer

Lillyn Brown debuted her sixty-year career in 1896, singing character songs in minstrel shows. Her performances embraced the Harlem Renaissance era and enriched the work of other black entertainers of that time, including those who appeared on Broadway. Because of her heritage, one of her billings was the "Indian Princess." As an eleven-year-old entertainer, her repertoire included performing as a male impersonator named Elbrown as the "Youngest Interlocutor in the World." She showcased her talents in vaudeville shows, in nightclubs, at Carnegie Hall, and in venues in Europe.

Born in Atlanta, Georgia, Lillyn was the daughter of Ben Thomas, an Iroquois Indian, and Ella Bronks, a black French woman. In 1918, Fisk University alumnus Irvin Miller introduced her to musical theater when she replaced vaudeville singer Esther Bigeou in his show *Broadway Rastas*. Backed by her band, the Jazz-Bo Syncopators, Brown recorded the first blues record for the Emerson label in 1921. She worked with her husband William DeMont Evans, and the two performed as Brown and DeMont. In 1924, Brown appeared in *Dixie to Broadway*.

Brown was called the "Kate Smith of Harlem." During the 1930s, she and DeMont wrote and she starred on Broadway in *Black Aces*. Other credits include roles in the musical *Kiss Me Kate* and the drama *Regina*. Brown was an entrepreneur, directed plays for Harlem's Abyssinian Baptist Church, was a member of the Negro Actors' Guild of America, and ran a school for performing arts.—GLORIA HAMILTON

BUCKINGHAM [HARPER], MINNIE

(May 15, 1886–February 10, 1978) Politician

True to the spirit of seizing opportunities for change during the era of the Harlem Renaissance, Minnie Buckingham Harper, a housewife in Keystone, West Virginia, was called upon and agreed to complete her husband's term in political office. Harper subsequently became the first African American woman to serve in a legislative body in the United States. Harper was born in Winfield, West Virginia, on May 15, 1886. She later moved to an area known as the coalfields of McDowell County. With the death of her husband in 1928, Harper, although a homemaker and resident of Keystone, West Virginia, was unanimously recommended by the McDowell County Republican Executive Committee to fill her husband's vacant post in the House of Delegates. As a delegate, she served for less than a term, but her appointment helped to advance the expanding role of African American women in the political system in West Virginia during the Harlem Renaissance era and the continuation of coalitions as an important part of state politics. She chose not to run in the next election.

Harper later married miner John B. Patterson and resided in Norfolk, Virginia. She returned to her birth place after the death of her husband in 1956.—LEAN'TIN L. BRACKS

BURGOYNE, OLGA "OLLIE"
(June 12, 1872–April 2, 1974) Dancer, actress

Ollie Burgoyne made her mark during the Harlem Renaissance as a performer in such shows as *Follow Me* (1923), developed by Mamie Smith, and through her involvement with the short-lived Negro Art Theatre. She was born in Chicago, in 1878. As early as the age of six, she performed in minstrel shows called pick shows. She danced internationally in Germany, France, and Turkey, and participated in vaudeville shows. When she returned to the United States, Burgoyne was highly acclaimed for her exotic dances, which included the snake and Brazilian and Spanish dance. She lived in Russia in the early 1900s and had many admirers of her performances there. Around 1904, she was part of a six-member black female (plus one backup person) troupe, along with Coretta Alfred and Emma E. Harris, called the Louisiana Amazon Guards. In St. Petersburg, Burgoyne was able to earn a living as a dancer and had the opportunity to do something she likely could not have done in the United States: purchase a lingerie shop.

Often the lone African American (generally as a domestic character) in her shows, Burgoyne appeared in numerous Broadway dramas between 1920 and 1930. All-black dramas that she had roles in during this time included *Make Me Know It* (1929) and *Constant Sinner* (1931). As a member of Hemsley Winfield's Concert Dance Group (the first African American modern dance company in New York), Burgoyne became known for her memorable role in *Run Lil Chillun* (1933). Along with Edna Guy, she was one of the leading female dancers in the group. Unlike many of her peers, Burgoyne's career spanned nearly fifty years. In her later years, she taught Russian dances and worked behind the scenes in the movie industry. She died in Oxnard, California.—ANGELA M. GOODEN

BURKE, GEORGIA
(February 27, 1878–November 28, 1985) Entertainer

For more than three decades, including the Harlem Renaissance years, Georgia Burke made contributions to the entertainment industry. Born in Atlanta, Georgia, to a Methodist minister and a nurse, she had seven siblings and attended Atlanta public schools, Clark University, and Claflin College. Burke taught grade school in Wilson, North Carolina, for six years. Because of a friend's encouragement while on a trip to New York, she auditioned for *Blackbirds of 1928* and was hired immediately.

Burke received many supporting roles in Broadway shows, including *Mamba's Daughters*, *The Grass Harp*, *Anna Lucasta*, *Mandingo*, and *Porgy and Bess*. In her role as Maria in George Gershwin's *Porgy and Bess*, she shared the stage with famed entertainers Cab Calloway and Leontyne Price. She performed with Ethel Waters in *Mamba's Daughters*. In addition, Burke played the role of Lily on the radio soap opera *When a Girl Marries*. This series was heard on major networks, including NBC, CBS, and ABC, from 1939 to 1957.

In the spring of 1952, *Jet* magazine highlighted Burke in an article about body image and black female entertainers. The writer of the article commented on Burke's weight not being an issue, as she had been frequently cast in Broadway roles. Hattie McDaniel and Mahalia Jackson were also featured.

Burke was a resident of the DeWitt Nursing Home until her death, where she was a member of their chorale. She entertained other residents by singing Fats Waller tunes. Although confined to a wheelchair in her last years, she was still lively and energetic.—JEMIMA D. BUCHANAN

BURLIN, NATALIE CURTIS [NATALIE CURTIS]
(April 26, 1876–October 23, 1921) Ethnomusicologist, Harlem Renaissance supporter

Natalie Curtis Burlin was born on April 26, 1876, to Edward and Augusta Curtis. At the dawn of the Harlem Renaissance, she contributed to the scholarship on spirituals and Negro folk music. With her passion for music and skills as a composer and pianist, she took a departure from her European classical music ventures and began studying the music of Native Americans and the Negro. Burlin completed the majority of her research related to folk music and spirituals on the campus of Hampton Normal and Agricultural Institute in Virginia. During this time, Hampton's students consisted of newly freed men and women, Native Americans, and Africans. Her works, *Songs and Tales from the Dark Continent*, completed in 1920, and *Negro Folk-Songs*, a four-part series published between 1918 and 1919, are listed in the bibliographic section of Alain Locke's *The New Negro*.

Burlin came from both a paternal and maternal family with strong political and business ties to the elite of New England and New York, as well as Pennsylvania. She was reared in the beliefs of transcendentalism and early twentieth-century feminism. Molded by her family's involvement in abolitionism and the popular suffragist and religious movements of her day, Burlin developed an inquiry for a variety of topics rather than settling on a singular strong conviction of the world. She studied at the Bearly school and received private instruction. Her education continued in Europe, where she further honed her talent as a pianist and composer of European classical music.

Burlin's musical maturation took place during an era that focused on creating a national identity. This led to her study of folk music of Native Americans and the

Negro. She was supported financially by prominent Harlem Renaissance patron Charlotte Osgood Mason. George Foster Peabody, another wealthy patron of Burlin, served on the Board of Trustees at Hampton Institute. Hampton's commitment to the preservation and promotion of black and Native American music further attracted Burlin.

Burlin worked closely with Hampton's director of music, R. Nathaniel Dett, as she conducted her research for her books. It was with the help of Hampton's principal, Hollis Frissell, and other Hampton standouts like Booker T. Washington and Robert Moton, that she founded the Music School Settlement for Colored People in 1911, located in New York. Other black luminaries who contributed to the development of this school were scholar W. E. B. Du Bois and journalist Lester A. Walton. Minister Adam Clayton Powell Sr. was also on the school's board. Musicians and composers James Reese Europe, J. Rosamond Johnson, and Harry T. Burleigh were involved in the promotion of the school, as was noted tenor Roland Hayes, who sang "On-Away, Awake, Beloved!" at one of the school's benefit concerts at Carnegie Hall. In 1917, Natalie married artist Paul Burlin.

As a white woman in the early twentieth century, Burlin held prejudices with regards to the intellectual capabilities of blacks, Native Americans, and other groups. Despite her beliefs, she was able to observe and appreciate their humanity and the contribution that each group made to American culture through their music. She was killed in a car accident in Paris.—SARAH-ANNE LEVERETTE

BURRILL, MARY P. "MAMIE"
(c. 1884–March 13, 1946) Playwright, educator, activist

During the early 1910s, Mary P. Burrill, who already had an interest in theatrics, began to write plays and joined other playwrights of the Harlem Renaissance era who became important in theater history. She was one of the first black women to promote social change through her plays.

Burrill was born around 1884, in Washington, D.C., the daughter of John H. and Clara E. Burrill. In 1901, she graduated from the popular M Street School, later renamed Dunbar High School. While there, she developed an interest in literature and the theater. She received a diploma from the Emerson College of Oratory (later Emerson University) in 1904, and a bachelor of literary interpretation in 1929. Beginning in 1904, Burrill taught school in her hometown for nearly forty years, alternating between her alma mater and Armstrong Technical High School, finally becoming permanent at Dunbar. There the eloquent orator gave lessons on theatrical performance, speech, and diction, and she inspired her students to become dramatists.

Although Burrill is said to have written many plays, only two are known to be extant. *They That Sit in Darkness* was published in 1919, and may be the first known feminist play by a black woman. It advocates education for black women and calls for women's access to birth control. Her other play, *Aftermath*, was published in the same year in the left-wing periodical *Liberator*. During the 1920s, the Krigwa Players of New York and the Workers' Drama League produced the play. This play centers on a black soldier's return to South Carolina after World War I. Burrill's work confronts important social issues that remain problems in the black community.—JESSIE CARNEY SMITH

BURROUGHS, NANNIE HELEN
(May 2, 1879–May 20, 1961), School founder, civil rights activist, feminist, religious leader, clubwoman

Nannie Helen Burroughs

An influential leader in the African American community, Nannie Helen Burroughs belonged to a network of southern black female activists who helped to shape the thought and work of Harlem Renaissance participants. She was perhaps most influential as a school founder and strong proponent of women's rights at the National Baptist Convention. She also challenged men to "glorify" women and refrain from treating them as slaves.

Born in Orange, Virginia, Burroughs was the daughter of former slaves John Burroughs, a farmer and itinerant preacher, and Jennie Poindexter Burroughs, a cook. In 1883, she and her mother relocated to Washington, D.C., where she graduated from M Street High School (later renamed Dunbar) in 1896. She studied business and, in 1907, received a honorary A.M. degree from Eckstein-Norton University in Kentucky. Her career began as a secretary for the Baptist *Christian Banner* in Philadelphia. From 1898 to 1909, she was bookkeeper and editorial secretary for the Foreign Mission Board of the National Baptist Convention in Louisville. While there, she organized the Women's Industrial Club for black women, which became a vocational school.

In 1900, Burroughs helped found the Woman's Convention, an auxiliary to the National Baptist Convention, and was its corresponding secretary for forty-eight years. Her ambition since childhood to establish an industrial school for black girls was realized on October 19, 1901, when the National Training School for Women and Girls opened in Northwest Washington, D.C. It came after her successful persuasion of the Women's Convention to underwrite the initiative. The school, which she served as principal, prepared black women for domestic work, which led to some criticism by black people; however, Burroughs encouraged the young women to be respectable workers and remain proud of themselves and their work. The institution eventually changed its emphasis and abandoned the old trade-school curriculum; in 1964, it was renamed the Nannie Helen Burroughs School, in Burroughs's honor. The school was designated a National Historic Landmark in 1991.

While acting as corresponding secretary of the Women's Convention, in 1907, Burroughs proposed the Women's Day Celebration, which brought her condemnation for wanting to set aside only one day to celebrate women. The convention accepted her resolution, however, and the celebration became popular throughout the black church as a time to promote black women and their leadership.

Burroughs came under the scrutiny of the federal government in 1917, simply because she was an outspoken advocate on many political and social issues. She urged black men and women to vote and for the end of the lynching and racial discrimination that was so prevalent during her time. She chaired the National Association of Colored Women's Antilynching Committee and belonged to the Women's Division of the Committee on Interracial Cooperation. She was also a charter member of the Antilynching Crusaders and became president of the National League of Republican Colored Women. In 1934, Burroughs launched the first self-help project for blacks in Washington, D.C.

Among her writings are the undated works *Grow: A Handy Guide for Progressive Church Women* and *Making Your Community Christian*; in 1948, *Words of Light and Life Found Here and There* was published. Burroughs was in great demand as a speaker. She died in Washington, D.C, after a lifetime of agitation for the rights of black women.—JESSIE CARNEY SMITH

BUSH, ANITA
(1883–February 16, 1974) Dancer, actress, theater company founder

A theatrical milestone of the Harlem Renaissance was reached in 1915, when Anita Bush established the Lafayette Players, a professional African American dramatic company. The stock company generated opportunities for African American actors and produced plays for black audiences. Bush was born in Washington, D.C., in 1883, and raised in Brooklyn, New York.

When Bush was a teenager, she began dancing in Bert Williams and George W. Walker's vaudeville shows, which were performed on Broadway, and also in England and Scotland in 1903 and 1904. When the Williams and Walker shows ended in 1909, she formed a dance group that performed in various venues from 1910 until 1913. In 1915, Bush founded the Anita Bush Stock Company; after moving from the Lincoln Theater to the Lafayette Theater later that year, the Harlem-based company was renamed the Lafayette Players. The repertory company produced at least 250 plays during its seventeen-year existence, and Lafayette Players touring companies appeared in various cities. Bush starred in numerous productions during the Lafayette Players' early years. In addition, she starred in two films: *The Crimson Skull* (1921), the first African American Western, and *The Bull-Dogger* (1922). She also appeared in several plays for the Works Progress Administration Federal Theatre Project in the 1930s.—LINDA M. CARTER

BUSH-BANKS, OLIVIA WARD
(May 23, 1869–April 8, 1944) Writer, educator

Olivia Ward Bush-Banks wrote, published, and taught during the last decades of the nineteenth century and continued to do so during the Harlem Renaissance. She was born in Sag Harbor, New York, on May 23, 1869, to Abraham and Eliza Draper Ward; both parents were of African American and Montauk Indian descent. After her mother's death in November 1869, and her father's subsequent marriage, Bush-Banks was raised by her aunt, Maria Draper, in Providence, Rhode Island. Bush-Banks graduated from Providence High School before she married Frank Bush in 1889. The couple divorced, and Bush-Banks supported her two daughters, her aunt, and herself by working various jobs in Providence and Boston until 1915 or 1916. She married Anthony Banks and lived in Chicago until 1928. She returned to New York and resided in New Rochelle and New York City until the 1940s.

Bush-Banks was an assistant drama director in Boston. In Chicago, she taught drama in public schools and established the Bush-Banks School of Expression. In New York City, she was the drama coach at Abyssinian Baptist Church's Community Center. Bush-Banks wrote for the *Colored American, Citizen*, and *Westchester Record-Courier*. She also published two volumes of verse, *Original Poems* (1899) and *Driftwood* (1914), as well as *Memories of Calvary* (1915), an Easter pageant. In addition, she wrote "Indian Trails; or, Trail of the Montauk," an unpublished play, and the "Aunt Viney Sketches." She died in New York.—LINDA M. CARTER

BUTLER, ANNA MABEL LAND
(1901–1989) Editor, journalist, poet

Anna Mabel Land Butler's poems were published in the *Pittsburgh Courier* during the Harlem Renaissance. Little is known about this woman, although her works endure as a tribute to her talent and the rich body of literature that was produced during one of the most prolific eras in African American history.

Raised in Atlantic City, New Jersey, Butler was not the only one in her family with poetic ability. Her father, John Weaver Land, who worked as a hotel doorman, also published poetry. As an adult, Butler was employed as an elementary teacher from 1922 to 1965. While teaching between 1936 and 1965, Butler worked as a newspaper correspondent for the *Pittsburgh Courier*. Founded in 1907, by Edwin Nathaniel Harlston, the paper grew into one of the country's most widely circulated African American newspapers. Robert Lee Vann, the paper's publisher and editor, made sure that the *Pittsburgh Courier*, like many other African American newspapers, contributed to the Harlem Renaissance during the 1920s and 1930s. Publishing new and established writers was a popular way to participate in the renaissance and expose audiences to black talent. During this time period, Butler published several poems.

In the decades that followed the end of the Harlem Renaissance, Butler continued to work in journalism and produced more poetry. In 1965, she worked as an editor and reporter for the *Philadelphia Tribune*. She published three volumes of poetry, including *Album of Love Letters—Unsent. Volume 1: Morning 'til Noon* (1952), *Touchstone* (1961), and *High Noon* (1971). Her poems touch on such universal themes as love and death, as well as race.—GLADYS L. KNIGHT

BUTLER, SELENA SLOAN

(January 4, 1872–October 7, 1964) Educator, children's advocate, advocate for education, organizer

The Harlem Renaissance era was enriched in part by the work of Selena Sloan Butler as an advocate for the uplifting of black people and their community, as well as the education of blacks, particularly children.

Butler was born in Thomasville, Georgia, to a white father, William Sloan, and an African American and Indian mother, Winnie Williams. She was educated in Thomas County, in a mission school, Spelman Seminary, later Spelman College, from which she graduated in 1888, and began teaching English and elocution in Georgia and later Florida. In 1893, she married Henry Rutherford Butler Sr. They moved to Massachusetts, where he studied medicine at Harvard; they returned to Atlanta in 1895, and he established his practice and became a prominent doctor. In 1899, their son, Henry Rutherford Butler Jr., was born. Butler's actions following the discovery that there was no adequate preschool available for her son are illustrative of the New Negro in her assertiveness, self-reliance, and racial/community uplift. She started a kindergarten in her own home. When young Henry entered Yonge Street Elementary School in 1911, Butler organized the first black Parent–Teacher Association in the United States and encouraged parents to become involved in their children's education. These experiences served as the impetus for her life's focus of working to improve educational issues for everyone.

In 1926, Butler established a statewide black Parent–Teacher Association. When the National Congress of Parents and Teachers became a part of the National Parent–Teacher Association in 1970, she was recognized as one of the founders. Butler was appointed by President Herbert Hoover to serve on the Committee on the Education and Training of the Infant and Preschool Child for the White House Conference on Child Health and Protection, 1929–1930. When her husband died in 1931, she moved to London with her son, where she worked with the Nursery School Association. During World War II, Butler moved to Fort Huachuca, in Arizona, to join her physician son; there she organized the first black women's chapter of the Grey Lady Corps.

Other achievements include editing and publishing the *Women's Advocate*, a monthly newspaper devoted to issues and concerns of black women; serving as the first president of the Georgia Federation of Colored Women; acting as a delegate to the National Association of Colored Women; organizing the Phyllis Wheatley Branch of the Atlanta Young Women's Christian Association (YWCA); and cofounding the Spelman College Alumni. The Yonge Street Elementary School was renamed in honor of her husband, and, in 1966, the park adjacent to the school was named in her honor. In 1995, Butler was inducted into Georgia Women of Achievement. Her portrait hangs in the state capitol.

Butler died of congestive heart failure in Los Angeles, California. She is buried beside her husband at Oakland Cemetery in Atlanta, Georgia.—HELEN R. HOUSTON

C

CALLOWAY, BLANCHE DOROTHEA JONES
(February 9, 1902–December 16, 1978) Singer, band leader, entrepreneur

An active participant in the Harlem Renaissance, Blanche Dorothea Jones Calloway became popular in the 1920s when she joined the national tour of the all-black musical revue *Plantation Days*, featuring Florence Mills, her idol since childhood. She was also inspired by blues singer Ida Cox. She moved to Chicago in 1927, and, between 1931 and 1938, formed, led, and directed her own orchestra, becoming the first woman to lead an all-male orchestra. She became one of the most successful bandleaders of the 1930s.

Calloway was born in Baltimore, one of four children born to Cabell Calloway, a lawyer, and Martha Eulalia Reed, a music teacher. She was the older sister of bandleader Cab Calloway, an icon of the Harlem Renaissance. She studied piano during her childhood and, in her teens, sang with a church choir. Calloway enrolled in Morgan State College (now University) in Baltimore but dropped out of school in the early 1920s to develop her interest in show business and a musical career that lasted fifty years.

While in Baltimore, Calloway performed in local nightclubs, revues, and stage shows. In 1921, she performed with Eubie Blake and Noble Sissle of Harlem Renaissance fame in the musical *Shuffle Along*. Her career blossomed when she joined and toured with the revue *Plantation Days*. When the show ended in 1927, Calloway remained in Chicago, which, by then, had become the jazz music capital. Blanche introduced her brother Cab to the entertainment world, and for a time they had their own act; he was bandleader and she was vocalist. Blanche became a popular attraction in clubs and also toured and performed at venues like the Crib Club in New York. She performed to packed houses in Atlantic City, Boston, Kansas City, New York, Pittsburgh, and St. Louis. Calloway's all-male band performed at the Lafayette Theater in New York in 1931, 1932, and 1934, and at the Apollo Theater in 1935, 1936, 1937, 1938, and 1941. Race records became a public craze, which, in 1925, led her to record two records with her new group, Blanche Calloway and Her Joy Boys. They recorded "Lazy Woman Blues" and "Lonesome Lovesick Blues." Her group featured some of the emerging young talent of the day, for instance, trumpeter Louis Armstrong and drummer William Randolph "Cozy" Cole. Calloway eventually renamed her group Blanche Calloway and Her Orchestra and led them to be considered one of the nation's best musical groups.

The racially segregated and male-dominated musical world contributed to Calloway's downfall. While on tour in Yazoo, Mississippi, in 1936, she used a ladies room at a local service station, and she and an orchestra member were then jailed for disorderly conduct. Her team abandoned the band. Her flamboyant performance style was considered inappropriate for female performers. By the mid-1930s, Calloway had difficulty getting bookings. In 1940, she assembled an all-girl orchestra, but the group was unsuccessful. After that, she settled in Philadelphia with her husband, became a socialite, and engaged in community activities before relocating to Florida in 1953. Calloway became a disc jockey in the 1950s and then founded a cosmetics company. She remarried in the last year of her life and returned to Baltimore, where she died of breast cancer.—JESSIE CARNEY SMITH

CAMPBELL, HAZEL VIVIAN
(1935–?) Short story writer

Hazel Vivian Campbell is best known for the two short stories that were published in *Opportunity*, a prominent African American magazine. One of the foremost mediums that operated during the dazzling Harlem Renaissance era, the magazine featured the literary works of male and female writers. Although some writers rose to prominence, for example, Zora Neale Hurston, many others, like Campbell, did not attain far-reaching success and notoriety. Consequently, little is known about Campbell.

Campbell's short stories are significant in that they narrate the sobering realities of poverty and struggle in black life. Her first short story, "Part of the Pack: Another View of Night Life in Harlem," was published in the *Opportunity* in August 1935. "The Parasites" was published in September 1936. In "Part of the Pack," a couple grapples with poverty, unemployment, and a race riot, issues and events that loomed even during the glamorous days of the Harlem Renaissance. In "The Parasites," a family contends with welfare and the wretchedness of their living environment. Both stories are featured in Judith Musser's anthology, *"Tell It to Us Easy" and Other Stories* (2008). This seminal anthology includes the complete short stories of women that were published in *Opportunity* magazine between 1923 and 1948.—GLADYS L. KNIGHT

CARTER, EUNICE HUNTON
(July 16, 1899–January 25, 1970) Lawyer, community leader, women's rights advocate

During the Harlem Renaissance and years thereafter, the African American community in New York and New Jersey benefitted from the work of Eunice Hunton Carter. She had a keen interest in equal rights for women and government reform. As a social worker, she served many family service agencies before taking her degree in 1932 from Fordham University School of Law.

The Atlanta-born Carter was the daughter of William Alphaeus Hunton, an executive with the Young Men's Christian Association (YMCA), and Addie Waites Hunton, a field worker for the Young Women's Christian Association (YWCA). The Atlanta race riots of 1906 spurred the Huntons to relocate to Brooklyn. Carter graduated from Smith College in 1921, with both bachelor's and master's degrees. With an interest in government reform, her master's thesis is entitled "Reform of State Government with Special Attention to the State of Massachusetts." She spent the next eleven years in public service. In 1924, she married Lisle Carter, a practicing dentist in New York.

Carter was admitted to the New York bar in 1934, and had a brief tenure in private practice but continued her interest in civic organizations and Republican politics. She joined the National Association of Women Lawyers, National Lawyers Guild, New York Women's Bar Association, and Harlem Lawyers Association. She held membership in these organizations between 1935 and 1945. After the Harlem riots in 1935, Mayor Fiorello LaGuardia named her secretary of the Committee on Conditions in Harlem. Carter also investigated rackets and organized crime in Harlem, having been named to an extraordinary grand jury by special prosecutor Thomas E. Dewey. She was the only black and the only woman on the investigative committee. From 1935 to 1945, Carter was deputy assistant district attorney for New York County, and she distinguished herself as a trial prosecutor.

In 1945, Carter returned to private practice and devoted much of her time to working with civic and social organizations, and seeking to secure equal rights for women. Her friendship with school founder Mary McLeod Bethune led her to become a charter member of the National Council of Negro Women (NCNW), which Bethune and twenty other women founded in 1935. Carter was a member of the executive board and a trustee of NCNW. She held membership in many other organizations, including the Roosevelt House League of Hunter College, Urban League, and International Conference of Nongovernmental Organizations of the United Nations. She attended conferences held in foreign countries and held such posts as advisor to women in public life for the German government. Like her parents, she had a keen interest in YMCA work. She was a member of the YWCA national board, as well as the Administrative Committee for the Foreign Division, and cochair of its Committee on Development of Leadership in other Countries.

Carter retired from law practice in 1952, but her interest in women's organizations and equal rights for women never waned. After a few months' illness, she died in New York City.—JESSIE CARNEY SMITH

CASELY-HAYFORD (AQUAH LALUAH), GLADYS MAY
(May 11, 1904–1950) Poet

Gladys May Casely-Hayford, African by birth, contributed her poetry to the literary movement in Harlem in the 1920s and 1930s and further expanded, through her work, such themes as the strong sense of African cultural beauty and strength, as well as a feminist perspective inclusive of her own personal and sexual honesty. She was born on May 11, 1904, in Amix, Gold Coast, to parents who were activists in their community. Her father, Joseph E. Casely-Hayford, was a Pan-Africanist and a lawyer, and her mother, Adelaide Smith Casely-Hayford, was a Victorian feminist and educator. Although born with a malformed hip joint that resulted in being slightly lame in one leg, Casely-Hayford was not limited by this affliction. She spent her early years of education in Ghana and went to college at Colwyn Bay College in Wales, England.

Casely-Hayford's interest in poetry began at an early age, fostered by her love of reading. At fifteen, she wrote a poem entitled "Ears," which garnered much attention from the school's headmistress and resulted in a call to her mother about this accomplishment. After completing her college education, she returned home in 1926, and taught African literature and folklore at her mother's Girls Vocational School in Freetown, Sierra Leone. In 1927, after sending some of her poetry to Columbia University and having three of her poems published in *Atlantic Monthly*, thanks to her mother sharing her poetry with a friend in Cambridge, Casely-Hayford received an invitation to attend both Columbia University and Radcliffe College. Although she never made it to New York, her work was so impressive that it was published in such periodicals as *Crisis*, *Opportunity*, and the *Message*, and it was included in Countee Cullen's book *Caroling Dusk* in 1927. Her most noted poems are "Creation" (1926), "Nativity" (1927), "Rainy Season Love Song" (1927), and "The Serving Girl" (1941).

Casely-Hayford's poetry, published in the early years under the pseudonym Aquah LaLuah, was highly sought after, as it incorporated strong and beautiful African images and spoke directly about issues of women with an air of political sophistication. As an African writer who shared such pride in her homeland and a personal honesty about her experiences, her work had a direct effect on the literary works of African Americans from the 1920s through the 1940s as they sought a connection with their African heritage. Casely-Hayford spent most of her life in Sierra Leone, having later married and given birth to a son. While serving as caretaker for her mother and raising her son, she died in 1950, from black water fever or cholera.—LEAN'TIN L. BRACKS

CATO, MINTO [LA MINTO CATO]
(August 23, 1900–October 26, 1979) Opera singer, producer, performer

Minto Cato was a mezzo-soprano opera singer who became known for performing show music during the Harlem Renaissance from the 1920s until the late 1940s.

Cato was born in Little Rock, Arkansas, in the late summer of 1900. She received musical training at the Washington Conservatory of Music, in Washington, D.C., and began her career by teaching piano in public schools in Arkansas and Georgia. In 1919, she opened a music studio in Detroit.

Cato began to work in show business at Detroit's Temple Theater in 1922, when she performed with the B. F. Keith vaudeville circuit. She worked and toured with impresario Joe Sheftell, and they were married around 1923. She gave birth to a daughter, Minto Cato Sheftell, around 1924. During the 1920's, Cato performed in many of Sheftell's shows, including the *Creole Bronze Revue*. They conducted a worldwide tour of Europe, Alaska, Canada, and Mexico as the *Southland Revue*.

By the end of 1927, Cato had separated from Sheftell and was working in various venues. She had a solo act in 1929, at Chicago's Regal Theater and worked as an impresario with such shows as the *Frivolities of 1928*. She also worked as a vaudeville producer in the United States and abroad. Cato was a successful singer, and she performed with Louis Armstrong in the *Blackbirds* shows from 1920 to 1930. In May 1936, she performed in the role of Azucena in the opera *Il trovatore*, which she also staged and directed. She went on to perform in many operas, singing the role of Aida with the Hippodrome Opera Company in New York. In 1938, Cato sang the role of Queenie in *Show Boat* and Liza in *Gentlemen Unafraid* with the Municipal Opera Society of St. Louis. Cato performed in *La traviata* with the National Negro Opera Company in 1947, and this was one of her last major opera performances.

In the mid-1940s, Cato returned to show business performances, but her career in the United States was in a state of decline, in part because the opera world was not offering roles to African American performers at this time. She returned to Europe and toured as part of a trio and a solo performer until the early 1950s. As the years passed, Cato remained active with the National Association of Negro Musicians. After her death in 1979, she was buried in Hawthorne, New York.—FAYE P. WATKINS

CAUTION-DAVIS, ETHEL [ETHEL M. CAUTION]
(1880–1981) Poet

As African American women began to follow their passion in the world of poetry, Ethel Caution-Davis was among those who had the talent and determination to add her work to the diverse poetry of the Harlem Renaissance era. Ethel M. Caution was born in 1880, in Cleveland, Ohio. After the death of her parents, she was adopted and later took on the surname Davis. Caution began her work in poetry while attending Wellesley College.

While in college, Caution produced short poems and essays that were published in *Wellesley Magazine* and *Wellesley News*. After graduating from college in 1912, she began to use the name Caution-Davis. She began her work experience as a teacher in Durham, North Carolina, and later taught in Kansas City, Kansas, before accepting a position as dean of women at Talladega College in Alabama. After three years, Caution-Davis moved back to the Northeast and then took up residence in New York, working for the public assistance program. She remained in New York until her retirement and continued to work with programs that helped single women.

Caution-Davis produced only a limited amount of poetry, but it was favorably received and published in such periodicals as *Crisis*, the *Durham Advocate*, and *The Brownies' Book* for children. Her most notable poem, "Long Remembering," is known for its complexity and a regard for showing diverse experiences. In her later years, Caution-Davis was nearly blind, but she kept up with literature and issues of the day through a volunteer reader and audio books. She died at 101 years of age in New York City.—LEAN'TIN L. BRACKS

CHAPPELLE, JUANITA STINNETTE
(June 3, 1899–June 4, 1932) Singer

Juanita Stinnette was a vaudeville performer, as well as coproducer of the Chappelle and Stinnette Revue and the Chappelle and Stinnette record label during the Harlem Renaissance era. In 1912, Stinnette toured with Salem Tutt Whitney and Homer Tutt's Smart Set Company, a vaudeville and musical comedy act. She later married the man that convinced her to join the show, Thomas Chappelle. The couple toured together for several years and, by 1922, had their own revue, the Chappelle and Stinnette Revue. The couple starred as a dancing team in such revues as *Yaller Gal* (1924) and *Kentucky Sue* (1926). Music was provided by the Jazz Hounds, who included Bobby Lee, Percy Glasco, Seymour Errick, and Fleming and Faulkner. In 1926, the couple produced nine blues discs under their label Chappelle and Stinnette, manufactured by C&S Phonography Record Company. The song "Decatur Street Blues," by Clarence Williams, is the only song recorded that was not sung by the duo. Chappelle also appeared in a few Broadway shows, including *How Come?* (1923), *Deep Harlem* (1929), and *Sugar Hill* (1931). Chappelle died of peritonitis the day after her thirty-third birthday in 1932.—AMANDA J. CARTER

CLARK, MAZIE EARHART [FANNIE B. STEELE]
(1874–1958) Poet

Mazie Earhart Clark was a poet who published poems and collections of poetry during the Harlem Renaissance. Born in Glendale, Ohio, to David and Fannie Earhart, she lost her mother at the age of five. As a young adult, she studied chiropody in Cincinnati. She later opened a shop and married George Clark, a U.S. Army sergeant; he died in 1919. She experienced another loss with the death of her sister.

Poetry and religion, however, helped Clark transcend her sorrow. Although a lesser-known poet, she was a copious writer. Her poems were published in several periodicals. Notable collections include *Life's Sunshine and Shadows* (1929), published under the pseudonym Fannie B. Steele, and *Garden of Memories* (1932). Her poems address assorted themes, including romantic love, patriotism, nature, religion, and family. Some poems also cover African American life and themes about southern living.—GLADYS L. KNIGHT

CLIFFORD, CARRIE WILLIAMS
(1862–November 1934) Writer, editor, educator, clubwoman, civil rights and women's activist

Prior to and during the Harlem Renaissance, Carrie Williams Clifford worked to abolish racial and gender discrimination through various organizations and publications. The daughter of Joshua and Mary Williams, Clifford was born in Chillicothe, Ohio, in 1862. The family moved to Columbus, Ohio, when Clifford was approximately eight years old, and she attended the city's public schools. She was a schoolteacher in Parkersburg, West Virginia, prior to her marriage to William H. Clifford, a lawyer and Republican state legislator, in 1886. They resided in Cleveland, where their two sons were born, until 1908. The family moved to Washington, D.C., after Clifford's husband accepted employment as an auditor at the War Department.

Clifford's earliest efforts to battle racial and gender discrimination were visible through her work with the National Association of Colored Women in the late 1890s, and the Ohio Federation of Colored Women's Clubs (OFCWC), which was founded in 1900, with Clifford as the organization's first president. Clifford edited the OFCWC's *Sowing for Others to Reap: A Collection of Papers of Vital Importance to the Race* (1900). Active in national and local activities of the National Association for the Advancement of Colored People, she presented (along with Mary Church Terrell) the organization's antilynching resolutions to President William Howard Taft in 1911.

Clifford published two volumes of verse. Her first book, *Race Rhymes* (1911), was published 138 years after Phillis Wheatley's *Poems on Various Subjects, Religious and Moral* (1773), and fifty-four years after Frances E. W. Harper's *Poems on Miscellaneous Subjects* (1854). Thus, following in the tradition of Wheatley and Harper, Clifford was one of the first black women to publish a book of poetry. In addition, she was one of the first African American women to publish a volume of verse during the Harlem Renaissance, for her second book, *The Widening Light* (1922), was published four years after Georgia Douglas Johnson's *The Heart of a Woman* (1918) and the same year as Johnson's *Bronze: A Book of Verse*. Clifford's poems were vehicles for her to protest racial and gender injustice, as well as pay tribute to notable African Americans. Both volumes were published posthumously as *The Widening Light* (1971). Clifford died in Washington, D.C.—LINDA M. CARTER

CLOUGH, INEZ
(c. 1860s or 1870s–November 24, 1933), Singer, dancer, actor

The first black show to appear in a legitimate theater rather than a burlesque theater was John Isham's *Oriental America*. When it opened on Broadway in 1896, Inez Clough was among its cast, and she toured with the show in the United States. Her work on the musical stage continued through the most productive years of the Harlem Renaissance.

Clough's date and place of birth are uncertain. She was born in the 1860s or 1870s, probably in Worcester, Massachusetts. Little is known about her family. After *Oriental America* opened, Clough and the company went to London in 1897. Although the company disbanded in 1898, Clough remained in London until 1902. When she returned to New York, she joined the Bert Williams and George Walker's company until 1911, and appeared in the troupe's performances of *In Dahomey*

Inez Clough

(1902–1904), *Abyssinia* (1906–1907), *Bandanna Land* (1908–1909), and *Mr. Lode of Koal* (1909). In 1906, she toured with Cole and Johnson Brothers' *Shoo-Fly Regiment*. Clough spent several years in vaudeville, ending such engagements when she became a member of the Lincoln Stock Company in New York, and later a charter member of the Lafayette Players.

During the most productive years of the Harlem Renaissance, Clough was active in dramatic and musical productions, and she appeared in two movies, one in 1921, and another in 1932. She joined the road company of *Shuffle Along* in 1922, and two years later she appeared on Broadway in *The Chocolate Dandies*, with Josephine Baker, Valaida Snow, and Elizabeth Welch. Her other appearances included *Earth* (1927), *Wanted* (1928), and *Harlem: An Episode of Life in New York's Black Belt* (1929). Clough retired from show business in the late 1920s and died in Chicago.—JESSIE CARNEY SMITH

COLEMAN, ANITA SCOTT
(November 27, 1890–March 27, 1960) Essayist, poet

During the height of the Harlem Renaissance, Anita Scott Coleman was a literary contributor from the Southwestern United States who won numerous prizes for her short stories, essays, and poems. She was born in Guaymas, Mexico, on November 27, 1890, to William Henry Scott, a retired Buffalo soldier in the well-known 9th Calvary Regiment, and Mary Ann Stokes. Coleman grew up on a ranch in New Mexico, matriculated from the New Mexico Normal School, and later began working as a teacher.

On October 16, 1916, she married James Harold Coleman, a printer and photographer originally from Virginia. She then ended her teaching career. She published her first writings while living in New Mexico from 1919 to 1925. Coleman published her first story, "Phoebe and Peter up North," in *Half-Century Magazine* in 1919. During this time period, she published thirteen short stories. Her most famous story, "The Little Grey House," was published in 1922.

Coleman relocated to Los Angeles to join her husband, who had moved there for work. In Los Angeles, where she lived from 1926 until her death in 1960, she raised four children, ran a boarding house, and published her most sophisticated work.

Despite living in New Mexico and later in Los Angeles, Coleman published numerous essays, short stories, articles, and poems in the major race journals advocating the uplift of the African American race, including *Crisis*, *Messenger*,

Competitor, and *Opportunity*. She also published in several major African American newspapers, namely the *Pittsburgh Courier*, *Nashville Clarion*, and *Messenger*. Coleman, who won several literary prizes, knew many writers of the Harlem Renaissance era, including Langston Hughes and Wallace Thurman. She also corresponded with Countee Cullen, who was an assistant editor for *Opportunity*.

Coleman produced more than thirty short stories during the Harlem Renaissance period. Her best stories include *The Brat* and *Three Dogs and a Rabbit*. Although she never lived in Harlem, her work epitomizes the goals of the writers of that time. Her stories focus on racial pride and issues important to black women, and explore such issues as employment discrimination, lynching, and segregation.

Coleman died relatively unknown in Los Angeles in 1960; however, her writing was an important contribution linking the Southwest to the Harlem Renaissance. Her writings give us a glimpse into the lives of African Americans living in the Southwest during that time.—ANDREA PATTERSON-MASUKA

COLEMAN, BESSIE [ELIZABETH]
(January 26, 1892–April 30, 1926) Aviator

Early aviator Bessie Coleman is often associated with the Harlem Renaissance and its participants, perhaps due to the iconic role that she played in American aviation and the admiration that her race had for her notable accomplishments. In 1921, she was the first black American woman to become an aviator and gain an international pilot's license. She was also the first black woman stunt pilot, or "barnstormer." She joined the group of blacks who opposed racial segregation, especially during performances by blacks, and became a role model for women with an interest in aviation. For a brief period during the Harlem Renaissance, Coleman was widely promoted in the press as a popular heroine.

Born Elizabeth Coleman in Atlanta, Texas, Bessie, as she was popularly known, was the daughter of George Coleman, a day laborer of Indian descent, and Susan Coleman, a domestic. The family relocated to Waxahachie, Texas, but her father left the family and returned to the Indian Territory in Oklahoma that he knew. This left Susan to care for her family. After completing high school, Bessie spent one semester at Langston Industrial College (later Langston University) but dropped out due to financial problems. In 1917, she joined her two brothers in Chicago, studied manicuring at Burnham's School of Beauty Culture, and worked at the White Sox Barber Shop. She later managed a small restaurant.

Coleman married Claude Glenn in 1917. Meanwhile, her brother Johnny told her stories about female pilots in France during World War I. An avid reader since childhood, she also read about aviation and thus developed an interest in the then-fledgling field. Determined to learn to fly and earn a pilot's license, she sought admission to various aviation schools but was rejected due to her race and gender. Robert S. Abbott, founder and editor of the *Chicago Defender*, and black banker Jesse Binga became her staunch supporters and provided the finances needed to study aviation in France, where female aviators were encouraged. Coleman accepted their support, learned French, and was trained at the School of Aviation in

Le Croto, the most famous flight school in France. She had both French and German aviators as her teachers.

The French Federation Aéronautique awarded Coleman international pilot's license number 18310 on June 15, 1921, making her the first black woman to hold such recognition; this was only ten years after the first American woman had earned her pilot's license. She returned home in September 1921, but left again for Europe for advanced training in stunt performance and parachute jumping. She was back home in August 1922, with the continued sponsorship of Abbott, Binga, and the *Chicago Defender.*

Coleman's first exhibition in the United States was at Garden City, New York, on Labor Day 1922, when she flew a Curtiss aeroplane. By this time, she owned three army surplus Curtiss biplanes and performed in the Chicago region in October of that year. She also gave successful exhibitions throughout the Midwest. Coleman met David Behncke during her third exhibition in Gary, Indiana. Behncke, president of the International Airline Pilots Association, became her manager. During Coleman's first exhibition flight on the Pacific Coast, flying from Santa Monica to Los Angeles, her engine failed and her plane was demolished when it fell 300 feet to the ground. As Coleman recuperated, she went on a lecture tour.

Her performances continued, as she performed in Columbus, Ohio, Memphis, Tennessee, Cambridge, Massachusetts, and elsewhere. When she performed, she drew large crowds and thrilled spectators as much with her flying outfit (cap, helmet, goggles, long jacket, and pants) as with her skill. She became known as "Brave Bessie." Coleman endured another airplane accident while flying from San Diego to Long Beach and, as before, lectured to churches and schools while recuperating. As often as she could, she lectured on the opportunities for blacks, including black women, in aviation. She also appeared in many news documentaries during this time.

An invitation from the Negro Welfare League brought Coleman to Jacksonville, Florida, in April 1926, to perform in an airshow for the upcoming First of May celebration. When she learned that blacks were forbidden to attend her show, she refused to perform. Because local agencies refused to rent a plane to blacks, she decided to use her Jenny plane instead. After the flight from Texas to Jacksonville, her plane developed mechanical problems during a practice run, and Coleman fell out of the plane and to her death. She was highly celebrated at services following her death, and organizations and clubs have been formed and air shows held in her honor. Coleman is buried in Chicago's Lincoln Cemetery. In 1995, the U.S. Postal Service issued a stamp in the Black Heritage Series honoring Coleman.—JESSIE CARNEY SMITH

COLE-TALBERT, FLORENCE
(June 17, 1890–April 3, 1961) Opera singer, educator

After deciding at the age of fifteen to be a become a singer, Florence Cole-Talbert went on to become the first African American to perform the challenging title role in Verdi's *Aida*, the opera that inspired her decision. Her commitment to music also influenced her to teach and support the talents of other aspiring singers in their careers.

Florence Cole-Talbert

Born in Detroit, Michigan, on June 17, 1890, Cole-Talbert came from a family of musicians, her father a singer, basso, and dramatist reader, and her mother a singer and mezzo-soprano who traveled extensively with the Fisk Jubilee Singers and became well known for her talents. Once she decided to become a singer, Cole-Talbert attended high school in Los Angeles. After participating in her school's music programs and graduating, she completed her college degree at Chicago Musical College in 1916. She briefly married Wendall Talbert, and after their relationship ended she decided to keep his surname for professional reasons.

Between 1918 and 1925, Cole-Talbert accomplished a great degree of success. She made her New York debut concert appearance on April, 18, 1918, at Aeolian Hall, and continued to make appearances in Detroit, Los Angeles, and throughout the United States. As a well-received performer, she had excellent reviews in the local papers. Cole-Talbert also recorded on several record labels. These included Broome Special Phonograph, created to support the work of black artists; the Paramount label; and the Black Swan label. In 1925, Cole-Talbert decided to embark on a two-year stay in Europe for additional vocal study, which included her singing the title role in *Aida* at the Teatro Comunale, in Consenza, Italy. Although Italian audiences were known for their strong and sometimes negative responses to performances, Cole-Talbert was triumphant and given critical acclaim for her role.

Cole-Talbert returned to the United States in 1927, married Dr. Benjamin F. McCleave, and became stepmother to his four children. She continued to do recitals until 1930, when she accepted a position as music director at Bishop College in Dallas, Texas. Throughout the years, she also had teaching positions at Fisk University, Tuskegee Institute, and Alabama State College. She mentored aspiring students during her career, most notably Vera Little, a mezzo-soprano who debuted as Carmen in Berlin, Germany, in 1957, and Marian Anderson, whom she encouraged and further helped by raising funds with a concert for Anderson's voice training.

Cole-Talbert remained active in the music world and served in the National Association of Negro Musicians and the Memphis Music Association. She served as an example to many who faced the challenges and barriers of being the first to achieve in areas where black Americans were not known and not always welcomed. Cole-Talbert, a pioneer for black concert artists, died in Memphis, Tennessee.
—LEAN'TIN L. BRACKS

COOPER, ANNA JULIA HAYWOOD
(August 10, 1858–February 27, 1964) Educator, writer, feminist, activist

Prior to, during, and after the Harlem Renaissance, Anna Julia Haywood Cooper improved the quality of life for generations of African Americans, as she obdurately and persistently challenged prevailing notions of African American intellectual inferiority and gender discrimination. She was born in Raleigh, North Carolina, on August 10, 1858, to Hannah Stanley, a slave, and George Washington Haywood, a slaveholder. In 1868, she was a member of the inaugural class at St. Augustine's Normal School and Collegiate Institute (now St. Augustine's University), where she received her primary and secondary education. Cooper earned her bachelor's degree in 1884, and her master's degree in 1887, from Oberlin College, as well as her Ph.D. from the University of Paris (Sorbonne) in 1925. Her two-year marriage to George Cooper, who was the second African American ordained as an Episcopal minister in North Carolina, ended with his death in 1879. Decades later, Cooper, at the age of fifty-seven, adopted five children, ranging from infancy to twelve years, who were the grandchildren of her half-brother, and raised them in Washington, D.C.

Cooper's career as an educator (teacher and administrator) lasted more than seventy years. She exhibited pedagogical promise as a child at St. Augustine's when she tutored other students. Upon graduating from St. Augustine's, she taught at the school prior to her matriculation at Oberlin. After she received her Oberlin degrees, she taught at Wilberforce College in 1884, and returned to Saint Augustine's in 1885. Two years later, Cooper joined the faculty of the Preparatory High School for Colored Youth (renamed M Street High School in 1891, and then Dunbar High School in 1916) in Washington, D.C., where she was appointed principal in 1902. During her tenure, a number of M Street students were accepted to Ivy League institutions; however, when Cooper refused to deemphasize academics in favor of manual training, racism and sexism led to her dismissal in 1906. Cooper taught at Lincoln University in Missouri until 1910, when she returned to M Street and taught until 1930. That same year, Cooper, who was in her early seventies, was appointed president of Frelinghuysen University, located in Washington. After Frelinghuysen lost its building lease, Cooper allowed classes to be held in her home. She remained president until 1941, and then served as Frelinghuysen's registrar until the mid-1950s.

Cooper did not limit her efforts on behalf of her fellow African Americans to academe. She was also a prominent and prolific lecturer. At the 1886 meeting of African American Episcopal ministers in Washington, her discourse centered on womanhood and race; that lecture appears as the lead essay in her *A Voice from the South, by a Black Woman of the South* (1892), a landmark African American feminist publication by a woman who challenged gender discrimination as early as her days as a student at St. Augustine's, and subsequently as an undergraduate at Oberlin College. In 1893, Cooper lectured on the intellectual advancement of African American women at the Congress of Representative Women at the World's Fair in Chicago. She addressed African American issues at the first Pan-

African Conference, which was convened in London in 1900. She also lectured at the 1895 National Conference of Colored Women in Boston, the 1896 National Federation of Afro-American Women in Washington, and the 1902 Biennial Session of Friends' General Conference in Asbury Park. In addition to her activities as an educator and lecturer, Cooper was a founder of the Colored Women's League of Washington in the late nineteenth century, and the Colored Women's Young Women's Christian Association in the first decade of the twentieth century. She was also a trustee of the Colored Settlement House, founded in 1905, and situated in Washington. In addition, she was the Women's Department editor for the African American magazine *Southland*, founded in 1890. Aside from the aforementioned *A Voice from the South*, Cooper's publications include her memoir, *The Third Step* (c. 1945), as well as the two volumes *Personal Recollections of the Grimké Family* (1951) and *The Life and Writings of Charlotte Forten Grimké* (1951). Cooper's 1925 dissertation, written in French, was translated by Frances Richardson Keller and published in 1988 as *Slavery and the French Revolutionists (1788–1805)*. The educator, writer, and activist died in Washington.
—LINDA M. CARTER

COPELAND, JOSEPHINE
(?–?) Poet

Josephine Copeland is best known for her poem "The Zulu King: New Orleans," which contains her unique perspective of black life during the Harlem Renaissance. Born in Covington, near New Orleans, Louisiana, she moved to Chicago after completing a two-year teaching course at Dillard University in New Orleans. She published few poems in her lifetime but, nonetheless, left an indelible mark.

Although much of the literary works of this movement centered on life in the city or the South, Copeland added her intimate experience of life in her native Louisiana in her celebrated poem, "The Zulu King: New Orleans." This poem was included in Arna Bontemps's *Golden Slippers* (1941). New Orleans is known for its large African American population and distinct cultural traditions that meld influences of the Spanish, French, and Africans. Mardi Gras, a long-standing tradition in the city, is a celebration that is observed with floats, costumes, and much revelry. "The Zulu King" is Copeland's ode to the Mardi Gras Carnival tradition and the pride that the Zulu-inspired float generated in her.

"The Zulu King" was Copeland's second known published poem. Her first, "Negro Folk Songs," was published in *Crisis* magazine in 1940. The poem describes the tragedy of black oppression and discrimination in four gripping stanzas.—GLADYS L. KNIGHT

COWDERY, MAE VIRGINIA
(1909–1953) Poet

Although not as familiar as other writers of the Harlem Renaissance, Mae Virginia Cowdery published numerous poems in popular black magazines during the 1920s. Encouraged by both Langston Hughes and Alain Locke, she submitted poems to

Crisis, Opportunity, and other journals. Her works also appeared in anthologies containing works by such writers as Jessie Redmon Fauset and Zora Neale Hurston. Inspired by the work of Edna St. Vincent Millay, Cowdery became one of few black female poets of that time to publish an entire volume of her own works.

Born in Germantown, Pennsylvania, on January 10, 1909, Cowdery grew up in a family that valued the arts. Her father, Lemuel, worked as a caterer and post-office clerk. Her mother, a social worker, helped direct the Bureau for Colored Children. They enrolled Cowdery in a prestigious school for academically gifted students, the Philadelphia High School for Girls. There she began to develop her interests in literature and the visual arts.

In the spring of 1927, Cowdery's senior year, *Black Opals*, a black literary journal based in Philadelphia, published three of her poems. That same year, she earned first place in a poetry contest sponsored by *Crisis*, and she also won the Krigwa Poem Prize. She belonged to Philadelphia's Beaux Arts Club, a literary society that began in the 1920s and flourished during the next three decades. Cowdery went on to study design and the visual arts at New York's Pratt Institute.

While in New York, she visited Harlem and Greenwich Village frequently, spending time in the cabarets. Langston Hughes, Alain Locke, Benjamin Brawley, and others encouraged Cowdery in her writing. Other contemporaries included Nellie Bright, Idabelle Yeiser, Evelyn Crawford Reynolds, Ottie Beatrice Graham, and Arthur Huff Fauset. Throughout the early 1930s, *Crisis* and *Opportunity* published many of Cowdery's poems. Her work also appeared in *Carolina Magazine* and *Unity*. A January 1928 issue of *Crisis* includes a few of her poems and features a photograph of her on its cover. That year, *Black Opals* published her one-act play, *Lai-Li*.

Several of Cowdery's poems were also published in anthologies, including Charles S. Johnson's *Ebony and Topaz*, William Stanley Braithwaite's *Braithwaite's Anthology*, and Benjamin Brawley's *The Negro Genius*. In 1936, she collected her works, publishing a limited edition volume (350 copies) entitled *We Lift up Our Voices and Other Poems*. In Braithwaite's highly complementary introduction to the work, he characterizes Cowdery as a fugitive poet. Critics proved receptive to the work, some of them comparing her imagery to that of Angela Weld Grimké and other modernists. The book stands as Cowdery's last published work. She committed suicide at the age of forty-four.—MARIE GARRETT

COX, IDA PRATHER
(February 25, 1896–November 10, 1967) Blues singer

Called a "Queen of the Blues," the "Uncrowned Queen of the Blues," and the "Blues Singer with a Feeling," Ida Cox began performing as a child. By the time the Harlem Renaissance reached full swing, she had become a star solo performer. In the late 1920s and early 1930s, Cox took her own road show on tour and did versions of *Raisin' Cain* and *Dark Town Scandals*. She barnstormed throughout the South in the 1930s and into the 1940s, and often appeared with emerging musicians and performers.

Born Ida Prather in Tocca, Stephens County, Georgia, she spent some years in Cedartown, Georgia, and sang in the church choir. When only fourteen years old, she left home and toured under the names Velma Bradley, Kate Lewis, Julia or Julia Powers, Jane Smith, and other stage names. She appeared in blackface and played "Topsy" roles with the White and Clark Black and Tan Minstrels until 1910. She later appeared with the Rabbit Foot Minstrels, Silas Green Show, and Florida Cotton Blossom Minstrels. In 1916, Prather married Adler Cox and became known under the Cox name. After Adler Cox died in World War I, she married twice more.

Between 1923 and 1929, Cox recorded extensively with Paramount, producing seventy-eight titles. Lovie Austin and Her Serenaders joined her on early recordings; they were backed up by Coleman Hawkins, Fletcher Henderson, and others. Cox also recorded for both the Harmograph and Silvertone labels simultaneously.

In 1945, Cox suffered a stroke that slowed her performances tremendously, and she moved to Knoxville, Tennessee, with her daughter. Her performances between 1940 and 1960 were intermittent. In 1961, after spending time doing church work and a twenty-year hiatus from performances, Cox cut her final album, *Blues for Rampart Street*, backed up by Hawkins and other all-star band members. She suffered another stroke while living in Knoxville and died of cancer.—JESSIE CARNEY SMITH

CRIPPENS, KATHERINE "LITTLE KATIE" [ELLA WHITE]
(November 17, 1895–November 25, 1929) Entertainer

Katherine "Little Katie" Crippens was born on November 17, 1895, to John Crippens and Catherine Garden in Philadelphia, Pennsylvania. She had at least two siblings. As a teenager, she settled in New York and worked at Edmond's Cellar, the cabaret club where Ethel Waters rose to fame. She married Lou Henry, who also was a musician. Crippens was also known as "Ella White."

Crippens recorded with the Fletcher Henderson Orchestra on the Black Swan label in 1921. It was Katie Crippens and Her Kids that gave the legendary William "Count" Basic one of his first musical opportunities. He was pianist of the group. Crippens also did various tours in the 1920s with Dewey Brown. She also operated her own food concession to bring in additional income.

Crippens died in 1929 after a long battle with cancer.—JEMIMA D. BUCHANAN

CUNARD, NANCY
(March 10, 1896–March 17, 1965) British poet, writer, publisher, journalist, activist

In regard to the Harlem Renaissance, the British-born Nancy Cunard is best known for her seminal contribution, the anthology entitled *Negro* (1934). Indeed, the anthology was, at the time of its publication, a groundbreaking work in that it features a comprehensive examination of the history of African Americans, their contributions and achievements, and the controversial issues of slavery, race, and racial injustice. The leading African American writers and intellectuals in Harlem praised her work, while the mainstream media vilified Cunard for her public support of African Americans. Cunard's outspokenness in regard to unpopular topics and causes, as well as her scandalous reputation, made her an unconventional and complex figure. Nonetheless, she garnered respect from many in the Harlem community during the Harlem Renaissance and is remembered as a daring contributor to early twentieth-century African American literature.

Cunard was born in 1896, into a wealthy family. Her father, Sir Bache Cunard, was an heir to the Cunard Line shipping business. Her American-born mother, Maud Alice Burke, descended from a wealthy family. Nancy spent her early childhood on the family estate in Leicestershire and was mostly raised by maids and governesses. Her appetite for reading, poetry, and elite culture, for instance, the opera, was greatly influenced by her mother and novelist George Moore.

In 1911, Cunard moved with her mother to London after her parents separated. She obtained her formal education at elite European institutions in London, as well as France and Germany. Although her world was filled with parties and encounters with royalty and high society, she would not subscribe to conventional ideas concerning white superiority and supremacy with regard to marginalized groups. Such ideas were prevalent among the power elite.

While Cunard remained a part of this world, she also did as she pleased. She took different lovers throughout her life, only briefly settling into marriage in 1916. When jazz created by African Americans reached Europe, Cunard became enamored with the music. She wore African bracelets piled up on her forearms. Known for her beauty and status as a well-known socialite, she fascinated as much as she confounded mainstream society. She inspired poets, novelists, and artists, many of whom were her friends. She promoted literature through her small press, Hours Press, which she established in 1928. She fueled media coverage of her scandalous behavior, for instance, her taboo relationship with the African American jazz musician Henry Crowder.

After meeting and then forming a relationship with Crowder in the late 1920s, Cunard's life was changed. Through Crowder, she was introduced to racism, discrimination, and racial violence in the United States. Her interest and desire for action spawned the anthology *Negro*. In this work, Cunard assembled mostly African American writers who contributed more than 800 pages of poetry, fiction, nonfiction, and historical documents. In addition to visits to Harlem, Cunard befriended such high-profile individuals as writer and Harlem Renaissance proponent Langston Hughes.

Cunard supported the literary development of African Americans, as well as their struggle for equality. Through such efforts as fund-raising and journalism, she fostered other causes, including protesting fascism in Spain.

When Cunard died in Paris, she left the world many works. These include poems; *Black Man and White Ladyship* (1931), a pamphlet that protests her mother's disapproval of her relationship with Crowder; and such books as *Grand Man: Memories of Norman Douglas* (1954).—GLADYS L. KNIGHT

CUNEY HARE, MAUD
(February 16, 1874–February 13, 1936) Biographer, playwright, musician, musicologist, historian

Maude Cuney Hare became an influential figure in the Harlem Renaissance during the 1920s. She was a talented musician, a prolific author, and one of the first historians to investigate the African roots of American music. She also documented the performances and compositions of black women in music.

Cuney Hare was born in Galveston, Texas, on February 16, 1874, the daughter of Adelina Dowdie Cuney, a school teacher, and Norris Cuney, a prominent Texas politician. Norris was the son of a white plantation owner and Adeline Stuart, one of his slaves. Maude's father served as an alderman, ran unsuccessfully for mayor of Galveston, and later became chairman of the Texas Republican Party. In 1889, Norris was appointed collector of customs for the port of Galveston.

Cuney Hare had a pale complexion and European features. She could have passed for white, but her equally light-skinned father made sure that she was proud to be an African American. Cuney Hare's family was very affluent. She grew up in a comfortable home surrounded by books and music. After graduating from Central High School in Galveston in 1890, she traveled to Boston at the age of sixteen to study at the prestigious New England Conservatory of Music. After her arrival, some of the white students complained and pressured the school's administrators to bar her from living in the dormitory. Cuney Hare's father received a letter in October asking him to remove his daughter from the conservatory. Mr. Cuney promptly dispatched a response, flatly refusing to do so.

After learning about the matter, Boston's Colored National League convened a meeting at the Charles Street A.M.E. Church. The attendees adopted a forceful resolution condemning the conservatory's actions and noting that discrimination against students based on their race was prohibited by Massachusetts law. They delivered the resolution to the conservatory and demanded just treatment for the young girl. W. E. B. Du Bois, who was a student at Harvard at the time, joined a group of students who supported Cuney Hare. The conservatory backed down, and Cuney Hare graduated in 1895.

After completing her studies at the conservatory, Cuney Hare enrolled in the Lowell Institute at Harvard University, where she studied English literature. She socialized with Boston's circle of elite African Americans and was, for a while, engaged to marry Du Bois. The engagement did not last, but the two remained friends, corresponding regularly and collaborating on projects. Cuney Hare was one of the first women to join the Niagara Movement, a predecessor to the National Association for the Advancement of Colored People (NAACP).

In 1898, Cuney Hare returned to Texas, where she served as director of music at the Texas Deaf, Dumb, and Blind Institute for Colored Youths. In 1898, she married a physician, J. Frank McKinley, and moved with him to Chicago. The couple had one child, Vera, and divorced in 1902. Cuney Hare returned to Texas and worked for two years as a music instructor at Prairie View State College (now Prairie View A&M University). On August 10, 1904, she married William Parker Hare and returned to Boston. In 1908, Cuney Hare's daughter from her previous marriage died at the age of eight.

Cuney Hare performed regularly in musical recitals and lectured extensively. She accompanied baritone William Howard Richardson on concert tours for almost two decades. She also performed with other distinguished singers. A folklorist and music historian, Cuney Hare was interested in the African connection to European and American music. She traveled to Mexico, Haiti, Cuba, Puerto Rico, and the Virgin Islands collecting folk songs and dances.

In 1913, she published a biography of her father, *Norris Wright Cuney: A Tribune of the Black People*. She edited a poetry collection, *The Message of the Trees: An Anthology of Leaves and Branches*, in 1918. She also authored *Antar of Araby*, a play about a black Arabian slave, poet, and warrior. In 1921, Cuney Hare wrote the book *Six Creole Folk Songs*. In addition, she contributed articles to *Musical Quarterly*, *Musical Observer*, *Musical America*, and the *Christian Science Monitor*. Cuney Hare wrote a regular column on music and the arts for *Crisis*, the NAACP's widely circulated periodical.

In 1927, the playwright and musician established the Allied Arts Center in Boston to encourage the musical and artistic abilities of African American children. She continued to write, producing her best-known book, *Negro Musicians and Their Music*, in 1936. Cuney Hare's research traced the evolution of African American music from its ancient African roots to the creation of jazz in the early twentieth century. She died of cancer in Boston shortly before her book was published.
—LELAND WARE

CUTHBERT, MARION VERA
(March 15, 1896–May 5, 1989) Educator, organization leader, writer, activist

Black women of the early twentieth century were circumscribed by race and gender prejudice, leading some, for example, Marion Vera Cuthbert, to seek relief and develop a commitment to equality and interracial harmony. Such conditions were very much behind the thinking of those who encouraged a renaissance in Harlem to celebrate and promote black talent. Cuthbert's talent was also manifest in her advocacy for black women in the black academy and her work for justice through the Young Women's Christian Association (YWCA).

Cuthbert was born to Victoria Means and Thomas Cornelius Cuthbert in Saint Paul, Minnesota. She earned a baccalaureate degree from Boston University in 1920; a master's degree in 1931, from Columbia University; and doctorate from Columbia University's Teachers College in 1942. After teaching English and serving as assistant principal at Burrell Normal School in Florence, Alabama, Cuthbert left in 1927, to become dean of women at historically black Talladega College in Talladega, Alabama. She was present on March 1–2, 1929, at a historic conference at Howard University that gave birth to the Association of Deans of Women and Advisers to Girls in Negro Schools.

Cuthbert left Talladega in 1932, to take a leadership position with the national YWCA, where she helped guide others in leadership training. She conducted workshops on interracial relations in the United States and several foreign countries. Cuthbert blossomed as a writer in the 1920s while with the YWCA. She contributed articles to Woman's Press, the official publication arm of the association, and *YMCA Magazine*, and collaborated on the organization's numerous training publications. Her writings include a biography of Fisk University's dean of women Juliette Derricotte, entitled *Juliette Derricotte* (1933); *We Sing America* (1938); a book of children's stories; *April Grasses* (1936); and *Songs of Creation* (1949). Cuthbert's essays, poetry, short stories, and book reviews regularly appeared in periodicals from the 1930s through the 1960s. Her works deal with YWCA matters, education, black women, race relations, religion, social issues, and other then-timely topics.

Cuthbert continued to work in YWCA leadership but also returned to academia in 1942, when she joined the Brooklyn College Department of Personnel Services. She retired in 1961, moved to Plainfield, New Hampshire, and became an integral member of the community. She held membership in church organizations and lectured to groups about social issues and her new books. She moved to Concord, New Hampshire, in 1968, and then to Windsor, Vermont, and Claremont, New Hampshire.—JESSIE CARNEY SMITH

D

DAY, CAROLINE STEWART BOND

(November 18, 1889–May 5, 1948) Anthropologist, writer, educator

During the Harlem Renaissance, Caroline Stewart Bond Day wrote essays, short stories, plays, children's stories, and poetry that were published in both anthologies and magazines. As an anthropologist, she was interested in the life and problems of blacks, as well as those of mixed racial heritage, a concern she had as the result of her own racially mixed background.

A Montgomery, Alabama, native, Day was the daughter of Georgia Fagain and Moses Stewart. A light-skinned woman, she was a descendant of black, Native American, and white forebears. For several years, the family lived in Boston. After Moses died, the family moved to Tuskegee, Alabama, where Georgia taught school and later married John Percy Bond, whose last name Caroline assumed. Caroline graduated from Atlanta University, taught English at Alabama State College (now Alabama State University) in Montgomery, and worked for the Young Women's Christian Association (YWCA) in Montclair, New Jersey. When she applied to Radcliffe College of Harvard University to pursue a graduate degree, the school refused to accept her Atlanta credits toward the degree; she was instead admitted to the undergraduate program and, in 1919, received a second bachelor's degree.

After World War I, Day worked with W. E. B. Du Bois as executive secretary of the Circle for Negro War Relief, and she also became student secretary of the National Board of the YWCA. She moved to Texas, taught English, and served as dean of women at historically black Paul Quinn College. She then moved to Prairie View State College (now Prairie View A&M University) as head of the English Department. In 1920, she married Aaron Day, who taught chemistry at the college and later became a salesman for the National Benefit Life Insurance Company. She returned to Atlanta University as instructor of English, drama, and anthropology, where she remained from 1922 to 1929.

Day continued her studies at Harvard's graduate school of anthropology and, in 1930, received her master's degree. Her thesis, *A Study of Some Negro-White Families in the United States*, was published in 1932, and republished in 1970. Her examination of mixed-race families was a first in the field of anthropology. The Days moved to Washington, D.C.; adopted a teenage boy; and taught English at Howard University. Caroline was also a social worker and directed a local settlement house in 1934. Her work with the YWCA continued, as she was appointed general secretary of the local Phillis Wheatley "Colored" YWCA in 1937. Aaron rose to the head office of North Carolina Mutual Life Insurance Company in Durham; his family joined him in 1939. Caroline taught English and drama at North Carolina College for Negroes (later North Carolina Central University). Due to health problems that she had endured for many years, she began to teach only occasionally, published some of her works, and spent time with her family. She also read, engaged in gardening, and attended local club activities. Complications of her chronic heart condition led to her death in 1948. In addition to her contributions in the classroom, Day had also made a name for herself in the field of anthropology.—JESSIE CARNEY SMITH

DEAN, LILLIAN HARRIS ["PIGFOOT MARY"]
(1872–July 15, 1929) Food vendor, realtor

Known for her business acumen, Lillian Harris Dean became successful during the Harlem Renaissance by turning a small (five-dollar) investment in the food business into a fortune. Her entrepreneurial success is well documented in the literature of the era.

Dean was born in Tougaloo, Mississippi, in 1892, and became part of the major migration of African Americans from the rural, segregated South to the urban North, looking to improve their lives. She first moved to Chicago, then to Boston, and, according to her obituary in the *New York Amsterdam News*, arrived in New York City in 1896. Blessed with an entrepreneurial spirit and a willingness to work hard, Dean began a cooked food vending business based on her southern roots, which became popular and lucrative. Although she sold such soul-food favorites as fried chicken and hot corn, her most desired menu item, which brought her lasting fame, was boiled pigs feet. The food stand was located on 135th and Lenox, near a newsstand that was owned by John Dean, a postal worker who became her husband of twenty-three years. Known as "Pigfoot Mary" throughout Harlem, Lillian saved the money she made from her entrepreneurial cooking and gained a reputation for thriftiness and shrewd investments.

In 1911, the New York legislature passed a food act that outlawed the sale of cooked food on the streets. This caused Dean to go out of the food vending business. She and her husband decided to transition into the real estate business and began purchasing property in the New York area. In his book *Black Manhattan*, which was first published in 1930, the famed author and poet James Weldon Johnson writes that "Pigfoot Mary" purchased an apartment building with five stories near the corner of Seventh Avenue and 137th for $42,000 and made a profit of $30,000 when she subsequently sold it to a black funeral director. At a time when many African Americans were struggling in dire poverty, Dean was able to purchase an apartment building worth $100,000, as well other properties.

Although she attended the Mother Zion A.M.E. Church for several years, Dean later became a member of the Mount Olivet Tabernacle and belonged to such fraternal organizations as the Independent Order of St. Luke and the Household of Ruth. In her retirement years, Dean decided to pursue her dreams of traveling both domestically and abroad. She made many trips to California, Hawaii, and the Pacific Islands. Her newspaper obituary states that she died in Los Angeles on July 15, 1929, leaving her husband, daughter, son-in-law, and seven-month-old granddaughter to mourn her passing. The family brought her back to New York and buried her in Woodlawn Cemetery. An article that appeared in the *New York Amsterdam News* after her death reveals that her husband filed a petition to be given authority of her personal property, which was valued at $75,000. She owned properties in both California and New York. At the time of her death, John's newsstand was located on 145th Street and Eighth Avenue, and the couple was fondly remembered for the three-week whirlwind romance that led to their lengthy marriage.

The memory of "Pigfoot Mary" still lives in Harlem lore. She was portrayed by actress Loretta Devine in the 1998 movie *Hoodlum*, starring Laurence Fishburne and Vanessa Williams.—GLENDA MARIE ALVIN

DELANY, CLARISSA MAE SCOTT
(May 22, 1901–October 11, 1927) Poet, critic

Clarissa Mae Scott Delany is best known as a poet, as well as one of the best representatives of the New Negro model of excellence during the 1920s, as she contributed literary writings and social commentary on key issues during the Harlem Renaissance era. Although she only lived a short twenty-six years, her involvement and influence were important.

Born in Tuskegee, Alabama, on May 22, 1901, Delany spent her early years on the campus of Tuskegee Institute, while her father, Emmett Jay Scott, was secretary to the school's founder, Booker T. Washington, for almost two decades. At the age of fifteen, Delany left home to study at Bradford Academy in Haverhill, Massachusetts, from 1916 to 1919, and Wellesley College from 1919 to 1923. While in college, she was active in sports and various clubs, and got her literary inspiration from the Literary Guild in Boston, where, on one occasion, she heard and was inspired by Harlem Renaissance poet Claude McKay.

Delany graduated from Wellesley in 1923, Phi Beta Kappa, with a focus on poetry and social economics. With such high honors, her picture was placed on the June 1923 issue of *Crisis* magazine, representing young, educated black women of her time. After traveling in Europe, Delany spent three years teaching at Dunbar High School in Washington, D.C., before marrying Hubert T. Delany, a lawyer, in 1926, and moving to New York City. During this time, Delany wrote often and submitted essays, book reviews, and poems to *Crisis*, *Opportunity*, and *Palms*. One such essay, published in 1925, by *Opportunity*, addresses major issues of the period, including art and Pan-Africanism. In 1926, Delany became a social worker with the National Urban League and the Women's City Club, and she collected statistical data regarding delinquency among black children in New York.

Delany's poetry, which was considered subtle in presentation and often personal in content, was popular with the literary community. From her early poetry "Interim," which appeared in 1923, to her series of lyrical poems, which include the well-known work "Solace," a fourth-place winner in the first literary contest held by *Opportunity*, Delany's style was lauded by such familiar contemporaries as W. E. B. Du Bois, Alice Dunbar-Nelson, and Countee Cullen. Her work was subsequently published in Cullen's anthology of black poets, *Caroling Dusk*, in 1927, a collection that was actually compiled by Langston Hughes and Arna Bontemps. Only a small portion of Delany's poetry was published, and the remaining works were lost throughout the years. The poet and critic died from a kidney disease that may have been the result of a six-month bout with a streptococcal infection or possibly tuberculosis. Special tributes were written for Delaney by Anna Julia Cooper and Angelina Weld Grimké, who wrote the poem "To Clarissa Scott Delany," published in *Ebony* in 1927.—LEAN'TIN L. BRACKS

DICKINSON, BLANCHE TAYLOR
(1896–1972) Poet, fiction writer, teacher

Blanche Taylor Dickinson's work appeared in prominent publications of the Harlem Renaissance, including *Crisis*, *The American Anthology*, *Caroling Dusk*, the *Louisville Leader*, and *Opportunity*. In the September 1927 issue of the latter, she was awarded the Buckner Award for "A Sonnet and a Rondeau," and for her potential, and in October, *Opportunity* printed her biographical statement. She wrote that she had an intense interest in young black writers and kept in touch with them through the black press.

Dickinson was born in Franklin, Kentucky, and attended Bowling Green Academy and Simmons University in Kentucky. She taught for a period in Sewickley, Pennsylvania, where she lived with her husband, Verdell Dickinson (1898–1978), a truck driver born in Trenton, Kentucky.

In the biographical statement that ran in *Opportunity*, Dickinson indicates that she and her mother shared the desire to write poetry and stories. In the output from her brief public publishing period (1927–1929), she reflects the themes and issues of black female writers the likes of Marita Bonner and Georgia Douglas Johnson, as well as the realities of the time. She details the plight and pain of women suffering racial, gender, and psychological oppression, and beauty measured by white standards. The women in Dickinson's poems are invisible and without voice, trapped and living within themselves. They are isolated and vulnerable in a world that disregards their thoughts and feelings. In her poem "Fortitude," Dickinson portrays the woman of the silent scream, the denial of her person, and her acceptance with a countenance of pride and a broken spirit. In the poem "Four Great Walls," Dickinson focuses on curtailed liberty, freedom, and expectations. She is buried in Pleasant View Cemetery in Simpson County, Kentucky.—HELEN R. HOUSTON

DISMOND [HODGES], GERALDYN
(July 29, 1894–1984) Journalist, writer, editor

Also known as the "Harlem Hostess" and "Gerri Major," Geraldyn Hodges Dismond served as editor and society columnist for some of the key black publications in New York, Pittsburgh, Chicago, and Baltimore. Her work spanned the Harlem Renaissance era and well into the 1980s. Dismond was born July 29, 1894, in Chicago. She went on to graduate from the University of Chicago in 1915. She later married a local doctor. After spending time as a teacher and serving as a major in the Red Cross during World War I, Dismond found her true calling in journalism and writing about the black society scene. She wrote columns for such black newspapers as the *New York Amsterdam News* in 1925, the *Pittsburg Courier* from 1926 to 1927, and the *Baltimore Afro-American* in 1928.

In 1927, Dismond won first place in a "Survey of the Negro Press"; in 1928, she presented herself as a "publicity agent" and opened the Geraldyn Dismond Bureau of Specialized Publicity, and from 1928 to 1931, served as manager-editor of the *Inter-state Tattler*, and later as its associate editor. Under Dismond's leadership, her frank commentaries, specifically on gossip columns in the *New York Amsterdam News* from 1939 to 1944, on the activities of luminaries on one hand, and the bohemian lifestyle on the other, all while excelling in her literary commentary as a journalist, made her columns a key part of the events of the age. Dismond was a familiar figure at many social galas of the time and found the extravagant parties given by A'Lelia Walker at her Harlem townhouse, known as the Dark Tower, a showcase of the vibrant times. Dismond hosted numerous parties of her own and was dubbed the "Harlem Hostess." Not limited by print media in showcasing black culture, she also became the first black female radio announcer and hosted the program "The Negro Achievement Hour" on station WABC.

After working as an administrative assistant from 1934 to 1946 for the New York Health Department's Bureau of Public Health Information and Education, Desmond became society editor and associate editor of *Ebony* magazine in 1953. She then became known as Gerri Major. Her career lasted another twenty-five successful years and included coauthoring the book *Black Society*, published in 1976. Dismond died in New York City.—LEAN'TIN L. BRACKS

DRAPER, MURIEL
(1891–August 26, 1956) Hostess, writer

During the 1920s, Muriel Draper used her New York salon to entertain many young black artists and writers of Harlem. Each Tuesday, her renovated stable on 40th Street was the site of teas, with an abundance of refreshments provided by friends, as she entertained about a third of her guests.

The years of Draper's birth and death are variously recorded; some sources say she was born in 1891 and died in 1956, while others say she was born in 1856 and passed away in 1952. The wife of Paul Draper, a baritone whom she divorced in 1916, Muriel had become famous for her salon in London known as "Edith Grove." Musicians and writers, including Henry James, John Sergeant, and possibly Gertrude Stein, whom she befriended, were her regular guests. She became known as a writer, as well as a "worldly society hostess, arts aficionado, decorator, and memoirist." Draper returned to her native New York in 1915, and became an interior designer, serving wealthy clients. She was a talented public speaker and published essays in *Vogue* and *Town and Country* magazines. In addition to her talents, Draper was known for her "strange beauty" and ability to attract the public eye with her fashionable dress.

Draper was a welcomed guest at A'Lelia Walker's Harlem townhouse, known as the Dark Tower, and at her 80 Edgecombe Avenue pied-à-terre, along with such black luminaries as Langston Hughes, Zora Neale Hurston, and Florence Mills; white writers from downtown, for example, Carl Van Vechten and Witter Byrnner, and a mixture of African and European royalty would also be in attendance. Draper is among those white benefactors who supported the African Americans who were connected to the arts during the Harlem Renaissance.—JESSIE CARNEY SMITH

DU BOIS, [NINA] YOLANDE

(1900–1960) Teacher

Yolande Du Bois was the only surviving daughter of the esteemed activist and scholar W. E. B. Du Bois and Nina Gomer Du Bois, his first wife. She is also known for her lavish wedding to the acclaimed Harlem Renaissance poet Countee Cullen. The wedding was a milestone event in Harlem Renaissance history.

Born in 1900, Du Bois received a prestigious education. She attended the Bedales School, a British preparatory academy. Her father expected no less. Indeed, he had been the first African American to receive a Ph.D. from Harvard University, a predominately white institution. He went on to achieve spectacular fame as an activist fighting for equality and against racial violence. He published several books and novels, for instance, the seminal work *The Souls of Black Folk* (1903). He taught at Atlanta University and cofounded the National Association for the Advancement of Colored People (NAACP). As editor of the NAACP's magazine, *Crisis*, W. E. B. Du Bois became an influential voice for the African American people. In *Crisis*, he promoted writers, including the men and women of the Harlem Renaissance.

Yolande followed in her father's footsteps when she attended Fisk University in Nashville, Tennessee. Her father had received his undergraduate degree there in 1888. In 1924, she received a degree in fine arts. After graduation, she taught in the Baltimore public school system.

In 1928, Du Bois made headline news as she and her fiancé, Countee Cullen, prepared for their greatly anticipated wedding. Cullen, born in Harlem, was a luminary of the Harlem Renaissance, earning several awards for his literature. Due to Du Bois's famous father and celebrated fiancé, the wedding was the social event of the year. There were some 3,000 guests in attendance for the nuptials, which took place on April 9, 1928. Guests included such well-known figures as African

American writers Arna Bontemps, Langston Hughes, and James Weldon Johnson, and Mary White Ovington, a suffragist, journalist, and cofounder of the NAACP.

Following the wedding, the newly married couple traveled to several cities, including Philadelphia, Pennsylvania, Atlantic City, New Jersey, and Great Barrington, Massachusetts. They also traveled to France; however, in 1930, the couple divorced. Yolande married a second time and gave birth to daughter Du Bois Williams in 1932. After Yolande's death from a heart attack in 1960, her father buried her near her mother in Great Barrington.—GLADYS L. KNIGHT

DU BOIS, SHIRLEY LOLA GRAHAM [SHIRLEY GRAHAM]
(November 11, 1896–March 27, 1977) Writer, composer, playwright, activist

Shirley Lola Graham Du Bois contributed creative works during the Harlem Renaissance. She remained productive throughout the 1970s until her death in 1977. Du Bois is also known for her marriage to prominent scholar and activist William E. B. Du Bois and her activism.

Born Shirley Lola Graham on November 11, 1896, in Evansville, Indiana, Du Bois was nurtured from childhood to transcend the limitations that were imposed on her ethnicity and gender by society. She was born into a world that denied blacks and women equal rights and full inclusion into mainstream society; however, her father, David A. Graham, a minister in the African Methodist Episcopal Church, and mother, Etta Bell Graham, instilled in her a passion for reading, learning, and pursuing grand dreams. The family moved frequently. Each new experience in New Orleans, Louisiana, Nashville and Clarksville, Tennessee, and Spokane, Washington, yielded opportunities for Du Bois to explore her talents and broaden her outlook on life. At only eight or nine years of age, she received payment for contributing articles to a local newspaper. She won a contest for an essay entitled "Booker T. Washington" while in high school in 1912.

Several years later, Du Bois focused on family life. In 1921, she married Shadrach McCants. An ambitious individual, McCants owned a clothing store and worked for a newspaper. In 1923, Du Bois gave birth to their first son, Robert. A few years later, in 1925, they welcomed their second son, David; however, in 1927, Du Bois and McCants divorced.

While the Harlem Renaissance was still at its peak, Du Bois emerged a single mother intent on continuing her educational and creative goals. In 1929, she launched her educational experiences at the Sorbonne in Paris, where she studied music composition. In 1934, she graduated with a bachelor's degree in music from Oberlin College in Ohio. The following year, she received an M.A. in music history from the same institution. Throughout the 1930s, Du Bois was productive. A notable work includes her musical composition *Tom-Tom*, which she wrote in 1932. The production pays tribute to the history of African Americans from Africa to Harlem. In the 1930s, Harlem was still a vortex of African American talent in art, music, and literature.

Du Bois used her multiple talents in various ways. She taught music at Morgan College in Baltimore, Maryland (now Morgan State University), and music and arts at the Agricultural and Industrial State College in Nashville, Tennessee (now Tennessee State University). From the mid-1930s to the 1940s, she was also supervisor of the Negro Unit of the Chicago Federal Theater and a USO director at Fort Huachuca in Arizona. She was also a longtime national field secretary for the National Association for the Advancement of Colored People (NAACP). Her abundant writings include the plays *Coal Dust* (1938) and *Dust to Earth* (1941), as well as books on such eminent African American figures as George Washington Carver, Paul Robeson, Frederick Douglass, Booker T. Washington, and husband-to-be W. E. B. Du Bois (after his death).

In 1951, Du Bois married W. E. B Du Bois. At the time of their marriage, she was fifty-four; he was eighty-four years old and still deeply entrenched in the struggle for equality for African Americans. W. E. B. helped found and lead the NAACP and greatly supported the Harlem Renaissance. Stories, poems, and reviews by African Americans appeared regularly in the NAACP's magazine, *Crisis*, during a time when talented African Americans were largely ignored by the mainstream media. The lives of the newlyweds took a sudden turn following Du Bois's arrest for his association with Communism. Following his arrest, the couple traveled to Europe, the Soviet Union, and China. They eventually became members of the Communist Party and moved to Accra, Ghana, in 1962. In Ghana, Shirley helped her husband with his book, *Encyclopedia Africana*. He died in 1963.

Denied permission to return permanently to the United States, Shirley moved from Ghana to Cairo and China. She died in Beijing, China, of breast cancer. —GLADYS L. KNIGHT

DUNBAR-NELSON, ALICE RUTH
(July 19, 1875–September 18, 1935) Author, activist, educator

Alice Ruth Dunbar-Nelson was one of the most influential women of the Harlem Renaissance; she was a prolific writer (poet, short story writer, dramatist, novelist, essayist, journalist, and diarist), editor, educator, and lecturer, as well as a social and political activist. Dunbar-Nelson was born in New Orleans, Louisiana, on July 19, 1875, to Joseph Moore, a merchant marine, and Patricia Moore, a seamstress. She attended the city's public schools and completed the two-year teachers' program at Straight College (now Dillard University) in 1892. Dunbar-Nelson also studied at Cornell University, Columbia University, the Pennsylvania School of Industrial Art, and the University of Pennsylvania. She is also known as the widow of her first husband, Paul Laurence Dunbar.

Prior to Dunbar-Nelson's marriage to the most prominent African American poet of the nineteenth and early twentieth centuries, she taught school in her hometown from 1892 to 1896. During that period, her *Violets and Other Tales* (1895), a collection of essays, poetry, and short stories, was published. In 1897, she moved to Brooklyn, New York, where she taught at a public school. She also helped Victoria Earle Matthews with the founding of the White Rose Mission Home for Girls, located in Harlem, and met Dunbar face-to-face after a two-year correspondence initiated by the famous poet. They married on March 8, 1898, and lived in Wash-

Alice Ruth Dunbar-Nelson

ington, D.C., where they were considered the African American version of poets Robert and Elizabeth Barrett Browning. Dunbar-Nelson's second book, *The Goodness of St. Rocque and Other Stories* (1899), was presented in conjunction with Dunbar's *Poems of Cabin and Field* (1899) by his publisher. In September 1900, Dunbar-Nelson's first play, *The Author's Evening at Home*, was published in the *Smart Set*, a periodical edited by George Jean Nathan and H. L. Mencken. Alice and Paul legally separated in 1902, four years before his death at the age of thirty-three.

In 1902, Dunbar-Nelson moved to Wilmington to teach English and drawing at Howard High School, the only African American high school in Delaware. She later served as head of the English Department. In addition to working at Howard, Dunbar-Nelson ran the in-service teachers' summer sessions at the State College for Colored Students (now Delaware State University) for seven years, and she taught for two summers at Hampton Institute (now Hampton University). In April 1909, an excerpt from her Cornell thesis, "Wordsworth's Use of Milton's Description of the Building of Pandemonium," appeared in *Modern Language*.

On January 19, 1910, Dunbar-Nelson married Henry A. Callis, a fellow Howard High educator, Cornell University acquaintance, and cofounder of the Alpha Phi Alpha fraternity. The following year, Callis, who was twelve years younger than his wife, left Wilmington to attend medical school, and the couple subsequently divorced. Callis later became a physician and a Howard University professor of medicine. Dunbar-Nelson's tenure at Howard High School ended in 1920, when her political activism led to her termination after she returned from Marion, Ohio, where she participated in Social Justice Day events. Four years later, along with other members of the Federation of Colored Women, she established the Industrial School for Colored Girls (later named the Kruse Industrial School) in Marshalltown, Delaware, where she volunteered as a teacher and parole officer until 1928.

On April 16, 1916, Dunbar married Robert John Nelson, a journalist and widower with two children. The previously published writer continued to write during her second and third marriages. She also edited two books: *Masterpieces of Negro Eloquence: The Best Speeches Delivered by the Negro from the Days of Slavery to the Present* (1914) and *The Dunbar Speaker and Entertainer, Containing the Best Prose and Poetic Selections by and about the Negro Race* (1920). Dunbar-Nelson included eight of her works in *The Dunbar Speaker*, including the short story "The Praline Woman," the poem "I Sit and Sew," and the one-act play about

African American men fighting in World War I entitled *Mine Eyes Have Seen the Glory*. During the author's lifetime, her creative works were also published in such periodicals as the *Brooklyn Standard Union*, the *Southern Workman*, *Lippincott's Magazine*, *Leslie's Weekly*, *Crisis*, *Opportunity*, and *Harlem: A Forum of Negro Life*, as well as in anthologies. These include *Book of American Negro Poetry* (1922), edited by James Weldon Johnson; *Negro Poets and Their Poems* (1923), edited by Robert T. Kerlin; *Caroling Dusk* (1927), edited by Countee Cullen; and *Ebony and Topaz* (1927), edited by Charles S. Johnson. Dunbar-Nelson's articles appeared in various sources, namely *Education*, *A.M.E. Church Review*, *Messenger*, and the *Journal of Negro History*. She was a syndicated columnist for the *Pittsburgh Courier* in 1926, and for the *Washington Eagle* from 1926 to 1930. From 1920 to 1922, the Nelsons published and edited the *Wilmington Advocate*, an African American newspaper. Dunbar-Nelson's diary from the 1920s and early 1930s was edited by Gloria Hull and published as *Give Us Each Day: The Diary of Alice Dunbar-Nelson* (1984). It provides insight into the life of an African American female intellectual, writer, and activist, and offers Dunbar-Nelson's firsthand observations of early twentieth-century life.

Dunbar-Nelson remained steadfast in her determination to battle racism and sexism. She was a field representative for the Women's Committee of the Council of National Defense in 1913; a field organizer for the Middle Atlantic to campaign for women's suffrage in 1915; a member of the prominent African American group that met with President Warren Harding in the American Friends Peace Committee; and, in 1929, the first African American woman to serve as a Republican state committee member in Delaware. In 1932, when Robert Nelson was appointed a member of the Pennsylvania Athletic Commission, the family moved to Philadelphia. Dunbar-Nelson died at the University of Pennsylvania Hospital at the age of sixty.—LINDA M. CARTER

DUNCAN, THELMA MYRTLE [THELMA BROWN]
(1902–?) Playwright, novelist, short story writer, educator

Thelma Myrtle Duncan was a member of an elite group of university students and writers who formed the National Negro Theater at the beginning of the twentieth century. She was active in the New Negro Movement in Washington, D.C., an extension of the renaissance that was taking place in Harlem. She associated with other luminaries of that era, including Mae Miller, Georgia Douglas Johnson, and Zora Neale Hurston. She was also author of nine plays, some published and some unpublished.

Duncan was born in St. Louis, Missouri, in 1902, and graduated cum laude from Howard University with a degree in music. She later attended Columbia University. She became a music teacher as a necessity, although her true passion was writing. She taught music in North Carolina.

At the Civil War's end, 90 percent of African Americans lacked literacy. In the 1800s, 30 percent were literate, and, by 1890, 50 percent could read. With the improved literacy, a larger percentage of blacks were educated and produced an audience for black plays, poems, and other writings. The Harlem Renaissance, or New

Negro Movement, of the 1920s and 1930s was not strictly confined to the Harlem section of New York, but flowered in several urban areas.

At Howard University in Washington, D.C., students and faculty were active in literary and artistic pursuits. It was in this rich climate that Howard students were writing plays to be performed by the Howard Players and other theater groups. Duncan's *Death Dance* was one of the first plays put on by the Howard Players. It was performed in Rankin Memorial Chapel at Howard, and in the Douglass Theatre in Baltimore. Some of the New Negro one-act plays were performed at the 135th Street Branch of the New York Public Library.

Duncan wrote several one act-plays, including *The Death Dance* (1927). *Sacrifice* is the story of a character named Roy who sacrifices his good name so his friend can graduate from college. *Black Magic* is a comedy about superstition among blacks in the South. Duncan also wrote *Drifter: One-Act Plays of Lower Negro Life, Jinda, Payment*, and *The Scarlet Shawl*.

Duncan was mentored by Howard University professor and editor of *The New Negro*, Alain Locke. A second mentor was Thomas Montgomery Gregory, founder of Howard University's Drama Department. She wrote at least two more plays, *The Witch Woman* and *Hard Times*, with the wish that they be published in a collection by Montgomery. Her novel, *Ham's Children*, was never published.

The plays at National Negro Theater were of three different genres—the revelation class, contribution class, and conscience class. The revelation class was written to introduce the Negro world to the white world. The contribution class showed how important the Negro was to society as a whole. The conscience class attempted to appeal to Caucasian liberals to get them to join in the fight for equality. Duncan wrote three plays in the conscience category, with characters like Roy in *Sacrifice*. Duncan's mentor, Alain Locke, was probably disappointed in his students for trying to change white people's minds with one-dimensional characters in their plays.

Duncan traveled by automobile throughout New Mexico, Texas, and Mexico. She returned to her parents' home in La Junta, Colorado, in 1929, hoping to write full-time, but she was not successful, even though her play *Sacrifice* was published in *Plays and Pageants from the Life of the Negro in 1930*. She wrote a letter to her professor, Gregory, indicating her disappointment with her writing career. She wanted to write but was unable to make a career of it. Duncan's play *Black Magic* was published in *Yearbook of Short Plays*, edited by Claude Merton.

When she was thirty years old and living in Albuquerque, New Mexico, Duncan married a Mr. Brown in 1932. Here she started a novel and had some success with short stories; two of her stories were published. The date of her death is unclear.— ELIZABETH SANDIDGE EVANS

DUNN, BLANCHE
(April 1911–?) Socialite, actress

Blanche Dunn was recognized by many of her Harlem Renaissance contemporaries as one of the most beautiful and fashionable women in New York. She has been called the "it" girl of that era.

Dunn was born in Jamaica in 1911, and arrived in New York City in 1926, when she was fifteen or sixteen years old. She met Wilda Gunn, a fashion designer, who mentored the teenager and taught her how to dress appropriately and stylishly. Dunn was a showgirl in the Broadway musical *Blackbirds of 1930*, and she had a minor role in *The Emperor Jones*, the 1933 film starring Paul Robeson.

Dunn attended the opening nights of numerous Broadway productions, as well as many social events in Harlem and elsewhere in Manhattan, including parties hosted by such prominent figures as A'Lelia Walker and Carl Van Vechten. In addition to being a mainstay at Van Vechten's parties, Dunn posed for his photographs of her as early as January 1924, and as late as May 1941. There are at least two photographs from 1924 of Dunn's legs and shoes, in addition to a 1941 photograph of Dunn wearing Martinique attire. Her popularity guaranteed that a table was always reserved for her at the Hot Cha, a popular and exclusive Harlem nightclub. Dunn's beauty, personality, and sophistication enabled her to wear expensive clothes, shop in Paris, and travel to other European locales. In late January or early February 1953, for example, she returned to New York after a nine-month European vacation that included trips to Paris and the Riviera. She ultimately married and relocated to a villa in Capri.—LINDA M. CARTER

E

EASTMAN, CRYSTAL
*(June 25, 1881–July 8, 1928) Harlem Renaissance supporter, activist,
legal scholar, publisher*

Crystal Eastman was a feminist and activist whose quest for justice intersected with the Harlem movement through her association with Claude McKay, one of the genius poets of the Harlem Renaissance. Eastman advanced the black cause by appointing McKay as associate editor of the controversial journal the *Liberator*. She gave voice to the black experience. In 1919, the publication introduced McKay's poetry with the seminal work, "If We Must Die," an artistic expression of the response to the racial riots of the summer of 1919. It became a manifesto for the spirit of the Harlem movement.

Eastman was born to two ministers within the Congregational Church in Massachusetts. She received a graduate degree in sociology from Columbia University and a law degree from New York City University Law School. Eastman was a feminist lawyer with great concern about civil liberties for all people as a compassionate champion of the intersection of race, gender, and class. She was one of the founders of the Congressional Union for Women's Suffrage, the Women's Peace Party, the National Civil Liberties Bureau, and the American Civil Liberties Union. Her commitment and contribution to the women's movement was not to overshadow her commitment to workers' rights and civil rights for blacks. She understood the plight of the working poor woman of color. Her brother, Max Eastman, was a socialist writer and poet who was an active patron of the Harlem Renaissance.—SHEILA R. PETERS

ELLIS, EVELYN
(February 2, 1894–June 5, 1958) Actress

An actress on the stage, screen, and television, Evelyn Ellis had a successful thirty-five-year career that embraced the Harlem Renaissance era. Although her work was interrupted by the Great Depression, she made a comeback in 1937, and continued to be productive until 1953. Accounts of her work vary from that of minor actress and one whose name is not widely recognized in entertainment to that as an actress of outstanding talent and performance.

Born in 1894, in Boston, the facts of her family life and educational background are virtually obscure. Ellis made her professional stage debut in 1919, at the Lafayette Theater, appearing in a production of *Othello*. She then had parts in several Broadway shows, including *Roseanne*. Ellis appeared in the revival of *Goat Alley* in 1927, and played the role of Bess in the hit drama *Porgy*, the forerunner of *Porgy and Bess*. An actress in race films, she appeared in *Easy Money* (1921) and Oscar Micheaux's controversial *A Son of Satan* (1924).

In 1937, Ellis was cast in the comedy *Horse Play*, supported through the Works Progress Administration and its efforts to sustain the black theater. She continued with a number of successful performances, including *Native Son* (1941), *Blue Holiday* (1945), *Deep Are the Roots* (1945), *Tobacco Road* (which she also directed, 1950), and *Supper for the Dead* (1954). Ellis died in Saranac Lake, New York, of a heart ailment.—JESSIE CARNEY SMITH

EPPERSON, ALOISE BARBOUR
(March 21, 1889–July 13, 1953) Poet

As the audiences of the 1920s encouraged black women to offer their creative talents through poetry while confronting segregation and racist notions of the day, some preferred less confrontational approaches in their technique. Aloise Barbour Epperson is one such poet who, because of her devastating experiences in the racist South, chose to focus more on lyrical poetry using conventional and religious themes, while invoking a keen sense of observation. Although a recognized member of the Harlem Renaissance writers, publications of her work are unknown prior to her book of poetry, *The Hills of Yesterday*, in 1943. Epperson was respected for her poetry in her local community. She died from a cerebral hemorrhage and is buried in West Point Cemetery in Norfolk, Virginia. —LEAN'TIN L. BRACKS

EVANTI, LILLIAN [ANNIE LILLIAN EVANS]
(August 12, 1890–December 6, 1967) Opera singer, music educator

Following the advice of Jessie Redmon Fauset, a Harlem Renaissance novelist and editor, Lillian Evans combined her maiden and married names to become known professionally as [Lillian] Evanti. Annie Lillian Evans was born in Washington, D.C., on August 12, 1890, to Bruce Evans, a physician-turned-school principal, and Anne Brooks, a music teacher. She was educated at Miner's Teacher's College and received her degree in music in 1917, from Howard University. In 1918, she

Lillian Evanti

married Howard music professor Roy W. Tibbs and had a son, Thurlow E.

To pursue a career in opera, Evanti traveled abroad to Paris, France, and Italy, and she was among the first black Americans to sing abroad with the Nice Opera, a European opera company. In 1925, critical reviews were bestowed upon her when she performed the lead role in *Lakme*, by Delibes, at the Casino Theatre in Nice, France. While in France, and for the next five years, she studied voice with Madame Ritter-Ciampi, as well as acting with Monsieur Gaston Dupins.

Upon her return to Washington, D.C., Evanti continued to perform throughout the United States, Europe, and Latin America. In 1934, she gave a performance at the White House for President and Mrs. Franklin D. Roosevelt, something she repeated years later for presidents Eisenhower and Truman. When the National Negro Opera Company produced Verdi's *La Traviata*, Evanti received rave reviews for her performance as Violetta in 1943.

In addition to being a renowned opera singer, Evanti was also a songwriter who founded her own music publishing house, Columbia Music Bureau. She died in Washington, D.C.—SHARON D. BROOKS

F

FAUSET, JESSIE REDMON
(April 27, 1882–April 30, 1961) Novelist, editor, teacher, poet

Jessie Redmon Fauset

Born in New Jersey in 1882, Jessie Redmon Fauset, arguably one of the most underrepresented figures of the later Harlem Renaissance era, was the youngest of seven children born to a minister and his wife. After her mother's death, Fauset and the family moved to Philadelphia, where she experienced the impact of the color line as the only black student in her class. Such encounters proved inherently influential on Fauset's later novels, for instance, *There Is Confusion* (1924) and *Plum Bun: A Novel without a Moral* (1929), both examples of the Künstlerroman examining the themes of racial identity and class. Characterized by Langston Hughes as the literary midwife of the emerging Harlem Renaissance tradition, Fauset became an influential figure in the literary revival of her time, in part through her depictions of American color prejudice, as well as through her editorship of *Crisis* magazine from 1919 to 1926.

Graduating Phi Beta Kappa from Cornell University in 1905, the first black woman to attend and graduate from the university, Fauset was a teacher in Baltimore and later in Washington, D.C. In 1919, she graduated from the University of Pennsylvania with a master's degree in French and continued teaching before persuaded by W. E. B. Du Bois to become literary editor of *Crisis* later that same year.

Although her time with the magazine was relatively short, her impact was ultimately long-lived, shaping the literary careers of black authors, from Langston Hughes to Countee Cullen and Claude McKay. During this time, Fauset also served as literary editor for *The Brownies' Book: A Monthly Magazine for the Children of the Sun* from 1920 to 1921—a journal devoted to teaching black heritage to children. Through her editorship of these two magazines, Fauset provided emergent black writers with an opportunity to present their works and contribute to the burgeoning tradition of New Negro literature later known as the Harlem Renaissance.

In 1924, Fauset published her first novel, *There Is Confusion*—the first of four novels she composed largely focused on the black struggle for fulfillment and acceptance despite rampant racial prejudice within the black community and throughout the United States. Here, Joanna Marshall, the protagonist of the novel, strives to gain acclaim as a singer and dancer, even though her endeavors consistently clash with the American color line. The novel, Fauset's response to T. S. Stribling's controversial novel *Birthright*, reveals a different side of the African American experience than that presented in most Harlem Renaissance fiction. Instead, Fauset presents the life she knew: life in the black middle class, where the struggles for social mobility were just as present as among the working class. Such themes continue in her 1929 novel *Plum Bun: A Novel without a Moral*, as the character of Angela Murray temporarily turns to passing as a vehicle to escape the racial discrimination that interfered with the creation of her art. That same year, Fauset married Herbert Harris, a World War I veteran and insurance broker. The marriage produced no children.

Later, in 1931, Fauset published her third novel, entitled *The Chinaberry Tree*, arguably her least successful work. The novel presents the story of a slave woman whose feelings of love for her master soon dissipate after earning freedom and gaining a new understanding of self. Soon thereafter, in 1933, Fauset published her fourth and final novel, *Comedy: American Style*—a complex work depicting the tragic result of self-hate and intraracial color consciousness within the larger black community. Following the character Olivia, the novel illustrates the desperate and disastrous attempts she takes to pass as being white, denigrating her own son and even condemning her daughter to a marriage of veritable misery. These four novels attempt to complicate the portrait of the African American experience, moving beyond the simple tragic mulatto or gin-chasing primitive explored in other Harlem Renaissance works.

Fauset remained with Harris until his death in 1958, her role in the literary world ultimately diminishing during these years. Despite this, through her editorial and literary endeavors, she left an indelible mark on the Harlem Renaissance and the larger African American literary tradition before her death from a heart attack in 1961. Her works challenge the gender and racial limitations placed on black women of her time, as each novel focuses on the empowered black woman, from Joanna Marshall to Angela Murray, whose drive challenged the stereotypes of the not-so-distant past. Through this approach, Fauset's works present a necessary commentary on the dynamics of race, class, and gender in the United States.—CHRISTOPHER ALLEN VARLACK

FERNANDIS, SARAH COLLINS
(March 8, 1863–July 11, 1951) Social activist, poet, essayist

The New Negro of the Harlem Renaissance resented being seen as a social ward. Their response was reflected in racial assertiveness and consciousness and the rise of black social workers. For Sarah Collins Fernandis, the response was personal; she spent her life organizing welfare and public health initiatives, often across racial and class lines, that improved the lives of African Americans and communities at large. She founded the first Black Social Settlement House, a neighborhood social welfare agency designed to meet the specific needs of the people being served. She established the Baltimore Women's Cooperative Civic League to push for improved sanitation and health conditions in black neighborhoods, and in 1920, Fernandis was the first black social worker hired by the Baltimore Health Department. She was also instrumental in the opening in Baltimore of a tuberculosis sanitorium for black people, Henryton State Hospital, in 1923.

Born to Caleb Alexander Collins and Mary Jane Driver Collins in Port DePosit, Maryland, Fernandis graduated from Hampton Normal and Agricultural Institute (1882), attended the New York School of Philanthropy (1906), and married John A. Fernandis in 1902. She held teaching positions in Virginia, Tennessee, Georgia, and Maryland. She received her master of social work degree from New York University.

Fernandis's dedication to racial community uplift and optimism were not only evident in her work, but also in her writing, both prose and poetry. She wrote on social issues, nature, and black American achievements. Her work appeared in the *Southern Workman*, and in 1925, her books of poetry, *Poems* and *Vision*, were published. Among other topics, she targeted the plight of the poor and blacks, eulogized Booker T. Washington, and extolled the courage of black soldiers as American citizens. Fernandis continued her public service after her retirement by opening the National Administration office for housing homeless young women; she volunteered her services. Her methods and work were recognized both in the United States and England. Fernandis died at the age of eighty-eight in Baltimore.—HELEN R. HOUSTON

FIELDS, DOROTHY
(July 15, 1905–March 28, 1974) Lyricist, librettist

Dorothy Fields was born July 15, 1905, in Allenhurst, New Jersey, the daughter of Rose Harris Fields from Troy, New York, and Lewis Maurice Schoenfield, a Jewish immigrant from Poland. Lew Fields was a vaudeville star in the successful comedy team of (Joe) Weber and Fields at the end of the nineteenth century. This environment influenced both Dorothy and her brothers, who also became successful in theater: Joseph as a writer and producer and Herbert as a writer and Dorothy's sometimes collaborator. The team of Weber and Lewis broke up, and Lew Fields became one of the most important theater producers of the day. He produced approximately 40 Broadway shows and was called the "King of Musical Comedy."

Following graduation from the Benjamin School for Girls in 1923, Dorothy desired to become an actress, a choice her father was against and thwarted. In school, she had excelled in English and history and published her poetry in the school's literary magazine. Thus, she taught drama for a brief period and continued writing poetry. She published poetry briefly in the *New York World*. In 1924, she married Jack Weiner, a surgeon; they later divorced.

Fields was introduced to Jimmy McHugh by J. Fred Coots, a popular songwriter best known for his 1934 song "Santa Claus Is Coming to Town," and with whom Fields had written some unremarkable lyrics. McHugh asked her if she was interested in writing revues for the Cotton Club in Harlem. When they teamed up, Fields discovered her niche as a lyricist and launched a career that saw her gain success in writing songs for Tin Pan Alley, Broadway, and Hollywood. Fields and McHugh were a team from the late 1920s until the mid-1930s. They are credited with providing some of the most popular songs of the period. "I Must Have That Man," "Diga Diga Doo," and "I Can't Give You Anything but Love" from the *Blackbirds of 1928*, and from the 1930 *International Revue*, "Exactly Like You" and "On the Sunny Side of the Street" became favorites for the big bands of the period. The success of their songs was supported and furthered by Louis Armstrong, who used them when he began recording with big bands. The duo's success on and experience with revues on Broadway laid the foundation for a contract from Hollywood and their achievements in film. Fields and McHugh were credited for music that appeared in 39 films, *Love in the Rough*, *Singin' the Blues*, *Cuban Love Song*, *Clowns in Clover*, and *Every Night at Eight* (for which they wrote "I'm in the Mood for Love") being just a few examples. During this period, the team split, and Fields began collaborating with other composers.

Fields collaborated with such composers as Sigmund Romberg, Morton Gould, Harold Arlen, Oscar Levant, Fritz Kreisler, and Jerome Kern. Kern was both her favorite collaborator and friend. They partnered to write scores for *The Joy of Living*, *I Dream Too Much*, and *Swing Time*. The latter film includes the song "The Way You Look Tonight," which earned Fields and Kern the 1936 Academy Award for Best Original Song. In 1934, Fields married David Eli Lahm, a businessman, and the couple settled in Manhattan. They subsequently became parents of two children—David and Eliza. In the 1940s, Dorothy and her brother Herbert began collaborating on books for Broadway plays. Their efforts include *Let's Face It*, *Something for the Boys*, and *Mexican Hayride*, all Cole Porter shows, as well as *Annie Get Your Gun*, which grew from an idea Dorothy had and was scored by Irving Berlin. In 1945, Dorothy and Herbert wrote the book and Dorothy wrote the lyrics for Sigmund Romberg's operetta *Up in Central Park*.

In the 1950s, Fields worked with Harry Arlen on the film *Mr. Imperium* and composer Arthur Schwartz on the Broadway musical *A Tree Grows in Brooklyn*. During this same time period, she and her brother coauthored the book and wrote the lyrics for Schwartz's musical *By the Beautiful Sea*. In addition, Dorothy wrote both the book and lyrics for Albert Hague's *Redhead*, which won six Tony Awards. In the 1960s, Fields was asked by Cy Coleman to become part of the creative team for the Broadway show *Sweet Charity*, and from this show came two memorable songs: "Big Spender" and "If My Friends Could See Me Now." This was the highlight of the 1960s for her, although she was involved in some lesser collaborations. She collaborated once with her son David, as well as with Quincy Jones. Fields's final Broadway production was in the 1970s and was a collaboration with Cy Coleman on the musical *Seesaw*. On March 28, 1974, she suffered a fatal stroke.

Fields's career spanned more than fifty years, from the Jazz Age and the 1920s to the rock and roll of the early 1970s in radio revues, Hollywood film, Broadway musicals, and television. She excelled in a profession dominated by men. During her lifetime, she cowrote more than 400 songs and collaborated with more than eighteen composers. Many of her songs have become part of popular culture. Fields's longevity and versatility can be attributed to several factors. First, she was able to maintain relevance and popular appeal because of her talent for the vernacular and her ear for slang, everyday speech, and the urbane. Second, her ability to be sensuous, humorous, risqué, sentimental, and meticulous made her work successful and lasting. Third, she maintained both the traditional image of the woman while reflecting the new woman of the later twentieth century.—HELEN R. HOUSTON

FIGGS, CARRIE LAW MORGAN
(1878–1968) Poet, playwright

Before the Harlem Renaissance became a collective movement toward the literary and cultural defining of black Americans, there were those who had already put forth the ancestral legacy of black creative expression. Carrie Law Morgan Figgs, an early twentieth-century poet and playwright, not only contributed to the literary accomplishments of black America, but she self-published some of her work to insure its availability.

Figgs, who was born in 1878, went on to become a teacher at Edward Waters College in Jacksonville, Florida. As a teacher and community leader, she used her poetry to confront racial issues and uplift the race. Her early collections of poetry include *Poetic Pearls* (1920) and *Nuggets of Gold* (1921), which address Jim Crow laws, contributions of African Americans, and the injustices of racism. Also as a playwright, Figgs clearly sought to reach the community, as she stated in her collection of self-published plays, which includes *Santa Claus Land*, *Jepthah's Daughter*, *The Prince of Peace*, and *Bachelors Convention* (1923), that the plays were free for use by amateurs, but for professionals the author reserved her rights. Her plays used biblical themes or messages that catered to moral instruction.

Although Figgs was not directly involved in the Harlem Renaissance, her work as a poet and playwright during this early era of the twentieth century unquestionably helped to set the stage for the cohesive movement of art for racial uplift and political commentary.—LEAN'TIN L. BRACKS

FLEMING, SARAH LEE BROWN
(January 10, 1876–January 5, 1963) Activist, educator, writer, poet

Sarah Lee Brown Fleming joined those writers of the Harlem Renaissance who had something to say about the race problems in American society and who achieved in spite of the odds being firmly against them. She was born on January 10, 1876, in Charleston, South Carolina, and moved to Brooklyn, New York, as a child. Although raised in poverty, she achieved a college education, becoming the first black teacher in the Brooklyn school system. On November 5, 1902, she married Richard Stedman Fleming and had two children, Dorothy (1903) and Harold (1906). She and her family moved to New Haven, Connecticut, where she organized the New Haven Women's Civic League in 1929. Her husband, a dentist, was the first African American to practice in Connecticut.

In her position as community activist and organizer, Fleming was cited on numerous occasions for her many contributions. These honors include election as Connecticut's "Mother of the Year" in 1952; she was the first African American female to be awarded this distinct honor. In 1955, Congress acknowledged her municipal achievements.

Although not primarily known as a writer, Fleming had a notable literary history. She used her writing as a voice of expression regarding racial disparity and pride in her people. Her first novel, *Hope's Highway*, was published in 1918. She is also known for her poetic work, *Clouds and Sunshine*, published in 1920, and dedicated to her children. A talented yet unsung artist, she also wrote songs, skits, and musicals, much of which are still unpublished.—MARSHA M. PRICE

FORSYNE, IDA
(1883–August 19, 1983) Dancer

A diminutive dancer, Ida Forsyne and many other talented black performers lived in Europe and sometimes had critical success there, before returning to the United States. Forsyne's success at home, however, never equaled what she had known in Europe, and at times she found that other blacks discriminated against her because of her dark complexion.

Born in Chicago in 1883, Forsyne was billed early on as Ida Forcen and Ida Forsyne Hubbard. As she watched rehearsals at a local theater, she learned to dance. When only ten years of age, she danced and sang for small sums on the street, at candy stores, and at rent parties, and she also cakewalked at the Chicago World's Fair. Forsyne became a singer and dancer with the Black Patti Troubadours when she was sixteen years old and, from 1898 to 1902, toured with them on the West Coast before going to New York. In 1902, she joined the original cast of *Smart Set*, which helped establish her as a popular performer, and continued in 1904 in *Southerners*. Forsyne had a long-term contract with a booking agency in Europe and performed there continuously for nine years with great success and to much acclaim. She returned to the United States in 1914, to what she called "black prejudice," which restricted her ability to become a headliner. She toured with Sophie Tucker (1920–1922), Mamie Smith (1924), and Bessie Smith (1927). Following her touring, she had minor roles and then worked as a domestic and elevator operator. After living in a rest home for some time, Forsyne died in Brooklyn.—JESSIE CARNEY SMITH

FULLER, META WARRICK

(June 9, 1877–March 18, 1968) Sculptor, designer, arts and civil rights activist

Meta Warrick Fuller

A noted African American artist of the 1920s and 1930s, Meta Warrick Fuller used the prevailing neoclassical approach to sculpture to render important scenes from black history. Exposure to her works allowed for a new generation of Americans to become aware of the many facets of black life in African history.

Fuller was born on June 9, 1877, to William Henry Warrick, a barber, and Emma Jones, a hairdresser. In addition to studying at the Pennsylvania Museum and School of Industrial Arts (later the Philadelphia College of Art), she trained in Paris at the Académie Colarossi and studied under Jean Antonin Charlés. While in Paris, Fuller spent many hours studying the human form by observing and drawing classical statues in the Louvre and other museums. Her life and career as a sculptor stands as one woman's determination to fight the challenges of being black and female in a male-dominated profession.

Fuller's marriage to physician Solomon Fuller in 1909 produced sons Solomon Jr. and William Thomas. She and her husband settled in Framingham, Massachusetts, where she built a studio. Upon the death of her sister, she adopted her thirteen-year-old niece, Margaret. Although family was most important in her life, she was also committed to following her artistic passion and telling stories that proved personal, challenging, and uplifting. Fuller served as a role model to others, especially women who aspired to become artists. She inspired sculptor Augusta Savage and mentored painter and designer Lois Mailou Jones. As a young artist, she benefitted from the racial pride and dedication to training demonstrated earlier by pioneering black sculptor Edmonia Lewis.

Early in her career, Fuller sought out the folklore and history of black people, which fed her creative energies. In 1907, she created a series of sculptures that were placed in dioramas for the Jamestown Tercentennial Exposition, held in Virginia. This series of installations showcased the contributions of black people to Virginia, as well as the United States, and they were presented as "Landing of the First Twenty Slaves at Jamestown," "An After Church Scene," and "Commencement Day."

Fuller began her work with universal themes, many from American history, but built on her passion for the human experience by adding the rich and complex story of black people. Through her association with W. E. B. Du Bois, she was encouraged to share the black experience through art. This thematic platform, along with her ability to cast a trained eye on the human form, resulted in three-dimensional statements that spoke to the courage, sacrifice, and determination of African Americans. In 1919, as a tribute to the life of Mary Turner, a pregnant black woman who had recently been lynched, she created *Mary Turner: A Silent Protest against Mob Violence*. Although many of her early works focus on despair and tragedy, Fuller's portfolio grew to embrace the more uplifting themes, for instance, her Emancipation sculpture, which portrays a black woman and man looking proud and standing tall. In 1920, Fuller was commissioned to create a bust of poet Paul Lawrence Dunbar for Dunbar High School in Washington, D.C.

In 1902 and 1903, Fuller's works were exhibited in Paris at the American Girls' Art Club and the Société Nationale des Beaux Arts, and she received special notice at the Paris Salon. Other early venues included Veerhoff's Gallery and the Corcoran Gallery of Art in Washington, D.C., as well as the 135th Street Branch of the New York Public Library. She also exhibited at the National Academy of Design in Philadelphia in 1916 and 1928.

Fuller's approach to sculpture was typical of the period—realistic portrayals of people and events. Her art training in the United States focused on capturing the essence of the human form with emotional overtones. At the Philadelphia Museum and School of Industrial Arts, Fuller learned to draw from modestly draped nude models and plaster casts. She traveled to Paris for training in 1899, following the tradition of many American artists. Although she encountered some racism in the city, her stay there was largely without incident. While in Paris, American sculptor Augustus Saint-Gaudens encouraged her to first concentrate on drawing as a means of achieving the visual perspective needed for sculpture. Although design was part of her coursework, it remained secondary to her interest in capturing the three-dimensional image.

Fuller also followed the teachings of Alain Locke, who advocated the study of and focus on the majesty of traditional African art. She joined black artists Aaron Douglas, Palmer Hayden, Richmond Barthé, and others in depicting a variety of historical and cultural themes from the continent. The concept of the Egyptian mummy inspired her to create *Ethiopia Awakening*, which speaks to the awakening of the African American consciousness. It remains her most recognized work from the Harlem Renaissance period. The five-foot bronze statue was displayed at the 1922 Making of America Exposition, held in New York. In 1937, she created *Talking Skull*, which was inspired by an African folktale that she remembered from her childhood.

During the Harlem Renaissance period, Fuller found several ways to promote her work. An association with the Harmon Foundation, which exhibited and promoted the works of professional and self-taught artists beginning in 1928, allowed her to serve as a judge in 1929 and participating artist in 1931 and 1933. Works exhibited through the Harmon Foundation include *Dark Hero*, *The Doctor*, *Water Boy*, and *W. Monroe Trotter*. Through this organization, her works were shown with sculptor Nancy Elizabeth Prophet, painter and art historian James A. Porter, print-maker Albert Alexander Smith, photographer James Latimer Allen, and numerous others. These associations allowed her to follow the careers of those whose cultural experiences she shared. *Opportunity* magazine, the literary organ of the National Urban League, featured Fuller's work during the 1920s.

Throughout her life, Fuller continued to infuse romanticism and emotionalism into her sculpture, which narrates the richness of the black experience. For the last fifteen years of her life, she created art intermittently and wrote poetry.
—Robert L. Hall

G

GEE, LOTTIE
(1886–?) Entertainer

Lottie Gee's name and brief mention of her performances appear in the literature of the Harlem Renaissance. She performed in musicals and revues alongside well-known female entertainers of that era.

Gee was born in 1886, in Millboro, Virginia. The details of her family and life remain obscure. Her career began in the early twentieth century as a dancing girl for Aida Overton Walker. In 1904, Gee appeared in James Weldon Johnson's musical comedy *The Red Moon* and other shows of that time. With Effie King and Lillian Gillman, she formed a trio, and then a sister act with Gillman. The two toured in vaudeville shows, and Gee then became a soloist with the Southern Syncopated Orchestra. When Gee, who played the part of Jessie Williams, introduced the song "I'm Just Wild about Harry" in the original Broadway musical comedy *Shuffle Along* (1921), she was immediately elevated to stardom. She reportedly said that she was unable to sing the song in the tempo in which it was written. As a result, she was responsible for Eubie Blake's changing the beat from original waltz-time to the up-tempo beat that made it a hit. Gee and Blake enjoyed a close friendship. For one year, *Shuffle Along* also preempted and held New Yorkers' interest in black theatricals.

Throughout the 1920s, Gee appeared in other revues. Notable among these was *Chocolate Dandies* (1924), a musical comedy in which she played the part of Angeline Brown. Edith Spencer and Gee teamed up in 1928, and advertised themselves as "Harlem's Sweethearts." When Lew Leslie's *Blackbirds* revue was mounted beginning 1926, it helped advance the career of several famous Harlem Renaissance artists, including Florence Mills, Aida Ward, and Lottie Gee. When Mills died in 1927, Gee was one of her honorary pallbearers.—JESSIE CARNEY SMITH

GEORGE, MAUDE ROBERTS
(ca. 1892–ca. 1945) Music critic

Maude Roberts George was one of the pivotal voices of the Harlem Renaissance. Her work as a classical music critic and advocate of this music made her an influential force in the African American community. Her reviews in the columns of the prestigious African American-owned newspaper the *Chicago Defender* appeared with regularity, shining the light on the extraordinary talents of African American men and women.

Like so many women who made a profound impact on the African American renaissances of Harlem and Chicago during the early twentieth century, little is known about the personal life of George. Her work, however, is remembered through her thriving public work. Born circa 1892, during the tumultuous post-slavery era, George was destined for a life that transcended the degradations experienced by many blacks and the forced limitations that were imposed on them by white society. Many other African Americans refused to succumb to the oppressive forces and pursued rich and satisfying careers as doctors, artists, and teachers; they headed prominent clubs and organizations, and owned businesses and newspapers.

George's career began in teaching. She taught at Walden University, an institution in Nashville, Tennessee, from which she had graduated. Founded in 1865, Walden University was originally known as Central Tennessee College. This institution was one of several historically black colleges and universities that served African American students; however, the school closed in 1925.

During the 1920s, George moved to Chicago. Her arrival coincided with the flowering of Chicago's cultural and artistic black renaissance. Like Harlem, Chicago was where many African Americans settled during the first wave of the Great Migration that occurred between 1910 and 1930. George was part of this massive migration of blacks who left the South for opportunities in the North. Indeed, George found opportunity as one of the most influential African American music critics in the city. Her reviews appeared in one of the most prominent and longest-running daily papers owned by an African American, the *Chicago Defender*. Founded in 1905, by Robert Sengstake Abbott, the *Chicago Defender* covered an array of subjects concerning black life, politics, and talent. A number of writers associated with the Harlem Renaissance, including the well-known Langston Hughes, were also featured.

Not only did George enjoy a long stint with the paper in a career that spanned the 1920s and 1930s, she brought to light the contributions of blacks to classical music through this popular medium. Although not traditionally associated with classical music, African American men and women have made important contributions to this genre. Their contributions, however, were often overlooked by mainstream society. Thanks to George, such African Americans as baritone Theodore Charles Stone and composer Florence Beatrice Price were regularly recognized for their accomplishments. In 1933, George underwrote a performance entitled "The Negro in Music," featuring Price in a groundbreaking concert. This act marked Price as the first African American female composer whose symphony was performed by a major American orchestra. In her role as music critic and president of the National

Association of Negro Musicians, George advocated and supported African Americans in classical music. When George died in 1945, she left a remarkable legacy to the world.—GLADYS L. KNIGHT

GILBERT, MERCEDES
(1889–March 1952) Actress, poet, songwriter, playwright, novelist

During the 1920s and 1930s, Mercedes Gilbert became known for numerous appearances in Broadway plays and on the radio. She gave one-woman performances and wrote and published songs, poetry, plays, and, finally, in 1938, an obscure novel.

Born in Jacksonville, Florida, in 1889, Gilbert was the daughter of Daniel Marshall Gilbert, who had a furniture business, and Edna Earl Knott Gilbert, who owed a dressmaking business. She was apparently homeschooled by a nurse during her kindergarten and primary years. She then entered the fourth grade at a local girl's seminary. When she was six years old, Gilbert began to write poetry and recited her works at the family's African American Episcopal church. The family relocated to Tampa, where Gilbert attended Orange Park Normal and Industrial School. She later graduated from Edward Waters College in Jacksonville. She then graduated from Brewster Hospital Nurses Training School and, for two years, served as assistant superintendent for the school. While still a student, she wrote a book of poems, *Looking Backward*, and several plays.

In 1916, Gilbert moved to New York, took additional training at Lincoln Hospital, and then worked as a private nurse. By then, her interest in the arts had blossomed fully, and she worked with songwriter Chris Smith, who helped her put her poetry to music. "They Also Ran the Blues" became their first effort—and a hit. Gilbert also recorded with Arto Records to produce "The Decatur Street Blues" and "Got the World in a Jug."

Gilbert married Arthur J. Stevenson on July 19, 1922, continued songwriting, and began contributions to the Associated Negro Press. She made her debut on Broadway in 1927, with an acting career in vaudeville and motion pictures, and appeared with a mostly white cast in *The Lace Petticoat*. After appearing in several other plays, she began memorable stage portrayals in 1930, playing the part of Zipporah in *Green Pastures*. Gilbert succeeded Rose McClendon in the 1935–1936 Broadway season of Langston Hughes's play *Mulatto*. *Lysistrata*, *Tobacco Road*, and, in 1938, *How Come, Lawd* were among her other appearances.

A collection of her writings, *Selected Gems of Poetry, Comedy, and Drama*, was published in 1931. Beginning 1941, Gilbert went on tour with her one-woman dramatic presentations. She also lectured on black history at various colleges. In 1938, she published her single novel, *Aunt Sara's Wooden God*, which portrays southern life and intraracial prejudice. After contributing widely to African American cultural history, Gilbert died in Jamaica, New York.—JESSIE CARNEY SMITH

GOODEN, LAURETTA HOLMAN
(?–?) Poet, entrepreneur

During the 1920s and 1930s, waves of the Harlem Renaissance rippled to black communities throughout the United States and inspired black writers. Lauretta

Holman Gooden was not spotlighted on the national stage, as were Zora Neale Hurston and Nella Larsen; however, Gooden holds the distinction of being published in the first anthology of Negro verse published in Texas, J. Mason Brewer's *Heralding Dawn: An Anthology of Verse*. Gooden's "A Dream of Revenge" and "Question to a Mob" appear in the anthology. Neither poem was published previously, nor have researchers excavated proof of Gooden's poetry appearing in any other publication.

In "A Dream of Revenge," the narrator suffers the pangs of being spurned by a lover. Her anger, conflicting emotions, and hurt pride cause her to plot revenge. The dark thoughts intensify as a raging storm breaks upon the beach where she is contemplating her feelings. She eventually reasons the futility to mourn a love that she never possessed and decides to forget him. Gooden proposes thought-provoking ponderings in "Question to a Mob." This poem questions the vicious activities of the Ku Klux Klan, no doubt Gooden's reflection on her parents' decision to leave Sulfur Springs, Texas, where she was born, and migrate to Texarkana, Texas. The move was prompted because of rigorous Klan activity in the community.

Gooden lived with her family until she married John Gooden and moved to Dallas. There she and her husband raised and educated one son and the children of Lauretta's deceased sister.—JEWELL B. PARHAM

GOODWIN, RUBY BERKLEY
(October 17, 1903–May 31, 1961) Actress, writer

During the Harlem Renaissance, Ruby Berkley Goodwin became the first accredited African American correspondent in Hollywood, writing a syndicated movie column for several years. Goodwin was born in Du Quoin, Illinois, to Braxton Berkley and Sophia Jane Holmes. After high school, she attended San Diego State Teacher's College in Imperial Valley, California. During the 1920s, Goodwin won a short story contest, an accomplishment that encouraged her writing career. Her first publication was a series of sketches about black life and accompanied *Twelve Negro Spirituals* (1937), by noted composer William Grant Still. Goodwin began attending Fullerton College in 1931; while there she wrote *From My Kitchen Window* (1942).

Goodwin was publicist for Oscar-winning actress Hattie McDaniel and gospel singer/actress Ethel Waters, from 1936 to 1952, which benefited her acting career in the 1940s. She appeared in several films and television programs, including *The Life of Booker T. Washington* and *The Loretta Young Show*. During this decade, she also wrote a musical and radio plays based on the lives of black leaders. She received a degree from San Gabriel State College and lectured about race relations, black music, and literature. She later published an acclaimed autobiography entitled *It's Good to Be Black* (1953), stressing the positive influence of family relationships.

Goodwin was equally committed to her family. She married Lee Goodwin in 1924, and had five children and adopted another. The mother of five was named "Mother of the Year" by the state of California in 1955. Goodwin died in Los Angeles, California.—AISHA M. JOHNSON

GORDON, EDYTHE MAE
(1896–?) Writer, poet

Edythe Mae Gordon was known as a writer who utilized the political, social, and economic circumstance of women, as influenced by race, class, and gender, to challenge many of the social norms of the Harlem Renaissance era. Her work was also influenced by her husband, Eugene Gordon, whose Marxist philosophy also centered on equality regarding class, race, and gender.

Gordon was born in 1896, in Washington, D.C., and received her secondary education through the instruction of such accomplished individuals as Anna Julia Cooper, Carter G. Woodson, and Jessie Redmon Fauset at the well-known M Street School, where many prominent African Americans attended. In 1916, Edythe married Eugene Gordon.

Edythe's first publication was in 1928, in the *Saturday Evening Quill*, a literary magazine published three times per year in Boston. Her husband served as the magazine's editor, while Helene Johnson and Dorothy West were among the founders. Of the short stories that Gordon contributed to the magazine, "Subversion" was noted by the O. Henry Memorial Award Committee as one of the best short stories of 1928.—LEAN'TIN L. BRACKS

GRAHAM, OTTIE BEATRICE
(1900–?) Playwright, short story writer

During the first decade of the Harlem Renaissance, Ottie Beatrice Graham published at least two plays and three short stories in a literary magazine and two prominent African American periodicals. Details about her literary works and life are scarce. She was born in 1900, in Virginia, and was the daughter of the Reverend W. F. Graham. Ottie attended public schools in Philadelphia, and after she matriculated at Howard University and Columbia University, she returned to Philadelphia, where she was a member of the Beaux Arts Club, a literary society.

At Howard University, Graham joined the Howard Players, an acting troupe established in 1919, by Thomas Montgomery Gregory, an English professor. Two years later, Graham was involved with the Howard Players' inaugural production, Ridgely Torrence's *Simon the Cyrenian*. In 1922, she was choreographer for the Howard Players' production of Torrence's *The Danse Calinda*. Graham's one-act play *The King's Carpenters* (1921) was published in the May 1921 edition of the *Stylist*, a student literary publication founded by Gregory and his English Department colleague, Alain Locke. Four years later, Locke published his edited anthology, *The New Negro*, which was a landmark publication of the Harlem Renaissance. Graham's one-act tragedy *Holiday* (1923) was published in the May 1923 issue of *Crisis*. The play reveals the devastating consequences for two women after the light-skinned mother, an actress, abandons her darker-skinned daughter and passes for white. *Holiday* was one of four one-act plays included in the production of *Beauty Is the Best Priest: Short Plays of the Harlem Renaissance*. The other three plays were Alice Dunbar-Nelson's *Mine Eyes Have Seen the Glory*, Zora Neale Hurston's *Color Struck*, and May Miller's *The Bog Guide* (Miller was also a member of the

Howard Players). *Beauty Is the Best Priest* was presented by Austin Community College's Department of Drama, and the performances were held at the Boyd Vance Theater at the George Washington Carver Museum in Austin, Texas, from February 22, 2013, to March 3, 2013.

Graham's "To a Wild Rose" won the top prize in the Delta Omega Chapter of the Alpha Kappa sorority's short story competition for African American students. The judges for the competition were Arthur B. Spingarn, prominent attorney and civil rights activist; Jessie Redmon Fauset, literary editor of *Crisis*; and W. E. B. Du Bois, editor of *Crisis*. After their unanimous decision, Graham was awarded fifty dollars, and "To a Wild Rose" was published in the June 1923 issue of *Crisis*. Graham's prize-winning narrative focuses on love, as well as slavery's aftermath. "Blue Aloes," her short story about love and defiance, was published in *Crisis* in July 1924. It was followed by the November 1924 publication of "Slackened Caprice," Graham's tragic story about an African American soldier. Graham's short stories, ignored for decades after the Harlem Renaissance, began appearing in such late twentieth-century anthologies as *The Sleeper Wakes: Harlem Renaissance Stories by Women* (1993), edited by Marcy Knopf, and *Harlem's Glory: Black Women Writing, 1900–1950* (1996), edited by Lorraine Elena Roses and Ruth Elizabeth Randolph.—LINDA M. CARTER

GREELY, AURORA BOREALIS
(1905–?) Dancer

Aurora Borealis Greely was a youthful sensation during the 1920s through the 1940s, as she had a natural talent for dance and choreography that left a lasting impression on her contemporaries.

Greely was born in 1905, in Jacksonville, Florida, and her family later moved to New York. She knew early on that she wanted to be a dancer, but her request for lessons was refused by her mother. After her third year at Wadleigh High School, Greely left home and joined the Irvin C. Miller theatrical production of *Liza* in 1924, as part of the chorus. After six months, she was asked to take the starring role when the leading lady got sick. Although she had to be convinced to take the role, Greely went on to star in several more Miller productions, for example, *Broadway Rastus* and *Running Wild*. In 1927, Greely teamed with dancer LeRoy Bloomfield, and they became a successful duo, touring in Philadelphia, Chicago, and Los Angeles. In 1927, the team developed the stage show for the Frank Sebastin's Cotton Club in Los Angeles, and they remained together until 1931.

Although little is known of Greely's career after 1931, the *Baltimore Afro-American* noted in 1931 that she was one of the wealthiest women in the West due to an inheritance from her grandfather.—LEAN'TIN L. BRACKS

GREEN, CORA
(?–?) Singer

Cora Green used her rich contralto voice to become known as a singer during the Harlem Renaissance. Little is known about her early life. While in school, however, she sang in school productions in Baltimore. By the age of fourteen, she began her career in vaudeville in an act known as Green and Pugh. Green joined Florence Mills and Ada "Bricktop" Smith to form the famed Panama Trio, a singing group that included legendary pianist Tony Jackson. Others occasionally performed with the group. The group apparently took its name from the Panama Club in Chicago. The trio had a flourishing act and might have continued their performances at the Panama indefinitely if the café had not closed due to a scandal involving a shooting incident. Although Chicago was an exciting city at the time and a center of black migration from the rural South, white gangsters controlled the black community's cabarets. New jazz music was also fostered at these cabarets. The Panama, however, became a center of vice. From 1916 to 1919, the Panama Trio conducted a tour of the United States on the white Pantages Circuit. The tenure of "Bricktop" and Mills was seemingly short, as the group later disbanded.

Green continued to perform. She appeared in *Put and Take* (1921), *Strut Miss Lizzie* (1922), *Dixie to Broadway* (1924), *Nobody's Girl* (1926), and *Vaudeville at the Palace* (1927). At some point, she went on tour in Europe. In 1929, she starred in *Ebony Showboat* and, much later, on Broadway in *Policy Kings* (1938). Green also appeared in two films by black filmmaker Oscar Micheaux: as Minnie in *Swing* in 1938, and as Amanda "Mandy" Jones in *Moon over Harlem* in 1939.
—JESSIE CARNEY SMITH

GRIMKÉ, ANGELINA WELD

(February 27, 1880–June 10, 1958) Poet, playwright, educator

Angelina Weld Grimké was a prolific poet whose verse was published in late nineteenth-century periodicals, as well as the most prominent Harlem Renaissance magazines and anthologies. Her three-act drama *Rachel* was written, produced, and published during the Harlem Renaissance and was one of the earliest plays by an African American woman.

Grimké was born in Boston on February 27, 1880, to Archibald Henry Grimké, an attorney, diplomat, and civil rights activist, as well as former slave, and Sarah (née Stanley) Grimké, a white writer from Boston. Angelina was the paternal granddaughter of Henry Grimké, a slave owner and lawyer, and Nancy Weston, a slave; she was the niece of Francis Grimké, a minister and former slave, and his wife, Charlotte Forten Grimké, a diarist. Angelina was the great niece of abolitionists Sarah Moore Grimké, Angelina Grimké Weld, and her husband, Theodore Weld, who was also an abolitionist. Archibald and Sarah Grimké's only child was named to honor the memory of her great aunt.

After her parents' marriage ended during her early childhood, Angelina was raised by her father. She attended the Fairmount Grammar School in Boston until her father was appointed U.S. consul to Santo Domingo (1894–1898); Grimké then stayed at the Washington, D.C., home of Francis and Charlotte Forten Grimké and enrolled in one of the city's public schools before attending the Carleton Academy in Minnesota, Cushing Academy in Massachusetts, the Boston Girls' Latin School, and the Boston Normal School of Gymnastics (which became the Department of

Hygiene at Wellesley College) in 1902. Grimké completed summer English courses at Harvard from 1904 to 1910. In each educational environment, she was the rare, if not the only, African American student.

In 1902, Grimké began her career as an educator, teaching physical education courses at the Armstrong Manual Training School in Washington, before transferring to the city's prestigious M Street School (later known as Dunbar High School) in 1907, where she taught English. M Street was known for its outstanding faculty, and Grimké's colleagues included historian Carter G. Woodson and three women, like Grimké, who would also be associated with the Harlem Renaissance: Mary Burrill, Anna Julia Cooper, and Jessie Redmon Fauset. Among Grimké's students were three future Harlem Renaissance writers: May Miller, Willis Richardson, and Bruce Nugent. Although Grimké endured a chronic injury after a 1911 train accident, she continued to teach until 1926. Her medical problems, along with her role as her father's caretaker during the final years of his life, led to her retirement. After her father's death in 1930, Grimké moved to Brooklyn, New York.

Grimké's first published poem, "The Grave in the Corner" (1893), was published in the *Norfolk County Gazette* (*NCG*) when she was thirteen, and additional juvenile poems were published during the next two years in the *NCG* and *Boston Sunday Globe*. During the first decades of the twentieth century, Grimké's verse was published in the *Boston Transcript, Pilot, Crisis,* and *Opportunity,* as well as four edited collections: Robert T. Kerlin's *Negro Poets and Their Poems* (1923), Alain Locke's *The New Negro* (1925), Countee Cullen's *Caroling Dusk* (1927), and Charles S. Johnson's *Ebony and Topaz* (1927). In addition to writing approximately 300 poems, Grimké wrote such short stories as "Black Is, As Black Does: A Dream" (1900), which was published in *Colored American Magazine,* as well as "The Closing Door" (1919) and "Goldie"(1920), printed in *Birth Control Review.* Furthermore, her essay "A Biographical Sketch of Archibald Grimké" (1926) was published in *Opportunity.* Grimké's signature work is *Rachel: A Play in Three Acts.* The antilynching play debuted in Washington, D.C., where it was sponsored by the local chapter of the National Association for the Advancement of Colored People and performed in March 1916, at the Myrtilla Normal School; it was also put on in April 1917, at the Neighborhood Theater in Harlem, and in May 1917, in Cambridge, Massachusetts. *Rachel* was published in 1920; a second antilynching play, *Mara,* remains unproduced and unpublished.

Grimké died in New York City. In 1991, ninety-eight years after her debut publication, *Selected Works by Angelina Weld Grimké,* edited by Carolivia Herron, was published.—LINDA M. CARTER

H

HAGAN, HELEN E.
(1893–1964) Pianist, composer

As the Harlem community's nightclubs and theaters offered jazz, blues, and theatrical performances showcasing extraordinary black talent, the concert hall in New York City can be counted among those opportunities to see great black talent, for instance, pianist and composer Helen E. Hagan. Hagan began her musical career at the age of thirteen when she began study at Yale University under the instruction of Horatio Parker. Her training as a pianist at Yale expanded to include study abroad, as supported by two university scholarships. Although Hagan had to return to the United States as a result of World War I, she went on to become the first black pianist to earn a bachelor of music degree from Yale University. In 1921, she made her New York debut at Aeolian Hall. Her performance served as a further extension of theatrical talents showcased in the production *Shuffle Along*, a new and successful musical comedy that was sweeping the theater community at the same time. Hagan, who won critical acclaim both in the United States and abroad, toured extensively into the 1930s and successfully wrote a full concerto for piano and orchestra. She later became a teacher in the black college system.
—LEAN'TIN L. BRACKS

HALL, ADELAIDE
(October 20, 1901?–November 7, 1993) Singer, actress

The Harlem Renaissance was an important time for Adelaide Hall, a multitalented performer in early black shows of the 1920s. Among her contemporaries were Valaida Snow, Florence Mills, Eubie Blake, Duke Ellington, Thomas "Fats" Waller, and Edith Wilson. Hall made her Broadway stage debut in Sissle and Blake's pioneering musical revue *Shuffle Along* and had a career that spanned more than fifty years.

Born in Brooklyn, New York, the exact date of Hall's birth is uncertain; it is either 1901 or 1904. She was the daughter of William Hall, whose background has been identified as white with German roots and German and African American; her mother, Adelaide Elizabeth Gerrard, was of African American and Native American descent. The family relocated to Harlem during the 1910s, and Hall and her younger sister sang at school concerts and other events. Adelaide's career began to bud when she sang in J. Homer Tutt and Salem Tutt Whitney's troupe and appeared in a number of their original musicals. Then she moved on to Broadway.

Hall was so successful in her Broadway debut that she was given a feature role in Miller and Lyle's *Runnin' Wild* (1923). She had two major successes at Club Alabam in New York City in 1925, and then was cast in Sam Wooding's *Chocolate Kiddies* and toured Europe with the latter group. While on tour, she met and later married Trinidadian Bert Hicks, who became her manager. In 1926, Hall appeared in *Tan Town Topics*, and the next year in *Desires of 1927*. Around this time, she performed and recorded with Duke Ellington's orchestra, singing "Creole Love Call." After her contemporary, Florence Mills, known for her starring role in Lew Leslie's *Blackbirds*, died, Hall was asked to return to Broadway with dancer Bill "Bojangles" Robinson in *Blackbirds of 1928*. She sang "I Can't Give You Anything But Love" and "Diga Diga Doo."

Hall appeared in several film shorts, including *Dancers in the Dark* (1932) and *All Colored Vaudeville Show* (1935), and she then toured Europe, becoming one of the few black female entertainers to be successful there and in the United States. Hall remained in Paris but returned to New York for appearances in the show *Brown Buddies*. She and her husband settled in London in 1938, where they opened clubs. She had her own radio series in London but continued to return to the United States for performances. Her one-woman show, created in 1977, led her to tour widely. Hall's career was so successful that she was the subject of *Sophisticated Lady*, a documentary made for the British Broadcast Company in 1989. She died in London in 1993.—JESSIE CARNEY SMITH

HALL [LONG], JUANITA

(November 6, 1901–February 28, 1968) Singer, actress, choral director

Harlem Renaissance figures knew well the name Juanita Hall, who began singing in New Jersey clubs in the 1920s, and then joined popular black productions on Broadway and elsewhere. She still received acclaim later on and set the stage for African Americans to be included in the golden age of musical theater.

Juanita Long Hall was born in Keyport, New Jersey, to Abram Long and Mary Richardson on November 6, 1901. Her birth date has also been reported as 1902. Her heritage was African American and Irish. Hall began singing early on in church choirs and the local community. She had heard Negro spirituals sung at a revival meeting in New Jersey when she was twelve years old and developed a love for them. Two years later, she taught singing at Lincoln House in East Orange, New Jersey. While in her teens, she married actor Clement Hall, who died in the 1920s; she never remarried. Hall's classical music training was at the Julliard School of

Music, where she took courses in orchestration, harmony, theory, and voice; she also had private teachers in voice and acting.

Noted pioneers in black music with whom Hall had contact were Hall Johnson, Eva Jessye, and William C. Handy. In 1928, she broke into the chorus of the Ziegfield production of *Show Boat*, which helped catapult the talented performer into popularity. In 1930, she worked with the Hall Johnson Choir in the choral production of *The Green Pastures*, and from 1931 to 1936, she was the show's soloist and assistant director. In 1935, Hall formed her own group, the Juanita Hall Choir, which was sponsored by the Works Progress Administration. She directed a 300-voice church choir at the 1939 World's Fair in New York.

During the 1940s, Hall appeared in a number of dramatic and musical roles on the stage. These included *The Pirates* (1942); *Sing Out, Sweet Land* (1944); *The Secret Room* (1944); *Deep Are the Roots* (1945), and the film *Miracle in Harlem* (1949). Also in 1949, she was cast in the role of Bloody Mary in the Pulitzer Prize-winning play *South Pacific*, which propelled her into even greater fame. In 1954, she appeared in *The House of Flowers* and *Flower Drum Song*, both by Rodgers and Hammerstein. Hall's numerous television appearances included on *The Ed Sullivan Show*, *The Coca-Cola Hour*, and *The Perry Como Show*. During the 1950s, she made a number of stage appearances. Her public appearances appear to have ended in 1966, with her one-woman show *A Woman and the Blues*. Hall died in Bay Shore, Long Island.—JESSIE CARNEY SMITH

HAMPTON, MABEL

(1902–1989) Dancer, activist

As the Harlem Renaissance welcomed the free and creative spirit of the new age, many individuals were also open with their creative and sexual choices. Mabel Hampton was a dancer in the nightclubs and theater groups of Harlem and part of the gay and lesbian community.

Hampton was born in Winston-Salem, North Carolina, in 1902, but with the passing of her mother while she was an infant and the later passing of her grandmother when she was seven, she developed a strong sense of self-reliance and independence. In 1909, at the age of seven, she moved to Greenwich Village, in New York City, and was placed in the care of her aunt and uncle, who was a minister. After being sexually abused by her uncle, Hampton decided that she had to leave. She subsequently purchased a bus ticket, thanks to a nickel from a stranger, and fled to New Jersey. On the same day that she arrived in New Jersey, Hampton met a kindly woman, Bessie White, who cared for her until she was seventeen. With the death of White, Hampton, who was again on her own, made a living as a domestic worker.

In 1920, Hampton was falsely arrested during a prostitution raid and sentenced to two years at the Bedford Hills Correctional Facility for Women. She was later sentenced to a second term for attending parties with other women, which was considered illegal. As a young woman, Hampton continued her relationship with other women, while being drawn into the excitement of the renaissance. She danced in the all-black chorus line at the "Garden of Joy" nightclub; became an actress at the Cherry Lane Theater; sang as a member of the Lafayette Theater Chorus; and performed with such well-known artists as Gladys Bentley, who was also part of the gay and lesbian community.

Throughout the years, Hampton continued to support the black community by contributing money to the civil rights movements and volunteering with the USO. She is also credited with being one of the founding members of the Lesbian Herstory Archives in 1974.—LEAN'TIN L. BRACKS

HARMON, FLORENCE MARION
(1880–1936) Short story writer

Florence Marion Harmon published two stories, "Belated Romance" and "Attic Romance," in the late 1920s, during the era of the Harlem Renaissance. Her stories were published in the *Saturday Evening Quill*, a literary journal based in Boston, Massachusetts.

Harmon was born in Lynn, Massachusetts, in 1880. In 1924, during the time that she attended Gordon College of Theology and Missions in Boston, her story "The House of Mirth" was published in the Gordon College yearbook. Her zeal for writing prompted her to join the Saturday Evening Quill Club. In 1928, she served as the secretary of this club. During the same year, her story "Belated Romance" appeared in the club's literary journal. In 1929, another story, "Attic Romance," was published in the *QUILL*. Although she published no additional stories, her published works reappeared in anthologies in subsequent decades; her biographies, while brief because little is known about her, appeared in such books as *The Harlem Renaissance* (1984). At the time of Harmon's death in 1936, she was working as a dressmaker.—GLADYS L. KNIGHT

HARRISON, HAZEL LUCILE
(May 12, 1883–April 28, 1969) Musician, educator

The fifty years that Hazel Lucile Harrison performed as a concert pianist spanned the early part of the Harlem Renaissance and extended into the years after that cultural revolution ended. During her career, she became known in the African American community as the "Dean of Native Pianists."

Harrison was born in 1883, in La Porte, Indiana, to Hiram and Olive (Wood) Harrison. Her father was a barber before becoming a business owner, and her mother operated a beauty shop at home. Hazel's musical talent was recognized during her early years, and she honed her skills by taking music lessons. By the age of twelve, she often appeared on musical programs and gave dance music at social occasions. While still in high school, she studied with Victor Heinze of Chicago, who helped to boost her skills. In March 1902, she gave a recital in Chicago's Studebaker Hall.

After graduating from high school in 1902, Harrison became a full-time piano teacher in La Porte, and in the fall of 1904, she embarked on a German tour, climaxing with an appearance in Berlin with the Berlin Philharmonic Orchestra. She returned to La Porte the next year and continued to teach piano. In late 1911, she returned to Berlin and gave a series of recitals. When war broke out in 1914, she returned home and was hailed by the black press as the "world's greatest pianist." She then began her concert career in her homeland.

As Harrison continued to give recitals and go on tour, she also taught at Tuskegee Institute (now Tuskegee University) in Alabama from 1931 to 1936, Howard University from 1936 to 1955, and Alabama State College (now Alabama State University) from 1958 to 1963. While most of her concerts were in black churches, in high school gymnasia, and on black college campuses—all due to limitations imposed by racial segregation—she made some appearances with major white orchestras, but under special circumstances. Harrison retired from Howard University in 1955, lived in New York City for three years, and continued to coach students. Her last major appearance came in 1959, in the campus auditorium of Alabama State College. After a brief illness, she died in Washington, D.C. She had two marriages, both ending in divorce.—JESSIE CARNEY SMITH

HARRISON, JUANITA
(December 28, 1891–?) Writer

As people from different parts of the world came to Harlem, New York, seeking to be entertained and enjoy the celebration of black culture, style, and creativity, Juanita Harrison traveled the world with a curiosity equal to those who came to Harlem.

Harrison was born on December 28, 1891, in Mississippi. With only a few months of schooling before the age of ten, she spent her life in a continuous role as housekeeper and maid. After seeing pictures of different places in foreign lands, her dream became one of a world traveler beginning at the age of sixteen. By the time Harrison reached the age of twenty-six, she had learned Spanish and French from the Young Women's Christian Association and traveled to Canada and Cuba. At one point, she had saved $800 to further pursue her travels but lost it when the banking industry failed. In spite of this, she was able to earn and save enough money to generate $200 a year in interest, which allowed her to travel the globe. Her employer, George W. Dickson, and his wife Myra were instrumental in helping her achieve this goal.

In 1927, at the age of thirty-six, Harrison began her trip throughout the world and recorded her experiences in twenty-two countries in a journal. She was later encouraged by an employer, Mildred Morris, to publisher her works, inclusive of grammar and other errors, resulting from Harrison's lack of education. In 1936, Harrison published her journal, *My Great, Wide, Beautiful World*. She shared her exuberance regarding her travels by relating everything from the food she ate to her ease in making friends. Although familiar with a world of racism and hate, Harrison's work focuses on the richness of her experiences and offers no consideration of race as a hindrance in her travels. Her recorded adventures end in Hawaii, and little is known about whether her travels actually ended there or if she decided to continue to explore the world. Her work lends itself to the era of the Harlem Renaissance since only through a sense of self-actualization and determination could a little black girl from the South feel empowered and determined to follow her dream of seeing the world.—LEAN'TIN L. BRACKS

HARVEY, GEORGETTE MICKEY

(1882–February 17, 1952) Singer, actress

Georgette Mickey Harvey was born in St. Louis, Missouri, to unknown parents. During the heyday of the Harlem Renaissance, she created a singing group called the Creole Belles that included Emma Harris. Her contralto voice was first recognized in her St. Louis church choir. Harvey longed for greener pastures and decided to use her gift as a theatrical performer, making her way to the bright lights of New York. She later formed a group, and her five girls traveled abroad to Belgium, England, France, and Germany. After success there, they returned to the United States as vaudeville performers and were in much demand. Harvey served as business and personal manager to the group. Around 1911, she moved her talented squad back to additional European countries and Russia. As an astute businesswoman, she wooed and amazed her clientele by being able to speak their language. Her troupe was particularly favored by Russian royalty. This heyday was short-lived, however, as the Russian Revolution swept through and changed everything. Harvey and her troupe were forced to flee with only small belongings. Her group traversed Siberia and was eventually separated. Harvey continued on through several Asian countries before returning to the United States. Although not as wealthy as before, she skillfully structured a new quartet of girls.

In 1927, Harvey played the role of Maria (created by Harvey herself) in *Porgy and Bess*, and she later appeared on Broadway in *Mamba's Daughters*. She also performed in *The Party's Over* (1933) and the powerful *Stevedore* (1934). *Lost in the Stars* (1949) was the last production Harvey appeared in. She died in New York City.—ANGELA M. GOODEN

HAWTHORNE, SUSIE

(1896–December 5, 1963) Performer

Susie Hawthorne was a popular performer best known as the other half of the popular comedy duo with Jodie Edwards, her husband of more than forty years. The twosome, known as Butterbeans and Susie, primarily performed for African American audiences, touring numerous cities, among them Harlem, New York, during the era of the great Harlem Renaissance. Their performances, however, were not enjoyed by everyone, particularly Harlem's most influential and race conscious.

Born in 1896, in Pensacola, Florida, Hawthorne took to the stage in the early twentieth century. Prior to marriage, she and her future husband had established their own careers. Hawthorne performed in the African American theater and sang blues; Edwards performed as a singer and dancer. On May 15, 1917, the couple married on the stage of the Theater Owners' Booking Association theatre in Greenville, South Carolina.

In the wake of the marriage, Hawthorne (who had taken her husband's surname) and her husband performed Butterbeans and Susie, which was a spectacular success, in minstrel and tent shows and theaters. In Harlem, they performed at the famous Lafayette Theater and the Cotton Club. Their Butterbeans and Susie comedic routine consisted of singing, bantering, and dancing. Their act, which entailed comedic conflict between the characters, who, like them, were husband and wife, was infused with sexual innuendo, violent threats, and complaints. At the end of the routine, the couple would make up; Hawthorne would sing an affectionate song, and Edwards would perform the laugh-generating dance known as "The Itch." The Butterbeans and Susie routine was augmented through the stark visual contrast between the couple. Hawthorne wore a long and stylish gown, while her husband wore comical attire consisting of tight pants that were too short and a derby hat. In response to the popular pair, some critics, for example, some proponents of the New Negro concept in Harlem, were none too pleased. They complained that the Butterbeans and Susie routine played into the stereotypes that white society had imposed on blacks. In contrast, the New Negro was an image of a positive, progressive, and dignified African American. This concept was fleshed out in Alain Locke's *The New Negro* (1925).

Although Butterbeans and Susie did not project the image of the New Negro, Hawthorne and Edwards's routine resonated with many African Americans. Indeed, their popularity spawned several shows that were performed in several major cities in the South, on the East Coast, and in the Midwest. They also recorded blues songs and comedy routines on records. Hawthorne and Edwards continued to perform into the 1960s. Hawthorne was the first of this dynamic duo to die, ending their long and successful partnership.—GLADYS L. KNIGHT

HAYNES, ELIZABETH ROSS
(July 30, 1883–October 26, 1953) Sociologist, social worker, organization official

Elizabeth Ross Haynes

During the Harlem Renaissance period, Elizabeth Ross Haynes worked through various organizations to address the plight of black women in the work force to bring about social justice and remove racial restrictions in the Young Women's Christian Association (YWCA).

Born in 1883, in Lowndes County, Alabama, Haynes was the only child of Henry and Mary (Carnes) Ross. She graduated from State Normal School in Montgomery (later Alabama State University), Fisk University in Nashville, and, much later, Columbia University in New York. Haynes was a volunteer worker with the YWCA, and in 1908, she began work for its student department of the National Board. She held this position until around 1925. In 1910, she married Fisk schoolmate George Edmund Haynes, a sociologist and a founder of the National Urban League. When he became director of Negro Economics, a division of the U.S. Department of Labor, she served as his assistant director. Elizabeth was also a volunteer for the Women's Bureau of the Department of Labor. From January 1920 until May 1922, she was domestic service secretary in the U.S. Employment Service and became keenly interested in the plight of black women, particularly with regards to labor. In 1922, she wrote "Two Million Negro Women at Work," which identifies the three main areas in which women in the labor force were engaged.

Haynes and her husband relocated to New York City in 1921. She remained active in her areas of interest and became the first African American member of the YWCA National Board, a post that she held from 1924 to 1934. This came at a time when the organization was highly segregated, and more than twenty years would pass before black women would be integrated into the life of the association. Haynes was active in interracial work with the Commission on Race Relations and the Federated Council of the Churches of Christ in America. She also had a keen interest in the black women's club movement, particularly those social service activities that related to her background and experience. She chaired the National Association of Colored Women's Industry and Housing Department. In 1935, Haynes was elected coleader of the 21st Assembly District in New York County. In addition, she was appointed to several commissions, including the New York State Temporary Commission on the Conditions of the Urban Colored Population and the New York City Planning Commission. She published two important black biographical works: *Unsung Heroes* (1921) and *The Black Boy of Atlanta* (1952). Haynes died in New York Medical Center.—JESSIE CARNEY SMITH

HAZZARD, ALVIRA
(1899–1953) Writer

Alvira Hazzard was part of a thriving black writers' literary group in New England from the 1920s to the 1940s that provided a writer's community and publication opportunities for those artists seeking to express themselves.

Hazzard was born in Northfield, Massachusetts, in 1899, the oldest of six children. She graduated from Worchester Normal School in Massachusetts. After completing her education, she moved to Boston and worked for a while as a Boston Public School teacher, and she was later employed at Boston City Hospital. Hazzard became a member of the *Saturday Evening Quill*, a black writers' group in Boston and Roxbury that included noted Harlem Renaissance writers Dorothy West and Helene Johnson. The group, which originated in 1925, published an annual journal under the name of the group to support the publication of their members' work. Hazzard's first published work was the play *Mother Liked It* in 1928, followed by *Little Head* in 1929, both published in the journal. She also published several short stories in the *Boston Post*, which was supported by the group's president, who was one of the paper's editors. Generally speaking, Hazzard's plays and writings explore varying themes inclusive of those that dealt with the persistence of racial stereotypes and their limiting effect of devaluing individuals within society. She died from lymphatic leukemia.—LEAN'TIN L. BRACKS

HEGAMIN, LUCILLE
(November 29, 1894–March 1, 1970) Singer

"Harlem's Favorite," as Lucille Hegamin was known in the early 1920s, was a refined and torchy blues singer whose career flourished after she moved to New York City around 1919. She graduated from singing in Harlem's cafes to making appearances at major events and became a popular recording artist before a society with a rich appetite for blues singers. In *Blues Who's Who*, Sheldon Harris writes that she had a "vigorous, powerful voice, deep and resonant, youthful and exuberant." Hegamin remained popular during the most prolific periods of the Harlem Renaissance, the 1920s, but her career began to fade by the end of the decade.

Born in Macon, Georgia, on November 29, 1894, Hegamin became a popular local singer without formal music training. She sang in churches and theaters and, in 1909, began touring, performing in tent shows throughout the South with the Leonard Harper Minstrel Stock Company. She married her pianist, Bill Hegamin, and by 1914. he accompanied her as she sang in clubs and cabarets in Chicago. The "Georgia Peach," as she was known then, performed at the Elite No. 2 Theater on South Side Chicago, with New Orleans pianist Tony Jackson. Hegamin popularized his classic "Pretty Baby" and W. C. Handy's "Saint Louis Blues." With her own band on backup, she sang in Seattle and Los Angeles in 1918 and 1919.

After Hegamin moved to New York in 1919, her recording career blossomed. Her ability to wail appealed to audiences, for voices like hers were popular in the emerging commercial fad for blues. Behind the "Mother of the Blues," Gertrude "Ma" Rainey, Hegamin was the next African American woman to record the blues. Hegamin promoted record sales during her tours and, in May 1922, teamed up with company of the show *Shuffle Along*. The next year, she joined the musical comedy *Creole Follies* in appearances in New York and Washington, D.C. By now she had become solo, as her marriage and business relationship with Bill Hegamin had ended. Between 1922 and 1926, Hegamin recorded extensively, cutting more than forty sides for Cameo Records. She then became known as the "Cameo Girl" and appeared in several shows held at the Lafayette and Lincoln theaters. These included *Lincoln Frolics* with Adelaide Hall in 1926, *Midnight Steppers* in 1928, and *New Year's Revels* in 1930. For two seasons (1933 and 1934), she sang at the Paradise in Atlantic City.

When Hegamin's popularity began to decline in the late 1920s, she gave up singing and became a nurse until she was rediscovered in the 1960s, when the blues were back in demand. In 1962, she recorded again, this time with Alberta Hunter and Victoria Spivey on the Spivey label. Her voice still had appeal both on recordings and during the few personal appearances that she made. The now revered blues elder died in New York City.—JESSIE CARNEY SMITH

HENDERSON [HENDERSON], KATHERINE
(June 6, 1909–?) Actress, singer, entertainer

Katherine Henderson was born in St. Louis, Missouri, in 1909, and at eight years of age, she started performing in minstrel shows and on the vaudeville circuit. As the niece of famed blues singer Eva Taylor and music producer Clarence Williams, and under the pseudonym Catherine Henderson, she found success under their guidance after moving to New York City. She worked with Taylor on her radio shows and made several recordings with Williams. As an actress, Henderson first appeared on Broadway in the musical revue *Bottomland* in 1927, and with the Kathleen Kirkwood in the Underground Theatre in Greenwich Village in 1928. She also acted in the theatrical production *Keep Shuffling* in 1929. Henderson continued as an entertainer until 1944, when she returned to St. Louis and went on to get married and have a family.—LEAN'TIN L. BRACKS

HENDERSON, ROSA
(November 24, 1896–April 6, 1968) Blues singer, vaudeville entertainer

Rosa Henderson, born Rosa Deschamps in Henderson, Kentucky, is considered one of the best classic blues singers; she recorded more than 100 tracks. In the 1920s, female blues singers created a huge market for commercialized music by fusing qualities of rural music with elements of vaudeville and minstrelsy. Thus, music was as essential to the Harlem Renaissance in its use of folk culture as literature. This fusion is seen in the performances of Henderson, who entered the entertainment circuit by joining her uncle's traveling circus in 1913. She was located in Texas until her marriage; little is known about this period.

In 1918, Henderson married Douglas "Slim" Henderson and became a member of a touring revue, the Mason Henderson Show. They toured throughout the South, performing in vaudeville productions prior to moving to New York. Here she appeared in black revues at the Lafayette, Alhambra, and Lincoln theaters, the major theater companies of the Harlem Renaissance, and was a popular singer with black audiences, as indicated by the number of songs attributed to her. She began a recording career that spanned nine years, from 1923 to 1931. During these years, she recorded on various labels, including Victor, Vocalion, Paramount, Ajax, and Columbia. Accompanists on these recordings include the instrumentalists Fletcher Henderson (piano, no relationship), Coleman Hawkins (tenor saxophone and bass saxophone), Bob Fuller (clarinet), Tom Morris (cornet), and Fats Waller (piano), as well as such groups as Fletcher Henderson's Jazz Five, Fletcher Henderson's Orchestra, the Three Hot Eskimos, the Three Jolly Miners, the Choo Choo Jazzers, the Kansas City Five, and the Four Black Diamonds. Recordings included "Afternoon Blues" (1923), "Doggone Blues" (1931), "Do Right Blues" (1924), "He May Be Your Dog But He's Wearing My Collar" (1923), "Hey, Hey and He, He, I'm Charleston Crazy" (1924), and "Papa If You Can't Do Better (I'll Let a Better Papa Move In)" (1926). Henderson recorded under her name and several pseudonyms, including Flora Dale, Sally Ritz, Mamie Harris, and Josephine Thomas.

Henderson decreased her number of performances in the late 1920s after her husband's death and, by the 1930s, had almost disappeared from the stage, although she performed for charities and benefits into the 1960s and began working in a department store. The mother of two children, she died of a heart attack in Roosevelt Island, New York, and is buried in Frederick Douglass Memorial Park.—HELEN R. HOUSTON

HEYWARD, DOROTHY KUHNS
(June 6, 1890–November 19, 1961) Playwright, author

During the Harlem Renaissance, the opera *Porgy and Bess* debuted on the American stage and became known as one of the greatest dramatic works of the era. It showcased the talents of playwright Dorothy Kuhns Heyward. A playwright, Heyward was born in Wooster, Ohio, on June 6, 1890. As a young adult, she moved to New York City to attend Columbia University with dreams of becoming a playwright. She worked for a brief time as a member of a chorus but soon stopped because of arthritic pain. She was awarded a fellowship in 1921, to spend the summer at the McDowell's Colony in Peterborough, New Hampshire. During her time at the colony, she met DuBose Heyward, who desired to be a poet and novelist. Kuhns and Heyward were both extended an offer to return to McDowell's Colony in 1923. Heyward proposed to the young writer during their time there. The couple married in September 1923. During that same month, Dorothy was awarded a Harvard Prize for drama for her play *Nancy Ann*. A year later, the play opened on Broadway but closed after a few shows.

The couple returned to the McDowell Colony during the month of June. Dorothy tried to write a novel during this time, while beginning to adapt the novel *Porgy*, written by DuBose. The novel was developed into a play in 1927, and then an opera in 1935, with the contributions of Ira and George Gershwin. The opera, known as *Porgy and Bess*, was favorably received and viewed as a success. The play was seen as empathetic to the plight of blacks during this time period; however, it was later seen as stereotypical. The novel, set in DuBose's hometown of Charleston, South Carolina, is based on the waterfront. The novel and play effectively use the Gullah dialect. The play was known as one of the great testaments of the American stage. In 1939, Dorothy later collaborated with her husband to adapt his novel *Mamba's Daughters* as a play.

DuBose died in 1940; however, Dorothy continued adapting plays and writing. In 1943, she coauthored with Howard Rigsby the play *South Pacific*, which subsequently went into production. Unfortunately, the show only lasted for a few performances.

Heyward was, for the most part, unknown, except for her contributions as a playwright with *Porgy and Bess* and *Mamba's Daughters*.—ANDREA PATTERSON-MASUKA

HILL, CHIPPIE [BERTHA]
(March 1905–May 1950) Dancer, singer

During the Harlem Renaissance, Chippie Hill stepped onstage at Leroy's Club in Harlem, showcasing her talents as a dancer. Traveling with vaudeville shows in the 1920s, she worked with the Rabbit Foot Minstrels and the Theater Owners' Booking Association. Her later move to Chicago marked the beginning of her recording career.

Born in Charleston, South Carolina, in 1905, Hill's family moved to New York a little more than ten years later. Her parents were John Hill and Ida Jones. In 1925,

Chippie recorded "Low Land Blues" with New Orleans natives Louis Armstrong on cornet and Richard M. Jones on piano. They also recorded "Kid Man Blues" in that same year for Okeh Records. They went on to record a string of songs the following year, including "Trouble in Mind," "Lonesome, All Alone, and Blue," "Georgia Man," "Pleadin' for the Blues," "Pratt City Blues," "Mess, Katie, Mess," "Lovesick Blues," and "Lonesome Weary Blues." "Trouble in Mind," penned and composed by Jones, has endured the test of time via covers from such artists as Ruth Brown, Nina Simone, and Jerry Lee Lewis. Hill recorded with Thomas A. Dorsey on "Weary Money Blues" and "Christmas Man Blues." While in Chicago, she performed with Joe "King" Oliver at the Plantation Café. The Elite No. 2 Club in Chicago was another night spot where she performed.

Hill married and had seven children. Around the finale of the Harlem Renaissance, she took time off from her career and did not return to performing until the late 1940s. She was hit by a car in 1950 and died.—SARAH-ANNE LEVERETTE

HITE, MATTIE [MATIE HITE, NELLIE HITE]
(c. 1890–c. 1935) Blues singer, cabaret singer

Mattie Hite's history beyond her performance is sparse. She was born in New York City and thought to have been the niece of Les Hite, a 1930s saxophonist and big-band leader, and to have recorded under the name Nellie; some say this might have been her sister. Hite was known for her emotion-fraught renditions, risqué style, and performance of "St. Joe's Infirmary," which broadened the scope and opportunities for black female singers. Her popularity grew with her emotion-packed rendition of "St. Joe's Infirmary," the story of a dead lover, a tune later popularized by Cab Calloway.

Hite moved to Chicago for a brief period around 1915. She performed at the Panama Club and worked with such performers as Florence Mills and Alberta Hunter. She returned to New York City in 1919, and performed in cabarets and revues, both on Broadway and off. In 1921, she began her recording career on Victor Records with Julian Motley, but the recording was not released. Hite recorded with Fletcher Henderson in 1923, on the Pathe label; in 1923–1924, on the Bell label; and in 1930, with Cliff Jackson for the Columbia label. In spite of her innovative contributions, she was not financially successful; however, her voice has recently appeared on reissues and collections, for instance, the multivolume set *The Female Blues Singers* (vol. 9, on the Document label). This selection includes a cut of "St. Joe's Infirmary (Those Gambler Blues)." Her last known performance was in New York City at the Lafayette Theater in 1932; little is known of her whereabouts after this.—HELEN R. HOUSTON

HOLIDAY, BILLIE [ELEANORA FAGAN]
(April 7, 1915–July 17, 1959) Jazz singer, composer

Even though she was a child during the 1920s heyday of the Harlem Renaissance, Billie Holiday emerged as a major jazz talent during the 1930s. Her earliest musical

Billie Holiday

influences were Bessie Smith and Louis Armstrong in terms of developing her unique singing style.

Born as Eleanora Fagan in either Philadelphia or Baltimore, Holiday's father, Clarence Holiday, had been a guitarist and banjoist with Fletcher Henderson, another Harlem Renaissance musical figure who contributed to the careers of Bessie Smith, Louis Armstrong, Benny Goodman, and other artists as a pianist, arranger, and bandleader. Her mother, Sadie Fagan, was not married to Clarence when their daughter was born, but they did marry for a brief period during her early childhood.

Holiday spent the remainder of her childhood in Baltimore with other relatives while her mother sought domestic work in Philadelphia and New York. Holiday also did domestic work, babysitting, errands, and other odd jobs, but she was placed in juvenile detention for frequent school absences and suffered the trauma of rape before reaching her teenage years. Even with these early hardships, she developed an interest in music and singing after hearing the music of Smith, Armstrong, and others on a Victrola (early record player) while working as a maid in a brothel.

In the late 1920s, Holiday's mother sent for her to come and live with her in Harlem; however, she had given up domestic work to become a prostitute. Both Holiday and her mother were arrested for vagrancy, a charge often associated with prostitution, in May 1929. While her mother was eventually released, Holiday was given a short prison sentence before the pair moved to Brooklyn. She then started working as a singing waitress in 1930, and gave herself the stage name "Billie," after Hollywood actress Billie Dove, while her mother returned to domestic work.

After an unsuccessful audition at Harlem's famed Small's Paradise nightclub, Holiday eventually became a featured singer at other venues, including Covan's, Mexico's, Pod and Jerry's, and the Hot Cha Restaurant. Around this time, she was introduced to such drugs as marijuana, yet she continued to draw attention for her singing talent. In 1933, the music entrepreneur John Hammond became interested in furthering Holiday's career, which led to her first recording session with a small band led by Benny Goodman. His black pianist, Teddy Wilson, would play on and produce a number of important recordings for Holiday in later years.

The following year, she met saxophonist Lester Young, who became such a dear friend and musical collaborator that she later nicknamed him the "Prez" (short for president) of the tenor saxophone. Young had also played with Fletcher Henderson, and he and Holiday would later team up as members of the Count Basie Orchestra, as well as on other performances and recordings. He was also credited with giving Holiday her famous nickname, "Lady Day."

In 1935, Holiday made her debut performance at the Apollo Theater on 125th Street, and after this success she became a national sensation, crossing the "color line" to tour as featured vocalist with the white Artie Shaw Orchestra, yet reacting strongly when she was exposed to racial discrimination, as well as other hardships, when the band toured in the South and other areas that supported segregation. The singer also appeared with Duke Ellington in the short film *Symphony in Black*, and her idol, Louis Armstrong, in the musical *Stars Over Broadway*.

Holiday's successful records with Wilson led to her own contract with Vocalion in 1936, and even provided her with the opportunity to record with her father on at least one occasion. In late 1938, Holiday opened at Café Society, and the next year she recorded the controversial and daring song "Strange Fruit" for Commodore Records, whose lyrics describe a lynching in the South. The song was later noted as the greatest jazz vocal recording of the twentieth century in a poll conducted by National Public Radio. In the early 1940s, Holiday continued to work with other great jazz musicians, namely pianist Art Tatum, trumpeters Roy Eldridge and Buck Clayton, vibraphonist/bandleader Lionel Hampton, and saxophonist/trumpeter/arranger Benny Carter during the heyday of New York's West 52nd Street as "Swing Street" and the "Jazz Capital of the World." She also had affairs, brief marriages, and other problematic relationships with other men she encountered in the world of entertainment and nightlife.

Holiday's drug addiction intensified, as she also became a heroin user in the early 1940s, and after her mother's death in 1945. Some years earlier, an argument with her mother regarding money prompted Holiday to say, "God bless the child that's got his own," which she later turned into a composition that became one of her most famous songs. Except for a few true friends, Holiday was on her own in dealing with her problems and addictions (which also included heavy drinking), yet she was somehow able to continue performing at major events, including the Esquire Magazine Jazz Concert, Jazz at the Philharmonic, and performances at New York City's Town Hall. In addition, she recorded for such labels as Columbia and Decca and appeared in another film, *New Orleans*, with Louis Armstrong.

Her romantic relationship with musician and fellow drug user Joe Guy led to Holiday's arrest after a performance at the Earle Theater in Philadelphia in May 1947. Guy betrayed her to the Federal Bureau of Narcotics and had legal representation to secure his release, but Holiday was sentenced to prison at the Federal Reformatory for Women in Alderson, West Virginia, where she remained incarcerated until March 1948. Her conviction also resulted in the loss of her New York City cabaret card, a legal work permit for entertainers, which further jeopardized her performing career.

Supporters rallied behind Holiday after her release in March 1948, as she scored critical and commercial successes with a sold-out concert at Carnegie Hall later that month and a reunion with the Count Basie Orchestra at the Strand Theatre, but she was forced to travel to other cities for nightclub work until her New York City work privileges were reinstated. In 1949, Holiday was again arrested for narcotics possession while working at a club in San Francisco; however, she was later cleared of the charges.

As the 1950s began, Holiday was dropped from Decca, and she recorded for the Clef and Verve labels. Some music critics thought that her voice had been ruined by her alcohol and drug abuse, while others said that her artistry and interpretation of the songs and music reflected the realities of her life and transcended any technical limitations in her singing voice. Holiday persevered despite her personal issues and health problems, and achieved her dream of performing in Europe during a 1954 jazz tour of Scandinavia, Germany, Holland, Belgium, France, Switzerland, and England, including an appearance before thousands at the Royal Albert Hall in London.

She returned to the United States to perform at the first Newport Jazz Festival during the same year and received an award from *DownBeat*, the nation's top jazz publication. Holiday's personal life included the publication of her life story, *Lady Sings the Blues*, with author William Duffy in 1956, and a relationship with Louis McKay, who helped bring some stability to her life. Holiday married McKay in Chihuahua, Mexico, on March 28, 1957, and later that year, she reunited with Lester Young for a memorable television performance of the song "Fine and Mellow" as part of the CBS production *The Sound of Jazz*.

In 1958, Holiday completed an album entitled *Lady in Satin*, with a full orchestra led by Ray Ellis. *Lady in Satin* became one of her all-time best-selling recordings, and she made another brief European tour but was unable to complete what would have been her last public performance at the Phoenix Theatre in 1959, after attempting two songs. On May 30 of that year, she was admitted to Harlem's Metropolitan Hospital, where she died on July 17. A requiem mass was held for her at New York's St. Paul Roman Catholic Church on July 22, 1959. Her final album, *Last Recordings*, was released after her death.

Holiday's last accompanist, pianist Mal Waldron, is one of many artists who have recorded musical tributes to Holiday in the years since her death. Singer/actress Diana Ross portrays Holiday in the 1972 film also titled *Lady Sings the Blues* and received an Academy Award nomination for Best Actress. Poems by Harlem Renaissance author Langston Hughes ("Song for Billie Holiday") and Frank O'Hara ("The Day Lady Died") were among the first of many literary tributes to the late singer and composer, including a critically acclaimed stage play, "Lady Day at the Emerson Bar and Grill."

Other posthumous awards and recognitions for Holiday include the Grammy Lifetime Achievement Award in 1987, and an official U.S. postage stamp in 1994, fitting tributes to a woman who overcame an ongoing series of issues, challenges, and tragedies to achieve lasting fame and iconic status in the world of art, music, entertainment, and culture as arguably the "greatest female jazz voice of all time."
—FLETCHER F. MOON

HOLLOWAY, LUCY ARIEL WILLIAMS [ARIEL WILLIAMS]
(March 3, 1905–1973) Poet, musician, educator

The Harlem Renaissance was enriched by the work of such poets as Lucy Ariel Williams Holloway, who, like countless other black female poets, had their works showcased in the journals *Opportunity* and *Crisis*. Holloway also shared her talent as a music teacher with black students in the South, where she taught for a time.

Holloway, also known as Ariel Williams, was born in Mobile, Alabama, to H. Roger Williams, a physician, and Fannie Brandon Williams, a teacher. She graduated from Talladega College in Alabama in 1902, and received a bachelor of music degree from Fisk University in Nashville in 1926. She then studied at the Oberlin Conservatory of Music and received a second bachelor of music degree, with a major in piano and a minor in voice, in 1926. She did further study at Columbia University.

While a senior at Fisk, Holloway received fleeting national attention when she published the dialect poem "Northboun'" in *Opportunity* magazine's 1926 contest; she was cowinner of the first and second prizes for writing. The poem was later published in anthologies by Countee Cullen, Arna Bontemps, James Weldon Johnson, and others. Holloway was director of music at North Carolina College for Negroes (later North Carolina Central University) from 1926 to 1932. She also taught music at Dunbar High School in Mobile from 1932 to 1936, Fessenden Academy in Florida in 1936–1937, and Lincoln Academy in North Carolina in 1938–1939. Fessenden and Lincoln were both under the auspices of the American Missionary Association. Holloway was the first supervisor of music for the Mobile Public School System, from 1939 to 1973. In addition to teaching, she was a pianist and gave local performances in Alabama. Lucy married Joaquin M. Holloway in 1936, and they had one child.

During the Harlem Renaissance, Holloway contributed to numerous periodicals and anthologies. Five of her poems were published in *Opportunity*, the official publication of the National Urban League and one of the leading journals that published works by and about African Americans during the Harlem Renaissance, between 1926 and 1935. Her works also appeared in Countee Cullen's *Caroling Dusk* (1927) and James Weldon Johnson's *Book of American Negro Poetry* (1922). In 1955, Holloway published *Shape Them into Dreams: Poems* (1955).—JESSIE CARNEY SMITH

HOLT, NORA [LENA DOUGLAS]
(1890 or 1895–January 25, 1974) Music critic, teacher, singer

Nora Holt became one of the pivotal figures of the Harlem Renaissance. Through her scholarship, writings, and commitment to making music a key component of African American culture, she was one of the great proponents of musical excellence, and her social connections made her a celebrity during the Harlem Renaissance era.

Born Nora Lena Douglas in Kansas City, Kansas, Holt was the daughter of the Reverend Calvin N. Douglas, a minister in the African Methodist Episcopal Church, and Gracie Brown Douglas. She enjoyed a good deal of freedom during her childhood, and her parents encouraged her pursuit of music. Following high school,

Nora Holt

Holt attended Chicago Music College, where she earned her bachelor of arts in 1917, and her master of arts in 1918, making her one of the first African Americans to earn a master of music degree. While she studied for her master's degree, she began writing music reviews for the *Chicago Defender*, a post she would hold from 1917 until 1921. In 1919, Holt cofounded the National Association of Negro Musicians (NANM). This organization was dedicated to making concerts and recitals necessary parts of the Harlem Renaissance movement. NANM was geared toward developing talent in young musicians and promoting African American musical expression. The organization was successful, expanding to more than twenty branches by the 1930s. In 1921, Holt edited and published the magazine *Music and Poetry*. The magazine gave her the space she needed to work on some of her own compositions, as well as highlight outstanding young, black artists. Holt worked to make African American music an institution, rather than a passing trend.

In New York City, Holt was known on the social scene for her sensual singing, platinum blonde hair, and love life. She married at least five times, and her affairs offered good sport for gossip columnists. Of all her marriages, the one with the wealthy Joseph L. Ray on July 29, 1923, attracted a good deal of attention. In photographs of that wedding day, Holt is wearing six-carat diamond earrings from her husband, and a black eye, rumored to be from her lover Gordon Jackson. The marriage to Ray lasted nineteen months, and their divorce was feature news for the tabloids.

Holt was one of the principal socialites of the Harlem Renaissance. Of all her friendships, the one she formed with Carl Van Vechten contributed significantly to her overall legend and legacy. The two first met in a Harlem speakeasy, and they went on to become lifelong friends. One of the great photographers of the Harlem Renaissance era, Van Vechten shot a series of portraits of Holt that captured her urbanity, sophistication, and beauty. At parties hosted by Van Vechten, she was known for offering a particularly sensual rendition of "My Daddy Rocks Me (with One Steady Roll)," a song that had been popularized by blues legend Trixie Smith. While more a critic and scholar than singer, Holt possessed good skill and virtuosity, and her performances were always playful. Her performances were also important in bringing the music of the Harlem Renaissance to social circles that perhaps would not otherwise have heard those songs. Holt's influence on the Harlem Renaissance was so notable that she appears in Van Vechten's 1926 novel *Nigger Heaven* as the character Lasca Sartoris, a beautiful and wayward young woman. This depiction added to the image of Holt as a modern woman.

Holt was actually anything but wayward. She was a serious scholar dedicated to the craft of music and cultural expression. Despite the attention she received in the gossip columns, she sought to live life on her own terms—and she did, enjoying a broad range of freedom and always exercising her intellect for the greater good. By 1937, having experienced firsthand the jazz and blues of Harlem Renaissance musicians, Holt moved to Los Angeles, where she taught music in public high schools until 1943. For a short stint, she also owned a few beauty parlors in Los Angeles.

When she moved back east, Holt became the first music critic for the *New York Amsterdam News*, and she wrote music reviews for the publication from 1943 until 1956, as well as for the *New York Courier*. In 1945, she was elected as a member of the New York Music Critics Circle. She remained one of the most influential advocates for African American artists, hosting and producing radio shows that highlighted emerging black musicians. When her voice was first heard on the air as she interviewed young musicians, she became one of the earliest black women to host a radio show.—DELANO GREENIDGE-COPPRUE

HOPE, LUGENIA BURNS
(February 19, 1871–August 14, 1947) Organizer, activist

Lugenia Burns Hope, an activist and reformer, exemplified just what an effective community organizer could accomplish. Her commitment, actualized during the Harlem Renaissance era, resulted in many positive changes for the African American citizens of Atlanta, and it was a model of resistance against segregation and racism.

Hope was born Lugenia Burns on February 19, 1871, in St. Louis, Missouri, and her family later moved to Chicago as a result of difficult financial times. Hope had to quit school and work full time, which fostered her involvement in such community organizations as Kings Daughters and Hull House in Chicago. She continued her education by attending the Chicago Art Institute, the Chicago School of Design, and the Chicago School of Business, before meeting John Hope in 1893, marrying him in 1897, and moving to Nashville, Tennessee. Both John and Lugenia taught at Roger Williams University in Nashville.

After a year in Nashville, John and Lugenia moved to Atlanta, where John took a position with Atlanta Baptist College (later Morehouse College). John eventually became president of Atlanta University, the first black graduate school in the United States. Lugenia continued her community work, using the strategy of first discovering what the community needs were, in particular the West Fair neighborhood near the college. After sending Morehouse students door-to-door gathering information, she was able to secure space from the college to provide the community with childcare facilities, kindergartens, and recreational facilities. The core group of this effort became the Neighborhood Union, with Hope at the helm as chairperson from 1908 to 1935.

Hope's organization worked with other groups, including women's clubs and church groups, to address discriminatory practices and provide needed services that were unavailable to blacks. During World War I, the Neighborhood Union served African American soldiers through the Young Men's Christian Organization

(YMCA), but in 1920, Hope led a campaign against the YMCA for its segregation practices. Hope also collaborated with the Association of Southern Women against Lynching. In 1924, also under her leadership, the first African American high school in Atlanta and first public housing in the United States for African Americans were established. As her organization grew in accomplishments and prominence, Hope's leadership became nationally known, and many of the innovative practices served as examples for other groups seeking reform and access. Hope's prominence resulted in an appointment to President Herbert Hoover's Colored Commission in 1927, and in 1932, she was selected as the first vice president of the Atlanta Chapter of the National Association for the Advancement of Colored People (NAACP). In this role, she introduced citizenship schools on voting and the constitution that were later utilized throughout the various branches of the NAACP.

Hope was a tireless activist and social reformer who became leader of the first female-run agency for the enhancement of the African American community in Atlanta. In her later years, and after the death of her husband in 1936, she experienced poor health. She moved several times to be near family and died of heart failure in Nashville, Tennessee.—LEAN'TIN L. BRACKS

HORNE, LENA [LENA MARY CALHOUN HORNE]
(June 30, 1917–May 9, 2010) Singer, actress, civil rights activist

Lena Horne

Lena Horne began her career as an adolescent performer at the Cotton Club, Harlem's most prestigious nightclub during the Harlem Renaissance. She went on to achieve enormous fame as a mainstream celebrity.

Horne's beginning in life was fraught with difficulties. She was born Lena Mary Calhoun Horne in Brooklyn, New York, on June 30, 1917, to Edna and Edwin "Teddy" Horne. The couple divorced during Lena's early childhood. Her father eventually moved to Seattle, Washington, and remarried; her mother struggled as she pursued her dream to be an entertainer and make a home for herself and her daughter. For much of her childhood, Horne was shuttled from home to home throughout numerous states, including New York, Georgia, and Florida (Miami). She lived intermittently with her father's parents, in foster homes, with an uncle who was dean of students at Fort Valley Normal and Industrial School, and with her mother. Her grandparents, Edwin and Cora Horne, provided a stable life and exposed Horne to a comfortable lifestyle. Their light skin color (a product of racial mixing), education, economic standing, and manners planted them firmly in the community of blacks known as the black bourgeoisie or black elite. Cora participated in many African American organizations, for example, the National Association for the Advancement of Colored People, the Urban League, and the National Association of Colored Women. These groups promoted racial uplift and equality and protested racism and discrimination.

The stability Horne experienced with her grandparents was fleeting. Although her father sent her gifts and her mother promised her a permanent home, Horne periodically experienced loneliness, emotional trauma, and loss. She observed and experienced some of the indignities many blacks suffered in the racist white world. She suffered humiliation when some blacks ridiculed her for her light skin color. Even when Horne lived for brief periods with her mother, life was a desperate struggle. While Horne's mother briefly made a meager sum as an actress working in Harlem's famed Lafayette Theater, her dreams of stardom never came to fruition, and finding stable work was an ongoing trial. Nevertheless, Horne's fate turned when her mother married Miguel Rodriguez, a Cuban. Horne finally found a permanent home with her mother and stepfather in New York City.

Work was still hard to come by for Horne's parents. With not enough money to provide for the necessities of life, a decision had to be made. Either at Horne's insistence or her mother's, Horne was sent to the Cotton Club to audition for the covetous role as a chorine, also known as a chorus girl, in 1934. Although Horne discloses in her autobiography that she thought she did not sing or dance well, she had had some grooming. During her childhood, she had received dance lessons and some exposure to acting. Moreover, at a mere sixteen years of age, she was pretty, slender, and young. As it was widely apparent, Cotton Club dancers had to adhere to stringent rules: They had to be beautiful; at least five-feet, five inches tall; thin; and twenty-six years of age or younger. The young women also had to be light-skinned. The restrictions reflected the intensely discriminatory definitions of the ideal woman. The color restrictions spoke specifically to the color barriers that existed in mainstream society and the African American community. To Horne's surprise, she was added to the Cotton Club's payroll despite the fact she was underage and felt that she was without talent. Her employment with the club fulfilled the immediate need for financial support, as well as Horne's ambitions for stardom.

Entrance into the star-studded Cotton Club was a stupendous achievement. Founded in 1923, by Owney Madden, an Irish gangster, the club was one of a handful of white-owned Harlem nightclubs that primarily catered to white audiences. The few African American customers that were allowed inside sat in the back of the room; the rest of the blacks worked as performers and waiters. The Cotton Club featured the chorus girls and other entertainment, including solo and group acts, singing, and comedy and dance routines. Such legendary band conductors as Cab Calloway and Duke Ellington set the bar high for fashion, music, and charisma. The dancers were notorious for their beauty, glamorous but scant wardrobes, and elegant dancing. Horne's voice may have lacked maturity and skill, and her dance routines sometimes foundered, but the audience and management adored her.

Working at the Cotton Club was not easy. The obvious discriminatory practices at the establishment were generally not addressed by the African American stars, but it offered steady pay, recognition, and prestige. Menacing-looking mobsters sat in tables among the well-to-do, the occasional celebrity, and the predominately white clientele. Horne was sheltered from the myriad grown-up influences and potential harm by her ever-present mother and the other performers; however, the young performer had to work long and grueling hours and endure poor working conditions. The dancers had to share a cramped dressing room, and they were forbidden from using the nightclub restroom.

The difficulties of working at the Cotton Club were compensated, in part, by the money that Horne made and the opportunities that came her way as a result of her nightclub experience. She won a brief appearance in the movie short *Cab Calloway's Jitterbug Party* (1934) and the role of a victim of a voodoo sacrifice in *Dance with Your Gods* (1934).

The following year, Horne left the Cotton Club. She sang and danced with Noble Sissle's dance band, one of the hottest African American orchestras in the nation. Sissle helped groom Horne's talents. Voice and dance lessons would play an important part in transforming the inexperienced Horne into a tremendous talent. Until then, Horne would have to endure many more trials and difficult times.

Horne was not an overnight success. Although she appeared to be a rising star, her status did not shelter her from hard times and discriminatory treatment. In 1937, she married Louis J. Jones. The marriage produced two children, Gail and Edwin "Teddy," but the union was rocky from the start. Horne was ill-prepared for her new role as wife. Cooking, cleaning, and bending to the will of a demanding husband was new territory for her. Adding to her woes was the fact that her husband, like many African American men, had trouble finding work and respect in the white-dominated world. When Horne returned to her former employment as an entertainer, tensions mounted in the marriage. The couple eventually divorced in 1940, after a long separation, and the children were split. Jones kept their son, while Horne raised their daughter.

As she forged ahead, Horne broke new ground for African Americans in the industry and helped challenge the way African American women were depicted in films. Her work included singing, dancing, and acting in the all-black musical *The Duke Is Tops* (1938), as well as the Broadway musical *Leslie's Blackbirds* (1939). In 1940, she sang with an all-white band, Charley Barnet's Band. That same year, she worked in the Café Society Nightclub, an integrated club.

More opportunities awaited Horne in the 1940s. In 1942, she recorded her first album, *Moanin' Low*. In the same year, she moved to Hollywood and signed on with the film giant MGM. She appeared in such classic films as *Cabin in the Sky* (1942) and *Stormy Weather* (1942), and mainstream magazines like *Time* and *Life*. Few African American women of her time received as much exposure in mainstream society. In the media, she was depicted as beautiful and talented. In many of her films, she took on roles that defied the mammy stereotype to which black women were usually relegated.

In the latter half of the decade, Horne performed for U.S. troops. She especially enjoyed performing and mingling with the all-black troops. In 1947, she married Lenny Hayton, a Jewish composer and conductor for MGM.

The 1950s were productive despite the fact Horne had been blacklisted for alleged association with Communism. She toured the nightclub circuit in the United States and Europe. She recorded four albums in 1957. Also in 1957, her name was removed from the Hollywood blacklist.

In successive decades, Horne climbed the heights of success and took part in civil rights activism. She appeared in television specials and programs and films, performed concerts, recorded albums, and received several honors. One of her most memorable roles was as Glinda the Good Witch in the musical film *The Wiz* (1978). Based on the American classic *The Wizard of Oz*, *The Wiz* recasts the film with black performers and soulful music. Other memorable moments included the times she made guest appearances as herself on such popular black television sitcoms as *Sanford and Son* (1972–1977) and *The Cosby Show* (1984–1992).

Amidst Horne's busy schedule, she took time to get involved with the Civil Rights Movement of the 1960s. She met with civil rights leaders and was outspoken in her support of black equality. She participated in the March on Washington in 1963, and lent her voice and influence at civil rights rallies.

In the years following the movement, Horne remained a tour de force in popular culture into the new millennium and a symbol of pride for African Americans. She was ninety-two years old when she died.—GLADYS L. KNIGHT

HOUSTON, VIRGINIA A.
(?–?) Poet

Virginia A. Houston's work was a regular presence in *Crisis* and *Opportunity* magazines from 1929 and 1931, but little is known about her life. Her work was highly respected because of its technical sophistication and sensitive presentation. Her content often criticizes black characters who disrespected themselves and denied their heritage, as she describes in her poem "Troubadour," published in the July 1930 edition of *Crisis*. Houston's poetry was also selected by Beatrice M. Murphy for her anthology of young Negro poets, *Negro Voices*, published in 1938. Late in life, Houston is known to have lived in Cleveland, Ohio, and she worked for the social service area of the city police department.—LEAN'TIN L. BRACKS

HOWARD, GERTRUDE
(October 13, 1892–September 30, 1934) Actress

Gertrude Howard was an actress during the 1920s and 1930s, during the era of the Harlem Renaissance. She transcended boundaries as an African American actress, appearing in several predominately white films. Controversially, she was often cast in stereotypical roles that reflected the unequal social status of African Americans in mainstream society.

Born in Hot Springs, Alabama, on October 13, 1892, Howard appeared on Broadway in *The Wife Hunters* in 1911. In 1919, she moved to Hollywood to work in the world-famous film industry that was dominated by whites, necessitating African Americans to create their own film companies featuring all-black casts. Howard, however, broke through the barriers, appearing in a long list of films. She portrayed Aunt Chloe in *Uncle Tom's Cabin* (1927). She also appeared as Queenie in *Show Boat* (1929), as well as in *Hearts in Dixie* (1929). Her character Beulah in *I'm No Angel* (1933) was a popular archetype that depicted African American women as the submissive mammy figure. The mammy figure, which originated during slavery times, was based on the African American women who were forced to care for the children of middle-class and upper-class white families. The figure, however, is problematic because the caricature is based on the presumption that these women were docile and content in their role as caretakers and in their inferior status to whites.

The problematic roles notwithstanding, Howard established a career that was available to few African Americans. She paved the way for others, for instance, Hattie McDaniel, who made their mark in the film industry. Howard died in Los Angeles, California.—GLADYS L. KNIGHT

HUNTER, ALBERTA
(April 1, 1895–October 17, 1984) Singer, composer, nurse

When the Harlem Renaissance reached full bloom in the 1920s, Alberta Hunter was already a seasoned performer and peer of such artists as Bessie Smith and Ethel Waters, as well as a survivor of a variety of hardships. Born in Memphis, Tennessee, as the second child of Charles E. Hunter, a sleeping-car porter who abandoned his family shortly after her birth, her mother, Laura Peterson Hunter, a domestic worker, resorted to work as a maid in a brothel to support herself and two daughters, including Alberta and older sister La Tosca.

The early life of Hunter became more complicated when her mother remarried between 1906 and 1907, as Hunter gained a stepfather and much younger stepsister. Hunter disliked the rest of her family, but she hated her stepfather, in particular, because he was abusive to her mother. Hunter was also sexually abused by the white boyfriend of their family's white landlady and a black school principal. As a result, the future singer and composer became fiercely independent and aggressive, protesting her treatment by becoming disinterested in her personal cleanliness and appearance. She was eventually given the nickname "Pig."

Hunter was offered the opportunity by one of her teachers to move to Chicago, with her mother's permission. She did not ask her mother and left her hometown while still a teenager. Another woman she knew from Memphis helped Hunter get domestic work at a boarding house in the Hyde Park neighborhood, where she earned six dollars a week. Hearing that singers could make as much as ten dollars a week, she started looking for opportunities to perform, despite her inexperience. Several months later, she started singing at a brothel called Dago Frank's, even though she only knew two songs when she was first hired.

By 1915, Hunter had sung at several other Chicago clubs and cabarets, and she reestablished a relationship with her mother when she came to Chicago to live with her. At the Panama Club, a top Chicago nightspot similar to the Cotton Club in Harlem, as it featured black entertainment for white patrons, Hunter became a popular attraction. She was one of the first to sing Maceo Walker's "Sweet Georgia Brown" and W. C. Handy's "St. Louis Blues," and she later worked with such notable jazz musicians as trumpeter and bandleader Joe "King" Oliver and pianist Lillian "Lil" Harding Armstrong.

Hunter continued to enjoy success in Chicago by being very professional in her "show business" affairs and discreet in her personal life and relationships, but she also wanted to establish herself in New York. In May 1921, she made her first recording with the city's Black Swan label, but she switched to Paramount the next year because she felt Black Swan favored Ethel Waters. She recorded her original composition, "Down Hearted Blues," for Paramount, but it became an even bigger hit when recorded by Bessie Smith. Hunter received little (if any) compensation as composer of the song.

Despite their rivalry, in early 1923, Hunter appeared with Waters in a short-lived show called *Dumb Luck*. After a brief return to Chicago, Hunter returned to New York in April to open a new show known as *How Come?* at the Apollo Theater (then located at 42nd Street and Broadway). She settled permanently in New York and continued to work in revues and vaudeville on the Keith Circuit, which allowed her to tour less frequently and record for Okeh after she was dropped from Paramount for contract violations. Hunter's presence on the Harlem scene led to associations with personalities the likes of Langston Hughes and A'Lelia Walker, but she also traveled to Europe in the late 1920s, where she performed in Paris and then London, where she worked with Noble Sissle and costarred with Paul Robeson in the touring production of the landmark musical *Show Boat*.

Hunter's popularity began to decline during the 1930s, but she continued to perform in New York on the stage (in *Mamba's Daughters*, with Ethel Waters) and radio, as well as record for Decca with Lil Armstrong. She also traveled to perform in major European cities, including Amsterdam and Copenhagen, as well as Paris and London, until the onset of World War II. During the war, she performed in parts of Asia with a USO tour and received the Asiatic-Pacific Campaign Ribbon for her services.

Hunter continued to write religious and secular songs, and in 1952, she became one of the first of her race and sex elected to membership in the American Society of Composers, Authors, and Publishers. She also went on another USO tour to Europe, Korea, Japan, and Okinawa during the Korean War era; continued to work in New York on Broadway and in clubs; joined a Colored Methodist Episcopal church, as it was known then, which met in the former Lafayette Theater; and continued to share a New York apartment with her mother until Laura's death in January 1954.

Hunter then retired from show business to volunteer at a Harlem hospital; reported her age as being twenty years younger to qualify for a nurse training program; received her license as a practical nurse in 1957; and worked for twenty years until being "forced to retire" in 1977, at the age of eighty-two. Later that year, pianist Bobby Short invited her to appear at an event for another veteran singer,

Mabel Mercer, which led to her rediscovery by the entertainment world and a personal "renaissance" as an acclaimed performer and celebrity in her last years, with numerous live and television performances at such venues as Cookery nightclub, Carnegie Hall, and the Newport Jazz Festival. She traveled to Europe and Brazil and even made a return to her birthplace in Memphis. In addition, she appeared on the *Today Show* in New York City,

In 1980, Hunter received the Handy Award as Traditional Female Blues Artist of the Year, but health problems forced her to retire from public performance in 1984. On October 17 of that year, she was found dead in her apartment. According to her wishes, she was cremated and interred next to her mother at Ferncliff Cemetery in Hartsdale, New York.—FLETCHER F. MOON

HUNTER, JANE EDNA HARRIS
(December 13, 1882–January 19, 1971) Organization founder and director, nurse, black women's rights activist

The plight of black women during the Harlem Renaissance was a tenuous one. Jane Edna Harris Hunter's efforts to improve the lives of these women during that era was most noticeable in her work in the nursing profession and her success in bringing about complete integration of the Young Women's Christian Association (YWCA) for the benefit of black women.

Born in Pendleton, South Carolina, Hunter was the daughter of sharecroppers Edward and Harriet Milner Harris, who lived on the Woodburn plantation. After her father died when she was ten years old, her work as a live-in nursemaid and cook became necessary. She had preferred to continue her education at that time. She did so later and graduated with the equivalent of a secondary-education diploma from Ferguson-Williams College in Abbeyville, South Carolina. Jane married Edward Hunter, who was forty years her senior, but never let the loveless marriage deter her from pursing nursing training. She worked in Charleston and then enrolled in Cannon Street Hospital and Training School for Nurses. In 1904, she pursued advanced training at the Dixie Hospital and Training School for Nurses at the Hampton Institute (later Hampton University) in Virginia. A year later, Hunter relocated to Cleveland, Ohio, where she was once again forced to work as a domestic servant due to racial segregation in health care facilities. Still later, she was hired as a private duty nurse and masseuse for Cleveland's wealthy families.

Hunter's mother died in 1910, before the two could reconcile differences they had experienced early on. Hunter had been troubled by her own racial heritage (her father was the son of a plantation overseer and a black woman) and the snobbery she witnessed as a child when skin tone made a difference in her own church. Hunter finally accepted her background and began to devote her life to supporting the needs of black women. She called together eight of her friends who a similar backgrounds, and they founded the Working Girls' Home Association, with Hunter as president. These women already belonged to the YWCA. The organization flourished and, in 1912, became the Phillis Wheatley Association to honor black poet Phillis Wheatley. It offered employment services and training in various professions to black women, and between 1913 and the 1960s, thousands of women lived there and received training. After moving to larger and larger quarters, the organization finally erected an eleven-story building. The association became a model for self-help groups through the United States.

In 1925, after completing studies at Cleveland Law School, Hunter passed the Ohio bar and then used her legal training and superb fund-raising skills to enhance other programs for black women. In addition, she became involved in real estate, stocks, and the black-owned Empire Savings and Loan Company. Hunter's book *A Nickel and a Prayer* (1940) recounts the stages that led to the founding of the Phillis Wheatley Association. She officially retired in 1947 and, in 1960, moved to a rest home, where she died.—JESSIE CARNEY SMITH

HUNTON, ADDIE D. WAITES

(June 11, 1875–June 21, 1943) Activist, educator, organization official, clubwoman

During the Harlem Renaissance, Addie D. Waites Hunton was a staunch crusader for the advancement of the black race, particularly the causes of black women. Like several of her black female contemporaries, for instance, Elizabeth Ross Haynes, she worked through the Young Women's Christian Association (YWCA) and the National Association of Colored Women to achieve her goal.

Born in Norfolk, Virginia, in 1875, Hunton was the daughter of Jesse and Adelina (Lawton) Waites. Her father was the successful owner of a shipping business. After her mother died while Addie was still a young child, she lived with a maternal aunt in Boston. In 1899, she became the first African American woman to graduate from Spencerian College of Business in Philadelphia. For one year, she taught school in Portsmouth, Virginia, and then moved to Normal, Alabama, where she continued to teach and also became principal of State Normal and Agricultural College (later Alabama Agricultural and Mechanical State University). In June 1893, Addie married William A. Hunton, who had moved to Norfolk to become the first black professional youth secretary of the Colored Men's Department of the International Committee of the Young Men's Christian Association (YMCA). The couple relocated to Atlanta and began their family of four children.

Addie worked at local Clark University and traveled with William when he attended YMCA conferences. This brought her some attention in the YMCA. She began to speak out publicly against racial segregation and wrote articles on black women's issues. Violence in the area, including the Atlanta riot of 1906, left the parents anxious about the family's safety, and they left for Brooklyn, New York, that same year. Addie was appointed secretary to the YWCA's National Board in 1907, and she took tours of the South and Midwest in 1907–1908, during which she conducted a survey for the organization. From 1907 to 1910, she and her children studied in Europe. When she returned home, she continued her work with the Y and studied at the College of the City of New York. After her husband died in 1916, Addie worked in Brooklyn canteens as a volunteer to aid black soldiers. She joined two other black women—Helen Curtis and Kathryn Johnson—who were invited to France as YWCA workers, but they were assigned to supply units rather than the fighting units that they preferred. While there, Hunton offered a literacy course and discussion programs on race leaders, art, music, religion, and other subjects to the men who felt the sting of isolation and racial segregation practices in military service.

After returning home in August 1919, Hunton devoted the remainder of her life to matters of race and African American women. She and Kathryn Johnson coauthored *Two Colored Women with the American Expeditionary Forces* (1920), which reveals the racial segregation that black soldiers and black female volunteers experienced in France. She also held leadership positions on many national boards and in numerous organizations, among them the Council of Colored Work of the YWCA National Board, the International Council of Women of the Darker Races (president), and the National Association for the Advancement of Colored People (vice president and field secretary). Hunton was a founder and organizer of the National Association of Colored Women and a staunch suffragist. Her other writings include a biography of her husband entitled *William Alphaeus Hunton: A Pioneer Prophet of Young Men* (1938).

Hunton's last known public appearance was at the 1939 New York World's Fair, where she presided over a program honoring outstanding women of her race. She died in Brooklyn of complications resulting from diabetes.—JESSIE CARNEY SMITH

HURST, FANNIE
(October 1889–February 23, 1968) Novelist, short story writer, activist

Fannie Hurst was a prolific and highly successful author of Jewish descent who championed African American writers and causes as early as the Harlem Renaissance. The daughter of Samuel and Rose (née Kopel) Hurst, she was born in Hamilton, Ohio, and raised in St. Louis, Missouri, where her father was a shoe manufacturer. Hurst graduated from Washington University in 1909, and she moved to New York the following year to pursue a writing career. Although she married pianist Jacques Danielson on May 5, 1915, the couple maintained separate residences, and Hurst did not publically reveal her marriage until her fifth wedding anniversary. Hurst continued to use her maiden name, and she was determined that marriage would not interfere with her professional life.

Hurst's career as a writer was characterized by longevity, popularity, and wealth. She published eight collections of short stories (1914 to 1937) and eighteen novels (1921 to 1964). More than twenty films (1918 to 1961) were based on Hurst's narratives. *Imitation of Life* (1933), one of Hurst's most popular novels, was adapted for the screen in 1934, and starred Claudette Colbert, as well as African American actresses Louise Beavers and Fredi Washington. In the book and film, two widows earn a living and raise their daughters, yet Peola, the African American daughter, abandons her mother and passes for white. Among the most prominent responses to the novel and/or film by Hurst's African American contemporaries are Sterling Brown's "*Imitation of Life:* Once upon a Pancake" (1935), which faults Hurst for her inclusion of stereotypical images, and Langston Hughes's "Limitations of Life," a satirical skit that was performed at the Harlem Suitcase Theater. The 1959 remake of the film features a white actress as Peola. By the end of the 1920s, Hurst received as much as $4,000 per short story, and her first novel, *Star-Dust: The Story of an American Girl* (1921), commanded $50,000 for book, film, and magazine rights.

Hurst used her celebrity status to encourage African American writers (including Zora Neale Hurston and Dorothy West) and to support their causes. When she served as a judge for *Opportunity* magazine's writing contest in May 1925, she met Hurston, who was awarded two second-place prizes and two honorable mentions. While attending Barnard College, Hurston worked briefly as Hurst's secretary, as well as her chauffeur and traveling companion. More than a decade later, Hurst wrote the introduction to *Jonah's Gourd Vine* (1934). Three years later, Hurston wrote "Fannie Hurst: By Her Ex-Amanuensis," which appeared in an October issue of the *Saturday Review of Literature*. After Hurston's death in 1960, Hurst's "Zora Neale Hurston: A Personality Sketch" was published in the *Yale University Gazette* (1961). Hurst was a member of the Writers' League against Lynching, which was founded in 1933; the Board of Directors for the National Health Circle for Colored People; and the National Urban League. In a 1934 meeting of the New York Urban League, she advocated the use of federal funds for housing improvements in Harlem, and on August 4, 1946, her *New York Times* article, "The Other and Unknown Harlem," sought to dispel misconceptions of residents after the Harlem Riot of 1943.

Although Hurst was a feminist and social activist, writing remained her passion. Her autobiography, *Anatomy of Me: A Wonderer in Search of Herself* (1958), was published six years after the death of her husband. At the age of seventy-seven, Hurst was working on manuscripts until a brief illness claimed her life.—LINDA M. CARTER

HURSTON, ZORA NEALE
(January 7, 1891–January 28, 1960) Folklorist, playwright, short fiction writer, essayist, novelist

The author of four novels, two books of folklore, several short stories, essays, plays, and one autobiography, Zora Neale Hurston holds a place as one of the Harlem Renaissance's most talented and productively diverse writers, offering audiences an in-depth look at folk life. Although most of her work was published after the period, her most influential texts appeared during the heart of the movement, and she was certainly one of the most prolific women of the time period.

Hurston was born to Reverend John Hurston and Lucy Potts Hurston on January 7, 1891, in Notasulga, Alabama. In 1894, the family moved to Eatonville, Florida, an African American town near Orlando; this setting became a central character of many of her works from which she drew her personal experiences and situations she witnessed.

As the second daughter of eight children, Hurston's childhood was surrounded by a large family, and her parents were important figures in the community—John Hurston served as Eatonville mayor and Lucy Hurston as a schoolteacher. Zora attended Hungerford School and later a boarding school in Jacksonville, Florida, until

Zora Neale Hurston

the death of her mother in 1904. Her father remarried six months after becoming a widower, which Hurston disapproved of immensely. After her mother's death, Hurston moved from relative to relative; this wandering may have contributed to the nostalgic picture she paints of Eatonville, Florida, in many of her texts. She once joined a Gilbert and Sullivan troupe as a personal maid, developing her love of the dramatic arts. The troupe ended in 1916, and Hurston grounded herself in Baltimore, enrolling in Morgan Academy (now Morgan State University). After graduating in 1918, she entered Howard University, became a member of the Howard Players, joined Alain Locke's literary club, and was a regular member of Georgia Douglas Johnson's literary salon, along with many other writers who would make up the younger generation of the New Negro writers.

At the encouragement and support of Locke, Hurston became a known figure during this time through her award-winning short stories. Her first, "John Redding Goes to Sea," appeared in *Stylus* in 1921; set in Florida, Hurston shows the beginning of her talents with dialect that she would continue to use throughout her writing career. "Drenched in Light" (1924) appeared in *Opportunity* and won second prize; it was in 1924 that Hurston was persuaded to move to New York, at the height of the Harlem Renaissance. The following year, she was once again an award recipient for her work "Spunk," also appearing in *Opportunity* and reprinted in Locke's anthology *The New Negro* (1925). Spunk Banks is a bold character who bullies and humiliates the mild-mannered Joe Kanty by parading in public with Mrs. Lena Kanty, Joe's wife. When Joe finally takes a stand, Spunk fatally shoots him, but soon thereafter, he suffers an accident at the sawmill. Hurston also enrolled in Barnard College on scholarship and studied anthropology under Frank Boas; in 1928, she was the first African American graduate of the institution. In 1927, Hurston married Herbert Sheen, a fellow Howard student, but they divorced in 1931.

"Sweat" (1926), published in the one issue of *Fire! A Quarterly Devoted to the Younger Negro Artists*—a literary magazine that Hurston coedited—is one of Hurston's frequently anthologized short stories and often considered her finest short piece. Delia Jones is a God-fearing woman in an abusive marriage. Her husband Sykes torments her with snakes in hopes of getting her to leave their home, leaving Sykes to do as he pleases with his mistress. As Sykes' abuse increases, Delia's resolve to not be moved is also strengthened. Divine justice delivers death to Sykes through a rattlesnake bite meant for Delia, and he is all the more aware that she refuses to assist him to his last breath. Also in that issue, Hurston published a one-act play, *Color Struck: A Play*.

In need of financial support from 1927 to 1931, Hurston accepted the patronage of Charlotte Osgood Mason (called "Godmother"), a wealthy woman in New York, but the conditions included control of how Hurston's research would be used. Also during this time, she collaborated with fellow period writer Langston Hughes on the dramatic comedy *Mule Bone: A Comedy of Negro Life*, based on Hurston's short story "The Bone of Contention." Disagreement regarding the content caused their split as friends and working partners. Hurston eventually wrote a new version of the play, which led to arguments about authenticity and authorship. The play was not produced until 1991, at Lincoln Center.

Another popular story, "The Gilded Six-Bits" (1933), published in *Story*, examines a young married couple almost destroyed by a slick newcomer in town. Joe and Missy May are young and in love, satisfied at first with just one another and their clean, small home, but when Otis Slemmons comes to town and opens an ice cream parlor wearing a fancy suit and sporting a "solid gold piece" on his watch chain, both Missy May and Joe are seduced by his charms and pretty words, changing their definitions of success and happiness. Missy May is soon discovered with Slemmons when Joe comes home early from work; although Slemmons is chased away, the marriage is strained, and the couple begins to look at each other differently. When Missy May discovers she is with child, her fears of losing Joe increase all the more. The two find their way back to one another through the strength of their love, the hope in the future represented in their child, and the realization that the "solid gold piece" was, in fact, gold-plated. The story drew the attention of an editor who asked Hurston if she had a novel in the works; she immediately began working on her first book, even though she had reassured him that she had one already completed.

Jonah's Gourd Vine (1934) is Hurston's first published novel; the text is loosely based on the tumultuous marriage of her parents and the philandering ways of her father. The novel offers a glimpse inside the struggles and triumphs of African American families in postslavery, early migration from places of birth to begin anew, and the birth of all-black townships and what would eventually be called the "New Negro." John Buddy Pearson, the protagonist, is a larger-than-life character in love with Lucy Potts, an upper-class girl who inspires him to better himself. From different backgrounds, John and Lucy marry despite the disapproval of her parents. John's biggest flaw is his inability to control his wandering eye and stay faithful to his wife. The couple and their three children relocate from Alabama to Florida as a means of beginning anew—John finds his calling as a preacher and leads Zion Hope Church, with Lucy as first lady. His leadership skills also move him into the role of mayor of the all-black town of Eatonville, with the support and advice of his wife, but her sudden death weakens his resolve and he soon succumbs to his previous negative ways. When his reputation is lost, he turns to a former lover for support and remarries; this union ends in divorce, and John also loses his church position. The novel ends with a third marriage, another adulterous encounter, and John's death by train accident.

Mules and Men (1935), Hurston's first published book of folklore, solidified the author as versatile and enmeshed in folklore. Her mentor and anthropology professor at Columbia University, Frank Boas, supported her work as a unique contribution and new voice in the discipline. Hurston's approach of a nonjudgmental persona as narrator allows the reader to enter into a world perhaps unfamiliar with a personable guide. The text is divided into two sections—the first in Florida and the second in New Orleans. The narrator returns home to Eatonville and neighboring Polk County to collect tales of Brer Rabbit and Brer Bear and set them to print before they are lost to the world. The collection includes seventy folktales as cultural artifacts. In section two of the text, the narrator journeys to New Orleans in hopes of collecting information on hoodoo, and with the assistance of Luke Turner—nephew of Marie Leveau, hoodoo priestess—she completes a personal initiation by lying face down on a snake for sixty-nine hours. This section also includes rituals for the reader's interest, including how to get a man and how to keep a husband faithful. Hurston's text was criticized by some as more fiction than folklore, but it also helped present her as an authority on African American folk life. Ultimately, this is the first book of folklore by an African American author, and its success propelled Hurston into demand by other anthropology scholars.

In 1936, Hurston received a two-year Guggenheim Fellowship, with which she traveled to Jamaica and Haiti for further research on diasporan folklore and voodoo. It was during this time, in a seven-week stint, that Hurston wrote what is considered her best and perhaps most important work: *Their Eyes Were Watching God* (1937), her second novel. It explores the journey of Janie Crawford from young girl to woman and her desire to establish a voice and live her dreams. Raised by her aging grandmother, Nanny understands the life of black women as akin to the life of a mule, she explains to Janie; she longs for her granddaughter to have a different experience, one that she believes will come with marriage and protection. Janie instead believes that marriage should be like the honeybee pollenating the pear blossoms—a partnership for mutual fulfillment. But Nanny's fears force Janie into a marriage with Logan Killicks, who is considerably older and a property owner. Despite protests, Janie acquiesces to the doomed marriage and allows Nanny to die in peace. The union is uneventful, with Janie relegated to the kitchen and house and Logan taking care of the farm, until he purchases Janie a mule of her own with which to plow alongside him. Janie quickly realizes that this does not fit her dreams, and she is easily persuaded to abandon that life and join fast talker and big dreamer Joe Starks, who is on his way to help start up the all-black town of Eatonville.

For Janie, Joe represents newness and the New Negro, leaving behind what Nanny wanted for her. Joe does indeed live up to his ego—becoming mayor and opening a general store and post office—but he also relegates Janie as part of his conquests, separating her from the community as Mrs. Mayor Starks. Joe strips her of any developing identity, silences her in public, and also insists that she cover her hair. He establishes himself financially, and they are able to live comfortably for many years. But his aging body and failing health make him insecure around his much younger wife, and he soon becomes verbally and eventually physically abusive. Janie refuses to continue her submissive role and finally matches his personal insults in front of the townsfolk, which then forces Joe into hiding and hastens his inevitable demise. Janie plays the grieving widow for a respectable amount of time but quickly moves on, taking charge of the store her husband left behind.

Reluctantly at first, Janie allows herself to be courted by Tea Cake, a much younger man who comes closest to Janie's vision of the bee and the pear tree blossom. Although the townspeople suspect that he is simply after her money and she is acting like a foolish old woman, Janie boldly decides to move with him to the Everglades and work as a migrant worker. Her change in appearance suggests a newfound sense of freedom—free-flowing hair and overalls—but their union is marred by an incident of domestic violence in which Tea Cake hits her, an act he justifies as necessary to prove a point to others. Their union is nonetheless presented as passionate young love. In an attempt to survive a powerful hurricane, Tea Cake is bit by a rabid dog while protecting Janie and thereby goes mad despite medical attention. Janie must shoot and kill him in self-defense and is acquitted of the devastating act against her lover. The novel ends with Janie's return to Eatonville, walking proudly in her overalls and unencumbered hair; she confidently tells her life story to her best friend Pheoby and is not concerned with the busybody talk of others. She has developed an authorial voice and is satisfied with her life as she looks out on the horizon.

Tell My Horse (1938) is Hurston's second book of folklore—the culmination of her research in Jamaica and Haiti—and was not as favorably received as the first. Criticism of the text included that it contains too much political commentary and history of the islands in the first two-thirds; the latter third presents insight into voodoo practices in Haiti and descriptions of zombies. The text was successful in England.

In 1939, Hurston published *Moses, Man of the Mountain*; the biblical tale of Moses and Exodus always appealed to the African American community because of the experience with slavery and later Jim Crow segregation and the ultimate triumph of the oppressed. Going against the popular notion of the time, Hurston rewrites Moses as African and ultimately as a great conjurer. Here, Hurston is able to combine her talents as a fiction writer and folklorist. Moreover, she incorporates humor into the tale, further connecting the plight of the biblical Hebrews to the African American experience.

Hurston's *Dust Tracks on a Road* (1942) chronicles her life through her fifties but begins in her beloved Eatonville, not her birthplace Alabama. The omission of her actual birthplace begins the illusion of revealing herself to the reader. She expresses a desire to explore the world and support herself as a writer, and she has much to say about love, religion, race, and politics. Although the original edition omits chapters that the publisher determined to be irrelevant to her life story, a more complete version of her memoir was published in 1955. Such a decision was perhaps an attempt to conform the text to the more traditional linear format. But as had already become Hurston's style, the text is nontraditional, blending folklore, essay, and narrative. As the title suggests, the text explores Hurston's journey from child to woman and the paths along the way. Once again, Hurston received mixed reviews; white critics gave favorable critiques, and the *Saturday Evening*

Post awarded her the Ansfield-Wolk Award and $1,000. Black intellectuals were critical of the racial views she espoused and the omissions of the struggles of black life, and many claimed she was pandering to a white audience. New readings of the memoir have determined Hurston to be an expert at disguise and the text as an attempt to find an authorial voice as a black female writer.

Seraph on the Sewanee (1948) is Hurston's final published novel and, although set in Florida, it departs from her traditional theme of African American communities and folklore; this novel explores white Florida "crackers," descendants of the original pioneer settlers, and she attempts to show similarities between white and black Southern culture. Arvay Henson is a shy and emotionally dependent young woman who falls for Jim Meserve, a town newcomer whom she marries under duress even though Jim is condescending about Arvay's background. They relocate to pursue citric farming and are prosperous; their first-born son, Earl, is born mentally challenged, and in a tragic sequence of events, Earl (as a teenager) sexually assaults a local girl, hides in the swamp, and is fatally shot by his father. Earl's death leaves Arvay devastated and withdrawn for many years. Jim, unable to accept her passive state, leaves the marriage, which thereby propels Arvay to return to her roots, a process through which she comes to appreciate her background and gains a self-confidence that has been missing all along. Only then can she and Jim reconcile and redefine their relationship.

During that same year, Hurston was indicted for allegedly committing immoral acts with a ten-year-old boy; the accusation was proven groundless, but having to defend herself caused the author to withdraw from society. In the 1950s, much of her productivity was spent on conservative political essays published in the *Saturday Evening Post*, *American Legion Magazine*, and *Negro Digest*. Her most caustic essay was against the 1954 *Brown v. Board of Education* decision, published in the *Orlando Sentinel*, in which Hurston argues that desegregation would harm the study of black culture.

With her health failing, Hurston suffered from hypertension and had a stroke in 1959, which left her debilitated. She died in Fort Pierce, Florida, and is buried in an unmarked grave in the segregated cemetery of Garden of Heavenly Rest. As her work was reexamined, she became recognized as a leading female figure of the time; in 1973, Alice Walker marked her gravesite with a stone that reads, "A Genius of the South."—ADENIKE MARIE DAVIDSON

I

ISAACS, EDITH JULIET RICH

(March 27, 1878–January 10, 1956) Harlem Renaissance supporter, editor, critic

Edith Juliet Rich Isaacs was born on March 27, 1878, in Milwaukee, Wisconsin. Her mother was Rose Sidenberg Rich, and her father, whose family emigrated from Hungary, was Adolph Walter Rich, a successful manufacturer and philanthropist who loved the arts. Edith was highly influenced by a home that promoted the love of music, literature, and art. After graduating from Downer College in 1899, she initially worked for the *Milwaukee Sentinel*, first as a reporter and then, in 1903, as the literary editor. By 1904, she had married New York lawyer and composer Lewis M. Isaacs.

While living in New York, Isaacs wrote for the *Ladies Home Journal*, became drama critic for *Ainslee's Magazine*, and in 1918, became editor of the publication *Theater Arts*. During her tenure at *Theater Arts*, which lasted until 1946, she became a recognized and respected voice in the theater, and she saw her role as one means toward social change. Isaacs believed in a national American theater rooted in the folk traditions of the nation and recognized the absence of black culture. Her commitment to this idea found her collaborating with Alain Locke on the exhibition *Primitive African Art of the Blondiau Theater Arts Collection* during the 1920s. Recognizing that once the exhibition closed the pieces would be scattered to different buyers, Isaacs bought the entire exhibit and ultimately divided the works between the Arthur Schomburg Collection of Negro Culture at the New York Public Library and Howard University in Washington, D.C. She believed that black communities were vital to the national theater. In 1942, offering further support to the black theater, she published an entire issue of *Theater Arts* dedicated to the Negro in the American theater. The issue consists of photographs of prominent black artists and a narrative written by Isaacs, in spite of her bout with arthritis. Her work with this issue became the basis for her book *The Negro in the American Theatre*, published 1947.

Isaacs was a champion for the cause of recognition and inclusiveness of black art in the national theater, and through her efforts she provided opportunities and exposure for this brilliant show of artistry and talent found in black culture. She successfully helped create the American National Theater and Academy in 1935, and served as its first president.—LEAN'TIN L. BRACKS

J

JACKSON, MAE HOWARD
(May 12, 1877–July 12, 1931) Sculptor

The art of Mae Howard Jackson helped dissipate recurring stereotypes of African Americans so prevalent during the Harlem Renaissance, a goal that those who brought forth the cultural revolution sought to achieve. Her depictions of the "New Negro" were positive self-images of what she saw in society.

In 1877, Jackson was born in Philadelphia, Pennsylvania, to Floarada Howard and Sallie Dunham. She first graduated from Professor J. Liberty-Tadd's Art School in Philadelphia and, in 1899, from the Pennsylvania Academy of Fine Arts. After marrying William T. S. Jackson, a teacher and high school principal in Washington, D.C., she moved to that city, maintained a studio, and pursued her career as an artist between 1899 and 1931. Jackson taught and also captured the images of a number of African Americans who were, or would later become, legendary. She taught art to students in the District of Columbia. She also lectured to students at Howard University, where one of her students was Sargent Johnson, the orphaned nephew of her husband, who had lived with the Jacksons at one time. Among her sitters were such notable black leaders and educators as W. E. B. Du Bois, Paul Laurence Dunbar, Francis J. Grimké, Jean Toomer, and Kelly Miller. In 1928, Jackson received the bronze medal from the Harmon Foundation for her bust of Miller.

In 1913, Jackson participated in the Emancipation Exhibition at the Corcoran Gallery in Washington, D.C. She was active at a time when race relations in the United States were tenuous, and her natural tendency to be withdrawn was intensified by the racial prejudices that she both saw and encountered. She was denied membership in the Washington Society of Fine Arts, and although some of her work had been showcased there in 1916 and 1928, she was denied other opportunities to

exhibit at the National Academy of Design. Jackson died in Long Beach, New York.
—JESSIE CARNEY SMITH

JARBORO, CATERINA
(July 21, 1898–August 13, 1986) Opera singer

Caterina Jarboro

Few opportunities were available to African American concert singers during the Harlem Renaissance; nevertheless, Caterina Jarboro enjoyed some success in the United States and Europe during that time. She became known on Broadway during the early 1920s, when she appeared in two popular Broadway shows.

The facts of Jarboro's early life are confusing due to accounts that she gave in an interview in 1972, and to various published sources. She is said to have been born Katherine Yarboro, in Wilmington, North Carolina, on July 21, 1898, but she changed her name when she became a singer later on. In addition to changes in her surname, her given name may have been changed to Caterina or Catarina. Her parents were John Wesley Yarborough, a barber, and (Ann?) Elizabeth Harris Yarborough. Caterina was orphaned at an early age and raised in Catholic convents and orphanages. While in a convent, her talent was recognized, and at the age of thirteen, she began to receive serious training in voice.

In 1921, Jarboro appeared in the Broadway musical *Shuffle Along*, as well as in *Running Wild* of 1923. She continued her education in Paris in 1926, and in 1928, she became the pupil of Nino Campinno in Italy. Jarboro made her debut at the Puccini Opera House in Milan on May 21, 1930, where she sang *Aida*, and she had moderate success in the opera houses of Europe. She returned to the United States and enjoyed more success in a series of concerts. Jarboro performed with the Chicago Opera Company, and in 1933, she sang *Aida* at the Hippodrome Theater in New York. With the latter performance, she was the first African American to sing a principal role with an all-white opera company. After two more performances of *Aida* at other New York sites, she returned to Europe to continue her career. The outbreak of World War II forced her to return home. Jarboro then became an interpreter for the U.S. Army. Little is known about her activities from then onward, although she appears to have settled in New York. She gave two town hall concerts in her hometown of Wilmington in 1943 and 1944. She was honored with a plaque

that, in 1982, was placed on her childhood home. Jarboro died in Manhattan.—JES-
SIE CARNEY SMITH

JEFFREY, MAURINE LAWRENCE
(1900–unknown) Poet, educator

   Maurine Lawrence Jeffrey was a poet and teacher from Texas whose work
emerged during the Harlem Renaissance era. Born in 1900, in Longview, Texas, her
family moved to Dallas when she was three years old. She attended Dallas grammar
schools, including J. P. Stacks Elementary School. Jeffrey lost her father just after
graduation but, upon her mother's insistence, still attended four years at Prairie
View State College (now Prairie View A&M University), where she enjoyed her
music, history, and English classes. After graduating with high marks, she taught in
Dallas public schools for nearly three years. She resigned from teaching when she
married Jessie W. Jeffrey, the son of a professor.

   Jeffrey began writing poetry when she was twelve years old and had her first
poem published in 1924. She then worked on the staff of such local newspapers as
the *Dallas Express*. Many of her poems were published in Texas newspapers, but
two that were published in the *Dallas Express* newspaper, "My Rainy Day" and
"Pappy's Last Song," were later published in J. Mason Brewer's *Heralding Dawn:
An Anthology of Verse* (1936). Jeffrey's poetry focuses on family and religion using
standard prose, as well as dialect.—AMANDA J. CARTER

JESSYE, EVA ALBERTA
(January 20, 1895–February 21, 1992) Choral director, composer

   Eva Alberta Jessye's contribution to the music world for more than three-quarters
of a century left an indelible mark of perfection on the sounds and tradition that
black culture offers to the world. She was born on January 20, 1895, in Coffeyville,
Kansas. Jessye was already aware of where life would take her, as she began to play
the piano at five years of age and direct singing groups before she was thirteen. She
studied music, both choral and theory, at Western University in Quindaro, Kansas,
and completed her studies in 1914. She received her lifetime teaching certificate
from Langston University in Oklahoma and spent several years teaching in segregated black schools.

   In 1926, Jessye moved to New York and joined the Dixie Jubilee Singers, which
later became the Eva Jessye Singers. She also became a protégé of Will Marion
Cook, an early black classical jazz composer. His guidance supported and enhanced
her skills in writing and composing work for her group and other projects. Jessye's
group performed extensively, singing a variety of black musical forms, including
spirituals, blues, jazz, work-songs, and opera, and they made both stage and radio
appearances. In 1936, the Dixie Jubilee Singers were featured in the first all-black
musical motion picture, *Hallelujah*, by King Vidor. Jessye's group continued to gain
acclaim, and she was selected as choral director for Virgil Thomson and Gertrude
Stein's *Four Saints in Three Acts* (1934), as well as George Gershwin and DuBose

Heyward's all-black folk opera *Porgy and Bess*, which premiered in New York City at the Alvin Theatre. No major production of *Porgy and Bess* was performed from 1938 to 1958 without the choral direction of Eva Jessye. Under Jessye's direction, the group maintained its prominence well into the period of the Civil Rights Movement in the 1960s.

Jessye's published compositions consist of *My Spirituals* (1927), *The Life of Christ in Negro Spirituals* (1931), and *Paradise Lost and Regained* (1934). Her most notable work, *Paradise Lost and Regained*, uses spirituals to create the sounds of the production in a way that Jessye called "folk oratorio." Her compositions engage every aspect of black music, and with her expert abilities in harmonics, she added richness and authenticity to any production that sought to express black life.

In Jessye's later years, she became an artist-in-residence at Pittsburg State University in Kansas and contributed a large portion of her memorabilia to the university. She was awarded an honorary degree from Eastern Michigan University, among many other awards, for her contributions to the arts. Jessye died in Ann Arbor, Michigan.—LEAN'TIN L. BRACKS

JOHNSON, DOROTHY VENA
(May 7, 1898–c. 1970) Poet, educator, activist

Dorothy Vena Johnson was born on May 7, 1898, to James M. Vena and Namie Plumb Vena, and she lived in California. Her education began in a convent; she later attended the University of Southern California, where she received her A.B. degree, and the Teachers College at the University of California, Los Angeles. Johnson married a lawyer who eventually became a U.S. attorney. She taught junior high school journalism and creative writing for forty years and encouraged her students to both write and publish. Thus, the poetry of Johnson's students frequently appeared in *Nuggets*, a bimonthly children's magazine of poetry by and about children. In both her teaching and her writing, she sought to influence students' attitudes about race.

Johnson's writing was candid, somber, rhythmic, straightforward, and lacked embellishments. This simple style often masked her poetry's depth of meaning, social consciousness, and complexity. In spite of the fact that she began writing and publishing at the end of the Harlem Renaissance, she maintained contact with Langston Hughes and Arna Bontemps. In addition, both her writing and life demonstrate signature themes of that period. She brought attention to history, ancestry, lynching, and the disenfranchised segment of the population. Harlem Renaissance themes are evident in "Epitaph for a Bigot" and "Post War Ballad," in which a statue of American Revolutionary soldier Crispus Attucks laments the dearth of change in the racial climate. These works are printed in *Ebony Rhythm*. Johnson's poetry also appears in such magazines and anthologies as *Golden Slippers*, edited by Arna Bontemps; *Poems for Radio*, *Negro Voices*, edited by Beatrice M. Murphy; and the National Poetry Association's *National Anthology of Verse* (1949). The latter contains poetry by both high school and college teachers. Johnson was both a member and former treasurer of the Los Angeles Creative Writing Teachers' Association.

In 1939, Johnson's social consciousness and activist nature became apparent with the cofounding of the League of Allied Arts, the oldest existing black women's nonprofit arts organization in Los Angeles. The necessity for such a group in Los Angeles became apparent when Langston Hughes visited friends Juanita and Loren Miller. He wished to stage a play, but there was no venue for an African American to present a play. Juanita Miller and Johnson pooled their resources to make it possible for Hughes to stage *Don't I Wanna Be Free?* Loren Miller, an attorney, became Hughes's first literary agent. Dorothy and Juanita cofounded the League of Allied Arts to promote, support, and advocate for artists and the arts, and present cultural enrichment programs in the community that honor the accomplishments of black artists. The league raises funds and awards scholarships to high school and first-year college students in Los Angeles who are pursuing the arts.

As a result of Johnson's work in education as both a teacher and pioneering administrator, and her concern for community uplift, a school for at-risk students, Johnson Community Day School, was named in her honor. The school is similar to typical public schools in operation with grades seven through twelve, but its class sizes range from three to seventeen students. The facility accepts disabled students and students with minimal academic skills, and it provides a variety of counseling options. Johnson died as the result of a cerebral hemorrhage.—HELEN R. HOUSTON

JOHNSON, GEORGIA DOUGLAS [PAUL TREMAINE]
(September 10, 1877–May 14, 1966) Poet, playwright, short story writer, musician

Georgia Douglas Johnson

Georgia Douglas Johnson was the most famous female poet of the Harlem Renaissance, publishing three volumes of poetry during that period; the addition of twenty-eight plays and her role of literary salon host sets her apart as an important figure.

Johnson was born in Atlanta, Georgia, on September 10, 1877, to Laura Douglas and George Camp. She attended Atlanta University's Normal School and the Oberlin Conservatory of Music, where she studied violin, piano, and composition. She returned to Atlanta and married Henry Lincoln Johnson, a prominent attorney, with whom she had two sons.

In 1910, the Johnsons moved to Washington, D.C., and Georgia became intensely involved in literary life. Although New York was the center for the Harlem Renaissance, the District of Columbia played an important role, partly due to Johnson's "Saturday Nighters' Club" at her home—1461 S Street NW—where she hosted various writers and artists, both established and budding. Her first poetry volume (1918) examines gender issues, but not specific racial themes; her subsequent work explores racial violence, miscegenation, and black motherhood.

After the death of her husband in 1925, Johnson continued to write and publish while working full time, winning first prize in *Opportunity* magazine for the play *Plumes* (1927). From 1926 to 1932, she wrote a column called "Homely Philosophy," syndicated in twenty newspapers. Under the pseudonym Paul Tremaine, Johnson published short stories during the 1940s. Unpublished works include a novel and the biography of her husband. Johnson died of a stroke in 1966. Although much of her papers have been lost, she is recognized as a significant writer of the time.—ADENIKE MARIE DAVIDSON

JOHNSON, HELENE
(July 7, 1906–July 6, 1995) Poet

Helene Johnson is a lesser-known but no less highly esteemed poet of the Harlem Renaissance. She published thirty-four poems, covering love, race, nature, the life and people of Harlem, and other thoughtful musings exquisitely worded and often in free verse.

Johnson was born in Boston, Massachusetts, on July 7, 1906, to George William Johnson and Ella Benson Johnson. Both parents hailed from the South. Her parents' marriage dissolved not long after her birth. Childhood, nonetheless, was a productive and delightful period in Johnson's life. Although an only child, her home was filled with extended family. She was the oldest of several cousins who were also her playmates. She formed a special and long-lasting bond with her cousin, Dorothy West. West would become a seminal figure of the Harlem Renaissance.

Learning, as well as family, played an important part in Johnson's young life. Reading and learning were stressed at home, and she had a strong academic background. Johnson and West attended Boston's Lafayette School, the Martin School, and the Boston Girls' Latin School. At Boston University, they studied writing. In 1925, the two women joined the Saturday Evening Quill Club, an organization that fostered the literary pursuits of African American Bostonians. That same year, Johnson made headway in her writing. Her short story "Respectability" won first prize in a literary contest and was published by the *Boston Chronicle*, an African American newspaper. Her poem "Trees at Night" was published in *Opportunity*, a journal founded by the National Urban League.

If Boston set the foundation for Johnson's zeal for writing, New York City opened the door to opportunities for her to write and publish alongside some of the greatest talents of the time. Johnson had a strong debut in the literary world of the Harlem Renaissance. Both Johnson and West received invitations to the Urban League's prestigious *Opportunity* awards dinner in 1926. Johnson won first honorable mention for her poem "Fulfillment." For two other poems, "Magula," and "The Road," she won fourth and seventh honorable mentions. West tied with Zora Neale Hurston for the second-place prize for fiction. Both young ladies, Johnson and West, were under twenty years of age. Johnson was nineteen; West was eighteen. The following year, the cousins returned to New York City to pursue their literary ambitions in the Extension Division at Columbia University.

At the time of the cousins' arrival in New York City, Harlem was ripe with energy and talent. The neighborhood was home to a large African American community. Many black Harlemites had migrated from the South in search of better opportunities; many were motivated by dreams of performing in the sundry hotspots available for black artists and performers. Art and literature also played an enormous role during the Harlem Renaissance. Blacks published and were published in newspapers, magazines, and literary journals. The Harlem literati comprised men and women who brought to the world a new wave of African American literature. Zora Neale Hurston, a writer, anthropologist, and folklorist, was a major part of this wave. Hurston, who had met Johnson and West at the *Opportunity* dinner in 1926, was a friend and mentor to the young women. She introduced Johnson and West to other influential writers in the community. The young women immersed themselves in writing, Harlem, and their network of friends and connections.

While West's career flourished, Johnson's career was less spectacular. Lack of talent or material was not the reason for Johnson's limited success. Johnson's poems appeared in several magazines; she was praised by her peers and critics. Indeed, she crafted poems that reflected the vivacious world of Harlem and dignity of black life. She crafted poignant words and images from subtle, seemingly unspectacular experiences. She brought forth elegantly worded contemplations on love, life, and the human experience.

Johnson's many poems were published with some regularity until her marriage. In 1933, Johnson married William Warner Hubbell III. In 1934, her poem "Let Me Sing My Song" was published in *Challenge*. Other poems would not be published until 1963. Some have surmised that Johnson's career was stymied by circumstances beyond her control. Without patronage and grants to fund her writing, she was forced to make a living like the majority of working-class Americans. As a wife and mother (she gave birth to her only child, Abigail Calachaly Hubbell, on September 18, 1940), she had little spare time to devote to her craft.

Notwithstanding Johnson's responsibilities, she continued to write, but she remained, with few exceptions, out of the limelight. The exceptions included the publication of four of her poems in Arna Bontemps's *American Negro Poetry* (1963). In 1987, Johnson attended a poetry reading at Off Center Theater in Manhattan. She died on July 6, 1995. Half a decade later, Verner D. Mitchell brought this little-known poet out of obscurity with the publication of *This Waiting for Love: Helene Johnson, Poet of the Harlem Renaissance* (2000). The book, which includes Johnson's thirty-four published and thirteen unpublished poems, celebrates the life and works of this important poet.—GLADYS L. KNIGHT

JONAS, ROSALIE M.
(1861?–1953) Poet

Rosalie M. Jonas was born in 1861, or possibly 1862. Although little is known about her early years, she was a well-respected poet in Harlem, New York, and contributed to the artistic movement of the Harlem Renaissance. Her life experiences include time spent in New Orleans, as her letters from 1905 to 1909 to white illustrator Frederic Door Steele (1873–1944) contain statements about the octoroon balls of New Orleans. In this correspondence, she asks Steele to illustrate her "Negro verse" because of his sympathetic view of the Negro. One of her first works of poetry, "Little Mammy," was published in 1898, in *Harper's Magazine*, and one of her short stories, "New York Light and Shade," was published in 1917, in *Art World*. Jonas was able to have her work published in numerous magazines, inclusive of *McClure's Magazine*, *Century Magazine*, and *Smart Set*, well beyond the 1920s. She used dialect in her stories and poetry and the "N"-word only for poetic effect. She was known to support social projects and community issues in Harlem.

Jonas's work was favorably received, and many of her poems and stories are in a variety of publications' archives.—LEAN'TIN L. BRACKS

JONES, LOIS MAILOU

(November 5, 1905–June 9, 1998) Painter, textile designer, illustrator, educator

Lois Mailou Jones

Lois Mailou Jones was a formally trained artist who used her skills as a designer and impressionistic painter to create stories that reflect black experiences and her own life in Boston, the American South, the Caribbean, and Africa. Her involvement in the New Negro Movement enabled her to enrich its visual arts focus and pass on the Harlem Renaissance legacy to future generations through her many exhibitions and forty-seven-year teaching career at Howard University.

Jones was born in Boston, Massachusetts, on November 5, 1905, to Thomas Vreeland Jones, a lawyer and real estate entrepreneur, and Carolyn Dorinda Adams, a cosmetologist. She began her art training at the High School of Practical Arts and later won a four-year scholarship to the School of the Museum of Fine Arts in Boston. In 1953, she married Haitian artist Louis Vergniaud Pierre-Noel.

In spite of Jones's extensive training and strong portfolio, she was initially compelled to submit her work to businesses through a white artist. During the late 1920s, she worked as a freelance textile designer for the F. A. Foster Company in Boston, as well as the Schumacher Company in New York. Business policy, however, dictated that the design houses receive acknowledgment for the work created, not individual artists. In addition to her textile work, Jones illustrated black history stories for Associated Publishers of Washington, D.C., founded by historian Carter

G. Woodson. Jones's designs for paper mâché masks were inspired by traditional examples from throughout the world. She also designed masks for African dancer Asadata Defora's dance company.

Through an association with the Harmon Foundation and interactions with other black artists of the 1920s and 1930s, Jones explored the richness of the black experience early in her career. She was a participating artist in the foundation's exhibitions held in 1930, 1931, and 1933, and she won honorable mention in 1931 for *Negro Youth*, a charcoal drawing. Inspired by the stylistic leadership of fellow artists like Aaron Douglas, Jones's *The Ascent of Ethiopia*, painted in 1932, depicts the story of black history from ancient Africa to the arts-focused 1930s.

Jones's art career was bolstered by exhibitions at La Boheme Tea Room in New York (1927); the Salon of the Société des artistes français and Société des artistes indépendants in Paris (1938); the Robert C. Vose Galleries in Boston (1939); the Pennsylvania Academy of the Fine Arts (1935 and 1938); the Howard University Gallery of Art (1937); and Morgan State College (now Morgan State University, 1940). In 1941, the painting *Indian Shops, Gay Head, Massachusetts* won her the Robert Woods Bliss Prize for Landscape at the Corcoran Gallery of Art in Washington, D.C. A major retrospective of her work was held in 1990, at the Meridian International Center of Washington, D.C.

In 1930, Jones began her teaching career at Howard University, following her establishment of the art department at Palmer Memorial Institute in Sedalia, North Carolina. At Howard, she dedicated her time to teaching design, drawing, and watercolor painting. During her tenure, her students included artists Elizabeth Catlett, David C. Driskell, Earl J. Hooks, Stephanie E. Pogue, Tritobia Benjamin, and Malkia Roberts. Jones retired in 1977.

One of the architects of the Harlem Renaissance, Alain Locke, philosopher and department head at Howard, directed her attention to the history of black people. In her 1938 painting *Les Fétiches*, inspired by traditional African masks, Jones addresses the stately spirit of a continent that was often misrepresented by stereotypical images and long-standing cultural traditions. Just as Countee Cullen wrote about Africa in his poem *Heritage*, Jones's crusade for Africa's rich artistic legacy is reflected in her paintings.

Following the example of Aaron Douglass, Meta Warrick Fuller, and other American artists, Jones looked to Europe—most notably Paris—to further her arts education and training. In 1937, she received a General Education Fellowship and began a nine-month study at the Académie Julian under Pierre Montezin and Jules Adler. She also began a friendship with African American artist and expatriate Albert Smith, which lasted until his death in Paris. Although expatriate artist Henry O. Tanner died in Paris before she could benefit from his guidance, his remarkable artistic accomplishments nonetheless inspired her to have a memorable career. During this time, she developed an appreciation for painting in natural light and an outdoor environment. Jones was also encouraged by several established artists and received constructive criticism of her work. It was the Parisian experience that led to the artist's signature painting style of using bold colors and the expressive use of form in her paintings.

Jones's interest in the black experience in the Americas continued to be a factor in her lifelong quest to create art. Paintings that represent the diversity of the black presence include *Harlem Backyard*; *Negro Shack I, Sedalia, North Carolina*; *Negro Musician*; and *Brown Boy*. Her painting *Mob Victim–Mediation* is a poignant reminder of the horrors of lynching.

Living in Washington, D.C. allowed Jones to become active in a vibrant arts community. Her association with the notable Barnett-Aden Arts Collection, started by Professor James Herring of Howard University in 1943, allowed her works to be promoted during a time when black artists in the city were being excluded from most mainstream art galleries and museums. To reach the everyday man and woman, she exhibited in numerous public schools and libraries. Jones was an active member of the District of Columbia Art Association (DCAA), which began in 1961, and was primarily comprised of art educators working in the local public school system. Her membership in DCAA provided long-standing bonds with such artists as Delilah W. Pierce, Peter L. Robinson Jr., Richard Dempsey, Georgette Seabrooke Powell, and Alma Thomas.

Jones died in Washington, D.C.—ROBERT L. HALL

JONES, MAGGIE [FAYE BARNES]
(1900–?) Singer

While the career of the "Texas Nightingale" barely spanned a decade during the Harlem Renaissance era, Maggie Jones recorded numerous songs with such artists as Louis Armstrong, Fletcher Henderson, Charlie Green, and Gladys Bentley.

Born Faye Barnes in Hillsboro, Texas, around 1900, she changed her name to Maggie Jones in the early 1920s when she moved to New York City to pursue her singing career. To supplement her musical earnings, Barnes also co-owned a dress shop in the city.

On July 26, 1923, under the name Maggie Jones, the singer became one of the first women from Texas to record a song. During the course of the next three years, she recorded forty selections and alternate takes. Jones recorded with labels like Black Swan, Victor, and Paramount Recording. She toured with the Theater Owners' Booking Association, during which time she performed at the Princess Theater in Harrisburg, Pennsylvania. By 1927, Jones was working with the Clarence Muse Vaudeville Company. She appeared on Broadway in *Blackbirds of 1928* from 1928 to 1929. Much of her work is contained in a two-volume self-titled set: *Maggie Jones, Volume 1, 1923 to 1925* and *Maggie Jones, Volume 2, 1925–1929*. Some of her best-known songs include "Anybody Here Want to Try My Cabbage," "Good-Time Flat Blues," "Undertaker's Blues," and "Single Woman's Blues."

In the early 1930s, Jones moved to Houston, Texas, and opened her own venue. She also performed at All-American Cabaret in Fort Worth, Texas, among others. Nothing more is known of her after the mid-1930s.—AMANDA J. CARTER

JONES, MATILDA SISSIERETTA JOYNER [BLACK PATTI]
(January 5, 1869–June 24, 1993) Singer

A precursor of the Harlem Renaissance, the career of Matilda Sissieretta Joyner Jones began in the early 1890s. Her success paved the way for many classically trained singers who later emerged during the Harlem Renaissance as a result of her pioneering efforts.

Jones was born in Portsmouth, Virginia, in 1869, to Malachi Joyner, a Baptist minister, and Henrietta Beale Joyner. Although she had a naturally beautiful singing voice, she was also influenced by her mother, whose commanding soprano voice could be heard in the church choir. The family relocated to Providence, Rhode Island, when Jones was only five years old so that she could study classical voice. Where she actually studied is unclear; however, she had private lessons from various teachers in different cities and developed a voice of considerable power and quality. She was soon in demand as a singer, giving concerts in local churches. She married and later divorced David Richard Jones, a compulsive gambler who wasted the money his wife earned as a performer.

Jones gave her first professional performance while still a student in 1887, performing to race notices before 5,000 people at Boston's Music Hall. She also performed at Philadelphia's Academy of Music and gave a concert at Wallack's Theatre in Boston. She took an eight-month tour, performing to packed houses in Buffalo, Pittsburgh, and elsewhere. In addition, Jones toured the West Indies with the Tennessee Jubilee Singers, not to be confused with the Fisk Jubilee Singers. When she returned home, Jones became the star attraction at the Grand Negro Jubilee at Madison Square Garden in April 1892, and she then performed at the 1893 Chicago World's Fair. She continued to tour in the United States and throughout the world, singing before U.S. presidents and foreign royalty.

Henry Abbey, who was Jones's manager, had also managed the career of Italian opera singer Adelina Patti (1893–1919). Jones was often compared to Patti. Thus, she became known as the "Black Patti." Although she disliked the title, it followed her for the remainder of her career. Jones found the limited opportunities that she had to perform in white venues unacceptable and launched her own company of performers, the Black Patti and Her Troubadors. The Troubadors toured the United States from 1895 to 1916, and had tremendous drawing power in new black-owned theaters in the South's major cities. They toured abroad as well.

Around 1908, audiences tired of the unsophisticated buffoonery of the minstrel format and preferred standard musical comedy instead. The group reemerged as Black Patti Musical Comedy Company. Among the countless black performers who built their careers around one or both of the comedy vehicles were Aida Overton Walker, Gertrude "Ma" Rainey, and dancer Ida Forsyne. Jones made tremendous breakthroughs for black female performers and African Americans in general. The final show came in 1916, in New York's Gibson Theater. Yet, by then, financial difficulties had taken a toll on the company. Minstrelsy was dead. After that, Jones return to Providence and devoted herself to church work and a variety of causes. She died penniless in Providence's Rhode Island Hospital.—JESSIE CARNEY SMITH

JONES, MAUDE
(?–June 3, 1940) Entertainer

A little-known and minor personality on the Harlem Renaissance stage, Maude Jones performed dramatic portrayals and recitations in the New York area and was known as an "elocutionist." Duse' Mohammed Ali praised one of her performances in New York City at the Mother Zion Church on March 3, 1922. He admired her rendition of a poem by Edgar Allan Poe and enjoyed her attempt to express "Ode to Ethiopia," by Paul Laurence Dunbar; however, he was somewhat critical of her ability to adequately deliver it in authentic Negro dialect. He praised her interpretation of the "Cremation of Samuel McGhee," by Robert W. Service. During the evening, Jones also performed some of the male and female roles from Shakespeare's plays, including *Romeo and Juliet*. Ali extolled her as a genius and proclaimed her the "Colored Ellen Terry," comparing her to one of the most famous English actresses of that era.—GLENDA MARIE ALVIN

L

LARSEN, NELLA [ALLEN SEMI]

(April 13, 1891–March 30, 1964) Novelist, short story writer, folklorist

Nella Larsen was known as a skilled novelist and rising star in the Harlem Renaissance. She was born in Chicago, Illinois, to Peter Walker and Mary Hanson; her father was of Dutch Caribbean descent and her mother Danish. Larsen's family history—and later her personal life—was shrouded in secrecy, and some of what is known about her early life has been disputed by her biographers; but what is clear is that the interracial union of her parents, along with her heritage, is a major theme in most of Larsen's work. Her parents were working class with no formal education; her father worked as a cook and her mother as a seamstress, and they lived in a Chicago neighborhood known for vice activity. It is believed that Peter died soon after Larsen's birth; records show that her mother married a white man, Peter Larsen, soon thereafter and had another daughter. Some biographers argue that Peter Larsen and Peter Walker are one in the same, the latter passing for white; another biographer claims Peter Walker to be a different man, which then places Nella as the only person of color in her childhood home.

Larsen grew up in Chicago and paid a visit to her mother's homeland of Copenhagen in 1898, along with her half-sister. In 1907, at the age of sixteen, she enrolled in Fisk University Normal School in Nashville, Tennessee. Larsen spent only one year at Fisk and the next four years at the University of Copenhagen (1908–1912). Upon returning to the United States, she began studying nursing at New York's Lincoln Hospital and graduated with a nursing degree in 1915; she then accepted a position as assistant superintendent of nurses at Tuskegee Institute in Alabama. She returned to New York in 1916, to her alma mater, and continued her nursing career at Lincoln Hospital throughout the Spanish flu epidemic in 1919.

On May 3, 1919, Larsen married Elmer S. Imes, a prominent member of the Harlem elite and the second African American to earn a Ph.D. in physics. Through this union, Larsen became acquainted with the literati of the Harlem Renaissance, including W. E. B. Du Bois, Langston Hughes, and Walter White. It was also at this time that she began to pursue her love of literature and changed careers. She took a job as assistant librarian of the New York Public Library, 135th Street Branch, in 1922; by 1924, Larsen was named the children's librarian. In 1920, she published in *The Brownies' Book* two brief accounts of children's games that she had learned while traveling in Copenhagen, as well as a book review in the *Messenger* in 1923.

Larsen then began writing short stories, and the two of these were published in *Young's Realistic Stories Magazine* in 1926, both under the pseudonym Allen Semi (her name spelled backwards), perhaps in an attempt to conceal her gender. "The Wrong Man" examines the character Julia Hammond, a woman from a poor background who is married to a wealthy man and is also former mistress to another wealthy man. Accompanied by her husband at a dance party, she sees her former lover and is frightened that her secret past may be exposed. She calls for a meeting with her former lover in the shadows, where she pleads for mercy, only to later realize that she has confessed to a stranger. "Freedom" examines a male protagonist who chooses freedom by leaving his pregnant mistress. Upon his return two years later, he is greeted with the news that she died during childbirth on the very day of his abandonment. Unable to live with the guilt, he commits suicide by jumping out the window of a high-rise apartment building. That same year, Larsen published "Correspondence."

In 1928, Larsen published her first novel, *Quicksand*, in which the protagonist is of Danish and African-Caribbean heritage; Helga Crane is on a search for self and moves from Naxos (a fictional southern black college) to Chicago seeking white relatives, and then to Harlem, overseas to relatives in Copenhagen, and back to Harlem. She finally ends up in Alabama. The mixed race of the main character leads the reader to assume that the tale is largely autobiographical, and certainly Larsen explores issues of race and identity through Helga's personal angst and quest; but perhaps more groundbreaking for the time is Larsen's treatment of female sexuality and the notion of repressed Victorian womanhood that accompanied the movement of racial uplift and the New Negro. Helga is in search of a way to unite her divided racial self, but she is also seeking a solution to her alienation from her own sexuality, which, during this time period, could only be satisfied through marriage. The novel's conclusion—Helga is married to the unpleasant and unrefined Reverend Pleasant Green and about to give birth in a weakened state to her fifth child—is quite unsatisfying for readers who view Helga's position as reverting to self-doubt and helplessness, despite the progress she made toward self-assurance throughout the novel. Helga's failure is presented through reproduction; she is giving birth to her fifth child but has been unable to give birth to her own agency.

Larsen's second novel, *Passing*, published only thirteen months after her first, explores the contradiction of racial passing—those who have crossed the racial divide often long for a real connection to the black community. The novel also returns to the issue of female sexuality, as well as female friendships and a preoccupation with material wealth and respectability. Two characters, Clare Kendry and Irene Redfield, are dealing with these issues differently but feel they are kindred spirits because of the common struggle; the novel is divided into three sections—"Encounter," "Reencounter," and "Finale"—signaling the plot's movement through the relationship of the two women. Irene values obtaining middle-class standing over her marriage and chooses to pass for white whenever it is expedient. Clare, married to a wealthy white man who calls her "Nig" as a joke, is willing to risk her marriage and relationship with her daughter to feel a real connection to the African American community. Clare's risky behavior is not only racial, but also sexual, and there is unmistakable erotic desire between the two women, which Irene finds seductive but intimidating; Larsen forces readers to view sexuality and racial identity as fluid entities instead of fixed ones. Clare's identity and secret life is revealed as her racist husband finds her at a Harlem party, and moments later Clare falls to her death; Larsen leaves the ending open—has Clare jumped or been pushed, or is the fall accidental?

Larsen's two novels received favorable reviews, and she received the bronze medal from the Harmon Foundation 1929. This helped establish her as a major female writer of the time; she was also the first black woman to win a Guggenheim Foundation creative writing award in 1930, to complete a third novel, for which she planned to travel to France and Spain on a research trip. Before her trip, Larsen's final known work, "Sanctuary," was published in *Forum* in 1930. A black woman hides a young black man who is being pursued by the police; she later discovers that the fugitive murdered her only son. Larsen was accused of plagiarism; many readers found the story remarkably similar to a short story published by British author Sheila Kaye-Smith, "Mrs. Adis." Larsen published "An Author's Explanation" in self-defense of the allegations, but she never published subsequent to this. No manuscripts of her unpublished work have been found. Larsen is now considered a woman ahead of her time, exploring identity behind and despite societal labels.

Around the time of the literary scandal, Larsen's marriage showed signs of weakness; rumors of an affair between Imes and Ethel Gilbert, a white female Fisk University staffer, led to an ugly public divorce in 1933. Larsen's literary success was blamed in the press for the marital troubles, and she was accused of marital neglect. It is also rumored that Larsen attempted suicide twice during this tumultuous time. In 1937, seeking anonymity, Larsen attempted to disconnect from the community by announcing plans to immigrate to South America. Instead she returned to her nursing career in 1941, after the death of her former husband, working at several New York hospitals; her colleagues were unaware of her literary notoriety. She died in New York City.—ADENIKE MARIE DAVIDSON

LEVINGER, ELMA EHRLICH
(October 6, 1887–January 28, 1958) Supporter, playwright, poet

Elma Ehrlich Levinger, a white and Jewish poet and playwright, offered her artist view of the black experience in her work during the 1920s and 1930s.

Levinger was born in Chicago, Illinois, on October 6, 1887, and later attended the University of Chicago and Radcliffe College. She dedicated her creative works to cultivating a Jewish identity for middle-class women and the community at large. She wrote a collection of poetry that serves as an example of social purpose as a means to inspire and instruct her Jewish community. With no direct reason known for her motivation, Levinger was also inspired to write a poem in March 1924, about the black experience. This work is entitled "Carry Me Back to Old Virginny," and it was published in *Crisis* magazine. The poem satirizes the song and plays on the fact that instead of blacks being happy to return to the seat of white control, they would literarily have to be carried back. Much of the poetry that Levinger wrote regarding the black experience refers to the importance of religion and the hard work and faith that was needed to achieve goals. The ideas of hard work and racial identity were part of the social and artistic goals for both black and white communities.

Levinger was a member of the National Council of Jewish Women's Committee on Religion and a prolific writer of plays, short stories, and poetry. She died as she was returning home to Los Altos, California, after vacationing in Hawaii.
—LEAN'TIN L. BRACKS

LEWIS, LILLIAN TUCKER
(?–?) Poet

During the Harlem Renaissance, Lillian Tucker Lewis was one of the first African American female writers in Texas to contribute to newspapers and magazines.

Tucker was born in Corsicana, Texas. She was a graduate of Prairie View State College (now Prairie View A&M University), continuing with her postgraduate studies at the University of Denver and Kansas University. Committed to her craft, Lewis was a passionate member of the Priscilla Art Club, Ladies Reading Circle, and City Federation of Dallas. For more than fifteen years, she taught in the Dallas public school system. She also was a fraternal worker and cashier-bookkeeper for the Henderson Wren Funeral Home in Dallas.

Lewis had a long-standing interest in literature and dramatics, and she had been a writer for a number of decades. In her writings, there exists a sympathetic attitude, establishing man as the unfortunate one. Her work displays precision using clever skills in her portrayal of life's situations. Lewis's philosophy of life is revealed almost continuously in her works in an exceptional manner. She used her talent to protest against certain practices of society and demonstrate thrill with thoughts of love and its possibilities. In her poem "Longing," she deeply conveys her feelings about the momentary nature of unfulfilled aspirations in a way that enables the reader to experience the same emotions.

In the 1930s, Lewis was referred to as one of the most mature Negro writers in Texas. Her works, like those of poets Birdelle Wycoff Ransom, Lauretta Holman Gooden, and Maurine Jeffery, appear in an anthology of Texas poets entitled *Heralding Dawn*, yet merely a small sample is extant. Although she was regionally well known, Lewis and her works have slipped into obscurity.—AISHA M. JOHNSON

LIVINGSTON, MYRTLE ATHLEEN SMITH
(May 8, 1902–July 15, 1974) Educator, playwright, choreographer

The small town of Holly Grove, Arkansas, claims Myrtle Athleen Smith Livingston as one of its notable citizens, even though she and her parents, Samuel Isaac and Lula C. Hall Smith, moved to Denver when she was eight. Livingston is celebrated because of her role in the Harlem Renaissance theater movement and for her leadership in promoting women's sports long before Title IX forbade the exclusion of women from participating in interscholastic, intercollegiate, or intramural athletics.

Following her 1920 graduation from Denver's Manual High School, Livingston was accepted into the pharmaceutical program at Howard University and became a member of the Rho Psi Phi medical sorority, founded in 1922. She returned to Colorado and obtained her teaching certificate from Colorado Teacher's College. During her college days, Livingston's love for dance was exemplified. She was asked to form the dance club Orchesis. Her other extracurricular activity was participating in the Modern Willis writers' association.

Livingston began teaching in the Denver public school system before receiving her degree and taught there several years following her graduation. She would pursue dancing, teaching, and writing for the rest of her life.

Three events occurred in 1925 that impacted her career. She married physician William McKinley Livingston; submitted the one-act play *For Unborn Children* to the National Association for the Advancement of Colored People's (NAACP) Amy Spingarn Contest in Literature and Art; and submitted another play, *Frances*, to the Urban League's *Opportunity* magazine contest. *Frances* was first of her plays to be performed. *For Unborn Children* won third prize from the NAACP and first prize from the Urban League. It has the distinction of being the first play published in *Crisis* magazine. The main character of *For Unborn Children* is a young black lawyer living somewhere in the South who is engaged to a white woman. Other themes explored include the educated black middle class, family secrets, and black men sacrificing themselves for their women. This work, along with dramas of playwrights Georgia Douglas Johnson and Alice Dunbar-Nelson, helped create the antilynching genre. It is included in many Harlem Renaissance literature anthologies. Livingston was one of the first black playwrights to explore the subject of interracial marriage.

In 1928, Livingston joined the faculty of Lincoln University in Jefferson City, Missouri. The new assistant professor of health and physical education headed a department with no other staff. She spent the next forty-four years teaching health education and formalizing a program of intramural and competitive sports for female students. Described as a master teacher in Lincoln's *Alumni Bulletin*, she taught competency in basketball, soccer, track, baseball, volleyball, tennis, and hockey. She introduced the women to archery and golf and, in 1936, established the first chapter of Orchesis at a black college. The talents of her students were showcased in the Kansas and Missouri area. Livingston's plays were performed by sororities and fraternities throughout the United States. The Lincoln University Library included her in a 2009 women's exhibit, and Jefferson City named a park in her honor.—GLORIA HAMILTON

LOVE, ROSE LEARY
(1898–1969) Children's author

Rose Leary Love was born in 1898, and grew up in the Brooklyn neighborhood of Charlotte, North Carolina. She became a teacher and writer and devoted her life's work to teaching children and writing literature to encourage positive life experiences. Love was a teacher for thirty-nine years and wrote stories that present the healthy and stable lives of children, particularly through farm life, as a means for finding value in the characteristics of Southern black communities. She had a strong connection with working-class African Americans in the South through family and other relationships. Her uncle was Sheridan Leary, who died along with John Brown in 1859, at Harper's Ferry; her grandson was poet Langston Hughes; and her husband, George W. Love, was a friend of George Washington Carver. At one point in Love's career, she attempted to write a book-length biography of Carver for elementary-age school children, but it was not published.

Love's talents can be recognized in her stories and poetry, for example, the story *Nebraska and His Granny* (1939), published by a press affiliated with Tuskegee Institute, about a young black boy who grows up on a farm in the South. His race is reflective of the rich dark soil and the maternal love of his granny, and the story is filled with folklore and traditions of the Southern black community. Love's poetry helped support the movement of creating positive images for African American youth, which included children's literature by Jessie Redmon Fauset and W. E. B. Du Bois, as well as the children's publication *The Brownies' Book*.

Although Love died in 1969, her memoirs, *Plum Thickets* and *Field Daisies*, about her life in her Brooklyn neighborhood, were published in 1996. Her work serves as a record of the African American neighborhood of Brooklyn, which was demolished shortly after her passing.—LEAN'TIN L. BRACKS

LUCAS, MARIE
(1880s–April 1947) Music director, orchestra leader

Marie Lucas came from a family of musicians and became distinguished during the Harlem Renaissance as a music and dance director.

Lucas was born sometime in the 1880s, in Denver, Colorado. Her father was Sam Lucas, a well-known minstrel performer. Her mother, Carrie Melvin Lucas, was also a musician. Marie's musical education began with her parents, since her mother played the violin and cornet, and her father played the guitar. She received formal musical training at schools in Nottingham, England, and at the Boston Conservatory in Massachusetts.

In 1909, Lucas's father obtained a leading role in the musical *The Red Moon*, and Marie also made her debut in the show. She became the leader of the Ladies Orchestra in 1915, which performed at the Lafayette Theater in Harlem, New York. A year later, she became musical director of the Quality Amusement Corporation, which was responsible for managing several black theaters on the East Coast. Lucas also managed another all-female orchestra, which performed at the Colonial Theatre in Baltimore, Maryland; led a male dance band; and held a lengthy residency at Howard Theatre in Washington, D.C. In addition, she toured with the Merry Makers, an all-male group, during the 1930s. Lucas died in New York City.—FAYE P. WATKINS

M

MABLEY, JACKIE "MOMS" [LORETTA MARY AIKEN]
(March 19, 1894–May 23, 1975) Comedienne, dancer, singer

Moms Mabley, as she was popularly known, has long been known as more a comic than singer and dancer during the Harlem Renaissance years and beyond, and despite the tacky and cantankerous old woman that she played, she brought laughter to the vast audiences that she entertained. The sheer gall that she used in her jokes was as appealing as her messages.

Born Loretta Mary Aiken in Brevard, North Carolina, Jackie "Moms" Mabley was the daughter of Jim Aiken, a local businessman, and one of twelve children. Her mother's name remains unknown. Mabley's experiences growing up were trying; she was raped by an older black man when she was eleven years old, and again two years later by the white town sheriff. Children resulted from both rapes. Mabley left home when she was fourteen years of age and moved to Cleveland. Altogether, she had five children.

Mabley joined a Pittsburgh-based minstrel show in 1908, and two years later she worked in black theatrical revues. In Pittsburgh, she met the Canadian Jack Mabley and, although they never married, took his surname. In 1921, she became a part of the Chitlin' Circuit, or the theaters and clubs of the South that were owned and managed by blacks. During the 1920s, Mabley, who was already singing and dancing, developed her special act. Although she is said to have been pretty, she became a comedienne who played the character of a grumbly, grouchy, gravelly voiced, toothless, and dirty old lady with bulging eyes who wore a baggy dress, big shoes, a hat, and droopy stockings—and had a penchant for young men. She joined the Butterbeans and Susie (Jodie Edwards and Susie Hawthorne) dance duo, and Edwards and Hawthorne introduced her to the Theater Owners' Booking Association. The moniker "Moms" was given to her because of the motherly way she treated fellow performers.

While on the vaudeville circuit, Mabley performed with such legendary black entertainers as Pigmeat Markham, Cootie Williams, Bill "Bojangles" Robinson, and Clayton "Peg Leg" Bates. In the late 1920s, she worked in Harlem clubs, including the Savoy Ballroom and the Cotton Club. Bessie Smith, Cab Calloway, Duke Ellington, and Count Basie were among the entertainers with whom she appeared in these venues. Also during this period, she had bit parts in talking motion pictures. In 1931, Mabley appeared in *The Emperor Jones* and had a featured role in the Broadway musical *Blackbirds*. Other shows in which she appeared were *Fast and Furious* and *Swinging the Dream*. Her first album, *Moms Mabley—The Funniest Woman in the World*, was recorded in 1960, and sold more than 1 million copies. She recorded other LPs, including *Moms Mabley at the UN*.

The comedienne made her television debut in *A Time for Laughter*, an all-black comedy that Harry Belafonte introduced on the ABC network in 1967. She appeared on television, on shows hosted by the Smothers Brothers, Bill Cosby, and Flip Wilson. Offstage, Mabley was an attractive woman who dressed in furs and chic clothing, and she owned a Rolls-Royce; she was also an avid reader.

Mabley died of natural causes at White Plains Hospital. In November 2013, actress Whoopi Goldberg celebrated her life with an HBO documentary called *Whoopi Goldberg Presents Moms Mabley*. Goldberg's documentary reveals that Mabley was, at one point, an open lesbian. It also shows Mabley in a picture dressed in a man's suit, hair slicked black and looking sharp, and says that she often flirted with women during her shows and had several girlfriends. This in no way interfered with her relationship with her performer friends. It did not matter. Don't ask, don't tell.—JESSIE CARNEY SMITH

MARTIN, MRS. GEORGE MADDEN [MRS. ATTWOOD R. MARTIN]
(May 3, 1866–November 30, 1946) Harlem Renaissance supporter, activist, novelist

Mrs. George Madden Martin, the pen name of Mrs. Attwood R. Martin, was not only an accomplished author, born in the white community of Louisville, Kentucky, but she was also a champion of social justice. She began her career as a member of the Authors' Club in Louisville in the 1890s. Her most successful novel, *Emmy Lou*, published in 1902, which appeared in *McClure's Magazine*, confronts the issue of how instruction in schools did not meet the needs of children like "Emmy Lou."

Martin continued to write, but she became more involved in social and political issues in her community. In the 1920s, she maintained her active leadership role as a charter member while also serving on the board of the Commission on Interracial Cooperation for Louisville, which continued for fourteen one-year terms. Martin advocated that women be more politically involved, while also actively seeking to abolish racial discrimination. In her role as a teacher, she also tried to have Negro history taught in Kentucky schools, but this effort was unsuccessful. Her collection of eight sketches about black life in the South, *Children in the Mist* (1920), gives Martin's literary and political perspective about racism and economic exploitation throughout the South. As chairwoman of the Association of Southern Women for the Prevention of Lynching in the 1930s, Martin challenged the notion that lynching was for the protection of Southern womanhood, but that it instead was an excuse for racism and violence. She continued to publish and serve her community through her activism and writing.

With the death of her husband in 1944, Martin moved to live with friends. She died in Louisville.—LEAN'TIN L. BRACKS

MARTIN, SARA [SARA DUNN, MARGARET JOHNSON, SALLY ROBERTS]
(June 18, 1884–May 24, 1955) Blues singer, vaudeville performer

Sara Martin was considered one of the most popular singers of the 1920s, the height of the Harlem Renaissance, performing both blues and popular songs. Because she was able to perform both genres, she was often billed as the "Famous Moanin' Mama" and the "Colored Sophie Tucker." She was known for a deep, full voice that was often compared to Bessie Smith and Gertrude "Ma" Rainey. She made recordings with such jazz musicians as W. C. Handy, Clarence Williams, Thomas "Fats" Waller, and Joe "King" Oliver. She also recorded under the names Margaret Johnson and Sally Roberts.

Martin was born in Louisville, Kentucky, on June 18, 1884. Little is known about her family or early life. She began performing on the African American vaudeville circuit in 1915, in Illinois. In 1922, she signed a contract to record for the Okeh label and made her first recordings in October of that year, accompanied by pianist Clarence Williams. She recorded for Okeh until 1928. Martin toured the United States from the early 1920s until the early 1930s. She appeared in the films *Hello, Bill*, with Bill "Bojangles" Robinson, in 1929, and *Darktown Revue* in 1930. The latter film features an all-African American cast. With the fading of the blues fad in the 1930s, Martin retired from show business but continued to sing gospel music, performing with Thomas A. Dorsey in 1932. During the Great Depression, she returned to Louisville, Kentucky, where she ran a nursing home. She died of a stroke.—ANTHONY WILLIAMS

MASON, CHARLOTTE OSGOOD [CHARLOTTE LOUISE VAN DER VEER QUICK]
(May 18, 1854–April 15, 1946) Patron

Born in Princeton, New Jersey, Charlotte Osgood Mason was one of the most influential, as well as controversial, wealthy white patrons of the Harlem Renaissance. With major financial contributions to artists and writers of the first cultural flowering of African American artistic expression, she was distinguished for her generosity and the insistence that her gifts came with strings.

Mason (née Charlotte Louise Van der Veer Quick) married physician Rufus Osgood Mason, one of the most celebrated surgeons in New York City, in 1886. Following her husband's death in 1903, Mason used her inheritance to fund the development of what she called the "primitive." At the turn of the twentieth century, her main cause was Native Americans. She published *The Passing of the Prophet* in 1907, her reflection on life and death that grew out of her fieldwork with Native

Americans in the Southwestern United States. Returning east to her Park Avenue home, Mason found a "modern primitive" in that of African American writers, artists, and intellectuals. Spurred by Alain Locke, professor of philosophy at Howard University and editor of the landmark anthology *The New Negro*, Mason's primary intellectual, artistic, and philanthropic interests switched to that of the Harlem Renaissance. Locke, a Rhodes Scholar who was referred to by Mason as her "precious Brown Boy," with his winning personality and keen intelligence, served as Mason's liaison to the emerging stars of the Harlem Renaissance.

Mason's patronage of the Harlem Renaissance was significant. She contributed more than $100,000 ($1.3 million in today's money) beginning in 1927. Beneficiaries of her largesse included visual artists Miguel Covarrubias and Aaron Douglas; writers Langston Hughes, Zora Neale Hurston, and Claude McKay; and folklorist Arthur Huff Fauset, among others. Mason helped fund the education of Langston Hughes and Zora Neale Hurston, and her close connection to Alain Locke provided him with the funding necessary to support the emerging artists of the Harlem Renaissance, while also permitting Mason access to a world she found ever fascinating and intriguing.

Little, however, is known of Mason's personal life. A major reason for this lack of information is her insistence that her financial support be anonymous, and that those in her care were only to refer to her as "Godmother." If anyone under her financial care spoke of her personally, she would cut off the flow of funds. This anonymity made Mason one of the mystery women of the Harlem Renaissance, but she did make veiled appearances in Rudolph Fisher's 1928 novel *The Walls of Jericho*, as Miss Agatha Cramp. Fisher's depictions are pointed. "Miss Agatha Cramp," he writes, "had, among other things, a sufficiently large store of wealth and a sufficiently small store of imagination to want to devote her entire life to Service," and "For fifteen years Miss Cramp had been devoting her life to the service of mankind. Not until now had the startling possibility occurred to her that Negroes might be mankind, too."

One of the major recipients of Godmother's funding, Langston Hughes also disguised a depiction of Mason in his 1934 collection *The Ways of White Folk*. Free from the controlling nature of Mason, Hughes, Godmother's "most precious child," created the character of Dora Ellsworth, modeled after Mason, of whom he writes has trouble discerning whether beauty was from the young "creators or the creation." Hughes dramatizes his break with Godmother in a work of fiction that shows a black character losing the favor of a patron because of a preference for jazz rather than classical music. According to David Levering Lewis in *When Harlem Was in Vogue*, Aaron Douglas, on a similar note, left the lucrative court of Godmother, headquartered at her penthouse on 399 Park Avenue, for Merion, Pennsylvania, when she tried to tell him what "proper Negro art" was.

Because of her stringent demands on artists, Mason was not an ideal nurturer of artistic vision. In most cases, she treated art as a commodity, as something to be bought and sold, which is part of a capitalist economy. Mason's great flaw, however, was that she treated the artists she funded as personal employees to collect and produce art for her sole consumption. With the sizeable stipend of $200 a month, she expected Hurston to do research on Mason's behalf. Their relationship was volatile from the beginning.

In 1927, around the time Mason began to fund projects for Alain Locke, whom she met at an art talk, Zora Neale Hurston, with the support of a fellowship from the Association for the Study of Negro Life and History, published her first field report in the *Journal of Negro History*. That same year, Mason's interest turned from the Southwest American Indians to the "New Negro" of Harlem. For this work, Hurston received a stipend of $200 a month, with the understanding that all of the folklore Hurston collected belonged to Mason. Hurston traveled throughout the American South collecting African American folklore and publishing what she deemed appropriate, thereby disregarding the stipulations of Godmother. Although Mason funded Hurston's folklore research, Hurston maintained a strong sense of individualism that brought her to loggerheads with Mason. In the end, Hurston fell out of favor with Godmother and left Mason's payroll in 1932.

The legacy of Mason in the Harlem Renaissance is rich and complex. She was directly responsible for the launching of several brilliant artistic and literary careers that continue to shape the landscape of literature and art to the present day. Of Mason, Hughes remembered, "I told her I wanted to write a novel. She told me she would make it possible for me to write that novel. And she did by covering the expenses of my summer, so that I need do no other work during the vacation." The value of such a gift is immeasurable, but such a gift is also detrimental to artistic voice and vision when the stipulations are too great. Godmother helped launch many careers of the Harlem Renaissance, but the sustained conversation about art never occurred in her salon. The one view that mattered most to her was hers. She insisted that art remain apolitical, and her deep interest in the "primitive" limited the range of expression of the artists and writers she funded.

Mason died in New York City, in relative obscurity, but her mark on the Harlem Renaissance, one of light and shadow, will always remain.—DELANO GREENIDGE-COPPRUE

McBROWN, GERTRUDE PARTHENIA
(1898–1989) Playwright, poet, actress, educator

Sometimes called a little-known playwright, Gertrude Parthenia McBrown was part of the Boston circle of black writers whose works are considered along with the creative artists of the Harlem Renaissance. She was multitalented, however, and kept her skills updated by constantly studying. She spent her life sharing her knowledge of African American culture with others.

Born in Charleston, South Carolina, McBrown was influenced by the work of African American actor Richard B. Harrison, whose reading she heard early on. She decided to become an orator and actress. McBrown studied at the Emerson College of Oratory (later known as Emerson College) and graduated in 1922. A drama student there, she prepared to become a writer, educator, and performer. After receiving a master's degree from Boston University in 1926, she taught in Boston's public schools and began experimenting with writing children's poetry.

McBrown submitted several poems to the *Saturday Evening Quill* and *Crisis* magazine. She was also active in local dramatic and church activities, and directed the choral groups and theatrical productions at Ebenezer Baptist Church. She had a brief tenure at Palmer Memorial Institute in Sedalia, North Carolina, under the leadership of founder Charlotte Hawkins Brown, and staged a variety of productions. Her production of George Hobart's *Experience* brought excellent reviews. McBrown then succeeded her idol, Richard B. Harrison, as dramatic arts teacher at North Carolina Agricultural and Technical College (now North Carolina Agricultural and Technical State University) in Greensboro.

In the 1930s, McBrown moved to Washington, D.C., where she was known in literary and dramatic circles. She founded a dramatic studio; directed the Southeast Children's Theater and other groups; and taught in private institutions, including Frelinghuysen University, under the leadership of Anna Julia Cooper. During this time, her interest in children's poetry and theater escalated. She published her first book of poetry, *The Picture-Poetry Book*, in 1935, and her works appeared in *Opportunity*, *Popular Educator*, *Black Opals*, *Negro Women's World*, and *International Poetry Magazine*. *Parent–Teacher Magazine* named her managing editor, and she was a feature writer for the Associated Negro Press. Her one-woman dramatic recitals and impersonations of well-known African American heroines brought her national popularity. Suffering from crippling arthritis, McBrown was forced to curtail her activities.—Jessie Carney Smith

McCLENDON, ROSE [ROSALIE VIRGINIA SCOTT]
(August 27, 1884–July 12, 1936) Actress

Rose McClendon was one of the most highly acclaimed and prolific actresses of the African American theater during the Harlem Renaissance. She was a native of New York, but she had lived there only since childhood. Like many blacks in Harlem and elsewhere in the North, the actress had migrated to the North from the South.

McClendon was born Rosalie Virginia Scott in Greenville, South Carolina, on August 27, 1884. Her parents, Sandy Scott and Tena Jenkins, moved with their three children to New York in 1890, following the lynching of McClendon's uncle. Hostilities toward African Americans were widespread; in the South, in particular, blacks were experiencing especially difficult and pervasive problems, including racial discrimination, unemployment, and racial violence.

New York was not without its problems, but many African Americans thrived there. McClendon was one such person whose career began and flourished there. She was introduced to the theater early in life through the church, participating in plays and later directing and acting in plays. In 1904, she married Henry Pruden McClendon, a chiropractor and Pullman porter. In 1916, she received a scholarship to attend the American Academy of Dramatic Art at Carnegie Hall.

McClendon did not have to wait long to perform in her first production. She made her debut in 1919, at the Davenport Theatre in New York, in *Justice*. Following this debut, she appeared in a number of plays. Many of her performances left positive impressions on critics and audiences. This pattern started with the play

Roseanne (1924); however, the play *Deep River*, which opened in 1926, was considered a defining moment in her career. Critics raved about the scene in which McClendon, as Octavie, descended, dramatically and in silence, down a grand staircase.

McClendon repeatedly caught the attention of admirers and became a fixture in the black plays that appeared in Harlem and elsewhere in the United States and abroad. Notable plays included the Pulitzer prize-winning *In Abraham's Bosom*, *Porgy* (the predecessor of the musical *Porgy and Bess*), *House of Connelly*, and *Mulatto*. The play *Mulatto* was written by Langston Hughes, one of the most celebrated figures of the Harlem Renaissance.

McClendon's influence extended beyond her distinguished acting career. She was heavily involved in the promotion and development of the black theater and directed productions for the Harlem Experimental Theatre. McClendon helped establish the Negro People's Theatre in 1935. The Negro People's Theatre eventually merged with the Federal Theatre Project's Black Unit in Harlem. She also worked with the Theatre Union.

McClendon was not yet fifty years old and at the peak of her career when she died from pneumonia.—GLADYS L. KNIGHT

McCOY, VIOLA [AMANDA BROWN]
(1900–1956) Singer

Born in Shelby County, Mississippi, Viola McCoy grew up in Memphis, Tennessee, but moved to New York in the early 1920s to pursue a career in music. She launched her career in the music industry by working as a cabaret singer and appearing in different clubs in New York and Philadelphia. She also performed in a variety of musical revues in the New York area, including *This Way Out* at the Lincoln Theater and *Moonshine* at the Lafayette Theater. McCoy soon developed a solid reputation as a classic blues singer and made her mark on the vaudeville stage.

It is believed that the singer released recordings on several labels under different pseudonyms in the 1920s and 1930s. (History shows that women who performed during this time period and in this musical genre sometimes used an alias.) It is speculated that the name she used on the Columbia and Pathe labels, "Amanda Brown," is actually her birth name. Other reported pseudonyms used by McCoy were Daisy Cliff, Gladys White, and Fannie Johnson.

McCoy's solo discography includes such songs as "Back Water Blues," Bleeding Hearted Blues," "Buzzin' Round, Chirpin' the Blues," "Do Right Blues," and "Dyin' Crap Shooter Blues." In addition, her musical repertoire consists of recordings with bands like the Dixie Trio, Kansas City Five, and Choo Choo Jazzers.—SONCEREY L. MONTGOMERY

McKINNEY, NINA MAE
(June 16, 1912–May 3, 1967) Actress, singer, dancer

Probably best known as the seductress Chick from the movie *Hallelujah* (1929), Nina Mae McKinney was a multitalented performer of the Harlem Renaissance era whose career spanned two continents. An immensely talented entertainer who was billed as the "Black Greta Garbo" in Greece, she worked with Paul Roberson on two films, *Congo Road* and the English film *Sander of the River* in 1935; however, her career never fully blossomed due to the racism of Hollywood, which refused to create or even cast black actresses in leading or nonstereotypical roles.

McKinney was born on June 16, 1912, in Lancaster, South Carolina, to Hal and Georgia McKinney. When she was young, her parents left Lancaster and moved to New York City, leaving her in the care of her great aunt, Carrie Sanders. At twelve or thirteen years of age, she moved to the city with her parents. After graduating, McKinney joined the chorus line in Lew Leslie's hit Broadway show *Blackbirds of 1928*. Thereafter, she appeared in numerous films in the United States and England, including *Pie Gang Smashers* (1938) and *Straight to Heaven* (1939). In 1940, she met and married musician Jimmy Monroe while touring with her own jazz band in the United States. Her last film was *Pinky* (1949). McKinney died from a heart attack in New York City.—MYRON T. STRONG

MEYER, ANNIE NATHAN
(February 19, 1867–September 23, 1951) Patron, writer, college founder, women's activist

Several Harlem Renaissance artists and writers benefited from a number of patrons of that era, patrons who considered their work important and recognized their enduring struggle as they tried to advance. The patrons responded by supporting them financially and personally. Such figures included Charlotte Osgood Mason, Fannie Mae Hurst, and Annie Nathan Meyer, and at some point all of these women supported folklorist and writer Zora Neale Hurston.

Born in New York City, Meyer was the fourth child and second daughter of Robert Weeks and Annie Augusta (Florance) Nathan. Her parents were one of the first families in New York. They were also the "nearer approach to royalty in the United States." Although Annie had less than six months of formal education, she began to read widely while still a young child, and by the age of seven she was boasting that she had read all of Charles Dickens's works. She became self-educated and multitalented, and developed an abiding interest in writing, music, and education for women. She married Alfred Meyer, a prominent physician, on February 15, 1987, and they had one child, Margaret.

Meyer used the library at Columbia University to support the correspondence course that she took, and there she met renowned librarian Melvil Dewey in 1887. This meeting marked the beginning of her strategy to found a self-sustaining liberal arts college for women. On October 7, 1889, Barnard College, the women's division of Columbia University, was founded and named for Frederick A. P. Barnard, who was a strong advocate for coeducation. Meyer organized its board of trustees, appointed herself a member, and remained an active board member until 1950. At first an antisuffragist, when the Nineteenth Amendment was passed, she began to work with the League of Women Voters in support of is cause. Meyer was also a playwright, and in 1932, she finally published *Black Souls*, which focuses on sex and race; James Weldon Johnson called it "one of the most powerful and penetrating plays yet written on the race question."

Meyer considered herself an American Jew and had an abiding interest in minority rights. She resigned from the Daughters of the American Revolution because it sanctioned segregation. She also raised money for Jewish and black students. Working with National Association for the Advancement of Colored People officials Mary White Ovington, Roy Wilkins, Ernest E. Just, James Weldon Johnson, and others, she helped raise money for black college students. After she met Zora Neale Hurston, Meyer was instrumental in Hurston's admission to Barnard. Hurston wrote in her autobiography *Dust Tracks on a Road* that Meyer "did nobly by me in getting me in. No matter what I might do for her, I would still be in her debt." Meyer also solicited donors to support Hurston's studies at the college. Writer Fannie Mae Hurst, a founder of Barnard and philanthropist, was also a donor and continued her support of Hurston. Meyer and Hurston maintained correspondence and discussed Hurston's research and writing after Hurston graduated from Barnard in 1928. When Hurston published *Mules and Men* in 1935, she dedicated the book to Meyer, saying, "To my dear friend Mrs. Annie Nathan Meyer, who hauled the mud to make me but loves me just the same." Meyer died in New York City.—JESSIE CARNEY SMITH

MILES, LIZZIE [ELIZABETH MARY LANDREAUX]
(March 31, 1895–March 17, 1963) Singer

Lizzie Miles began her career traveling with minstrel shows and circuses before establishing herself as a blues and jazz singer. A native of New Orleans, she emerged from the region of the United States that birthed jazz and the blues. Like many black entertainers in the late 1800s and early 1900s, Miles and her husband, J. C. Miles, toured with vaudeville variety shows that featured actors, singers, dancers, and comedians. They worked with the Alabama Minstrels and the Cole Brothers Circus. After her husband's death from influenza in 1918, Lizzie recorded solo and collaboratively with fellow New Orleans natives Joe "King" Oliver, Jelly Roll Morton, Edward "Kid" Ory, and Armund J. Piron.

With a large stature and heavy voice, Miles delivered her songs in English and various forms of French. She began recording in 1922, after her move to New York. In 1923, she recorded a tune that addresses the mass exodus of blacks from the South to the North, entitled "Cotton Belt Blues." Many of her other songs feature themes related to bad relationships. Miles performed abroad in Paris and throughout Europe until returning to the United States in 1925. Throughout the remainder of the decade, she recorded and performed in New York. Her move to Chicago in the late 1930s marked her last activity during the Harlem Renaissance. Miles is the sister of blues singer Edna Hicks. Their brother Herb "Kid" Morand, a trumpet player, formed the Harlem Hamfats.—SARAH-ANNE LEVERETTE

MILLER, MAY [MAY MILLER SULLIVAN]
(January 26, 1899–February 8, 1995) Poet, playwright, educator

May Miller was among the many poets that emerged during the Harlem Renaissance. She was born to Kelly and Annie May Miller on January 26, 1899, in Washington, D.C. Her upbringing was immersed in progressive black life and the arts and literature. Her father was dean of the College of Arts and Sciences at Howard University, a prominent African American institution of higher learning. Influenced by her environment and supportive parents, Miller demonstrated her literary talents to the world during adolescence when a poem and a play, *Pandora's Box*, were published.

Education and writing played a large role in Miller's life. While studying drama at Howard, she obtained the Howard University Drama Award for the play *Within the Shadows*. Her learning continued as she mingled with such literary giants as Langston Hughes in Harlem during the 1920s. She added to her learning and literary development with postgraduate study in literature at American University and Columbia University, as well as participation in the poet-in-residence programs at three different universities during the 1960s and 1970s. Miller's career included teaching English, speech, and drama at Frederick Douglass High School in Baltimore, working as an arts coordinator in Washington, D.C., and serving on Folger Library's Advisory Committee. In 1940, she balanced her busy life with marriage to John Sullivan.

Educational goals and work did not stop Miller from pursuing her literary ambitions. She published several plays and volumes of poems throughout her lifetime. Her notable works include the plays *The Bog Guide* (1925) and *Stragglers in the Dust* (1933), and poems in *Into the Clearing* (1959), *Lyrics of Three Women: Katie Lyle, Maude Rubin, and May Miller* (1964), *Not That Far* (1973), *Halfway to the Sun* (1981), and *The Ransomed Wait* (1983). In 1976, she read poetry at the inauguration of President Jimmy Carter. Miller's last work, *Collected Poems of May Miller*, was published in 1989. She died from pneumonia.—GLADYS L. KNIGHT

MILLS, FLORENCE
(January 25, 1896–November 1, 1927) Singer, dancer

Florence Mills, the preeminent entertainer of the Harlem Renaissance during the 1920s, broke barriers for subsequent generations of African American female performers both nationally and internationally.

Mills was born in Washington, D.C., on January 25, 1896, to John Winfrey, a day laborer who died during Mills's childhood, and Nellie Winfrey, a laundress. Florence attended Garnet Elementary School, where Jean Toomer was several years ahead of her, and Duke Ellington enrolled after Mills began her matriculation. In 1905 or 1906, Mills, her mother, and older sisters Olivia and Maude left Washington for New York, where Mills attended school. After a brief marriage to James Randolph, a taxi driver, when she was a teenager, Mills married Ulysses "Slow Kid" Thompson, a dancer and comedian, in the early 1920s.

Decades earlier, Mills was regarded as a child prodigy known as "Baby Florence"; her family added the surname Mills as her stage name. When she was four years old, she appeared onstage at Washington's Bijou Theater; as early as age five, Mills won cakewalk and buck-dance competitions. She performed in the homes of diplomats and, in 1903, made a guest appearance in Bert Williams and George Walker's Washington production of *The Sons of Ham* and sang "Miss Hannah from Savannah," the song made famous by Aida Overton Walker. Approximately two years later, white entertainers Bonita and Hearn included Mills in their act as they performed on the vaudeville circuit; since Mills was still quite young, her mother traveled with her. In 1910, Mills continued on the circuit with Olivia and Maude, and they billed themselves as the Mills Sisters. Mills also performed as a solo act in the New York area. In 1914 she teamed with Ethel "Kinky" Caldwell, and they toured together until Caldwell's marriage. One year later, Mills became a member of the cabaret act the Panama Trio, with Cora Green and Ada "Bricktop" Smith. Mills then joined the circuit act the Tennessee Ten; Thompson was a member of the troupe, and he became Mills's manager. While Thompson served in the military, Mills toured with the Panama Trio; after World War I, Mills and Thompson rejoined the Tennessee Ten and became husband and wife.

In 1921, Mills performed at the Barron's Club in Harlem. That same year, Gertrude Saunders, the original female lead in Eubie Blake and Noble Sissle's hit Broadway musical *Shuffle Along*, left the show, and Mills replaced her in the role of Ruth Little. Mills's singing and dancing captivated *Shuffle Along's* audiences. She mesmerized various critics and enthralled such Harlem luminaries as James Weldon Johnson, Claude McKay, and Langston Hughes, who praised her in *Black Manhattan* (1930), *A Long Way from Home* (1937), and *The Big Sea* (1940), respectively. *Shuffle Along's* success transformed Mills into a highly sought after entertainer. She rejected an offer to perform with the *Ziegfeld Follies* because she knew that if she headlined shows with primarily African American performers instead, she could provide more opportunities for black entertainers. Mills starred at the Plantation Room, Broadway's first upscale African American cabaret; the enterprise then morphed into the Broadway show *The Plantation Review* in 1922.

Also in 1922, Mills became the first African American entertainer to star in *The Greenwich Village Follies*; while white cast members threatened to leave the show because they were upset by the amount of advance publicity for Mills; they did not. Mills then appeared in *Dixie to Broadway*, which was the first Broadway show developed for an African American woman, and she was the first African American headliner at New York's famed Palace Theater. In 1924, Mills's photograph appeared in *Vanity Fair* and was the only full-page picture of an African American in the magazine in the 1920s; the next was Paul Robeson in the 1930s. Mills traveled to London, where she starred in *From Dover Street to Dixie*; she returned to New York and headlined *Blackbirds of 1926*, before starring in the production in Paris and London.

Mills returned to the United States in September 1927, and befitting her stature as an international celebrity, saw thousands waiting for her when she disembarked from the *Ile de France* in New York. After entering the hospital in October, she died from a tuberculosis-related illness at the age of thirty-one. Harlemites were stunned. Thousands viewed her body at the funeral home during a five-day period, attended her funeral, and lined Harlem's streets the day of her funeral. At Carnegie Hall in 1943, Duke Ellington performed his tribute to the legendary entertainer, "Black Beauty (Portrait of Florence Mills)."—LINDA M. CARTER

MITCHELL [COOK], ABRIEA "ABBIE" [ABBEY MITCHELL]

(September 25, 1884–March 16, 1960) Singer, actress

A talented singer and actress, Abriea "Abbie" Mitchell's brilliant soprano voice got her noticed by agents Paul Lawrence Dunbar and Will Marion Cook. The two men cast her in their musical *Clorindy, the Origin of the Cakewalk* (1898), which was her first big break. A year later, she married Cook and was given the lead in *Jes Lak White Folks* (1899). Her most memorable role may be as Clara in George Gershwin's Broadway opera *Porgy and Bess* (1935), around the end of the Harlem Renaissance.

Mitchell was born on September 25, 1884, to an African American mother and Jewish German father in New York City. She went to convent school in Baltimore, Maryland. After graduating, she moved to New York and joined the Memphis Student, a playing, singing, and dancing group that opened at Proctor's Twenty-Third Street Theater, the Victoria Theater, and the Roof Garden. She also traveled and performed in Europe, at the Olympia in Paris, at the Palace Theater in London, and with the Schumann Circus in Berlin. Years after returning to the United States, Mitchell took a position as head of the voice department at Tuskegee Institute; this did not keep her from singing in concert. She appeared in *Coquette* with Helen Hayes in Chicago in 1929, and at Town Hall in New York in 1931. Mitchell died in Harlem.—MYRON T. STRONG

MOODY, CHRISTINA

(1894–?) Poet

At the tender age of sixteen, Christina Moody published a book of poetry that uses the dialect of her people and offers a proud view of her race. Her contribution and thoughtfulness added to positive conversations about the intellectual and creative abilities of black people. She addressed such issues as Negros pledging their allegiance to the flag in twentieth-century America, where black were not treated equally. Although little is known about the life of Moody, her poetry, which consists of the compilation *A Tiny Spark*, published in 1910, and *The Story of the East St. Louis Riot*, published in 1917, are tributes to her talent. Her works remain as cherished parts of African American and American poetry. Moody's work was later passed on to librarian Florabelle Williams Wilson by her son in 1981. Her works are part of Wilson's collection at the Indiana Historical Society. —LEAN'TIN L. BRACKS

MORYCK, BRENDA RAY

(1894–1949) Writer, educator, social activist

Brenda Ray Moryck's contributions to black women's literature include short stories, essays, newspaper articles, and book reviews published primarily in *Opportunity*, the journal of the Urban League, founded by Charles S. Johnson, and the National Association for the Advancement of Colored People's *Crisis* magazine, founded by W. E. B. Du Bois. As a columnist for the *New Jersey Herald* and *Baltimore Afro-American*, she reported on activities of Harlem Renaissance notables, including an evening when James Weldon Johnson read his poem "The Creation" for his guests—Countee Cullen, Jean Toomer, Walter White, and Paul Robeson.

Moryck was born in Newark, New Jersey. Educated at St. Vincent's Academy, Barringer High School, and Wellesley College, she was influenced by her family's literary heritage. Her great-grandfather, Reverend Charles Ray, a New York abolitionist and Congregational minister, was editor of the *Colored American Newspaper* from 1839 to 1842. Her grandmother, Henrietta Cordelia Ray, was a poet and educator, and her mother was a writer. Growing up in a family of intellectual, political, and social activism, and through her writings and lectures, Moryck passionately supported Harlem Renaissance movement issues.

In 1917, she wed Lucius Lee Jordan, who died during their first year of marriage. Moryck's second marriage was to Robert B. Francke, a lawyer and attaché in the Haitian Delegation in Paris. The Franckes lived in Brooklyn. Between her marriages, Moryck moved from New Jersey to Washington, D.C., where she was employed as vice principal of Armstrong High School and joined the black social scene.

Moryck's passion for writing began at the age of six. Her short story "Why" was featured in the *Wellesley College Magazine* in June 1915. It was later published in the January 1923 issue of *Opportunity* magazine. In addition, it is included in the anthology *Harlem's Glory: Black Women Writing, 1900–1950*. Some of her works were recognized with *Opportunity* and *Crisis* magazine awards. Contest judges recognized her vivid imagination and creative talents. The essay "A Man I Know" won second prize, and "When a Negro Sings" garnered second-place honorable mention. Published in the May 16, 1929 edition of *Crisis* magazine, Moryck's short story "Days," which tackles the subject of segregated housing and racial stereotypes, won second-place honors.

Moryck debated Langston Hughes on his views of the lack of a literary environment in Washington. In the essay "I, Too, Have Lived in Washington," she optimistically writes that culture exists in the city if one looks for it. Her composition "A Point of View: An Opportunity Dinner Reaction," published in August 1925, challenged white writers who considered themselves experts on black literature and placed limits on subjects for black writers. She argues that black writers know themselves better than whites and are capable of writing about subjects other than those of rural oral traditions.

In 1927, Charles S. Johnson edited an anthology that represents the artistic contributions of Moryck's contemporaries: Sterling Brown, Langston Hughes, Alice Dunbar-Nelson, Arna Bontemps, and Zora Neale Hurston. The collection includes Moryck's autobiographical essay "I," in which she explains her childhood awareness of prejudice and the discovery of herself as black, female, and human. By 1929, she was being described by the black press as an outstanding writer. Along with artist Aaron Douglas and writer Jessie Redmon Fauset, Moryck was a contributor to *Metropolitan*, a magazine issued in the early 1930s. Its mission was to publish articles and literary works depicting the New Negro Movement.

During her lifetime, Moryck was part of the women's self-help movement, and she held memberships in the National Association of College Women and the

National Council of Negro Women. She served as secretary of the Women's Committee of the National Association for the Advancement of Colored People and volunteered as a vocational guidance counselor. She also championed the causes of the Women's Interracial Committee of the Federated Council of Churches, the National Negro Nurses' Association, Harlem's Community Welfare Association, and the Young Women's Christian Association.

Moryck moved between Harlem, the intellectual Mecca of the New Negro Movement, and Washington, D.C., attending such social and cultural events as one honoring Arna Bontemps and serving as hostess at the wedding of Yolande Du Bois to Countee Cullen. Her strong views made her a sought after speaker and lecturer.—GLORIA HAMILTON

MOSES, ETHEL
(April 29, 1904—June 1982) Actress, dancer

During the Harlem Renaissance of the 1920s and 1930s, when Hollywood often cast blacks in demeaning roles, Ethel Moses portrayed black women in stronger roles. One of Harlem's most popular actresses, she played lead roles in "race films" produced by Oscar Micheaux, which feature stars including Lorenzo Tucker, Oscar Polk, Jacqueline Lewis, Laura Bowman, and Alec Lovejoy.

The daughter of New York Baptist minister W. H. Moses and his wife, Ethel was born in Staunton, Virginia. She had three brothers and three sisters. Ethel and two sisters, Lucia and Julia, danced in *Dixie to Broadway* (1924–1925), featuring Florence Mills. They also danced in the chorus line at Harlem's popular Cotton Club (1928–1933). Ethel danced at Connie's Inn and the Ubangi Club as well. She also performed with Cab Calloway's band and married pianist Bennie Payne. With the Lucky Millinder Orchestra, she toured abroad in Monte Carlo, Paris, Cannes, Nice, and Naples. She danced in the Broadway shows *Blackbirds* (1926), *Show Boat* (1927), and *Keep Shuffling* (1928) but dreamed of becoming an actress.

Moses's film career began with *Birthright* (1924), a silent movie produced by the often controversial Oscar Micheaux. Known as the "Black Jean Harlow," she starred in *Lem Hawkins' Confession* and *Temptation* (1935), *Underworld* (1937), *God's Step Children* (1938), and *The Policy Man* (1938). In her final role, she starred in the musical *Gone Harlem* (1939). She and Frank Ryan, her second husband, lived in Jamaica, Long Island. Moses died in Brooklyn, New York.—MARIE GARRETT

MOTEN [BARNETT], ETTA
(November 5, 1901–January 2, 2004) Actress, singer, philanthropist

Etta Moten's career was launched in the 1930s, in New York, while Harlem continued to enjoy its coruscating success. In ensuing years, the actress ascended to greater fame in film and, notably, in her famous role as Bess in the musical *Porgy and Bess*.

Moten was born in Weimar, Texas, on November 5, 1901, to Freeman F. Moten, a preacher, and Ida Norman Moten. She was the only child of college-educated parents. A life of immense responsibility began early for Moten. After graduating from high school, she married Lieutenant Curtis Brooks and gave birth to three daughters. After seven years of a challenging marriage, Moten dauntlessly pursued divorce and a new future. In the 1920s, she attended the University of Kansas. Her parents aided her by caring for her children during the week so she could focus on school. In 1931, Moten received her degree in voice and drama.

The young performer did not hesitate to follow her passion upon graduation. Like many African Americans of this period who were driven by the promise of stardom and bright lights, she moved to New York. In the 1930s, New York, specifically Harlem, offered African Americans numerous venues in which to perform and opportunities to test one's dreams. Moten started out as a member of the Eva Jessye Choir of New York. While in New York, she met the influential Claude Barnett, who founded the Associated Negro Press in 1919. While in New York, Moten performed in the Broadway musical *Fast and Furious* (1931) and went on tour performing in *Zombie* (1932).

Moten's career also took her to Hollywood, which, as the mecca of the U.S. film industry, was then, and continues to be to some degree, dominated by whites. The few African Americans who appeared in Hollywood films were often confined to negative and stereotypical roles. In the beginning, Moten primarily dubbed songs for white actresses in films, but her dignified performance as a widow in *Gold Diggers* (1933) was considered a milestone for African Americans in film. She was praised for her performance by the black community and mainstream society. In 1934, Moten became the first African American woman to perform at the White House when she sang at President Franklin D. Roosevelt's birthday party. That same year, Moten married Barnett.

Family life in Chicago was accentuated with more travels and experiences for Moten. Her most crucial role is considered to be her part as Bess in the musical *Porgy and Bess*. This musical was one of George Gershwin's most celebrated creations, particularly for African Americans who dominated the cast. Moten performed in this role from 1942 to 1945.

In later years, Moten remained active. She and her husband were avid supporters of African culture and independence. In the 1950s, Moten established her own radio show, *I Remember When*. She left an indelible mark on the United States and the world. Moten died from pancreatic cancer.—GLADYS L. KNIGHT

N

NANCE, ETHEL RAY
(April 13, 1899–July 19, 1992) Secretary, museum assistant, civil rights worker, writer

One of the lasting contributions of Ethel Ray Nance to the Harlem Renaissance was the influence that she had on the expansion of that movement. She encouraged young black intellectuals to go to Harlem and become part of the great cultural awakening that was developing during the first quarter of the twentieth century.

Nance was born in Duluth, Minnesota, to racially mixed parents, William Henry Ray and Swedish immigrant Inga Nordquist Ray. The Rays were among the few African Americans who lived in racially hostile Duluth, which stimulated Ethel's desire to move to a friendlier environment. After graduating from high school, she was a stenographer and then secretary for the Minnesota State Relief Commission from 1919 to 1922. Ethel's trip with her father to Toledo, Detroit, Rochester, Boston, and New York City in 1919 broadened her view of black people. She met union organizer A. Philip Randolph, writer George Schuyler, and other influential blacks in New York. She was then introduced to important black entrepreneurs the likes of insurance executive Charles C. Spaulding while visiting North Carolina. After returning home, Nance became stenographer for the Minnesota House of Representatives in 1923, and took a position with the Urban League in Kansas City from 1924 to 1925. She met more prominent blacks while in Kansas City, including Harlem Renaissance writer Eric Waldrond and Charles S. Johnson, editor of *Opportunity* magazine.

In 1925, Nance moved to New York and became Johnson's secretary and editorial assistant. Her work with Johnson, who was often called the "godfather of the Harlem Renaissance," brought her into the midst of the renaissance. Nance shared an apartment with Regina Anderson [Andrews], a librarian at the 125th Street Branch of the New York Public Library, and Andrews's friend Louella Tucker. They named their apartment at 580 Saint Nicholas Avenue their "Dream Haven." In Harlem Renaissance circles, the apartment became popularly known as "580," and it was clearly the place to be in Harlem. It attracted such scholars and writers as Jean Toomer, Countee Cullen, Langston Hughes, Zora Neale Hurston, Arna Bontemps, Aaron Douglas, Jessie Redmon Fauset, and countless others. Nance maintained a diary of their guests, National Urban League developments, and other activities.

Nance planned the first Opportunity Awards celebration in May 1926, which celebrated the creative and literary artists of the renaissance. She helped to edit *Opportunity* and reviewed manuscripts for the journal, served as a talent scout for new artists, nurtured young writers, and undertook research projects. People were only accessible to Charles S. Johnson through Nance. She returned to Duluth in 1926, to be with her ailing mother but continued her work with Johnson. In 1929, she married Clarence A. Nance and had two sons. From then onward her various positions took her to Saint Paul, Minnesota; Hampton, Virginia; Seattle; and San Francisco. She moved to Nashville in 1953–1954, and became administrative assistant to Johnson, who was then president of Fisk University. After leaving Fisk, Nance held positions elsewhere, worked as research assistant for several projects, and helped found the San Francisco Historical and Cultural Society. When she was seventy-eight years old, she became the oldest person to receive a bachelor's degree from the University of San Francisco. She also maintained her relationship with Regina Anderson [Andrews] throughout the years.—JESSIE CARNEY SMITH

NEWSOME, EFFIE LEE [MARY EFFIE LEE]
(January 18, 1885–May 12, 1979) Poet, children's writer, columnist, librarian

Effie Lee Newsome wrote primarily on nature, the outdoors, and the realities and normalcy of the black child's experience. Through her works published in the major African American periodicals of the Harlem Renaissance, she challenged the racial stereotypes depicting black children in the literature of the period by her authentic illustrations and depictions of African Americans and within the African diaspora.

Newsome was one of five children born to Benjamin Franklin and Mary Elizabeth Lee. Her father was the second president of Wilberforce University; he later became a chief editor of the *Christian Recorder*, the official publication of the African Methodist Episcopal Church. He ultimately became a bishop in the African Methodist Episcopal Church. A family with this intellectual bent and religious spirit instilled in young Mary Effie optimism, a love of nature and learning, and an appreciation for drawing and the liberal arts, as evidenced in her life's work. She attended Wilberforce University (1901–1904), Oberlin College (1904–1908), the Philadelphia Academy of Fine Arts (1907–1908), and the University of Pennsylvania (1911–1914). In 1920, she married Reverend Henry Nesby Newsome and began publishing under the name Effie Lee Newsome.

Newsome's first sketch appeared in April 1920, and her first poems in May 1920, in *The Brownies' Book*, W. E. B. Du Bois's magazine for children. The publication lasted for twenty-four issues. Newsome's work appeared almost monthly during its publication from 1920 to 1922. With the end of *The Brownies' Book*, she was asked to write the column "The Little Page" in *Crisis*. The content of this page continued the mission of *The Brownie's Book* through poetry, prose, and illustrations to develop racial pride, instill a code of conduct, demonstrate positive ways to spend free time, and inspire children. In addition to her poetry, the column included a prose section called "Calendar Chat." The column generally focused on a topic relative to the month. Yet, other sketches appeared from time to time on this page that highlighted race. This heated topic was not one where Newsome often addressed children; however, she did present racial sketches designed to teach racial pride in black American readers. Her writing for an adult audience addressed nature with nostalgia and racial themes. Her poems for adults are included in *The Poetry of the Negro, 1746 to 1949* (1949), edited by Langston Hughes and Arna Bontemps.

Gladiator Garden: Poems for Outdoors and Indoors for Second Grade Readers (1940), a collection which mirrors the optimism of the Harlem Renaissance, was Newsome's only published book. The racial pride voiced in her work is evident in her 1922 poem "The Bronze Legacy (To a Brown Boy)." Newsome is remembered as an early pioneer in children's literature, one who addressed children on issues of importance in language they could understand and appreciate. She and her husband lived in Birmingham, Alabama, for a period, where she taught elementary school and served as children's librarian. Following this stint, she became children's librarian at Central State College. In 1963, she retired as librarian in the College of Education at Wilberforce University. She died in Wilberforce, Ohio.—HELEN R. HOUSTON

O

OVINGTON, MARY WHITE

(April 11, 1865–July 15, 1951) Harlem Renaissance supporter, suffragist, journalist, organization cofounder

During the Jim Crow era, Mary White Ovington became active in the crusade for Southerners' civil rights after hearing Frederick Douglass speak in 1890. She extended her reform crusade to the North after hearing an address by Booker T. Washington in 1903. After two years at Radcliffe College, in 1895, Ovington helped found the Greenpoint Settlement in Brooklyn, where she remained until 1904, when she was appointed fellow of the Greenwich House Committee on Social Investigations. In subsequent years, she studied employment and housing problems in black Manhattan, resulting in her book *Half a Man* (1911). It was during her studies that she met sociologist and civil rights activist W. E. B. Du Bois, who introduced her to the founding members of the Niagara Movement, the forerunner of the National Association for the Advancement of Colored People (NAACP).

Ovington, influenced by the ideas of William Morris, joined the Socialist Party in 1905, where she met other activists who argued that racial problems were as much a matter of class as race. She wrote for several radical journals and newspapers, including the *Masses*, the *New York Evening Post*, and the *Call*. Ever the influenced and influential individual, after reading an article by socialist William English Walling entitled "Race War in the North," which calls for an influential body of citizens to rescue blacks, Ovington responded and met with Walling, among others.

The group launched a campaign that issued a plea for a national conference on the civil and political rights of black Americans on February 12, 1909. Many activists responded to the plea, leading to the establishment of the National Negro Committee, which held its first meeting from May 31, 1909 to June 1, 1909. It was during the second meeting of the National Negro Committee, in 1910, that an organizational structure and new name were adopted, the NAACP. Its initial purposes were to improve the economic and social conditions of black people in cities throughout the United States and promote blacks' rights as citizens. Ovington was appointed the NAACP's executive secretary, while remaining active in the struggle for women's suffrage and opposed to U.S. involvement in World War I. Ovington served the NAACP as board member, executive secretary, chairman, and treasurer.

Ovington, a journalist, made major contributions to the literature about blacks and other popular subjects with her scholarly research. Her publications include the book *The Status of the Negro in the United States* (1913); the book *Socialism and the Feminist Movement* (1914); an anthology for black children, *The Upward Path* (1919); biographical sketches of prominent African Americans in *Portraits in Color* (1927); the autobiography *Reminiscences* (1932); and a history of the NAACP, *The Walls Come Tumbling Down* (1947).

Ovington retired as a board member of the NAACP in 1947. The association declared her the "mother of the new emancipation." She spent decades of her life fighting for the equal rights of black Americans.—AISHA M. JOHNSON

P

PETERKIN, JULIA MOOD

(October 31, 1880–August 10, 1961) Novelist, short story writer, teacher, actress, Harlem Renaissance supporter

Julia Mood Peterkin, a writer of fiction, gained the attention of Harlem Renaissance notables W. E. B. Du Bois, Langston Hughes, Zora Neale Hurston, Countee Cullen, and Paul Robeson, among others. They marveled at the writings of a southern white woman who composed powerful stories about black folk life on plantations in the South Carolina Lowcountry. In such works as *Black April* (1927) and the Pulitzer Prize-winning *Scarlet Sister Mary* (1928), Harlem Renaissance intellectuals were impressed with Peterkin's character creations, realistic men and women of strength, compassion, courage, and heroism—qualities seldom depicted in black characters created by white writers. In addition, the novelist's use of Gullah, the creole language spoken by her characters, and portrayal of authentic black folk life did not go unnoticed.

Peterkin was born in Laurens County, South Carolina, on Halloween, to Julius Mood, a physician, and Alma Archer Mood; however, she was raised by her maternal grandparents following her mother's death from tuberculosis when Julia was only eighteen months old. In 1896, Peterkin graduated from Converse College in Spartanburg, South Carolina. She earned a master's degree a year later, at the age of seventeen.

Peterkin's stories are largely autobiographical, since much of her stories are reflections of personal experiences. For example, her understanding of Gullah was born out of being cared for by a Gullah-speaking nurse following the death of her mother. And the settings in her stories mirror the Lang Syne Plantation, the author's marital home.—JEWELL B. PARHAM

PETERSON, DOROTHY RANDOLPH
(June 21, 1897–November 4, 1978) Teacher, actress

Dorothy Randolph Peterson is considered a lesser-known figure of the Harlem Renaissance in modern times; however, in her day, she was popularly known as a staunch supporter of the extraordinary movement and a person of influence in Harlem circles. She also made important contributions to the Harlem Renaissance, cofounding the New Experimental Theater in 1929, and appearing in the play *Green Pastures* in 1930. Carl Van Vechten depicts her as a heroine in his novel *Nigger Heaven*.

Peterson was born on June 21, 1897, to Jerome Bowers Peterson and Cornelia S. White. Due to her father's work as the U.S. consul to Puerto Cabello, Venezuela, and deputy collector of the Internal Revenue Service in San Juan, Dorothy spent much of her childhood in Puerto Rico. After graduating from the Puerto Rico University, she attended New York University. In the 1920s, she moved to Harlem, initially to spread the teachings of George Ivanovich Gurdjieff, a fusion of Eastern and Russian thought.

While in Harlem, Peterson immersed herself in the world of the Harlem Renaissance. She became a patron of the short-lived black journal *Fire!!* She hosted several literary salons, initially in her father's home and then in her own. She and Regina Anderson [Andrews] founded the Negro Experimental Theater in 1929. The following year, Peterson appeared in the play *Green Pastures*. This was Peterson's only foray into acting. She taught for a living, teaching at a public high school in Brooklyn, New York, and Wadleigh High School in Harlem.

In the 1940s, Peterson promoted the achievements of African Americans. Her major projects included the James Weldon Johnson Memorial Collection of Negro Arts and Letters at Yale University, and the Jerome Bowers Peterson Collection of Photographs of Celebrated Negroes at Wadleigh High School in Harlem. Despite Peterson's commitment to the Harlem Renaissance, she spoke little about the movement in her later years.—GLADYS L. KNIGHT

PITTS, LUCIA MAE ["LADY CALLED LOU"]
(1904–1973) Poet

Lucia Mae Pitts was a member of a literary group in Chicago, Illinois, that called themselves "Lasers." They were diverse both in their professions and literary aspirations. Their work was most often published in the literary section "Lights and Shadows" of the *Chicago Defender*, a black newspaper. Among their members were literary artists Langston Hughes and Frank Marshall Davis. Pitts, who served as editor and contributor and often wrote under the pseudonym "Lady Called Lou," not only wrote poetry, but she also used her talents as a playwright and art critic.

Pitts was born in Chattanooga, Tennessee, in 1904, but she spent her early years in Chicago. During that time, she contributed to the *Chicago Defender* but later moved to New York during the height of the Harlem Renaissance. Her work as a poet was published in the journals *Challenge* and *Opportunity*, and it is also included in two anthologies of young Negro poets edited by Beatrice M. Murphy—

Negro Voice (1938) and *Ebony Rhythm* (1948). In 1933, Pitts moved to Washington, D.C., another vibrant community of black literary artists.

No major publications by Pitts are known, but her life experiences included serving among the first to join the Women's Army Corps during World War II. After the war, she started a personnel service and later worked for the U.S. Department of Public Housing in Los Angeles.—LEAN'TIN L. BRACKS

POPEL, ESTHER [ESTER POPEL SHAW]
(July 16, 1896–January 28, 1958) Poet, educator, orator

As part of the thriving Washington, D.C., arts scene, Esther Popel had a connection to other black writers of the Harlem Renaissance through the crafting of poetry and essays that comment on the racial and gender disparities in the United States during that time.

On July 16, 1896, Popel was born in Harrisburg, Pennsylvania. In 1915, while a senior at Central High School, she published her first book of poetry, entitled *Thoughtless Thinks by a Thinkless Thoughter*. Soon thereafter, she attended Dickinson College in Carlisle, Pennsylvania, as its first black female student. Excelling in languages, she graduated as a Phi Beta Kappa in 1919. After marrying William A. Shaw in 1925, Popel began a teaching career in Baltimore, Maryland, and then moved to Washington, D.C., where she was a French and Spanish teacher at Shaw Junior High School and Francis Junior High School. She and her husband had one daughter named Patricia, who, like her mother, was accepted into Dickinson but did not attend because the school refused to provide housing for a black student.

As a frequent visitor of Georgia Douglas Johnson's S Street Salon, Popel befriended other black writers, for instance, Langston Hughes, May Miller, Zora Neale Hurston, and Eulalie Spence. Like her contemporaries, she aimed to highlight a distinct black experience in the United States. From 1925 until 1934, her race-conscious poems were published frequently in *Opportunity* and *Crisis*. One of her most recognized poems, "Flag Salute," juxtaposes *The Pledge of Allegiance* with the lynching of George Arwood on Maryland's Eastern Shore. Other poems include "Blasphemy—American Style," "October Prayer," "Night Comes Walking," and "Little Gray Leaves." Her first and only collection, *A Forest Pool*, contains twenty-seven lyrical and political poems. It was published privately in 1934. In addition to writing poetry, Popel engaged in other writing and lecturing projects. She wrote six plays; was a review editor for the *Journal of Negro History*; authored the pamphlet *Personal Adventures in Race Relations*; and lectured at women's clubs in Washington, D.C., and New York City. She died in Washington, D.C., in 1958.—TANYA E. WALKER

PORTER, DOROTHY LOUISE BURNETT [WESLEY]
(May 25, 1905–December 17, 1995) Library curator, librarian, writer

Best known as Dorothy Porter for many years, this librarian, writer, and scholar played a pivotal role in the collection and maintenance of African American research resources. Her strong determination to promote scholarship led her to ensure that the original and secondary works by and about black people, including Harlem Renaissance writers, poets, artists, and others, were gathered in the libraries at Howard University and elsewhere. She single-handedly searched attics, basements, storage areas, and even trash piles to gather many of the materials now available to scholars in libraries and repositories.

Dorothy Louise Burnett Porter [Wesley] was born in Warrenton, Virginia, to Hayes Burnett, a physician, and Bertha Ball Burnett, an expert tennis player. She was educated in the middle-class suburban neighborhood of Montclair, New Jersey, and received a diploma from Miner Normal School in Washington, D.C. She received a bachelor's degree from Howard University in 1928, a bachelor's degree in 1931, and master's degree in 1932, the latter two in library science from Columbia University. She was the school's first black to graduate with a degree in library science. In 1930, she married James Amos Porter, an artist and later department head at Howard University. After his death in 1979, she was married again in 1987, to historian Charles Harris Wesley.

After serving as librarian of Miner Teachers College for one year, in 1925, Porter became cataloger at Howard from 1928 to 1930. At Howard, she was charged with the responsibility of building a library collection of black materials. The results of her efforts can be seen in the Moorland Foundation, the Negro Collection, and the Library of Negro Life and History at Howard. The most outstanding academic library of its kind anywhere in the world, it is now known as the Moorland-Spingarn Research Center (MSRC). It was named in honor of Jesse E. Moorland, who, in 1914, gave his private library to Howard, and bibliophile Arthur B. Spingarn, whose collection was given to the university in 1946.

Porter's publications include *North American Negro Poets* (1945); *Early Negro Writing, 1760–1837* (1971); several works on nineteenth-century abolitionists; bibliographical works on African American resources; and numerous articles in the *Journal of Negro History*, *Opportunity*, *Phylon*, and more. When she retired in 1973, the reading room of MSRC was renamed the Dorothy B. Porter Room in her honor. She died in Florida.—JESSIE CARNEY SMITH

POSTLES, GRACE VERA
(January 2, 1906–?) Educator, poet

Grace Vera Postles is notable for the poems she wrote during the late 1920s. She began publishing in 1928, while a student at the Emerson College of Oratory in Boston, Massachusetts, and a member of the Saturday Evening Quill Club. Her poems were published in the club's literary publication, the *Saturday Evening Quill*. The Boston-based publication had a broad sphere of interest, garnering the acclaim and respect of the major players of the Harlem Renaissance.

Postles was born in Philadelphia, Pennsylvania on January 2, 1906. She attended the William Penn High School for Girls and the Cheyney Training School for Teachers. In 1927, Postles began her studies at the Emerson College of Oratory. In 1928, the year that the *Saturday Evening Quill* was founded, she published five poems in the June edition of the publication. The poems "Moonlight," "Prayer," and

"Prisoner" are simple and brief but penetrating. The following year, she published five poems in April. In 1930, Postles published "The Scar," an imploring poem. Although the *Saturday Evening Quill* lasted only three years, such prominent figures of the Harlem Renaissance as W. E. B. Du Bois, an African American scholar and activist, praised the literary skill that was represented therein.

Postles's career in writing continued into the 1930s. Her articles appeared in the printings of the Associated Negro Press; however, her primary career was in education. She was a dramatics counselor at Camp Guilford Bower in New York, and she taught English and dramatics in South Carolina. In South Carolina, she headed the Department of English at Avery Institute, as well as the Department of Speech and Drama at the State Agricultural and Mechanical College in Orangeburg (now South Carolina State University).—GLADYS L. KNIGHT

PREER, EVELYN
(July 26, 1896–November 18, 1932) Actress

Actress Evelyn Preer blazed the trail for African American women in motion pictures as early as the 1920s, when the Harlem Renaissance was in full bloom. She was equally successful onstage and made several appearances on Broadway, where she was seen in works by Sissle and Blake, and Miller and Lyles.

Born in Vicksburg, Mississippi, on July 26, 1896, Preer soon relocated with her parents to Chicago. While in high school, she made her acting debut, appearing in *Lady American Minstrels*. Following graduation, she toured with the Orpheum Circuit. Later, Preer moved to New York City and spent two years with the Lafayette Players at the Avenue Theatre. She remained with the Lafayette Players throughout her life. She also appeared on Broadway in several productions, including *Porgy*. Her performance in *A Comedy of Errors* brought Preer a favorable review from a theater critic for the *New York Times*.

Preer performed in feature films as well, and was a pioneer black woman in cinema. Between 1917 and 1930, she appeared in several films by black filmmaker Oscar Micheaux, including *The Homesteader* (Micheaux's first black silent film), *The Brute*, and *Within Our Gates. The Devil's Disciple* is considered her best work. In addition, Preer performed in the leading plays of the Harlem Renaissance era, including *Salome*, in which she was billed as the "most beautiful colored woman in the world." In 1921, she appeared in *Shuffle Along*, by Noble Sissle and Eubie Blake.

The multitalented Preer also made a number of popular photograph records. She continued her work on the stage during this period and, in 1927, appeared briefly in *Rang Tang*, by Irvin C. Miller and Aubrey Lyles. When she died, Preer was survived by her husband and fellow actor, Edward, whom she married in 1924, and their daughter.—JESSIE CARNEY SMITH

PRICE, DORIS D.
(?–?) Playwright

Doris D. Price's career as a playwright in the 1930s was enhanced by her experiences at the University of Michigan in Ann Arbor. While a student, she took a production and playwriting class that included such distinguished black classmates as Robert Hayden and Elise Roxborough, as well as white classmates Arthur Miller, Harvey Swados, and Betty Smith. Price's one-act plays *The Bright Medallion* and *The Eyes of the Old* were reviewed in *Crisis* magazine in 1933, and critics noted her attention to Southern black life and the philosophical ideas of different generations in the black community.—LEAN'TIN L. BRACKS

PRICE, FLORENCE SMITH
(April 9, 1888–June 3, 1953) Composer, musician

A child prodigy who began musical studies with her mother in her birthplace of Little Rock, Arkansas, Florence Smith Price played her first public recital at the age of four and published her first original composition at the age of eleven. Her public school music teacher was Charlotte Andrews Stephens, who had studied music at Oberlin College and also taught William Grant Still, another African American who would become a classical composer during the Harlem Renaissance era.

Graduating as high school valedictorian in Little Rock, Price continued her musical education at the New England Conservatory of Music, where she wrote a string quartet and a symphony, and performed as an organist and pianist. After graduation, she taught music at Arkadelphia Academy, Shorter College in Arkansas, and Clark College in Atlanta, Georgia, before marrying Little Rock attorney Thomas Price and becoming the mother of three children. When her firstborn son died as an infant, Price composed a piece in his memory.

Due to racial violence, Price and her family relocated to Chicago, where she resumed musical studies at Chicago Musical College, the American Conservatory, the University of Chicago, and other area institutions. She was influenced by outstanding classical musicians, as well as such African American Harlem Renaissance artists as Langston Hughes, Will Marion Cook, and William Dawson. One of her protégés, Margaret Bonds, followed in her footsteps as an African American female composer, performing Price's compositions, in addition to her own original works.—FLETCHER F. MOON

PROPHET, NANCY ELIZABETH
(March 19, 1890–December 1960) Sculptor

Nancy Elizabeth Prophet was an accomplished sculptor and Harmon Foundation winner in 1929, for her bust *Head of a Negro*. The Harmon Foundation, which awarded African American artists prizes for their work, noted Prophet's work as the "Best Sculpture," acknowledging her studies at the renowned Rhode Island School of Design and the École de Beaux Arts in Paris.

Prophet was born March 19, 1890, in Providence, Rhode Island, as an only child. After graduating from public school in Providence, she attended design school and later moved to Europe, with the financial assistance of Gertrude Vanderbilt Whitney, to further study her craft as a sculptor. She remained in Europe from 1922 to 1932, and her work was well respected and subsequently shown in the Paris August Salons from 1924 to 1927, and the Salon d'Automne in 1931 and 1932. After returning to the United States, Prophet continued working, occasionally using models, but primarily creating from her imagination. She took a teaching position at Spelman College in 1933, after being encouraged to do so by W. E. B. Du Bois, and later taught at Atlanta University. She left Atlanta in 1939, and returned to Providence after becoming frustrated with trying to find a welcoming artistic community.

Prophet, whose images are of individuals of African descent, created in stone, marble, and wood mediums. She is best known for her piece *Congolaise* (1930), which is reminiscent of a Masai tribesman. In 1945, she had a one-woman exhibit at the Providence Public Library, but she later destroyed many of her works because she could not afford storage. Many of them were destroyed after bring left outside because of a lack of space. Prophet later fell into obscurity and died in December 1960. Her work is held in several collections in Rhode Island and at the Whitney Museum of Art in New York.—Lean'tin L. Bracks

R

RAINEY, GERTRUDE "MA" [GERTRUDE MELISSA NIX PRIDGETT]

(April 26, 1886–December 22, 1939) Blues singer, songwriter

Regarded as the "Mother of the Blues," Gertrude "Ma" Rainey was born Gertrude Melissa Nix Pridgett on April 26, 1886, in Columbus, Georgia. She was one of the most influential singers of the Harlem Renaissance era, with more than 100 recordings, and she reigned supreme as one of the top-selling female vocalists of the 1920s. As a testament to her significance, there is no record of anyone singing the blues before "Ma" Rainey.

It would seem that from birth Rainey was destined to perform. Her parents, Thomas and Ella Pridgett, were traveling minstrels from Alabama, so it is indeed likely that she was raised for a while on the minstrel circuit. At fourteen, she entered the family business as a member of "A Bunch of Blackberries," a traveling show. In 1904, she married William "Pa" Rainey, a minstrel performer, and together they pooled their talents and created "Rainey and Rainey: The Assassinators of the Blues," a song and dance act that ran until 1916, along with touring with the Rabbit Foot Minstrels. With the "Foots," one of the most popular black minstrel companies in the South, Rainey became the first performer to use blues music in vaudeville acts. After a season of touring, the Raineys would spend their winters in New Orleans, where they met such luminaries as Sidney Bechet, Louis Armstrong, and Joe "King" Oliver.

Selling out juke joints, singing for washboard bands and jug bands, and honing her vocal craft for roughly twenty-five years, "Ma" Rainey was ready for a broader stage, and she had the imagination, vision, and creativity to write and perform top-selling songs. In 1923, she signed a recording contract with Paramount Records, out of Chicago, and recording history was put down on vinyl. In the six years that followed, she would record more than 100 songs, create several pieces that remain standards in the blues lexicon, and single-handedly invent the blues idiom. Her recordings during this period included "Jelly Bean Blues," "Daddy, Goodbye Blues," "Slow Driving Moan," "Shave 'Em Dry Blues," "Levee Camp Blues," "Booze and Blues," "Toad Frog Blues," and "Moonshine Blues." These songs are snapshots of varied aspects of folk life, and the blend of humor and pathos in these compositions is notable.

Heard throughout Mississippi juke joints, as well as Harlem speakeasies, Rainey's classic blues style was favorably received and helped lay the foundations for those women who followed her. Pieces that capture her classic style are the comedic and autobiographical "Ma Rainey's Black Bottom"; "Bo Weevil Blues"; "See, See Rider," which she recorded with Louis Armstrong; and the landmark "Backwater Blues." Rainey was also a master collaborator who was respected by jazz musicians. She was a serious musician who was able to take varied aspects of African American vernacular culture and weave them into artistic statements. The same composition could have both a light mood and a heavy sentiment. Louis Armstrong played cornet on her "Jelly Bean Blues," "See, See Rider," and "Countin' the Blues," and John Smith can be heard on "Titanic Man Blues," "Stack o' Lee," and "Bessemer Bound Blues." The performer also played with pianists Fletcher Henderson and Lovie Austin, legendary saxophonist Coleman Hawkins, and Texas guitar legend T-Bone Walker. Her usual Georgia band consisted of Al Wynn, Dave Nelson, Ed Pollock, and Thomas A. Dorsey, and this group was an impressive group of musicians who had a range of sound that supported the voice of Rainey.

As a singer and songwriter, Rainey pulled from a wide range of sources—carnival songs and folk ballads—and a number of styles—minstrel, vaudeville, burlesque, country-blues—to produce a sound that was uniquely hers. Similar to such poets of the Harlem Renaissance as James Weldon Johnson and Langston Hughes, Rainey was a cultural synthesizer, borrowing from varied aspects of her travels and making statements that, in the end, offered hope. After all, blues music is not about feeling blue, but it is cathartic. Life might be a low-down dirty shame, but the thing to do is to make it swing. And "Ma" Rainey always did that. Her shows were a celebration of the life of Southern black folk.

As a musician, Rainey worked in a male-dominated world, yet she held her own. She had been out on the road making a living almost two decades before women even had the right to vote. And in her working relationships with male musicians, there existed a profound respect for Rainey as a musician. Louis Armstrong, especially, strongly admired her work. Even her explicitly sexual performances were never about demeaning herself. They were a source of empowerment.

In her performances, her voice, her very being "Ma" Rainey achieved one of the main tenets of the Harlem Renaissance: that African American folk culture was worthy of artistic treatment. This idea is illustrated wonderfully by Zora Neale Hurston, whose 1937 classic novel *Their Eyes Were Watching God* grew out of her field notes while working as an anthropologist. The mythic and epic stature of Rainey is captured in the 1932 poem by Sterling A. Brown, in which Rainey is a hero because when she sings, she sings for so many down-home people. With her gravelly voice,

Rainey could make an audience laugh or cry. She used field hollers and moans of work songs, and she believed that her work was more than mere entertainment. The minstrel stage served as a launching point for her creativity and optimism. She was unapologetically country. As she explained on a few occasions, blues were the sacred music of the poor Southern blacks who worked the land. With this belief in mind, Rainey paid homage to those who worked the land every time she sang.

Nonetheless, Paramount did not feel the same way. While the record label had aggressively marketed Rainey during her heyday, referring to her as the "Mother of the Blues," "Songbird of the South," the "Gold-Neck Woman of the Blues," and the "Paramount Wildcat," the recording landscape was undergoing a shift, and the love for "Ma" had gone with it. The executives at Paramount felt that Rainey could no longer compete with emerging male blues singers, and they believed that Bessie Smith, Rainey's mentee, outclassed her. There was also a growing belief that the raw style of Rainey was no longer in vogue. Whatever the case may be, Bessie Smith, widely regarded as one of the greatest blues singers ever to stand at a microphone, always credited Rainey with being her chief influence.

A blues woman to her core, Rainey did not complain. Instead, she decided to form her own show company, the Arkansas Swift Foot, which proved short-lived as a result of the Great Depression. But the singer still had fans, so she toured until 1935, when both her mother and sister died. Following this familial loss, along with a decline in her voice, she decided to retire as a vocalist, but not from entertainment. Rainey returned to her hometown, where she owned and operated two theaters until a massive heart attack took her life on December 22, 1939. She was fifty-three years old.

In 1983, Rainey was inducted into the Blues Foundation's Blues Hall of Fame, as well as the Jazz Hall of Fame. In 1990, she was inducted into the Rock and Roll Hall of Fame. She was admitted into the Georgia Hall of Fame in 1992, followed by the Georgia Women of Achievement the next year. Rainey's image made it onto a U.S. first-class postage stamp in 1994, and her song "See, See Rider" earned induction into the Grammy Hall of Fame in 2004.

But Rainey's legacy runs deeper than music. Alain Locke, professor of philosophy at Howard University and one of the framers of the Harlem Renaissance, saw the emergence of black art less than four decades after the trauma of slavery as a revision of preconceived notions of blackness. The Harlem Renaissance was the first time on American soil that a conscious effort had been initiated by African Americans to define their culture, and Rainey was a powerful force in this movement. Her nickname carries with it both an expression of power and sexuality. She was earthy, sensual, and aggressive. She embodied feminine strength as she celebrated her body and sang freely.

Rainey's commercial success during the nascent years of the music recording industry was equally vital. Her success and strength helped make space for other women who contradicted the norms of femininity established in a patriarchal society. In Rainey's own time, these women would have included Bessie Smith, Trixie Smith, Ethel Waters, and Billie Holiday. And her influence extended to her cultural and artistic daughters, women like Tina Turner and Janice Joplin. The blues idiom developed and mastered by Rainey is now an attitude toward life where a woman has to travel her own road and learn to sing her own song.—DELANO GREENIDGE-COPPRUE

RANDOLPH, AMANDA [MANDY]
(September 2, 1902–August 24, 1967) Actress, singer, comedian

Amanda Randolph enjoyed a long and fruitful career during and after the Harlem Renaissance. Born on September 2, 1902, in Louisville, Kentucky, she lived in many different places with her family during her childhood. Following the death of her father in 1920, she moved to New York and launched her career as an actress and singer.

Although mainstream society provided few and limited opportunities for African Americans in the entertainment industry, Harlem was chock full of opportunities for blacks during the 1920s and 1930s. During the height of Harlem's most prolific years, Randolph performed in such popular productions as *Shuffle Along* (1921) and *The Chocolate Dandies* (1921).

After the 1930s, the Harlem Renaissance began to fade. Blacks and whites suffered when the Great Depression hit the United States. Randolph, however, adapted to the changing times. She opened an eatery known as the Clam Shop with her husband and recorded music under the names of Mandy Randolph and Amanda Randolph. Her music career lasted from 1920 to 1945.

Randolph also performed on Broadway and appeared in films and on television. Notable appearances included movies like *Swing* (1938) and *The Notorious Elinor Lee* (1941), produced by the illustrious African American filmmaker Oscar Micheaux. Among her television appearances were the controversial mainstream series *Amos 'n' Andy* (1951–1953) and *The Beulah Show* (1945–1953). Critics argued that those television programs portrayed African Americans in derogatory and stereotypical ways. Criticism notwithstanding, Randolph was a groundbreaking celebrity in the history of African Americans of the Harlem Renaissance and mainstream American media.

Randolph's husband, Harry Hansberry, preceded her in death. She was survived by her two children, Joseph and Evelyn.—GLADYS L. KNIGHT

RANDOLPH [WALLACE], RICHETTA G.
(1884–1971) Secretary, office manager, researcher

As secretary of the National Association for the Advancement of Colored People (NAACP) from its inception, Richetta G. Randolph knew well the many important decisions of the organization. In the early years of the twentieth century, she began her work as personal assistant to the leaders and scholars of that era; at first she was private secretary to social activist Mary White Ovington. That position led to her post with the NAACP; she was the first member of the administrative staff and then office manager until the mid-1940s. She became private secretary to James Weldon Johnson and Walter White. Randolph became an "inspiring figure in Brooklyn," the Harlem Renaissance, and national history.

Randolph was born in Virginia in 1884, and relocated to the Bedford-Stuyvesant section of Brooklyn, New York, in 1933. Little is known about her private life, but records show that she married a man named Wallace, who died early on; she became known by her maiden name, which she retained. Randolph assisted James Weldon Johnson in collecting information for his writings, and he praises her in both publications, *Black Manhattan* (1930) and *Along This Way* (1933). He writes in *Black Manhattan* that Randolph gave him valuable assistance as she gathered and sifted through historical data needed for his work. In *Along This Way*, he calls her the "best confidential secretary I have known or know of." Randolph was more than a secretary, but a research assistant as well.

Randolph was also Johnson's confidante and mentor. When Johnson was away from the office and Walter White managed in his stead, Randolph complained and expressed her disenchantment of her temporary boss. She disliked his effort to take over fully, reading the office mail, and manic attention to detail. When Carl Van Vechten's *Nigger Heaven* was published in 1926, Randolph wrote to her vacationing boss that Van Vechten wrote about what those who do not know black people think of them and urged Johnson to offer a rebuttal. Johnson refused, saying that what Van Vechten had written was no more than a "copyrighted racial slur."

After retiring from her post at the NAACP in 1946, Randolph continued to contribute to the literary and artistic culture of black America. Her papers, which cover the years 1906 to 1971, housed at the Brooklyn Historical Society, document her work with Mt. Olivet Baptist Church in Manhattan, where she had leadership roles as a congregant and officer.—JESSIE CARNEY SMITH

RANSOM, BIRDELLE WYCOFF
(August 14, 1914–?) Poet

Little is known about the Texas-born poet Birdelle Wycoff Ransom. Her only poem to be published, "Night," can be found in J. Mason Brewer's *Heralding Dawn: An Anthology of Verse*. She was one of six women chosen by Brewer to be included in this 1936 anthology of African American poets.

Ransom was born in Beaumont, Texas, on August 14, 1914. In 1918, her family moved to Houston, Texas, where she attended Gregory Elementary School. In 1930, Ransom graduated salutatorian from Washington High School, which then enabled her to graduate as valedictorian from Houston Junior College at eighteen years of age in 1933. Upon graduating from college, she began writing poetry for the *Houston Informer* column "Lines of Life," only to discontinue the column within the same year once she was married in Galveston, Texas. Before dropping into obscurity, Ransom completed her master's thesis, "Charles Dickens as a Social Reformer," at Texas Southern University in 1956.—AMANDA J. CARTER

REYNOLDS, EVELYN CRAWFORD [EVE LYNN]
(1900–1991) Teacher, social worker, columnist, poet

As a member of the Beaux Arts Club, Evelyn Crawford Reynolds wrote under the pseudonym of Eve Lynn. The Beaux Arts Club was comprised of black writers and artists in Philadelphia. During the Philadelphia Renaissance, she wrote poetry, reported on black high society, and worked as a community social worker.

Reynolds was born in Philadelphia around 1900. She graduated from Girls High and continued her education at Temple University by completing a special physical training course. Reynolds then taught in the Bureau of Recreation for four years.

In December 1927, she married Hobson Richmond Reynolds, thrusting her into well-known social circles and the spotlight. A mortician by trade, Hobson, originally from North Carolina, was a court judge magistrate. He became a prominent member of the Pennsylvania legislature and was featured in *Ebony* magazine later on as one of the most influential blacks in the United States. He was a grand exalted ruler in the Elks and active in this organization for many years.

According to Vincent Jubilee's dissertation on literary circles during the Harlem Renaissance in the 1920s, blacks in Philadelphia read two weekly newspapers: the *Philadelphia Tribune* and *Pittsburgh Courier*. During that period, Reynolds wrote a column, "Eve Lynn Chats 'bout Society and Folks," geared toward black professionals and entrepreneurs. It appeared in the *Pittsburgh Courier*. She documented visits of important figures, commented on current fashion trends, and even reported on the food that was served. After being appointed as neighborhood secretary of the Armstrong Association, a forerunner to the Urban League, Reynolds began writing for the *Philadelphia Tribune*. Although she covered the social, cultural, and civic events of high black society, Reynolds was far more than an observer. She was a member of the black elite and lived in Philadelphia's South Side on St. Albans Street.

Reynolds published three books of poetry: *No Alabaster Box* (1936), *To No Special Land: A Book of Poems* (1953), and *Put a Daisy in Your Hair* (1963). Her themes were nature, God, patriotism, and occasionally racial discrimination. Benjamin Brawley, a literary critic, compared Reynolds's first book to Mae V. Cowdery's *We Lift Our Voices and Other Poems* (1936). While Brawley thought that Reynolds's poetry was beautiful, he considered Cowdery's to be more intense. Even though Reynolds actually published more than Cowdery, Reynolds's poetry, although somewhat pleasing, was not all that memorable. She also tended to republish poems from her first book in subsequent volumes. Two of Reynolds's poems have been used as lyrics for hymns. "There's No Me, There's No You" and "We're Growing" were arranged by Nolan Williams. Both appear in the *African American Heritage Hymnal* as # 618 and #619.

Reynolds also had a knack for promoting herself. She loved public relations and self-acknowledgement. She used her poetry to achieve social recognition and bring people together. She obtained forewords for her books from such famous people as Mary McLeod Bethune, founder of Bethune-Cookman College, and Marian Anderson, an opera star.—JOY A. McDONALD

RIDLEY, FLORIDA RUFFIN [AMELIA YATES RUFFIN]
(January 29, 1861–March 1943) Activist, feminist, writer, educator

A prominent member of such activist and literary societies of the Harlem Renaissance as the Saturday Evening Quill Club, Florida Ruffin Ridley was an established advocate for equality, regardless of race and gender, by the late 1800s. Born Amelia Yates Ruffin on January 29, 1861, to elite African American Bostonians Josephine St. Pierre and George Lewis Ruffin, she was the only daughter and second of five children. Ridley's mother was a prominent member of racial uplift and women's club movements, while her father was the first African American man to graduate from Harvard Law School, as well as the first African American municipal court judge.

The dedication to African American and women's rights advocacy within the Ruffin household was advantageous for Ridley's education and career development. She graduated from Boston Teacher's College and began teaching at Boston's Grant School in 1880. In 1888, she married Ulysses A. Ridley, and they had two children, Constance J. Ridley and Ulysses A. Ridley Jr.

Always interested in promoting and preserving oral and folk traditions of the African American community, Ridley and her husband founded one of the earliest groups of black folklorists, the Society for the Collection of Negro Folklore, in Boston by 1890. In 1893, Ridley, her mother, and Maria Baldwin founded the Woman's Era Club in Boston. Ridley was corresponding secretary for the organization, while Josephine St. Pierre Ruffin was president. Along with her mother, she coedited and copublished the monthly *Women's Era* for the club until 1910, and she spent three years in Atlanta, Georgia, organizing a kindergarten. From 1894 to 1898, Ridley was a member of Brookline Equal Suffrage Association.

In 1895, Ridley participated in the first Convention of Colored Women, which resulted in the formation of the National Federation of Afro-American Women (NFAAW). One year later, after a meeting in Washington, D.C., NFAAW merged with the Colored Women's League to form the National Association of Colored Women. This group included members like Sarah Garnet and Mary Church Terrell. *Women's Era* was the official publication for the organization, and their primary objective was to establish an African American sisterhood that would encourage joint efforts in racial uplift.

To support the war effort, Ridley attended Boston University's secretarial war course in 1916, and one year later she was appointed executive secretary of the Soldier's Comfort Unit, a position she held until 1919. She was later offered a paid position in War Camp Community Service of New York. From 1919 until 1925, Ridley was a member of the board of directors for the Robert Gould Shaw Settlement House. She also promoted and directed Boston Public Library's Exhibition of Negro Achievement and Abolition Memorials in 1923.

In 1925, Ridley was awarded second place in the "Personal Experience" category of *Opportunity* magazine's contest for her essay "An Experience." She published her works in the *Saturday Evening Quill* (the annual publication of the Saturday Evening Quill Club), *Our Boston*, and *Opportunity*, among other publications. "He Must Think It Out," published in June 1928, is her most well-known short story. Other stories include "Two Gentlemen of Boston" (1926) and "Two Pairs of Gloves" (1930). Some of her most well-known nonfiction stories, aside from "An Experience," are "Preface: Other Bostonians" (1928) and "Maria Peters:

A Peculiar Woman" (1929). Ridley's writing topics focus on African American history, passing, and racial pride.

Although Ridley was politically independent, she campaigned with the Flying Squadron for the Democratic Party in 1924. She served as editor of the Cooperative Social Agencies publication *Social Service News* in 1928. As a member of the Saturday Evening Quill Club, she socialized with Waring Cuney, Edythe Mae Gordon, Alvira Hazzard, Helene Johnson, and Dorothy West, among others. The writer and educator was one of the few African American members of the Twentieth-Century Club and the Women's City Club in Boston, and she also participated in the League of Women for Community Service. Ridley was elected secretary of the Lewis Hayden Memorial Association in 1929, and from 1931 through 1940, she presided over the Society of Descendants of Early New England Negroes.

Later in life, Ridley moved to Toledo, Ohio, to live with her daughter. She passed away there and was honored with memorial services in both Toledo and Boston.— AMANDA J. CARTER

ROBESON, ESLANDA [CARDOZA GOODE]
(December 12, 1896–December 13, 1965) Activist, writer

Eslanda Robeson

Eslanda Robeson, who became the wife of Paul Robeson in 1921, was an activist and writer who was not only outspoken, but one who protested against violence toward African Americans, the end of colonialism and oppression, and independence for African nations. Her international perspective advocated for the rights of the oppressed.

Robeson was born Eslanda Cardoza Goode in Washington, D.C., on December 12, 1896. The family moved to New York City in 1900, where she completed high school and graduated from Columbia University in 1923, with a major in chemistry. She became the first African American to be employed as an analytical chemist at Columbia Medical Center and later took on the role as manager of her husband's career. Along with her interests in science and creative interest in theater, she became involved in civil rights issues and political concerns throughout the world. Robeson protested at the United Nations to have violence against African Americans included as part of a conference on genocide; between 1933 and 1935, she expanded her knowledge by enrolling in the London School of Economics and earned a doctorate in anthropology from Hartford Seminary. She visited Africa in 1936, and wrote the book *African Journey*, published in 1945. She also traveled to Spain to support antifascist groups. After she and her husband were accused of being Communists, they were required to testify before the House Un-American Activities Committee. Following their testimony, they were reprimanded by chairman and senator John McCarthy in 1953. They moved to Moscow, Russia, and remained there for five years, away from persecution.

In 1963, Robeson was suffering from breast cancer. While returning to the United States, she stopped in East Germany and was honored with the German Peace Medal. Once in the United States, she continued her activism by speaking out against the Vietnam War until her death in New York City.—LEAN'TIN L. BRACKS

ROBINSON, IDA BELL
(August 3, 1891–April 10, 1946) Pastor, evangelist, bishop

By 1924, when Ida Bell Robinson was having visions of giving greater opportunities for women in ministry, the Great Migration of African Americans from the rural South to urban cities in the North had provided fertile ground for religious evangelization. It seemed like the right time for her to enter the scenes of history with her overarching vision of full equality for women. The1848 Seneca Falls Convention had opened the door for conversation about women's suffrage, and in 1920, the Nineteenth Amendment to the U.S. Constitution gave legal legs to full voting rights for women. At a time when a woman preacher was a rarity, she was a charismatic pastor, evangelist, and later bishop whose impact could not be contained in the United States. Robinson's work spoke to topics of concern to blacks during the Harlem Renaissance—women's rights and freedom from all kinds of oppression.

Born Ida Bell on August 3, 1891, in Hazlehurst, Georgia, Robinson spent her childhood in Pensacola, Florida and, after marrying Oliver Robinson in 1910, moved to Philadelphia to find better employment opportunities. From an early age, Robinson felt guided by the Holy Ghost, and it was in Pennsylvania that her affiliation with the United Holy Church of America began a holiness ministry that flourished into one of the largest Pentecostal movements started by a woman; however, moving from street evangelization in Philadelphia to the development of an accredited school and a flourishing denomination would not be an easy journey to make.

In 1919, even before women had the right to vote, Robinson was ordained as a pastor by a bishop of the United Holy Church of America, and she was later installed as pastor of Mount Olive, then an affiliated mission of the church. Officials had recognized her gifts for ministry and commitment to God. Nonetheless, others in the congregation were uncomfortable with the decision. Ultimately, to continue her ministry, Robinson decided to heed the call she heard from God and made plans to start her own church. In 1924, after seeking legal counsel, she established Mount Sinai Holy Church of America. Her newly founded church had a Board of Elders on which more than half the seats were filled by women. Soon, because of her fiery deliverance of the Word of God and urgent sense of responding to revelations from God, Robinson set about preaching, teaching, and growing churches along the entire East Coast. Her mission work later expanded to churches in Cuba and British Guiana (now Guyana), South America.

In 1946, after having given more than twenty years of service to God, the fruit of her work was evident: Women had become presiding bishops of her denomination, then comprising eighty-four churches and more than 160 ordained ministers, 125 of which were women. This was certainly a testament to the power of a sacred vision she believed was given to her by God and which she lived out daily by the aid of the Holy Ghost in trust, prayer, and fasting until her death.—VIVIAN MARTIN

ROBINSON [ROBERSON], LIZZIE WOODS
(April 5, 1860–December 12, 1945) Religious organizer/activist, church cofounder, school matron

Although born a slave on April 5, 1860, in Phillips County, Arkansas, Lizzie Woods Robinson, or Mother Robinson, as she later became known, clearly demonstrated how one Spirit-filled woman could inspire others to achieve. Her widowed mother's wisdom in sending her to a missionary school gave Robinson an educational advantage that led her on a path of remarkable service to God, although that path would not be easily forged. No one event, but rather many events, help to explain her impact—reading the Bible early in life, meeting missionaries and evangelists, and later being introduced to Bishop Charles H. Mason, founder of the Church of God in Christ. For black women, the Harlem Renaissance proved to be a fertile time for black female religious leaders, whose works helped them build self-respect and promote racial pride in their own works.

Robinson, previously with Baptist affiliations at the time of meeting Mason, nonetheless decided to join in Mason's work. But during that time, the church was a newly formed denomination not readily received by the faith community. Yet, feeling led by the Holy Spirit, Robinson accepted the bishop's proposal to create a national office that would allow her to provide leadership for women in the early development of the church. The possibility of improving lives through the traditions of self-help and self-determination resonated with her; however, although the bishop recognized her exceptional organizational skills, unique ability to inspire others, and outstanding reputation for knowing and pronouncing the Word of God, female leadership was traditionally relegated to roles other than pastor or preacher. While Robinson's role was seemingly limited to only educational responsibilities, it was in this capacity that her greatest work was done.

But it was Robinson's indomitable drive, even in spite of financial suffering, that enabled her to overcome opposition and ultimately earn the respect of both men and women as a pioneering servant of God. Today, the denomination recognizes her as the Women's Department First General Supervisor, 1911–1945, whose early efforts focused on promoting moral purity and holiness and led to the strengthening of prayer and Bible bands, sewing circles, and foreign mission bands as she traversed rural and urban areas from Arkansas to Nebraska to Memphis and beyond during the Great Migration. In 1916, Robinson cofounded the first Church of God in Christ in Omaha, Nebraska, where the Lizzie Robinson House is listed on the National Register of Historic Places.

In her own way, Robinson reaffirmed for African Americans a sense of self-respect, racial pride, and cultural identity through the selfless ways in which she sought to overcome the effects of slavery, poverty, and injustice by serving others.

Her ministry was bolstered by the hope that lay pregnant in her postslavery world, the hope of a better day through the fostering of community and education. Whatever title one wishes to bestow upon her, her early ministry training and teaching at Baptist Academy in Dermott, Arkansas, and the skills honed by her own experiences made her an endearing leader that history cannot ignore.—VIVIAN MARTIN

ROSE, ERNESTINE

(1880–19?) Harlem Renaissance supporter, library administrator

The black cultural strivings that became known as the Harlem Renaissance were significantly strengthened by the work of Ernestine Rose, a librarian who headed the 135th Street Branch of the New York Public Library, which played a significant role in the movement. Rose drew on the sources of the community, integrated the library staff, and supported connections between writers and readers at literary gatherings held in the library. Artists, playwrights, and performers showcased their talents at the facility. The book collection that began during Rose's administration became the nucleus of library's most enduring legacy for research on African American people.

Rose was a white woman from a rural background in Bridgehampton, New York, the daughter of a farmer and a school principal. She experienced racial diversity while growing up, which would serve her well later in life and document her fierce commitment to social equality. She received a bachelor's degree from Wesleyan University and a degree in library science from New York State Library School in Albany.

In 1920, Rose became librarian of the New York Public Library's 135th Street Branch, located in Harlem; its staff was entirely white. Some sources say that she was a founder of what became known as the Schomburg Center. Rose fought racism and hired Catherine Latimer in 1920 as well, making the 135th Street Branch the only branch in the library system that hired blacks as librarians. Rose added additional black librarians, including Roberta Bosely, shortly after Latimer's appointment, and then Sadie Peterson Delany of later bibliotherapy fame at the Veterans Administration Hospital in Tuskegee, Alabama. In 1921, the 135th Street Branch hosted Harlem's first exhibition of African Americans; it became an annual event. This attraction, along with Rose's quick move to integrate the staff once she was hired, helped make the library a "focal point [of] the burgeoning Harlem Renaissance."

Rose led her staff to concentrate on building the collection of African American materials. In 1923, she reported to the American Library Association that patrons had increased their request for books by and about blacks, and also demanded professionally trained black librarians. In 1926, Rose secured the support of the National Urban League and then successfully sought financial support from the Carnegie Corporation to pay Puerto Rican Arthur A. Schomburg $10,000 for his collection of black materials and then donate the books to the library. Schomburg donated approximately 5,000 items, which he said would document the experiences he had growing up that blacks did, in fact, have a history and that they were not inferior to other races. Schomburg went on to become curator of the collection, known as the Arthur Schomburg Collection of Negro Culture at the New York Public Library.

Around 1933, the library also began to host a Works Progress Administration writer's project. In 1940, the American Negro Theatre was founded and, through the efforts of Latimer and with Rose's approval, gave performances in the basement of the 135th Street Branch. When Rose retired in 1942, assistant librarian Dorothy Homer, who was African American, replaced her. Rose's stellar achievements at the 135th Street Branch, now known as the Schomburg Center for Research in Black Culture, helped enhance her professional image. Her friend Langston Hughes once called her a "warm and wonderful librarian . . . [who] made newcomers feel welcome."—JESSIE CARNEY SMITH

ROWLAND, IDA
(1904–?) Poet

Although Ida Rowland is known to have published only one book of poetry, her accomplishment as one of the few black women who earned a Ph.D. during this era and her commitment to publishing books for African American youth is of particular note.

Born in Texas and raised in Oklahoma, Rowland worked her way through school, having to complete high school while doing domestic work. She further pursued her education and earned from the University of Nebraska in Omaha a B.A. in 1936, followed by an M.A. in sociology in 1938. Rowland's academic performance earned her membership in the National Honorary Scholastic Sociological Fraternity. In 1948, she earned her Ph.D. from Laval University in Quebec, Canada.

Rowland's highly regarded collection of poetry, *Lisping Leaves*, published in 1939, features an autumn theme that includes landscapes reminiscent of the regions where she grew up and was educated. Because of her literary skill, in 1940, she was inducted into the Eugene Field Society, a national association of artists and journalists who have shown literary skill and craftsmanship and an interest in things literary and cultural. Rowland spent time teaching sociology and psychology at Langston University, in Langston, Oklahoma, and she also taught in Arkansas. After she retired, she started a company that published books for young African Americans. The year of her death is unknown.—LEAN'TIN L. BRACKS

S

SAUNDERS, GERTRUDE
(March 25, 1903–April 1991) Singer, actress

While her greatest fame and recognition came from being the original star of *Shuffle Along*, the groundbreaking musical and theatrical production by Eubie Blake, Noble Sissle, Flournoy Miller, and Aubrey Lyles in 1921, which some cite as launching the Harlem Renaissance, Gertrude Saunders went on to continue her varied show-business career in motion pictures, as well as with live stage performances.

Born in North Carolina, Saunders was still a teenager at the time she left studies at Benedict College in Columbia, South Carolina, to tour with stage and vaudeville entertainer and producer Billy King as a featured singer and comedienne, where her performances turned a number of his songs into hits, including "Wait 'Til the Cows Come Home" from the 1918 show *The Board of Education*, "Little Lump of Sugar" from *The Heart Breakers* (also in 1918), "Hot Dog" from the 1919 show *They're Off*, and "Rose of Washington Square" from the 1920 show *Town Top-Piks*.

Saunders also starred in another King production in 1919, *Over the Top*, which dramatized the state of African Americans at the time of the Paris Peace Conference and presaged other Harlem Renaissance efforts to stage serious theatrical works and musical revues. After Saunders was replaced by Florence Mills as the star of *Shuffle Along*, she continued to work in other revues during the 1920s and 1930s, including one financed by Bessie Smith's husband Jack Gee in 1929, which led to a fight with Smith. After suffering a nervous breakdown and returning to her home in Asheville, North Carolina, in 1931, to recuperate, Saunders resumed performing in such revues as *Red Hot Mama* during the 1930s and eventually appeared in several films, including a small, uncredited role as a servant in a mainstream Hollywood production, *The Toy Wife* (1938), starring Robert Young and Melvyn Douglas, as well as *Big Timers* (1945) and *Sepia Children* (1947), which were marketed to black audiences.

Little is known about Saunders's life after she left show business, but she was recognized at a 1964 event sponsored by the Negro Actors' Guild, along with fellow entertainment veterans Josephine Baker, Eubie Blake, and Noble Sissle. She died in Beverly, Massachusetts.—FLETCHER F. MOON

SAVAGE, AUGUSTA
(February 29, 1892–March 26, 1962) Sculptor, educator, arts activist

Augusta Savage

An important figure during the 1920s and 1930s, Augusta Savage challenged the negative images of African Americans by sculpting figures that speak to the achievements, struggles, and uniqueness of her race. Her commitment to social fairness and equality in the visual arts resulted in a continuing campaign of speaking out against gender and racial discrimination.

Savage was born the seventh of fourteen children to Reverend Edward and Cornelia Fells in Green Cove Springs, Florida. Green Cove Springs's brick yard provided her with the clay that became her earliest art material. Initially viewed as graven images, Savage's art eventually gained favor with her father when she began to sculpt figures inspired by the Bible. In 1907, she married John T. Moore, and from this union a daughter, Irene, was born. Moore died soon after the birth of their daughter. In the early 1920s, a second marriage to James Savage lasted only a few months. Following her quest to render the human form and tell stories through sculpture, she decided to join fellow black Southerners during the Great Migration and move to New York City.

Savage settled in Harlem and was offered opportunities to study and advance her career. In 1921, she gained admission to Cooper Union after studying for one year at Tallahassee State Normal School (later Florida A&M University). Although she was denied acceptance to a summer program in France due do her race, she made it her life's calling to fight injustice whenever it surfaced. Activist and scholar W. E. B. Du Bois became an early supporter of her work. Following the example of Harlem Renaissance artists Aaron Douglas, Palmer Hayden, Lois Mailou Jones, and others, she traveled to Europe to further develop her artistic perspective and skills. Through financial support provided by the Julius Rosenwald Fund, black women's groups, and black teachers at Florida A&M, Savage was able to pay for this advanced training and living expenses. Her international studies included the Académie la Grande Chaumière, a leading art school in Paris. In Italy, she studied with Felíx Benneteau-Desgrois, a noted winner of the Grand Prix of Rome.

Savage created naturalistic images that were in keeping with the period's mainstream art style. By countering the prevailing stereotypical images, she joined a growing number of artists who established a new and welcoming story of the "New Negro." This new movement, established by sociologist Charles S. Johnson and philosopher Alain Locke, allowed Savage to look to her own history and culture as inspiration for self-expression and exploration. Dignity and pride of the race, as espoused by Black Nationalist Marcus A. Garvey, became her lifelong mission.

In developing much of her portfolio, Savage looked to capture the images of those who symbolized the diversity of black life. The bust *Gamin*, one of her most well-known pieces, was modeled after a Harlem street-smart youth and later voted most popular in an exhibition of 250 works by black artists. Commissioned works include busts of fellow Floridian and poet James Weldon Johnson, W. E. B. Du Bois, and Marcus A. Garvey. Her most ambitious work is the *Lift Every Voice and Sing*, also known as *The Harp*. This six-foot-tall clay sculpture, which incorporates varying sizes of heads and bodies of black people that line up to form a harp, was commissioned by the 1939 New York World's Fair. In addition, Savage created sculptures of friends, European-inspired images, animals, and nudes.

Savage's exhibition schedule was supported by several national and international venues. An early supporter of her work was New York's Harmon Foundation, which promoted black artists from 1926 through 1967. Fellow exhibiting artists included Richmond Barthé, E. Simms Campbell, James Lesene Wells, Laura Wheeler Waring, and Nancy Elizabeth Prophet. Savage also exhibited at the Colonial Exposition in Paris, the 135th Street Branch of the New York Public Library, Argent Gallery in New York, Art Anderson Galleries in New York, and the American Negro Exhibition at Tanner Galleries in Chicago.

In the 1920s and 1930s, Savage contributed immensely to the cultural life of Harlem by establishing studio art programs and serving as a mentor. In 1931, her initial outreach was through the Savage Studio of Art and Crafts, one of the first Harlem art schools started by an African American. The school was also known as Savage Studios and the Uptown Art Laboratory, and it lasted until 1935. Later, while employed by the federal government's Works Progress Administration, she made a difference in the lives of 1,500 people of all ages by teaching art at the Harlem Community Art Center. Throughout the years, her students, which included Jacob Lawrence, Gwendolyn Knight, Ernest Crichlow, Norman Lewis, William Artis, and Elton Fax, became successful artists and art educators.

The sculptor and educator was also an arts activist and organizer throughout her career. In 1923, her application to attend a summer art school in Fontainebleau was rejected by the French government because of her race. Her protest of this decision proved especially effective and brought international attention to the biased actions of the Fontainebleau committee. Always determined, Savage became the first black artist elected to the National Association of Women Painters and Sculptures, and she played a major role in organizing the Harlem Artists' Guild and that organization's Vanguard Club.

Faced with many political and creative struggles, Savage continued to seek the success that would allow her an easier and more comfortable life; however, due to the extended family that she brought from Florida and the cost of being an artist, she continually encountered financial difficulties. Her inability to easily accept professional and personal slights did little to endear her to the art world. In spite of her many challenges, she managed to survive by getting whatever work she could.

In the 1940s, Savage moved to Saugerties, New York, where she began a reclusive life and produced little art work. She returned to New York City in 1961, to live with her daughter, and died a year later.—ROBERT L. HALL

SHELTON, RUTH ADA GAINES [RUTH GAINES SHELTON]
(April 8, 1872–1938) Playwright, teacher

Ruth Ada Gaines Shelton

Ruth Ada Gaines Shelton is a lesser-known writer of the Harlem Renaissance; however, her play *The Church Fight* (1925) generated buzz in Harlem circles when it won second prize in a literary contest in *Crisis* magazine in 1926. The play is notable for being one of the earliest comedies written by an African American.

Shelton was born in Glasgow, Missouri, on April 8, 1872. Her parents were Reverend George W. Gaines, an African Methodist Episcopal Church minister, and Mary Elizabeth Gaines. Shelton was raised by her father following the early death of her mother and nurtured by the tightly woven African American Midwest community. She received her education at Wilberforce University, an African American institution in Ohio, in 1895. Between 1894 and 1899, she taught in public schools in Montgomery, Missouri. She married William Obern Shelton in 1898. They had three children.

Shelton began writing in 1906. She predominately wrote church plays and plays for children. She is mostly known for the play *The Church Fight*. In this play, the main characters have names that associate them with a particular behavior and biblical names, for example, Brother Instigator, Sister Meddler, and Brother Judas. The work follows the lively exchanges between the church members concerning getting rid of the pastor and speaks to some of the universal experiences within the African American church, an institution that has played a central role in black life. The award that Shelton won from *Crisis* magazine for the play was an extraordinary achievement, as few opportunities existed for African Americans to display their talent in any meaningful way. *Crisis* played a large role during the Harlem Renaissance in showcasing new talent, providing enjoyment for African American audiences, and addressing news that was pertinent to African Americans and the struggle for equality. Works like *The Church Fight* that were published and awarded prizes were always of the highest quality.

Shelton also wrote other plays, including *Aunt Hagar's Children*, *The Church Mouse*, and *Parson Dewdrop's Bride*. She died in Montgomery, Missouri.—GLADYS L. KNIGHT

SHIPP, OLIVIA SOPHIE L'ANGE PORTER

(May 17, 1880–June 18, 1980) Musician, bass player

Olivia Sophie L'Ange Porter Shipp was a multitalented musician who performed in theater and orchestra and jazz bands, and she started her own band, the Jazz Mines, in the 1920s. She also founded the Negro Women's Orchestral and Civic Association, which helped female musicians find performance opportunities and supported other civic groups. Her contributions and influence span from the turn of the century to the early 1950s.

Shipp was born on May 17, 1880, in New Orleans, Louisiana. Her interest in music began as a child when she taught herself how to play the piano and took voice lessons from Abbey Lyons of the Fisk Jubilee Singers. Shipp was influenced and helped by her older sister May, who left home to join the Black Patti Troubadour Company and later settled in New York City, performing in vaudeville. When Shipp turned twenty, her sister sent for her as promised. Once in New York City, she began performing in vaudeville and, after hearing the cello, decided to take lessons. While taking lessons at the Martin-Smith School of Music, she also played both the piano and violin. In 1917, Shipp learned how to play the string bass and began performing in the Lafayette Theater Ladies Orchestra. To expand her opportunities even further, she learned to play the bass violin to perform in Marie Lucas's band.

The role as a musician and performer in show business was not considered the most respected of careers at the turn of the century. To protect her family from the negative connotations of her career, Shipp used the stage name Olivia Porter when she began appearing onstage. After her marriage to the son of actor Jesse Shipp, she used her married name. By the late 1920s, she had started her own band, the Jazz Mines, and she went on to establish the Negro Women's Orchestral and Civic Association. The organization was supported by the American Federation of Musicians Local #802, which flourished during the Harlem Renaissance.

Shipp died in New York City.—LEAN'TIN L. BRACKS

SMITH, ADA BEATRICE QUEEN VICTORIA LOUISE VIRGINIA [BRICKTOP]

(August 14, 1894–January 31, 1984) Entertainer, cabaret owner

Ada Beatrice Queen Victoria Louise Virginia Smith, also known as "Bricktop," was an entertainer and entrepreneur who performed in Chicago, New York, and elsewhere during the Harlem Renaissance era. In Paris during the 1920s, she entertained the "lost generation" of artists and writers. Her cabarets became the favorite of Europe's "Café Society." Smith was the toast of two continents, operating nightclubs in Paris, Mexico City, and Rome during a remarkable career that spanned five decades.

Smith was born in Alderson, West Virginia, on August 14, 1894. Her mixed-race mother had a light complexion, blonde hair, and gray-blue eyes. Ada had two sisters, Etta and Ethel, and a brother, Robert. Her father, who had a darker complexion and was slightly hunchbacked, was a barber who died when Ada was a young child.

Smith's mother moved the family to Chicago, where she operated a series of boarding houses. Ada was attracted to the stage at an early age. The family lived on Chicago's State Street, close to several saloons. The ambience of these establishments attracted Smith, who dreamed of becoming a saloon singer. When she turned sixteen, she dropped out of school and traveled the African American vaudeville circuit with a series of singing and dancing groups. This was a time of enforced segregation and discrimination against blacks.

Smith had a light complexion, red hair, and freckles. One night in Harlem, a saloon manager pointed to her flaming red hair and nicknamed her "Bricktop." From 1911 to 1921, Bricktop performed in saloons throughout the country. In 1922, she moved to New York, where she performed in nightclubs and speakeasies that defied Prohibition laws. During trips to Washington, D.C., she discovered a local band. Bricktop persuaded the owner of her nightclub to hire the group. The band's piano player, Edward "Duke" Ellington, went on to become one of America's greatest composers and performers.

In 1924, Bricktop received an offer from a Paris cabaret. The establishment, Le Gran Duc, was managed by Eugene Bullard, an African American who had been a fighter pilot in the Layette Escadrille during World War I. When she arrived at Le Gran Duc, Bricktop burst into tears of disappointment. The tiny room, with about twelve tables, was not what she expected. She was comforted by a busboy who took her to the kitchen for a meal. Years later, she learned that the busboy was Langston Hughes, one of the bright lights of the *Harlem Renaissance*.

After Bricktop's slow start, Fannie Ward, a wealthy former actress and Paris hostess, visited Le Gran Duc. She returned a few nights later with an entourage of wealthy friends. This was the beginning of what would become Bricktop's immense popularity. When F. Scott Fitzgerald discovered Bricktop's in 1925, the writers and artists that were his friends and acquaintances followed. Among them were such notables as Ezra Pound, Sherwood Anderson, Ernest Hemingway, and Pablo Picasso. Bricktop's club became the favorite night spot for the "lost generation."

In 1925, Josephine Baker arrived in Paris to appear in *La Revue Nègre*. When Baker performed *Danse Sauvage* almost nude, she became an overnight sensation. Bricktop took Josephine under her wing and showed her around Paris. When Baker began to consort with an Italian gigolo, Bricktop warned her about his unsavory reputation. This led to a dispute that ended Baker and Bricktop's friendship.

Bricktop married musician Peter Duconge in 1929. In 1931, she moved her cabaret to a nearby location and hired singer Mabel Mercer as an assistant. Sidney Bechet and Django Reinhart played in Bricktop's cabarets, as did Louis Armstrong,

Fats Waller, and Duke Ellington. Bricktop was known for her signature cigars and engaging personality. Her cabarets were known for their wealthy and glamorous clientele. She attributed her success to her friend and patron Cole Porter. She taught Porter's circle of wealthy friends how to dance the "Charleston" and entertained the "Café Society" at her cabarets and at private parties. Porter composed "Miss Otis Regrets" for Bricktop, and it became her signature song.

In 1939, Bricktop escaped Paris on one of the last departing boats before the German army invaded. In 1943, she moved to Mexico City, where she opened the Minuit, a popular nightclub. Bricktop returned to Paris after the war ended. In 1950, she opened a new cabaret, but it went out of business in December. In 1951, she moved to Rome, where she operated cabarets on the Via Veneto throughout the next two decades. Bricktop's clubs became the favorite watering hole for movie stars filming in Rome. She returned to the United States in 1965, where she made some unsuccessful comeback attempts, but when her health started to decline, she became less active. Bricktop died in her sleep in New York City.
—LELAND WARE

SMITH, BESSIE
(July 1892–April 12, 1937) Singer, entertainer, recording artist

Bessie Smith's performances were significant during the heart of the Harlem Renaissance in the 1920s and 1930s. She became known as the "Empress of the Blues" because of the strength and clarity of her voice, her unique phrasing, her performances while touring theatrical shows in the 1920s, and her pioneering career in the newly developing fields of phonograph records and motion pictures. Her high record sales greatly increased her influence, and her innovative styling made Smith more popular than others singing the same songs. She set high standards for other blues singers, developed the field, and became one of the highest-paid entertainers and a trendsetter. Her ability to improvise influenced the developing field of jazz vocalists.

Smith was a trailblazer in a new musical art form that became a mainstay of African American culture; it was a form of musical storytelling—the experiences of average African Americans artfully sung and explained—and it not only reflected African American culture, but also became a part of it. She often included "patter" in some of her songs—comments that add explanation and meaning to the song. Popular music, blues and jazz, was not highly valued by African American leaders in the 1920s and 1930s because it was not considered as "uplifting" as sculpture, painting, fiction, and poetry. Yet, popular music had substantial creativity, and Smith made an enormous contribution with frequent appearances in New York, Philadelphia, Chicago, Detroit, and other cities throughout the Northeast, Midwest, and South. She helped broadened the public's knowledge and acceptance of blues and popular music.

Smith was the daughter of William Smith and Laura Owens Smith, both born in Alabama. In 1870, they were living in Moulton, Lawrence County, Alabama; William was a part-time minister at a local Baptist church who earned a living as a laborer. Laura was the mother of five children and "kept house." Both parents worked at available jobs to support the family, probably on the Owens Plantation. By the 1890s, the family had moved to Chattanooga, Tennessee, where Bessie was born in 1892. In the absence of standardized birth certificates, the 1900 U.S. Census, which lists Bessie's birth as occurring in July 1892, is the first government record of her birth; however, the 1910 U.S. Census and subsequent records and references give April 15, 1894 as her birthdate. Smith herself gave the April 1894 date on her marriage certificate.

The size and composition of Smith's family is also uncertain. Bessie's father, William, died in the mid-1890s, after Bessie's birth. The 1900 U.S. Census indicates that her mother Laura had ten children, only seven of which were still living. After Laura's death in early 1900s, Bessie's sister Viola raised the younger children.

In addition, Smith's early activities as a singer and entertainer are unclear. Family legends state that Bessie and an older brother, Andrew, began entertaining on the streets, he playing the guitar while Bessie sang and danced to elicit donations to help with the family's finances. It is believed that Bessie quit school in the eighth or ninth grade and received no formal training in singing or dancing. Her success as a singer and entertainer depended on her natural ability, instincts, and superior ability to improvise.

According to family stories, Bessie's older brother Clarence joined the Moses Stokes traveling troupe around 1910 or 1911, when Bessie was too young to leave home. Clarence returned in 1912, and after an audition, Stokes hired Bessie as a dancer. Gertrude "Ma" Rainey, who was later called the "Mother of the Blues," was the featured singer in the Stokes troupe, and Rainey and Bessie formed a lifelong friendship. Bessie probably learned stage presence by watching Rainey, who is considered by many scholars as one of the greatest female blues singers in the history of the blues, second only to Bessie Smith.

In the early twentieth century, vaudeville was the dominant form of general entertainment for both local and touring groups. Vaudeville shows contained a variety of loosely related acts—singing, dancing, comedy, magic tricks, and group and solo performances. It is believed that efforts to develop a central booking agency for African American performers started with Sherman H. Dudley, a vaudeville performer who organized the Colored Actors' Union and began buying and leasing theaters in 1911. By 1913, he had developed the first black theatrical circuit, consisting of eight or nine theaters in Washington, D.C., and Virginia, half of which were owned or leased by Dudley. By 1916, more than twenty-eight theaters had joined the Dudley circuit, including some in the Midwest and South. This organization allowed black performers to book as many as eight months' worth of contracts through one office. It is believed that the better-known Theater Owners' Booking Association (TOBA), an interracial group, developed out of Dudley's pioneering efforts. TOBA was the dominant scheduling agency for black performers until its demise during the Depression era (the early 1930s).

In the 1910s, Smith worked as a singer and entertainer in a variety of places. As early as 1913, she was appearing at 81 Theater in Atlanta, which became a frequent stop and where she was favorably received by both the management and a growing set of local fans. By 1916, Smith was charting her own course, and her popularity was growing in each city in which she appeared. By 1921, she was alternating between appearing as a single with her own band and shows organized by others. By 1922, she had established an ongoing residence in Philadelphia and made it her home for the rest of her life.

Smith had a momentous year in 1923, as she started a stellar career recording phonograph records in February and married John Gee in June. Frank Walker, a white executive with Columbia Records, decided to expand the recordings of black female blues singers, believing that the records would sell profitably in the African American community and assuming a few whites would buy them. Records recorded by black musicians and singers for an anticipated African American public were labeled "race records." Smith's first recording session was on February 15, 1923, when she recorded two songs, "Downhearted Blues" and "Gulf Coast Blues." Walker and Columbia Records were pleasantly surprised when 780,000 copies were sold in a little more than five months. Walker scheduled Smith to record more songs, adding to her popularity and attendance at her shows throughout the United States. Smith recorded 159 songs for Columbia, one of the larger, more influential recording companies, with a distribution network much larger than other labels. From 1923 to 1931, Smith's recordings sold better than those of any other African American singer in the United States.

Making contracts for recording songs was unfamiliar to Smith and her future husband. After a false start working through pianist Clarence Williams, Smith was able to garner a more rewarding contract by working directly with Columbia Records through Frank Walker. Smith also asked Walker to be her business manager. He agreed, even though he should have been aware that it was a conflict of interest. Smith and other black entertainers and musicians were paid a flat fee for each side of the recording but no royalties for composing or performing the music; therefore, multiple sales of a record added to the income of the record company, but not that of the singers and musicians. Still, by 1924, Smith was commanding higher payments from Columbia Records and higher fees for shows. Smith's 1924 contract with TOBA made her the highest-paid black performer in the United States. She recorded with Columbia Records until a severe downturn in record sales due to the Depression ended their contractual relations in November 1931. Smith's last recording was arranged by John Hammond in November 1933. In addition, she was the star and central focus of a short seventeen-minute film, *St. Louis Blues*, in 1929.

On June 7, 1923, Smith married John Gee, frequently called "Jack," in Philadelphia. Jack worked as a night watchman, a job he quit two months after the marriage. As Smith's popularity and income grew, Jack benefitted and lived well. On three occasions, he was able to improve Smith's earnings by negotiating a better contract for her from Columbia Records, as well as higher fees for performances at theaters in Chattanooga and Detroit. Otherwise, his offers to help were largely counterproductive. By 1924, the marriage was strained, and mutual infidelity led to a permanent separation by 1929. Although Smith had romantic liaisons with several men and women at different times, Richard Morgan became her frequent companion and romantic interest from around 1931 until 1937.

From the mid-1920s through the onset of the Depression in 1929, Smith was in great demand and frequently traveled throughout the eastern half of the United States, giving a variety of performances. In most summers, she traveled extensively to towns with widely varying populations, putting on "tent shows"—highly organized and elaborate shows under a portable tent taken from city to city. Her older brother Clarence was especially valuable to the touring company. Since Smith was responsible for the entire company of performers and their supporting cast of workers, Clarence suggested that they buy a Pullman-type railroad car to take the show's members and the offstage workers from place to place. They purchased a seventy-eight-foot railroad car, custom made in Atlanta to Clarence's specifications. It could be attached to any train by prearrangement; had hot and cold running water; could provide traveling, dining, bathroom, and sleeping accommodations for forty to fifty people; and store the tent and other supplies used for the show. The car was painted bright yellow, with "Bessie Smith" scrolled on it in green letters. The car could be used in place of hotels on the road and helped avoid racial discrimination when trying to make travel arrangements and secure local accommodations. Clarence was also valuable on the road as a business manager, often helping to make up the payroll for the traveling troupe. Even though Clarence believed that the train car paid for itself on the first trip, economic factors dictated its sale by 1930.

The Depression greatly reduced the public's ability to afford the types of entertainment in which Bessie Smith thrived. Still, she was able to sing or participate in shows occasionally in the 1930s. In September 1937, she accepted a featured position in a traveling show, *Broadway Rastus*. Smith insisted on using her own automobile instead of riding the train. She did not drive and had Richard Morgan serve as her driver. At the close of a Saturday night show in Memphis, Tennessee, Smith insisted that Morgan drive them overnight to the next stop in Clarksdale, Mississippi. As they went down a narrow two-lane road, they encountered a slow-moving truck that was pulling back on the road. Morgan did not see it in time and could not stop before hitting the truck. The collision caused the Smith car to turn on its left side, throwing Smith onto the pavement and causing her severe bodily injury. A white medical doctor stopped at the scene of the accident and rendered all the assistance he could provide. She was taken by ambulance to a black hospital, but her injuries were too severe for her to recover.—DE WITT S. DYKES JR.

SMITH, CLARA
(1894–February 2, 1935) Singer, musician

Believed to be born in the Spartanburg, South Carolina, area, details of the early life of Clara Smith are vague. Reports of her performing in Southern vaudeville date to as early as 1910, and she sang in such venues as Dream Theatre in Columbus, Georgia. By 1918, she was a "headliner" (featured and lead performer) on the Theater Owners' Booking Association circuit, including venues in a number of U.S. cities that catered to African American audiences, for example, Howard Theatre in Washington, D.C., the Regal in Chicago, and the Apollo Theater in Harlem/New York City. Smith's unique performing style earned her the title "Queen of the Moaners," and she could also accompany her singing by playing the piano as necessary.

Despite her continued travels and tours, Smith settled in Harlem in the early 1920s, during the Harlem Renaissance era. There she initially performed at small clubs, cabarets, and speakeasies. She also furthered her career by becoming an entrepreneur, as well as a performer, managing herself while appearing in and sometimes producing numerous stage shows and revues, including the *Black Bottom Revue, Clara Smith Revue, Ophelia Snow from Baltimo', Swanee Club Revue,* and *Dream Girls and Candied Sweets* at such New York venues as the Lincoln, Lafayette, and Alhambra theaters. Smith eventually opened her own venue, the Clara Smith Theatrical Club, in 1924. It is also reported that future entertainment legend Josephine Baker began her show business career by joining one of Smith's traveling shows in Kansas City, Missouri, while still a teenager, assisting Smith with stage costumes and wardrobe before going onstage to participate in dance and comedy routines.

Smith made history as part of the first wave of African American women to make blues recordings, beginning with Paramount in 1923. While with Columbia, she recorded three duets with the legendary "Empress of the Blues," Bessie Smith, as well as solo sides with accompaniment by such legendary jazz musicians as trumpeter Louis Armstrong, saxophonist Coleman Hawkins, pianist/arranger/bandleader Fletcher Henderson, and pianist James P. Johnson. As with other female blues singers of the era, she sang songs with lyrics chock-full of sexual innuendos and double entendres, but Smith was also noted for bringing comedy, humor, and audience involvement into her performances, which added to her appeal and popularity. Despite her unique combination of talents, she was often mistaken for one of the other "Smith" female blues singers (Mamie, as well as Bessie) by less well-informed audiences. It did not help that Bessie and Clara sometimes pretended to be sisters, even though they were not blood relatives.

While Clara and Bessie never actually performed together in a live stage setting, their last duet recording, "My Man Blues," in 1925, reflects Clara's flair for humor, as they agree in the lyrics to "share the same man on the cooperation plan." They maintained a cordial friendship until a disagreement during a party later that same year. Accounts indicate that they got into an actual fist fight, and that one or both women may have been under the influence of alcohol at the time. From that point onward, they never spoke to one another.

Just as she was reported to be smaller in physical stature, Clara was also considered to be the second most accomplished female blues singer at Columbia Records, as her voice and style was lighter and less powerful than that of Bessie. Clara continued to record for Columbia until 1932.

Some of Smith's later appearances included singing with Charlie Johnson and his Paradise Band at the Harlem Opera House in 1930, performing with the pioneering African American comedienne Jackie "Moms" Mabley in an all-Negro Western

show *Trouble on the Ranch* at the Standard Theatre in Philadelphia in 1931, and taking part in the production *Harlem Madness* at the Harlem Fifth Avenue Theatre in 1933. Smith continued to perform until her death in Detroit from heart failure.
—FLETCHER F. MOON

SMITH, MAMIE [MAMIE ROBINSON]
(May 26, 1883–September 16, 1946) Blues singer

During the Harlem Renaissance era, Mamie Smith made history when she became the first woman and vocalist to record the blues. Her achievement was soon eclipsed by the other "Smith blues women" who followed her, most notably Bessie Smith, but also Clara Smith, Laura Smith, and Trixie Smith. Their varying levels of fame, success, and sometimes notoriety could cause confusion as to which Smith was being associated with various performances, recordings, and other activities, but Mamie's singular achievement retained her status as a pioneer recording artist in American music.

Born on May 26, 1883, as Mamie Robinson in Cincinnati, Ohio, it is reported that Smith left home around the age of ten to perform as a vaudeville singer and dancer with a white touring company called the Four Dancing Mitchells. As a teenager, she continued her career with a group known as "Salem Tutt Whitney's Smart Set" until 1912, and married her first husband, singer William "Smitty" Smith, during the same year.

Smith settled in New York the following year and, in 1918, was the featured and lead performer in a stage production by Perry Bradford entitled *Maid in Harlem*, which premiered at the Lincoln Theater in Harlem. By the age of thirty, Smith had established herself as a top New York vaudeville and cabaret entertainer, performing at such venues as Goldgraben's, Barron Wilkins's, Leroy's, Percy Brown's, and Edmund's. Bradford remained an important professional associate for Smith as a promoter, talent broker, composer, bandleader, and mentor who was instrumental in the process that led to Smith's landmark recording sessions.

Bradford approached managers at the two major companies, Columbia and Victor, regarding the possibility of making vocal, as well as instrumental, recordings. According to Bradford, Columbia was not interested, but on January 10, 1920, he convinced Victor to make a test recording of Smith singing his composition "That Thing Called Love."

Victor refused to release the record, but record dealers bootlegged the recording and received a tremendous response from the public. Bradford used this success as leverage with the General Phonograph Company's Okeh Records and rerecorded Smith singing "That Thing Called Love," plus another of his songs, "You Can't Keep a Good Man Down," on February 14, 1920. As a result, Okeh also made history as the first company to issue a vocal blues recording when the record was released during the summer of 1920. Their plan had been to record white singer Sophie Tucker first, but her illness provided Bradford with the opportunity to convince the label to record Smith instead.

In August 1920, Smith and Bradford returned to the studio to record what would become her most famous song, "Crazy Blues" (originally titled "Harlem Blues"), which sold an unprecedented 75,000 copies in the first month after it was released. This also established the African American community as a viable market for the music industry and a separate category called "race records." Columbia, Victor, and other companies quickly sought other African American female singers, while Smith continued her output with more recordings of vaudeville, as well as blues songs. Notable musicians who contributed to her recordings included pianists Willie "the Lion" Smith and James P. Johnson (the father of "stride" piano), saxophonist Coleman Hawkins, and trumpeter James "Bubber" Miley, who later gained fame as a member of Duke Ellington's orchestra. She also married two other times during the 1920s (comedian Sam Gardner and a man only known by his last name, Goldberg).

Smith's fame and popularity continued through the 1930s and 1940, and during her peak she commanded fees between $2,500 to $3,000 per performance when touring with her band, the Jazz Hounds. She also continued to appear in a number of Harlem musical revues at the Lafayette and Lincoln theaters; made a European tour around 1936; and took her talents to the silver screen by appearing in race-oriented films the likes of *Paradise in Harlem* (1939), *Mystery in Swing* (1940), *Murder on Lennox Avenue* (1941), *Sunday Sinners* (1941), and *Because I Love You* (1943).

During her final years, Smith suffered from an extended illness and died in Harlem Hospital in New York. She is interred at Frederick Douglass Memorial Park Cemetery on Staten Island, but her gravesite remained obscure until German jazz fans secured and transported a gravestone to the location between 1964 and 1965. The inscription reads as follows: "Mamie Smith/1883–1946/First Lady of the Blues/ Dedicated from the Hot Club and the city of Iserlohn."—FLETCHER F. MOON

SMITH, TRIXIE [TESSIE AIMES]
(1895–September 21, 1943) Blues singer, actress

Trixie "Tessie Aimes" Smith was born in Atlanta, Georgia, in 1895, to middle-class parents, and during her brief career, she performed with some of the leading musicians of the Harlem Renaissance. She attended college at Selma University in Selma, Alabama, and in 1915, she moved to New York City, where she performed in vaudeville and minstrel shows at the Lincoln Theater in Harlem.

In 1922, Smith signed with Black Swan Records, the same label as Ethel Waters. That same year, she finished first in the first-ever blues-singing contest held at Inter-Manhattan Casino in New York City, with the singing of her original song, "Trixie's Blues." She also gained notoriety with her recording of "My Man Rocks Me (With One Steady Roll)." The phrase "rock and roll" meant sexual intercourse in the black vernacular. In 1925, Smith recorded two songs, "Railroad Blues" and "The World Is Jazz Crazy and So Am I," both featuring Louis Armstrong on cornet. In addition, she made sides with Fletcher Henderson, Sidney Bechet, and the Original Memphis Five, an all-white band, as well as recordings with Decca Records and Paramount Records.

Smith made appearances in music revues, Broadway shows, and four films. She was multifaceted and deeply talented. One of the lasting testaments to her legacy is her train songs—"Freight Train Blues" and "Railroad Blues"—which capture the spirit of the Great Migration, as well as her own longing for a life of opportunity. —DELANO GREENIDGE-COPPRUE

SNOW, VALAIDA
(June 2, 1903–May 30, 1956) Singer, musician, dancer, actress

The versatile and talented Valaida Snow was popular during the Harlem Renaissance both in the United States and Europe. In music, she was best known for playing the trumpet, but she played as many as ten other instruments. Onstage, she performed with several luminaries of the Harlem Renaissance era, and in plays and musicals by some of the best-known black writers and musicians.

The daughter of John and Etta Snow, Valaida was born in Chattanooga, Tennessee, in 1903. Her early background is imperfectly known. Around 1920, she appeared in East Coast clubs and toured with Will Mastin's shows. By 1922, she had received widespread recognition as a performer. Among the variety shows and musicals in which she appeared were *Rambling Round* (1923), *Follow Me* (1923), and *In Bamville* (1924). Also in 1924, Snow appeared with Josephine Baker in Noble Sissle and Eubie Blake's *Chocolate Dandies*, the new name for *In Bamville*.

In 1926, Snow became understudy for Florence Mills in *Blackbirds* and performed in the show again in 1929 and 1934. She traveled the world and, in 1931, performed in Paris with Maurice Chevalier, who became her close friend. Snow was also known as an exceptional trumpet player, with a style that was compared to that of Louis Armstrong. She performed in Chicago's Sunset Café in 1928, when she played her horn, sang, and danced in the same show.

Snow's brief film career came in the late 1930s, when she was on the West Coast and briefly appeared in *Take It from Me* and *Irresistible You*. While she was in Europe later on, she appeared in *L'Alibi* (1936) and *Pièges* (1939), both French films, and established a brilliant reputation in Europe.

In 1934, Snow married dancer Ananais Berry, and in 1943 she married her manager and caretaker, Earle Edwards. She suffered a stroke in 1956, and died soon thereafter.—JESSIE CARNEY SMITH

SPENCE, EULALIE
(June 11, 1894–March 7, 1981) Writer, playwright, teacher

Known for her one-act plays, Eulalie Spence is considered an important figure in the history of African American female playwrights and drama of the Harlem Renaissance; she is one of the few female dramatists to receive formal training.

Spence was born on June 11, 1894, in Nevis, a British island in the Caribbean, the eldest of seven girls; her father was a sugar planter and her mother a well-educated storyteller. The family immigrated to New York after a devastating hurricane destroyed their crops and home. They struggled economically but maintained a supportive and nurturing home.

Inspired by the strength of her mother, Spence became interested in writing as a child and was encouraged to pursue education. She attended the New York Training School for Teachers in the early 1920s, and the Ethiopian Art Theatre School in 1924. A lifelong learner, in 1937, she graduated from New York University with a B.A., and she received an M.A. in speech from Columbia University in 1939; while at Columbia she also studied playwriting and was a member of the drama club.

Spence began working in the New York public schools in 1918, and was assigned to Eastern District High School in Brooklyn from 1927 until her retirement in 1958; there she taught English and dramatics and headed the drama group. Spence's place as a black teacher in a predominantly white school, along with her success as a productive and award-winning playwright, was groundbreaking.

A pioneer in the field, Spence may be considered one of the most prolific black female playwrights of her time, with fourteen known plays to her credit; at least eight of her works were published and seven produced during her lifetime. Her talent was recognized, and she received several awards. *Foreign Mail* (1926) placed second in *Crisis* magazine's literary competition, and *Fool's Errand* (1927), a satire on the gossip of church women, won $200 in the Fifth Annual Little Theatre Tournament. Also in 1927, Spence's dramas *The Hunch* and *The Starter* placed second and third, respectively, in *Opportunity* magazine's literature competition.

Most of Spence's works are set in Harlem. *Her* (1927) is a suspense drama about waiting for justice that also explores domestic violence, and *The Starter* explores the romantic relationship between an elevator starter and dress shop finisher. *Hot Stuff* (1927) presents Fanny King—prostitute, numbers runner, and peddler of stolen goods; *Episode* (1928) is an intimate and satirical look at negotiating time together in marriage, and *Undertow* (1929) presents an inside look at a married couple's conflicts.

Spence often created strong female characters who reflect inner strength and a defiant self-reliance, but she chose to work out of the conventional motif of protest of the period. The history of racial violence and oppression specific to the experience in the United States, especially the horrific acts of lynching, was unfamiliar to her because of her Caribbean heritage. She chose to focus on folk comedies and dramas instead of protest literature, creating characters familiar to the working-class audience. Many of her characters are victims of circumstances and indifference. Her use of black dialect in her works and onstage challenged the dominant notion of African American literature for racial uplift. This artistic commitment differed with W. E. B. Du Bois's philosophy; he attempted to persuade her to use her talents more in line with protest literature, but with no luck. Despite these differences, Spence was an active member of the Krigwa Players Little Negro Theatre, for which Du Bois served as chairman from its founding in 1926 to its closing in 1930, and three of her plays were produced there.

Many of Spence's plays were never published or produced until recently; other works include *Being Forty* (1920), *Brothers and Sisters of the Church Council* (1920), *La Divina Pastora* (1929), and *Wife Errant* (1928). Her only extant full-length play, the three-act comedy *The Whipping* (1932), is a dramatization of Roy Flannagan's 1930 novel of the same title; in it, Klansmen unsuccessfully attempt to run a promiscuous young woman out of town, and she in turn uses the media attention to launch a theatrical career. Spence personally secured the rights from Flannagan, as well as the same agent as Tennessee Williams to represent her. *The Whipping* was scheduled to open in Danbury, Connecticut, at the Empress Theatre but was canceled before the opening. Unable to move it into production, Spence eventually sold it to Paramount Pictures as a screenplay for $5,000. The writer and playwright devoted most of her life to community theater and her students; she died in Pennsylvania.—Adenike Marie Davidson

SPENCER, ANNE [ANNE BETHEL BANNISTER]
(February 6, 1882–July 27, 1975) Poet, teacher, librarian, activist, gardener

Anne Spencer began writing before the actual beginning of the Harlem Renaissance; however, she published in the major periodicals and anthologies of the era. In addition, she was a friend and confidante of the Harlem Renaissance literati.

Spencer was born near Danville in Henry County, Virginia, the only child of Joel Cephus Bannister and Sarah Louise Scales Bannister. After a period, the couple divorced, and Sarah and Anne moved to Bramwell, West Virginia. Sarah resumed her maiden name and, because of economic straits, placed Anne with William T. Dixie, a prominent black resident. Available to her in his household were newspapers and dime novels, which aided in her language development and appreciation of the power of words. Recognizing Spencer's achievements, her mother enrolled her in Virginia Seminary (previously the Lynchburg Baptist Seminary) in 1893. It was here that Spencer's independence of thought and intellectual aggressiveness were first exhibited. She questioned the religious teachings of the institution and wrote her first poem, "The Skeptic." Consequently, she was asked to give the 1899 valedictory speech at the seminary, even though she was not the valedictorian. During her years at the institution, she also met her future husband, fellow 1899 graduate Edward Alexander Spencer.

Spencer taught for two years in West Virginia and then returned to Lynchburg to marry Edward on May 15, 1901. The couple moved to 1313 Pierce Street, where they were to live out their married lives. Here they raised their three children, Bethel Calloway, Alroy Sarah, and Chauncey Edward. The Spencer home became a place for prominent artists and educators of the day who journeyed through the South at a time when Jim Crow laws limited hotel accommodations for traveling African Americans. Spencer cultivated a garden, which, in 1920, became a place of Edenic peace and meditation. Because she spent so much time in the garden retreat, her husband had a cottage erected called Edankraal, a combination of Edward, Anne, and the Afrikaan term for enclosure. She was hostess to numerous celebrities of the day, with such attendees as W. E. B. Du Bois, Georgia Douglas Johnson, Langston Hughes, and Paul Robeson. In later years, Spencer hosted Gwendolyn Brooks, Maya Angelou, and Lady Bird Johnson. She also tutored Ota Benga, a pigmy from the Congo who was sent to the Virginia Theological Seminary and College in Lynchburg in 1910, after being exploited as a curiosity. Spencer taught at her alma mater from 1910 to 1912.

Noted among the many personalities who visited Spencer was James Weldon Johnson. Johnson discovered Spencer's talent as a poet and encouraged her to publish. Even though she had written poetry at Virginia Seminary, it was not until she met Johnson that she published her first poem, "Feast at Sushan," a work based on the Book of Esther, in the 1920 issue of *Crisis*. Johnson also selected her pen name, Anne Spencer, and introduced her to H. L. Mencken, who was prepared to aid her; however, Spencer declined his assistance since he was not a poet. During her association with Johnson, who at the time was secretary of the National Association for the Advancement of Colored People, she worked with him to establish the Lynchburg Chapter. Spencer continued to demonstrate the same independence of thought and intellectual acumen that she had shown during her school days. Prior to the 1920s, she campaigned to remove white teachers from the all-black Jackson High School in Lynchburg, since black teachers could not teach in the white schools. She often challenged racism by refusing to ride segregated public transportation or follow injurious Jim Crow laws. Like Zora Neale Hurston, she spoke out against school integration in the 1950s. As librarian at Dunbar High School in Lynchburg from 1923 to 1945, Spencer exposed students to otherwise inaccessible books by using her own books and those borrowed from her employer. In spite of these actions and her push for the rights of all humankind, the majority of her poetry does not show this element of protest.

Spencer's poetry, which was often found on napkins, scraps of paper, paper bags, in margins, and in other unconventional locations, reflects her garden in its biblical and spiritual nature in the midst of the sordid realities of the world. She wrote about universal themes and nature, and periodically dealt with issues that cause her to be considered a feminist by some. This is evident in "White Things" (1923) and "Lady, Lady" (1925). Some of her poems indicate her absorption with nature, including "Lines to a Nasturtium (A Lover Muses)" and "Earth, I Thank You." Spencer's works are generally short, in traditional forms: elegies, sonnets, and epigrams, using varied rhythms and rhyme schemes. Her style is both modernist in its complexity and neo-romantic in its love of nature, of the simple and the ordinary, and its use of a strong imagination. She utilizes both biblical and mythological themes.

The height of Spencer's publication career came in the 1920s, when her work appeared in prominent periodicals and anthologies. Although a number of sources carried her poems, she did not publish a prodigious amount of poetry during her lifetime. She appeared in *Crisis*, *Opportunity*, *Lyric*, and *Survey Graphic*. The anthologies in which her work appears are James Weldon Johnson's *Book of American Negro Poetry* (1922), Robert T. Kerlin's *Negro Poets and Their Poems* (1923), Louis Untermeyer's *American Poetry since 1900* (1923), and Alain Locke's *The New Negro* (1925). An indication of the esteem in which she was held as a poet is evident in the fact that ten of her poems appear in Countee Cullen's *Caroling Dusk* (1927), a collection of black poetry. Her work also appears in *The Poetry of the Negro, 1746–1949* (1948), edited by Langston Hughes and Arna Bontemps.

Spencer almost totally withdrew from writing and life upon the death of her husband in May 1964. She died of cancer and is buried beside her husband in the family plot at Forest Cemetery in Lynchburg. The Anne Spencer House and Garden was designated a Virginia Historic Landmark in 1976; the site is open to the public daily and for tours. Spencer's works continue to be anthologized. Her papers are housed in the Albert and Shirley Small Special Collection Library at the University of Virginia at Charlottesville.—HELEN R. HOUSTON

SPILLER, ISABELE TALIAFERRO
(March 18, 1888–May 14, 1974) Musician, music educator

Born in Abingdon, Virginia, and educated in Philadelphia's public schools, Isabele Taliaferro Spiller was well-known in music circles. After graduating from the New England Conservatory of Music in Boston, she joined a popular vaudeville act, the Musical Spillers, in 1912. She eventually married the band's leader, William Newmeyer Spiller, and toured with the group throughout the United States. Although versatile and adept at playing several instruments, Spiller was best known as a saxophonist for the group. Although she was skilled in playing different musical instruments (sometimes while dancing), she was also recognized for her talent as a stern musical teacher. In addition to being the primary teacher for the band, Spiller gave music lessons to young, talented musicians performing vaudeville acts, as well as accomplished musicians who wanted to strengthen their craft. In the mid-1920s, her musical focus shifted from performer to educator.

Spiller's "official" career as music educator began in 1926, when she and her husband established the Musical Spillers School in their home in Harlem. Their school and home was thought to have been a sort of "unofficial headquarters" for much of the music that came out of Harlem in the 1920s and 1930s. During the late 1920s and early 1930s, Spiller established herself as a masterful educator of music. In addition to teaching music at the Musical Spillers School, she was director of music at the Brooklyn Young Women's Christian Association, as well as director of music at the Columbus Hall Center. As her career as a music educator gained momentum and propelled her into different arenas, Spiller supervised various music education projects, including New York City's Federal Music Project, the Breeze Hill Civilian Conservation Corps Camp, and music education projects at the 1939 World's Fair in New York. Other noteworthy accomplishments by Spiller during her lifetime include being awarded a scholarship and furthering her education at the Juilliard School of Music, being named conductor of the Wadleigh Senior High School Orchestra, and organizing and conducting the Harlem Evening High Orchestra. A well-rounded educator and scholar, she also wrote several articles on music pedagogy. Her works appeared in such publications as *Etude*, *Metronome*, and *Jacobs' Orchestra Monthly*.

By the time of her death in 1974, Spiller had made an indelible mark on the early Harlem musical scene. A pioneer and legendary figure in music education, she made positive contributions to African American music and music education that are still evident in today's African American music students.—SONCEREY L. MONTGOMERY

SPIVEY, VICTORIA

(October 15, 1906–October 3, 1976) Singer, entrepreneur, musical stalwart

Victoria Spivey was a blues songstress who used her musical expression to capture the spirit of the Harlem Renaissance. She was known as the "Queen of Blues" and used her musical talents as an adolescent to perform in clubs to help support her family. During the height of the Harlem Renaissance, Spivey expressed the pain, loss, and depression in combating racism and discrimination with her sultry voice. She performed in the 1929 musical *Hallelujah* and was also a songwriter, manager, producer, and underestimated businesswoman. Spivey recorded her first song, "Black Snake Blues," during the peak of the Harlem Renaissance. She worked as a writer for the St. Louis Publishing Company in the late 1920s and captured the spirit of the St. Louis expression of the blues.

Spivey brought to the blues the expression of pain and agony through her melodic groans and moans, birthed in her Texas upbringing. She began performing at the young age of twelve in Houston, Texas, her birthplace. She began working with Blind Lemon Jefferson. In her later years, Spivey was an active blues aficionado and remained so until her death. She provided researchers with an invaluable perspective on the development of the blues during the span of four decades. The pain that was communicated through the breakthrough of the Harlem Renaissance era would have a lasting legacy through the voice of Spivey. She is known for her performances with legendary musical geniuses Louis Armstrong, Gertrude "Ma" Rainey, and Bessie Smith.—SHEILA R. PETERS

STAFFORD, MARY

(ca. 1895–ca. 1938) Jazz singer, blues singer, band leader

Mary Stafford was a pioneering American jazz and blues singer in the cabaret style. Under the name Mary Stafford and Her Jazz Band, she was the first African American woman to record for Columbia Records. Her style was also a good rhythm for the foxtrot, a dance that was popular during the Harlem Renaissance.

There is scant information available about Stafford's life. She was born circa 1895. Sometime around 1915, she came to the East from Missouri. In Baltimore, she worked with famous composer and pianist Eubie Blake. She toured many venues throughout the Mid-Atlantic states during the 1920s and 1930s, and was backed by Charlie Johnson's Orchestra, in which her brother, George Stafford, was a drummer.

Jazz music began in New Orleans around the turn of the twentieth century. Between 1893 and World War I, jazz was so trendy that most records with the word *jazz* in the title were sure hits. Jazz was different from ragtime, marching music, and the blues because of its use of improvisation. The "discovery" of Mamie Smith in 1920 started the "race record" industry, which introduced jazz to the bigger community, including white listeners.

Stafford's style was a clear-voiced, airy vaudeville style; different from the "shouters" who sang in the hollering style of plantation songs, Stafford's music is dominated by reeds. This made her a natural for the early recording equipment of the 1920s jazz industry. She was accompanied by such future stars as Charlie Gaines, Charlie Johnson, and Ben Whitted.

Some of Stafford's early hits were recorded by the Pathe Actuelle Company, and in January 1921, she was signed by contract exclusively to Columbia Records, where she turned out a variety of hit records. Some of her most important songs are "Crazy Blues," "Ain't Got Nobody to Grind My Coffee," "Strut Miss Lizzie," and "Take Your Finger Off It."

In the Lafayette Theater in New York City, Stafford appeared in the *Rocking Chair Review* in 1931, as well as *Dear Old Southland* in 1932. Also in 1932, she worked in Atlantic City, New Jersey, with Bessie Smith. While Smith's death was honored with a superstar funeral in 1937, Stafford died in obscurity in Atlantic City, New Jersey away from the entertainment field.—ELIZABETH SANDIDGE EVANS

SUL-TE-WAN, MADAME [NELLIE CONLEY]
(September 12, 1873–February 1, 1959) Actress

The career of Madame Sul-Te-Wan was that of a talented actress both onstage and on-screen, and one that embraced and exceeded the Harlem Renaissance years. Despite her appearance in the controversial film *The Birth of a Nation*, she became the first African American to be hired by a major movie producer on a continuing basis.

Louisville, Kentucky, native Madame Sul-Te-Wan, whose given name was Nellie, was the daughter of Cleo de Londa, a washerwoman and later a burlesque dancer, and Silas Crawford Wan, a Hindu minister and native of Hawaii. Silas died when his daughter was young, and after that, Nellie and her mother moved to Cincinnati, Ohio. By then Nellie had already worked in an all-black novelty act, which perhaps helped Creole Nell, as she called herself, find vaudeville work in Cincinnati's German immigrant neighborhood. She performed in other local spots and later joined the Three Black Cloaks Company, which was touring in Cincinnati at the time. After that, she began to organize her own show companies. When she took the name Madame Sul-Te-Wan is unclear.

Sul-Te-Wan married around 1906, had three sons, and moved to California, but she soon became a deserted wife and mother. Struggling to make a living, she joined D. W. Griffith in his controversial and stereotypical movie *The Clansman*. In 1915, the film was renamed *The Birth of a Nation* and became a popular and financial success to all except the African American community. The extent of her contracts with Griffith is unclear; however, in 1916, she also appeared in his film *Intolerance*. Griffith accused Sul-Te-Wan of joining protests against his first film and fired her; she sued and was then rehired.

During the silent-film era, Sul-Te-Wan appeared in a number of films, including *Hoodoo Ann* (1916), *The Children Play* (1916), *The Lightning Rider* (1924), *Manslaughter* (1922), *The Narrow Street* (1925), and *Uncle Tom's Cabin* (1927). She continued to perform onstage and in films for more than seventy years and was seen late in life in *Rhapsody in Blue* (1945), *Carmen Jones* (1954), and *Porgy and*

Bess (1959). After three marriages and a highly successful career, Sul-Te-Wan died in California at the age of eighty-six.—JESSIE CARNEY SMITH

SYLVESTER, HANNAH [GENEVIA SCOTT]
(1900–October 15, 1973) Singer

Hannah Sylvester, also known as Genevia Scott (her mother's given name), was an accomplished singer, performer, and actress from the 1920s well into the 1960s, primarily in New York. Her performance as a singer consisted of sexy moves and bawdy lyrics that were replicated in her stage and film roles. She was often billed in films as the "Sepia Mae West."

Sylvester, born in Philadelphia, Pennsylvania, in 1900, began singing and dancing at the age of three. She was considered a child prodigy and performed throughout the city until her move to New York City in 1920. Once in New York, Sylvester performed in many of the major clubs in Harlem, for instance, the Cotton Club, Club Harlem, and the Nest Club. She also performed in such successful theater productions as *Look Who's Here* (1928), *Jazzola* (1929), *Ballyhoo* (1931), the *All Star Revue* (1933), and the *X-Glamour Girls Revue* (1962). She continued her singing and touring well into the 1950s, with the Snookum Russell Orchestra in the 1940s and occasionally with the Buddy Tate Band in the 1950s.

Sylvester worked well into the 1970s, until her death.—LEAN'TIN L. BRACKS

T

TALBERT, MARY MORRIS BURNETT
(September 17, 1866–October 15, 1923) Activist

Mary Morris Burnett Talbert's abilities as an organizer and commitment as an activist impacted many of the important issues of her day. She had such key roles as vice president of the National Association for the Advancement of Colored People (NAACP), chairman of the Dyer Antilynching Bill Committee, and delegate to the International Council of Woman.

Born in Oberlin, Ohio, on September 17, 1866, Talbert graduated from high school at the age of sixteen and went on to Oberlin College. Although literature was her focus in college, the institution encouraged her ideals regarding community service. Her classmates, who also benefited from their experience at Oberlin and became activists in their community, were well-known women, including Anna Julia Cooper, Mary Church Terrell, and Hallie Q. Brown.

Talbert graduated from Oberlin in 1886, and accepted a teaching position at Bethel University in Little Rock, Arkansas, a segregated school during that time. She was later appointed assistant principal at Bethel, making her the first woman to be named in this role in the state. The following year, she was named principal of Union High School in Little Rock. In 1891, Talbert married William Herbert Talbert and moved to Buffalo, New York. The couple had their first and only child in 1892. While in Buffalo, Talbert turned her interest more directly toward organizations and activism, since married women were prohibited from teaching in public schools.

In Buffalo, Talbert found many women to join with in addressing cultural and social concerns. She became a charter member and later president of the Phyllis Wheatley Club in 1899, an affiliate of the National Association of Colored Women (NACW); founder and president of the Empire State Federation of Colored

Women, which focused on prison reform from 1911 to 1916; and president of the Christian Culture Congress. Talbert's actions in confronting such issues as challenging an all-white board of commissioners for excluding African Americans from the Buffalo Pan-American Exposition earned her attention from the national NACW. She was elected president of NACW from 1916 to 1920. It was during her term as president that Anacostia, the home of Frederick Douglass in Washington, D.C., was purchased and restored. Talbert represented the NACW as a full member of the International Council of Women and addressed delegates in Christiana, Norway, in 1920. She also founded the International Council of Women of the Darker Races of the World in 1921, and worked tirelessly with the NAACP.

Talbert championed support of World War I efforts and fair treatment of African American soldiers, and from 1918 to 1923, she was elected vice president and board member of the NAACP. As vice president, Talbert was national director of the anti-lynching campaign that supported the Dyer Antilynching Bill. Although the bill was never passed by Congress, Talbert was able to organize the raising of enough funds to advertise a listing of the atrocities of lynching. This helped increase the support of many whites and empowered new female voters to support the bill.

Talbert committed her time and energy as an organizer, activist, and promoter of human rights for people of color throughout her life. She advocated for causes that were both national and international, and was honored in 1922, with the most prestigious recognition as the first woman to be awarded the Spingarn Medal from the NAACP. Talbert died of coronary thrombosis at her home in Buffalo, New York.
—LEAN'TIN L. BRACKS

TARRY, ELLEN
(September 26, 1906–September 23, 2008) Children's writer, autobiographer, biographer, journalist

Considered a minor figure of the Harlem Renaissance, Ellen Tarry contributed to the *New York Amsterdam News*, was active in Catholic social activist organizations in Harlem, and is considered a pioneer in African American children's literature.

Tarry was born in Birmingham, Alabama, on September 26, 1906, to John Tarry, a barber and deacon in the First Congregational Church, and Eula Meadows Tarry, a seamstress. In 1921, after the death of her father, she attended St. Francis de Sales, a Catholic boarding school in Virginia, where she converted to Catholicism. The social mission of Catholicism spoke to her and would increasingly become part of her work, as she was a contributor to *Commonweal* and *Catholic World*, examining issues that she felt to be obstacles to African Americans embracing the Catholic Church.

Tarry returned to Alabama and studied at the State Normal School for Negroes with plans to teach; she held several teaching positions in Birmingham and wrote for the *Birmingham Truth* in a regular column entitled "Negroes of Note," which explored African American heritage, celebrated key figures, and condemned racial segregation. In 1929, she decided to pursue writing full time, moved to New York and joined the Negro Writers' Guild, and befriended fellow writer Claude McKay.

Committed to using her writing to promote racial justice, Tarry attended the Cooperative School for Student Teachers on scholarship from 1937 to 1939, where she studied writing literature for children.

In New York, Tarry was also active in the Roman Catholic intellectual circles and the Friendship House missionary project, led by Catherine de Hueck. She regularly lectured at the Friendship House on racial injustice and assisted in opening a Chicago branch. Tarry was committed to promoting Catholic race relations and desegregating the Catholic Church. She was briefly married and had a daughter in 1944. She worked for the National Catholic Community Service, the USO, and the U.S. Department of Housing and Urban Development.

During her teaching years, Tarry recognized the dearth of children's literature, examining urban life from a realistic point of view. By the end of the 1940s, she had published three books that were favorably received. Her first book, *Janie Bell* (1940), examines an African American child who has been abandoned and the white nurse who adopts her. *Hezekiah Horton* (1942) tells the tale of a young African American boy and his love of cars, which he must admire from afar, until he develops a friendship with Mr. Ed and his convertible. *My Dog Rinty* (1946)—cowritten with Marie Hall Els—is the story of a young African American boy who is assisted by kind white strangers in finding his lost dog. Her last children's book, *The Runaway Elephant* (1950), is based on an actual news story and reunites readers with Hezekiah and Mr. Ed. Tarry avoided stereotypes, and the innocent interracial friendships in her texts seem simple but were shocking and groundbreaking for the time period; she desired to improve race relations by promoting such interactions as normal.

In addition to children's books, Tarry wrote biographies of figures whose stories were neglected. These include *Saint Katherine Drexel: Friend of the Oppressed* (1958), *Martin De Porres: Saint of the New World* (1963), *Young Jim: The Early Years of James Weldon Johnson* (1967), and *The Other Toussaint: A Modern Biography of Pierre Toussaint, a Post-Revolutionary Black* (1981).

In 1955, Tarry published her autobiography, *The Third Door: The Autobiography of an American Woman*, in which she uses her own life story to explore and document the impact of such issues as segregation, racism, and the Great Depression on the African American community, while remaining optimistic about the future. She also continued her campaign against religious prejudice as a Catholic and presented the internal conflicts of color and passing within an economic system in which class and race were entwined. Fully active late in life and honored as a "living legend," Tarry died in New York City.—ADENIKE MARIE DAVIDSON

TAYLOR [WILLIAMS], EVA [IRENE GIBBONS]
(January 22, 1895–October 31, 1977) Blues and vaudeville singer, stage actress

Born into a family of twelve children in St. Louis, Missouri, Irene Gibbons became a performer at an early age and traveled nationally and internationally with a vaudeville troupe under her stage name, Eva Taylor. While still a teenager, she appeared as a chorus girl in a 1911 production featuring entertainment legend Al

Jolson. By her mid-twenties, she had met and married Clarence Williams, a noted pianist, singer, songwriter/composer, arranger, bandleader, theatrical producer, promoter, and music publisher during the Harlem Renaissance era, and settled in New York City to continue an active singing career with her husband's trio and "Blue Five" groups, as well as other theatrical revues and productions.

Taylor successfully raised three sons, maintained her marriage and professional relationships with Williams, and made her own mark in show business with her husband and such other Harlem Renaissance entertainers as Noble Sissle, Eubie Blake, Florence Mills, Bessie Smith, Ethel Waters, Joe "King" Oliver, and Cab Calloway. She recorded for Columbia, Black Swan, Okeh, Victor, Edison, and other companies; was the first African American female soloist to broadcast on national and international radio networks; and hosted her own radio program during the 1930s.

After her husband's death in 1965, Taylor spent her final years in New York and was interred next to him upon her death. Their grandson, Clarence Williams III, went on to have a notable career as a television and movie actor.—FLETCHER F. MOON

TERRELL, MARY CHURCH [MARY ELIZA CHURCH]
(September 23, 1863–July 14, 1954) Educator, clubwoman, writer, activist, public speaker

Mary Church Terrell

Mary Church Terrell was born in 1863, the year of the Emancipation Proclamation, and died in 1954, the year of the U.S. Supreme Court's *Brown v. Board of Education* school desegregation decision. By the end of World War I, she was already fifty-five years old. Thus, at the flowering of the Harlem Renaissance, she had obtained a college degree, taught, traveled, and published.

Terrell had an exceptional childhood and education for a person of color in the nineteenth century. She was born Mary Eliza Church in Memphis, Tennessee, on September 23, 1863. She was the eldest child of Louisa (Ayers) Church and Robert Reed Church, both former slaves. With her family's aid, Mary received an excellent education, followed by extended travel in Europe. After obtaining her undergraduate degree, her father urged her to settle down for a life of leisure in his home, but Terrell wanted to work for the uplift of African Americans and women, and she braved her father's disapproval to do so. She married Robert Heberton Terrell in October 1891. They had one child.

During Terrell's long and notable life, she worked tirelessly to improve the social, economic, and political conditions for African Americans. Her excellent education equipped her for a career that began with teaching and continued with leadership positions in the Colored Women's League and later the National Association of Colored Women (NACW). She became founding president of NACW in 1895. Terrell worked vigorously for women's suffrage and women's rights, particularly black women's rights. She was an internationally known speaker and lecturer, a widely published writer, a member of numerous boards and associations, and a founding member of a church in Washington, D.C. The educator and activist was also a charter member of the National Association for the Advancement of Colored People.

In 1920, Terrell was asked by the Republican National Committee to be the supervisor of the work among black women in the Eastern United States. Her assignment was to talk with women's groups about exercising their newly acquired right to vote by supporting the Republican Party platform. Terrell continued to work with the Republican Party, campaigning in 1929, for Ruth Hannah McCormick, who ran unsuccessfully for U.S. senator from Illinois. In 1932, Terrell served as an advisor to the Republican National Committee during the Herbert Hoover presidential campaign. During the intervening years, she was active with the party, helping in whatever ways she could. She remained an active member of the Republican Party until she joined the presidential campaign of Adlai Stevenson, a Democrat.

Terrell led and won the fight to desegregate Washington, D.C., a struggle that was finally resolved by the U.S. Supreme Court in 1953, just a year before her death. Many of the major players—statesmen, politicians, teachers, and literati—in the century after the Civil War were Terrell's personal friends or acquaintances, including Booker T. Washington, Frederick Douglass, Nannie Helen Burroughs, Mary McLeod Bethune, and W. E. B. Du Bois. Numerous other noted African American leaders worked alongside Terrell in "racial uplift" endeavors.

In 1940, the culmination of Terrell's writing career involved the publication of her autobiography, *A Colored Woman in a White World*, with a preface by H. G. Wells. In this work, she traces her life from her early childhood days, emphasizing her experiences growing up and living in a white-dominated America. She dedicated much of the book to the discussion of the community activism in which she had been involved for much of her life.—DEBRA NEWMAN HAM

THOMAS, EDNA LEWIS
(1886–July 22, 1974) Actress, activist

Edna Lewis Thomas, a leader in the black theater movement of the Harlem Renaissance, was one of the most popular members of A'Lelia Walker's social circle and a close friend to Carl Van Vechten. She also acted in hundreds of vaudeville, black theater, and Broadway plays, and was a proponent of racial uplift through activism.

Thomas was born in Lawrenceville, Virginia, in 1886, before moving to Boston. At the age of sixteen, she married the son of J. H. Lewis, although he later died of tuberculosis. Thomas returned to school to study music before working as social secretary and tutor to Madame C. J. Walker. Through Walker, Edna met her second husband, Lloyd Thomas.

Thomas's talent for acting and singing was discovered by the Lafayette Players during her performance in a benefit for J. Rosamond Johnson's music school. In 1920, she accepted the lead role in *Confidence*, which launched her prolific career, involving more than 100 roles. During the span of nearly thirty years, Thomas acted with the Lafayette Players, the Ethiopian Art Theater, the Alhambra Players, and the Works Progress Administration (WPA) Federal Theater. She also appeared on Broadway. In addition, she made appearances in movies and on the radio. By 1936, Thomas caught the attention of Orson Welles, who cast her as Lady Macbeth in his WPA Federal Theater adaptation of *Macbeth*. In 1947, she appeared in *A Streetcar Named Desire* and its subsequent revivals, including the 1951 film. During the course of her career, Thomas was a proponent for civil rights. She worked as an administrative assistant and acting head supervisor for the WPA Federal Theater Project, was on the board of directors for the Negro Playwrights Company, and was a founding leader of the Negro Actors' Guild.

Between 1967 and 1968, Thomas lost the two people closest to her: Olivia Wyndham and Lloyd Thomas. The three had lived together since the 1920s. Thomas died of heart disease in New York.—AMANDA J. CARTER

THOMPSON, CLARA ANN
(1869–March 20, 1949) Poet, lecturer, teacher

During the 1920s, Clara Ann Thompson wrote and presented readings of her poetry, works whose themes echo those addressed by black female writers of the period. She was the daughter of former slaves John Henry Thompson and Clara Jane Gray Thompson. She was born in Rossmoyne, Ohio, one of five children. Two of her siblings, Priscilla Jane and Aaron Belford, wrote and published poetry; another brother, Garland Yancey, was a sculptor. Clara was educated at the Amity School and by a private tutor. She lived most of her life with her sister, Priscilla, and her brother, Garland. Thompson's time was spent writing poetry and holding readings; she published two volumes of poetry. Her membership in the National Association for the Advancement of Colored People, Baptist church, and Young Women's Christian Association indicate her social consciousness and commitment to politics and religion.

Thompson's first volume of poems, *Songs from the Wayside*, was published in 1908, and dedicated to Priscilla and Garland. In this collection appear "Uncle Rube on the Race Question," "Uncle Rube's Defense," and "Uncle Rube to the Young People." Uncle Rube is a wise old man who speaks in dialect to a silent white man and is similar to Charles Chesnutt's Uncle Julius McAdoo and Langston Hughes's Alberta K. Johnson. His broken English marks him as unlettered and disguises his wisdom. By using this masking technique, Uncle Rube, like Alberta K. Johnson, makes astute observations about race relations. Thompson shared with Hughes a veracity that was not one sided. Uncle Rube knows that the black man also has

weaknesses and faults, and needs to be free to act without having to answer to another or have his actions monitored.

In addition to the Uncle Rube poems, there are occasional and seasonal poems,
including "Memorial Day," "The Christmas Rush," "The Easter Light," and "The
Autumn Leaves." Thompson's use of dialect is not limited to Uncle Rube; a poem
like "Mrs. Johnson Objects" has the dialect, monologue, and racial criticism found
in the Uncle Rube poems. Just as the poet comments on the issue of race, she also
addresses Christianity, both the preaching and the practice. The promise and hope
in Christianity is sung in "Not Dead, But Sleeping," "Out of the Deep: A Prayer,"
and "I Follow Thee." "Lost Love," "Parted," and "If Thou Shouldest Return" are
poems that allude to love and relations, and are contemporaneous in theme with
those by such writers as Georgia Douglas Johnson.

Thompson's second volume of poetry, *A Garland of Poems*, was published by
a Boston press and reflects the social conditions of the twentieth century and the
human condition. *A Garland of Poems* includes poems about black men in World
War I, for example, "Our Soldiers" and "Our Heroes"; religion, for instance, "Consecration" and "Communion Prayer"; and elegies, with "Life and Death" and "Our
Deceased Leader" being examples. Here, Thompson uses dialect, gives advice,
makes observations about race relations, and writes about the human condition—
its foibles and pain.

Thompson spent her later years in Cincinnati, living with a niece and serving as a
catechism instructor at St. Andrews Episcopal Church, Mt. Healthy. She is buried
in the Colored American Cemetery in Oakley, Ohio.—HELEN R. HOUSTON

THOMPSON, ELOISE ALBERTA VERONICA BIBB
(June 28, 1880–January 8, 1928) Writer, journalist

The writings of Eloise Alberta Veronica Bibb Thompson are important in the
African American literary tradition seen during the Harlem Renaissance. Her works
reflect her faith in her race and her opposition to the racial inequality that she saw
in American society.

Thompson was born in New Orleans, Louisiana, on June 28, 1880, the only child
of Charles H. and Catherine Adele Bibb. While still a teenager, she published her
first book of verse, *Poems* (1895), and dedicated it to her contemporary, writer Alice
Ruth Moore [Dunbar]. Thompson studied at Oberlin College Preparatory Academy
from 1899 to 1901, and then returned to New Orleans, where she taught school for
two years. She entered the Teacher's College at Howard University and graduated
in 1908. From 1908 to 1911, she was head resident at the Colored Social Settlement in Washington. She married Noah Davis Thompson, a prominent journalist,
in 1911, and the couple relocated to California.

A rising star, Thompson held positions with the *Evening Express*, the *Morning
Tribune*, and the *Liberator*. She was also a feature writer for the *Morning Sun* and
Los Angeles Tribune, and as a freelance writer, contributed articles to *Out West*,
Tidings, and other magazines. Around 1915, Thompson turned to playwriting and

short fiction. Her concern for racial issues led her to write the play *A Reply to the Clansmen*, a response to Thomas Dixon's novel *The Clansmen*, on which filmmaker D. W. Griffith based his controversial film *The Clansmen*, later renamed *The Birth of a Nation*. Her play, however, was never produced.

During the early 1920s, Thompson produced three plays: *Caught, Africans*, and *Cooped Up*. They were staged in New York and California. When *Africans* (sometimes cited as *Africannus*) was staged in Los Angeles, it was the first play about an African country written by a black author designed for a black audience and realized by an all-black cast. Thompson's concern for racial issues was seen in her short fiction, as well as her plays. Two of her short stories, "Mademoiselle Tasie—A Short Story" and "Masks," were published in *Opportunity* magazine in 1925 and 1927, respectively. In 1927, the Thompsons relocated to New York City, where Noah became business manager for *Opportunity*. A year later, Eloise died suddenly. *Opportunity* referred to her work as among the best of its new writers.—JESSIE CARNEY SMITH

THOMPSON, ERA BELL [DAKOTA DICK]

(August 10, 1906–December 29, 1986) Writer, activist

Era Bell Thompson was a writer, editor, feminist, and trailblazing African American female journalist who flourished toward the latter years of the Harlem Renaissance era. She was born on August 10, 1906, in Des Moines, Iowa, to Stewart C. and Mary Logan Thompson. She enjoyed her Iowan childhood but, by 1914, moved with her family to Driscoll, North Dakota, to a farm. Her father then worked as a private messenger for Governor Lynn Frazier from 1917 to 1921. Two years after Thompson's mother died in 1918, she moved to Bismarck with her father, who operated a secondhand store.

Thompson attended Mandan High School for a few years before graduating from Bismarck High School in 1924. While attending the University of North Dakota from 1925 to 1927, she wrote for the school newspaper, the *Dakota Daily Student*, and excelled in athletics, setting five state intercollegiate women's track records and tying two. Due to poor health, Thompson had to leave school before graduating. The next year, her father died, and she returned to Bismarck to run his store until she was able to pay off his debts. In 1930, Thompson won twenty-five dollars in a bedspring-naming contest, which enabled her to visit friends in Grand Forks, North Dakota. In Grand Forks, she met Methodist pastor Reverend Robert E. O'Brian. When O'Brian became president of Morningside College, Thompson moved with his family to Sioux City, Iowa. In 1931, she was awarded the Wesleyan Service Guild Scholarship, which helped her return to college. Two years later, she graduated from Morningside College with a B.A. in social science and returned to Chicago.

Between 1933 and 1942, work was difficult to find in Chicago, so Thompson held a variety of odd jobs, beginning with the Settlement House under Mary McDowell. She later held various domestic positions, interspersed with working for the Illinois Occupational Survey, Works Progress Administration, Chicago Department of Public Works, Chicago Relief Administration, and Chicago Board of Trade. During this time, she was a correspondent for the *Chicago Defender* and would sometimes write in the "Lights and Shadows" column under the pseudonym Dakota Dick. Thompson also published an in-house newspaper during her time with the Works Progress Administration. From 1938 to 1940, she conducted postgraduate studies at Northwestern University's Medill School of Journalism. In 1942, Thompson became an interviewer for the United States and Illinois State Employment Services.

By 1945, Thompson had received a Newberry Library fellowship to write her autobiography, *American Daughter*, published in 1946. Her unique experiences as an African American Midwesterner caught the attention of John H. Johnson, publisher of *Negro Digest* and *Ebony* magazine. In 1947, she was persuaded by Johnson to join Johnson Publishing Company. Thompson held the position of associate editor of *Negro Digest* until 1951. She also wrote articles for *Negro Digest*, including the March 1951 article "Girl Gangs of Harlem." She then became the comanaging editor of *Ebony* until 1964, when she was promoted to international editor. Although she was semiretired after 1970, Thompson held the position until her death on December 29, 1986. She is buried in a family plot in Driscoll.

While working with *Ebony* magazine, Thompson, who is credited with using her unique perspective and insight on racial attitudes in various societies to promote racial understanding, published more than forty byline articles and visited 124 countries on six continents. In 1949, she was awarded the Bread Loaf Writer's Fellowship. In 1954, she published another book based on her tour of eighteen African countries, *Africa, Land of My Father*. By 1961, Thompson held a National Press Club citation. In 1963, she and another *Ebony* editor, Herbert Nipson, edited and published a collection of essays featuring such figures as William Faulkner and Jack Dempsey: *White on Black: The Views of Twenty-Two White Americans on the Negro*. These essays demonstrate attitude changes witnessed in *Ebony* during the mid-twentieth century. Two years later, Thompson was given the Iota Phi Lambda Outstanding Woman of the Year award and a honorary degree from Morningside College. Her August 1966 *Ebony* article entitled "What Weaker Sex?" demonstrates her avid feminism, while her September 1971 essay "I Was a Cancer Coward" shares her personal struggle with breast cancer and the experience of having a radical mastectomy. She hoped to help relieve fears of other women going through the same ordeal.

In 1968, Thompson was given Society of Midland Authors' Patrons Saints Award for *American Daughter*, and one year later she was granted a honorary degree from the University of North Dakota. From 1968 through 1976, she was featured in various *Backstage* columns and honored by Driscoll, North Carolina, in 1972. Thompson won the Distinguished Alumni Award from Morningside College in 1974, as well as the Theodore Roosevelt Rough Rider Award in 1976. The same year, she was inducted into the North Dakota Hall of Fame. Two years later, Thompson was inducted into the Iowa Hall of Fame and photographed and interviewed by Schlesinger Library for their black women's oral history project, "Women of Courage." Also in 1978, the University of North Dakota Cultural Center was named after her. By February 1986, Thompson had been selected as one of fifty black women to be featured in "Women of Courage," an exhibit at the Chicago Public Library's

Cultural Center. The writer and activist was also interviewed for Fisk University's Black Oral History Project, now preserved in Special Collections at the John Hope and Aurelia E. Franklin Library at Fisk University. Her papers are preserved at the Carter G. Woodson Regional Library in Chicago.—AMANDA J. CARTER

THOMPSON, PRISCILLA JANE
(1871–1942) Poet

Priscilla Jane Thompson, one of three poets in a family of six children, wrote poetry that focuses on the true character of her race. She was born in Rossmoyne, Ohio, in 1871, and spent her entire life in that community. Thompson and her siblings, Aaron Belford and Clara Ann, self-published their work. Priscilla published her first volume of poetry, *Ethiope Lays*, in 1900, followed by a second volume, *Gleanings of Quiet Hours*, in 1907. This second volume contains many of the poems from the first collection. Thompson's themes are inclusive of Christian faith, racial pride, morality, racial issues, and love. More than half of her work is in dialect. Even though it is not considered grammatically sound and "antiquated," it was favorably received. No other collections of poetry by Thompson are known to exist, despite the fact that one can only assume she continued to write.—LEAN'TIN L. BRACKS

THOMPSON PATTERSON, LOUISE ALONE
(September 9, 1901–August 27, 1999) Social activist

Louise Alone Thompson Patterson was an activist who devoted her life to fighting for equal rights for women and African Americans. She was born in Chicago, Illinois, on September 9, 1901. Her family moved to the West Coast, eventually settling in Berkeley, California. Thompson Patterson attended the University of California, Berkeley, where she graduated with honors in 1923. While a student at Berkeley, she attended a lecture delivered by the renowned African American intellectual and civil rights activist W. E. B. Du Bois and was so inspired that she decided to dedicate her life to fighting for race and gender equality.

After graduating, Thompson Patterson worked briefly at the Branch Normal College for Colored People (now the University of Arkansas at Pine Bluff). From there she moved to Hampton Institute in Virginia, where she worked for five years. Uncomfortable with the racial conservatism at Hampton, she moved to New York City to study social work.

In Harlem, Thompson Patterson became involved with the artists, writers, and intellectuals associated with the Harlem Renaissance. Her Harlem apartment was a gathering spot for a group she called the "Vanguard." Zora Neal Hurston, Wallace Thurman, Langston Hughes, and other renaissance luminaries were frequent guests. Thompson Patterson married Wallace Thurman but left him six months later after learning he was gay. In 1938, she founded the short-lived Harlem Suitcase Theater with Langston Hughes.

In 1930, Thompson Patterson was a delegate to the World Conference against Racism and Anti-Semitism in Paris, France. That same year, she enrolled in the Communist Party's Worker's School in New York City. In 1932, she organized a group of twenty-two African American artists and writers who traveled to the Soviet Union to film *Black and White*, a movie about race discrimination in the United States. The African Americans were treated as international celebrities during their time in the Soviet Union. The movie, which was to be produced by a Soviet film company, was eventually canceled for artistic or diplomatic reasons that remain unclear. Thompson Patterson spent ten months traveling in Europe and Central Asia. In the mid-1930s, she set out for Spain in a gesture of solidarity with the antifascist forces fighting the civil war in that country.

Thompson Patterson actively supported the "Scottsboro Boys," nine African American teenagers who had been accused of raping two white women in Alabama in 1931. She led marches and rallies to generate support for the accused. The case generated worldwide attention. The International Labor Defense, an organization associated with the Communist Party, handled the young men's appeals after they were convicted. Impressed by the Communist Party's antiracist stance and work on the Scottsboro cases, Thompson Patterson joined the organization in 1933. She went to work for the International Workers' Organization, a Communist-affiliated outfit that offered its members low-cost insurance and access to health clinics and educational activities.

In 1940, she married William L. Patterson, an African American lawyer who was head of International Labor Defense. After World War II ended, the Soviet Union and Communism were viewed as dangerous threats to American democracy. In 1948, the leaders of the American Communist Party were convicted and imprisoned for violating the Smith Act, a law that prohibited advocating the overthrow of the U.S. government. Thousands of Americans were accused of being Communists or Communist sympathizers. When the government launched a red-baiting campaign against African American singer and actor Paul Robeson, Thompson Patterson was his vocal supporter.

At the peak of the McCarthy era's "Red Scare," Thompson Patterson and others founded Sojourners for Truth and Justice, a black leftist and feminist organization. In 1951, a group of Sojourners pushed their way into the Department of Justice in Washington, D.C., demanding equality for African Americans. The Sojourners were mostly urban, middle-class, well-educated women with radical, leftist views, and they were unable to build a broad-based organization supported by working-class women. During the two-year lifespan of the group, it defied the Cold War political order. The Sojourners were seen as a subversive, Communist-influenced group. The government kept close tabs on members, and informants infiltrated the organization. Under mounting pressure from the government, the group disbanded.

Thompson Patterson maintained her ties to the Communist Party. In March 1971, when she was sixty-nine years of age, she organized support for Angela Davis, an African American professor who was a member of the Communist Party. Davis had been charged with murder, conspiracy, and kidnapping in connection with a failed prison escape in Marin County, California, in 1970. The Davis case became an international cause *célèbre*. In 1972, she was acquitted of all charges. Thompson Patterson remained a courageous activist until her death.—LELAND WARE

THORNTON, WILLIE MAE "BIG MAMA"

(December 11, 1926–July 25, 1984) Blues singer

Like many of the artists, writers, and intellectuals of the Harlem Renaissance, Willie Mae "Big Mama" Thornton strove for and achieved an authenticity of voice that was a celebration of both herself and African American folk culture. She not only sang the blues, but she lived them in a career that spanned four decades. While some scholars suggest that Thornton was born three years before the "end" of the Harlem Renaissance, her work places her within that tradition. Like Bessie Smith and Gertrude "Ma" Rainey, she brought sensuality and authenticity to her blues singing. Her daring stage presence, life on the road, and open lesbianism represent a freedom that few women enjoyed.

Thornton was born in the rural outskirts of Montgomery, Alabama, on December 11, 1926. With her father a minister and mother a choir member, she began her career as a gospel singer in her father's church. When her mother died, Thornton began working in a local saloon, cleaning and later filling in for the regular singer. And it was as a singer that her musical prowess was recognized.

When she was fourteen years old, Thornton joined the Hot Harlem Revue. As a member of that group, she was billed as the "New Bessie Smith," and she toured the Southeastern United States for seven years. Reflecting on her singing style, she would cite "Ma" Rainey and Bessie Smith as some of her chief influences.

In 1948, Thornton left the revue and settled for a while in Houston, where she was instrumental in the development of "Texas blues." With Houston as her base, she made her first recordings, had a regular gig at the Bronze Peacock, and began touring the Chitlin' Circuit, a collection of spots spanning from Harlem's Cotton Club to the juke joints of Mississippi that were safe for African American musicians.

Along with singing, Thornton could play several musical instruments, a rarity that earned her a five-year contract with Peacock Records. In 1952, she performed in the Harlem's Apollo Theater, and it was there that she earned the nickname "Big Mama." Standing at six feet tall and weighing 250 pounds, "Big Mama" became a marketing sensation along the lines of "Ma" Rainey. In August 1952, while in Los Angeles, she became a music legend when she recorded "Hound Dog," a twelve-bar blues laden with sexual references, with the Johnny Otis Rhythm and Blues Caravan. In that song, Thornton pays respect to the long tradition of field hollers that were part of the work songs in African American culture. Her version of "Hound Dog," a song that was later covered by Elvis Presley, sold more than 2 million copies and topped the R&B charts in 1953. This song also established her legitimacy as one of the major figures in blues music history, along with blurring the boundaries between blues and rock and roll.

In the late 1950s, rock and roll surpassed rhythm and blues in the popular music landscape, and "Big Mama" moved to San Francisco, where she continued to perform. In the mid-1960s, the San Francisco Bay Area was emerging as a hotbed for blues music as a result of Bob Dylan and the Rolling Stones, and Thornton continued to support herself as a musician. In 1965, she toured Europe as part of the American Folk Blues Festival. In the late 1960s, Janis Joplin extended Thornton's musical influence when she covered her "Ball and Chain," making the Thornton original a part of her musical repertoire. And she always had an open invitation to the Monterey Jazz Festival.

The latter part of Thornton's life is a testament to her creativity and the respect she fostered among musicians. She was a blues woman who lived an unconventional life, and the result was varied opportunities to see the world and bring African American folk culture to as wide an audience as possible. The little girl from Alabama had indeed become the "Big Mama," bringing the sounds of the South and African American folk culture to a broad audience. In the late 1960s, Thornton made three influential recordings: "Big Mama in Europe" (1966), "Big Mama Thornton with the Chicago Blues Band" (1967), and "Ball and Chain" (1968). She was one of the first blues women to travel outside the United States, and she performed in venues that included such performers as Janis Joplin, the Grateful Dead, and Santana. These distinctions were the result of her musical talent. Thornton's influence on Joplin is particularly poignant. Like Thornton, Joplin both sang and played musical instruments; Joplin was one of the bridges between blues and rock music, and her style built upon the foundation set down by "Big Mama" Thornton.

Thornton endured and continues to endure as one of the most prominent voices in blues history because of her voice; it was and remains a voice of substance. She was no flash, and in her forty-year career, she influenced Aretha Franklin, Janis Joplin, Grace Slick, and Stevie Nicks, to name just a few. Thornton died of a heart attack in Los Angeles, California, in 1984. A life of hard drinking finally caught up to her, and she was laid to rest in Inglewood Park Cemetery. That same year, she was inducted into the Blues Foundation's Blues Hall of Fame.

While "Ma" Rainey was often called the "Mother of the Blues," and Bessie Smith was widely recognized as the "Empress of the Blues," "Big Mama" Thornton acquired the unofficial moniker the "Heart of the Blues." Thornton had a big voice that was full of gusto, and the words she sang came from experience. In interviews, she often explained that no one taught her music, and that she learned to sing and play the harmonica, as well as the drums, through observation. But it was more than observation that made Thornton one of the most important blues singers of the Harlem Renaissance era. It was her ability to infuse music with her unique soul and personality that makes her one of the most memorable and revered figures in the history of blues music.—Delano Greenidge-Copprue

TURNER, LUCY MAE
(1884–?) Poet, essayist, educator

Although she has received little recognition, Lucy Mae Turner is noted as one of the last black poets of the Harlem Renaissance to publish a collection of dialect verse. Born in Zanesville, Ohio, in 1884, this granddaughter of Nat Turner, the slave-revolt leader, lived a modest life on her family's farm. Her father Gilbert, who was previously enslaved in Virginia, married Sarah Ellen Jones, daughter of a local Baptist minister. The couple had four children, but Lucy Mae and her older sister Fannie were the only ones to survive past infancy.

After high school, Turner left Zanesville to attend Wilberforce University, and she earned her degree in 1908. Shortly thereafter, she began teaching in East St. Louis public schools, notably the James Weldon Johnson School. She and Fannie purchased a home together, and their mother eventually moved in with Fannie. Turner went on to earn a B.S. from Ohio State University in 1934, and a master's degree from the University of Illinois in 1942. When St. Louis University began to admit black students into its law school, she enrolled and earned her law degree in 1950. Despite her impressive academic record, she was not granted admittance to the Illinois Bar Association and could not practice law.

On August 1, 1938, Turner published her only collection of poetry, entitled *'Bout Culled Folkses*. The volume features thirty-eight poems written in dialect, as well as Standard English. The influence of Paul Laurence Dunbar's *Lyrics of Lowly Life* on Turner's style is evident throughout the book, particularly in such dialect verses as "Pay Day," "Ebenezer," and "Evahbody's Got Troubles." She ends the volume with "Nat Turner, an Epitaph," which corresponds with black writers' recurrent use of revolt leaders in 1930s and 1940s literature. Beatrice M. Murphy, book reviewer for the *Baltimore Afro-American* newspaper, offered a favorable review of *'Bout Culled Folkses* and invited Turner to publish "A Bird Is Singing" in the anthology *Negro Voices*, also published in 1938. Turner's inclusion in the anthology illustrates her short-lived recognition as a race poet among the likes of Langston Hughes, Frank Marshall Davis, and Lucia Mae Pitts.

In 1955, the *Negro History Bulletin* published Turner's essay "The Family of Nat Turner, 1831–1954" in its March and April issues. Written forty years after her father's death, the essay chronicles his life following Nat Turner's insurrection and execution. Anecdotes about her father's later years in Marietta and Zanesville, both cities in Ohio, reveal a resilient man who worked diligently to secure employment in the field of iron manufacturing, overcome illiteracy, and become a pillar of his family's integrated community. To conclude the essay, Turner recalls the frequency with which her parents opened their home to formerly enslaved individuals who were in need of food and shelter. It was at the feet of her father and their guests where Turner became intrigued by the narratives and voices of slavery that would, one day influence the themes and language of her poetry. Her exact birth date, marital status, and cause of death are unknown.—TANYA E. WALKER

W

WALKER, A'LELIA [LELIA MCWILLIAMS]
(June 6, 1885–August 15, 1931) Entrepreneur, socialite

A'Lelia Walker

Skilled businesswoman A'Lelia Walker was not only the daughter of beauty industry pioneer Madame C. J. Walker and heiress to her hair care fortune, she was also an advocate for the arts and a socialite who brought together artists during the Harlem Renaissance, including poet Langston Hughes, author Zora Neale Hurston, actor Paul Robeson, and writer and photographer Carl Van Vechten.

Born Lelia McWilliams in Vicksburg, Mississippi, on June 6, 1885, Walker was the only child of Moses and Sarah Breedlove McWilliams. After the death of Moses in 1887, Sarah moved with her daughter to St. Louis, Missouri, where three of the Breedlove brothers ran a barbershop.

The McWilliams's transition to city life was aided by ladies from St. Paul African Methodist Episcopal Church, whose association with the National Association of Colored Women helped them better understand the plight of newcomers to the city. One of the women, Maggie Rector, matron of St. Louis Colored Orphans' Home, helped enroll Lelia in Dessalines Elementary School in 1890. In 1894, Sarah married John Davis, who was an abusive alcoholic from whom she was separated by 1903. Determined that her daughter have a solid chance at success, she saved enough of her washerwoman's salary to send Lelia to Knoxville College in 1902, right before she began working on her hair care product formulas.

In 1905, Sarah moved to Denver to become a sales agent for Annie Malone's Poro Company, a hair care products manufacturer that would later become a lifelong rival. One year later, Sarah married Charles Joseph Walker and began the Madam C. J. Walker Manufacturing Company in Denver, Colorado. Lelia soon joined her family in Denver to become one of the company's first employees, where she learned beauty culture and the hair-growing process. While she was not formally adopted by her mother's third husband, Lelia took the Walker name to establish and validate her connection to the family business. By September 1906, she had taken over the Denver mail-order operation, while her mother and stepfather traveled throughout the Southern and Eastern United States to promote the business. By 1908, Madam Walker had established the Lelia College of Hair Culture and a temporary headquarters in Pittsburgh, Pennsylvania, at which point Lelia moved east to become one of the company's first traveling sales agents.

In 1909, Lelia married John Robinson, a laborer, and became known as Lelia Walker Robinson. He left her within one year of their marriage, although they would not officially divorce until 1914. Madam Walker opened her permanent headquarters in Indianapolis, Indiana, in early 1910, so Lelia took over the Pittsburgh operation of the beauty school and sales agents' supply station.

During a visit with her mother in Indianapolis in 1911, Lelia was introduced to twelve-year-old Fairy Mae Bryant, whose long hair enabled her to be an ideal model for Madam Walker's hair care products and treatments. By October of the next year, the Walker women had adopted the child from her widowed mother, Sarah Etta Bryant, on the condition that she be formally educated and receive business training. Lelia changed the child's name to Mae Walker Robinson. Mae graduated from Spelman College in 1920, and became president of the Madam C. J. Walker Manufacturing Company upon Lelia's death in 1931.

By 1913, Harlem was just beginning to embody the African American political, social, cultural, and artistic mecca later known as the Harlem Renaissance. Seeing this, Walker convinced her mother to start a branch office on 136th Street, near Lenox Avenue in New York City, where they opened Walker Hair Parlor and Lelia College of Hair Culture. Walker oversaw the six-week training course at the college and managed the northeastern sales territory. During World War I, Walker followed her mother's lead in supporting black troops by hosting fundraisers and volunteering with the Colored Women's Motor Corps as an ambulance driver for formal occasions and parades honoring the troops. In 1917, Madam Walker hired Alpha Phi Alpha founder and one of the first licensed African American architects in New York, Vertner Woodson Tandy, to build a thirty-four-room limestone and brick Georgian-style mansion at Irvington-on-Hudson, New York. Walker's friend, opera singer Enrico Caruso, dubbed it "Villa Lewaro," based on the first two letters of Walker's name, Lelia Walker Robinson.

When Madam Walker passed away on May 25, 1919, Lelia became president of the Madam C. J. Walker Manufacturing Company and inherited most of her mother's estate. Days after her mother's funeral, Walker married Wiley Wilson, a Howard University Medical School graduate. As with her first marriage, they separated within a year after allegations of an affair with his former girlfriend, but the duo did not divorce until 1925.

A seasoned international traveler to Central America, the Caribbean, and Hawaii, Walker left in November 1921 to spend five months in Europe, Africa, and the Middle East. During the trip she visited London's Covent Garden; attended the coronation of Pope Pius XI in Rome; toured the Egyptian pyramids on camelback; and is said to be the first American to meet Ethiopian empress Waizeru Zauditu, daughter of the emperor who defeated an invading Italian army in 1896. Upon her return to the United States in 1922, and for unknown reasons, Walker changed her first name to A'Lelia.

In 1923, Walker began orchestrating a lavish wedding for her daughter. Walker chose Dr. Gordon Jackson to marry Mae in November of that year at the illustrious St. Philip's Protestant Episcopal Church. She distributed more than 9,000 invitations and held an extravagant reception with elaborate decorations; however, the marriage was short. Mae Walker and Dr. Gordon Jackson divorced in December 1926. By August 1927, Mae had married Marion Rowland Perry Jr., an attorney.

Walker married her third husband in May 1926. James Arthur "Artie" Kennedy was a Chicago psychiatrist and later a physician, as well as second in command at the Tuskegee Veterans Hospital in Alabama. Walker donated $25,000 to the Hampton-Tuskegee Endowment Fund when he moved to Alabama. They agreed to live separately but only visited one another a few times before divorcing in March 1931.

Always a socialite, Walker began a tradition of "at-home," where she would introduce her artist, writer, performer, and celebrity friends to one another. In October 1927, she converted one floor of her 136th Street townhouse into a literary salon, nightclub, and tearoom called the Dark Tower, based on Countee Cullen's column in *Opportunity* magazine. The centerpiece of the room was a bookcase designed by Paul Frankl in the shape of a tower and filled with first-edition copies of some of the best African American writers of the day. Walker intended for it to be a place for writers, artists, and performers to congregate and socialize. Between the Dark Tower and her smaller pied-à-terre at 80 Edgecombe Avenue, she hosted such visitors as Langston Hughes, composer and pianist Eubie Blake, Zora Neale Hurston, dancer Florence Mills, and Paul Robeson, as well as white writers the likes of Carl Van Vechten, Witter Bynner, Muriel Draper, and Max Ewing. On some occasions guests included African and European royalty. Since she held parties for the famous and not-so-famous, Langston Hughes called her the "joy goddess" of the Harlem Renaissance. The Dark Tower officially closed in October 1928, but it remained a venue for parties and meetings and was even the site of the wedding reception of W. E. B. Du Bois's daughter Yolanda to Countee Cullen.

Between 1927 and 1928, Walker Company trustees decided to build a million-dollar headquarters in Indianapolis, Indiana. Sales at the company were greatly affected after the Stock Market Crash of 1929, so Walker and the trustees were forced to auction off much of the contents of Villa Lewaro in November 1930. The results of the auction were less than satisfactory, so the next year the townhouse was put on the market to be sold. In 1932, Villa Lewaro was sold at auction to Companions of the Forest. After later being sold back into private hands, the townhouse eventually became a historic landmark.

On August 15, 1931, after a champagne and lobster celebration for a friend in Long Branch, New Jersey, Walker died of a stroke at forty-six years of age. Yet, even her funeral was a grand event, much like the parties she hosted. More than 11,000 people viewed her in her silver, orchid-filled casket. Reverend Adam Clayton Powell Sr. presided and read her eulogy, Langston Hughes shared his poem "To A'Lelia," and Hubert Fauntleroy Julian dropped bouquets of gladiolas and dahlias from a plane as her casket was lowered into the ground. Walker is buried next to her mother at Woodlawn Cemetery. Her daughter Mae became president of the Madam C. J. Walker Manufacturing Company. The company itself survived into the mid-1980s.

While Walker lived in her mother's shadow, the nearly six-foot-tall enthusiastic supporter of the arts was well-loved and created a social and cultural countenance of her own. She also established the role of the African American heiress. Walker's memberships included the Harlem Child Welfare League, the Music School Settlement, and women's auxiliaries of the National Association for the Advancement of Colored People and the National Urban League. Langston Hughes writes of Walker in his autobiography that she was the inspiration for Duke Ellington's *Queenie Pie*. Adora Boniface, a character from Carl Van Vechten's *Nigger Heaven* (1926), is based on her, and sculptors, photographers, and artists who have rendered her likeness include Richmond Barthé, Augusta Savage, Berenice Abbott, R. E. Mercer, and James Latimer Allen.—AMANDA J. CARTER

WALKER, MADAM C. J. [SARAH BREEDLOVE]
(December 23, 1867–May 25, 1919) Hair products entrepreneur

Sarah Breedlove, who became known as Madam C. J. Walker, was a pioneering entrepreneur who laid the foundation for generations of African American women to own and operate hair care salons. She began her career in the cotton fields of Louisiana. She later worked as a washerwoman and moved up to cooking in kitchens. Within a few years, Breedlove launched what would become an international sales and manufacturing enterprise that would make her the wealthiest black woman in the United States. She was in Harlem when the cultural revolution was in bloom, and she and daughter A'Lelia became well noticed among the contributors of that period.

Breedlove was born on December 23, 1867, in Delta, Louisiana. Her parents were Owen and Minerva Breedlove. Sarah had a sister, Louvenia, and four brothers, Alexander, James, Solomon, and Owen Jr. Her parents had been slaves on a Parish farm in Louisiana. In 1874, Minerva died during a yellow fever epidemic. The following year, Owen died from the same disease. Sarah, her sister, and her sister's husband moved to Vicksburg, Mississippi, in 1878, to escape plague. Sarah worked as a maid.

When she was fourteen, Sarah married Moses McWilliams, mainly to escape the abuse inflicted by her sister's husband. On June 6, 1885, she bore a daughter, Leila. When her husband died two years later, Sarah and Lelia moved to St. Louis, Missouri. Sarah married John Davis on August 11, 1894. That marriage ended in 1903.

Annie Turnbo Malone, an African American hair care entrepreneur based in St. Louis, had developed and manufactured her own line of hair care products for African American women. During the height of the Jim Crow segregation, Malone was able to establish a prosperous hair care business. Malone used her treatment to restore Breedlove's hair loss.

Breedlove began to work with Malone in 1903. In 1905, Breedlove moved to Denver, Colorado, as an agent for Malone. In January 1906, Breedlove married a newspaper sales agent, Charles Joseph Walker. After changing her name to Madam C. J. Walker, she established her own business and sold her own hair care product, Madam Walker's Wonderful Hair Grower.

Before the introduction of the straitening comb, African American women pressed and straitened their hair using a hot iron. Walker's hair treatment changed that. It consisted of shampooing a person's hair, applying a hair growing cream, and using heated iron combs to straighten the hair. When Malone learned about Walker's fledgling enterprise, she accused Walker of copying Poro's products. Walker denied the claims and struck out on her own.

In September 1906, Walker and her husband toured the United States, promoting their products and training sales agents. From 1908 to 1910, they operated a beauty training school, the Lelia College of Hair Culture, in Pittsburgh, Pennsylvania. The company's mainly female agents became familiar figures in cities and towns throughout the United States and the Caribbean. Thousands of agents set up their own in-home shops, where they used and marketed Walker's products.

The sales representatives made house calls wearing white shirtwaists and long, black skirts. They carried bags that contained hair care products. Madame Walker's Wonderful Hair Grower and a collection of other beauty products were stored in tin containers that were decorated with a portrait of Mae Walker Perry, the adopted daughter of Lelia Walker. Perry's long, attractive hair was the perfect advertisement for Walker's products. Walker advertised heavily in black newspapers and magazines. Her husband, who had been a newspaper salesman, provided advice about the company's marketing and advertising efforts.

Every summer, several African American professional, fraternal, and social organizations held national conventions in cities throughout the United States. These were elaborate, weeklong events where hundreds of delegates and their families and guests would gather. Business meetings were held during the day, while dinners, dances, and other social events took place in the evening. Walker attended several of these gatherings. After making sure that the event was in full swing, she would make a conspicuous entrance in her chauffeur-driven limousine, elegantly dressed in the latest fashions. These displays of wealth and success served as means of promoting her business.

In 1910, Walker moved the company's operations to Indianapolis. There she established Madam C. J. Walker Laboratories to manufacture cosmetics and train beauticians. These entrepreneurs operated independent salons in black communities throughout the United States, where they styled women's hair and sold Walker's products. Walker was one of the pioneers of direct sales marketing strategies and commission sales. She was an advocate of women's economic independence and created opportunities for thousands of African American women who otherwise would have been cooks or domestics or held other low-level positions. Walker organized clubs and held annual conventions for her sales representatives.

Walker constructed a building complex that covered an entire city block in downtown Indianapolis. The complex became the national headquarters and manufacturing site for Walker's products, employing 3,000 women. The complex also served as a community center that housed a ballroom, a theater, a hair salon, and corporate offices. The theater was a movie house and venue for jazz performances. The Walker complex was an important institution that contributed to the growth and development of Indianapolis's African American community.

In 1912, at the peak of her company's success, Walker wanted to address the delegates at the National Negro Business League convention in Chicago, Illinois. She arrived at the event in her chauffeured limousine. The league's founder, Booker T. Washington, was, at that time, the most powerful black leader in the United States. During the first two days of the convention, he ignored Walker's requests to address the delegates. On the final day of the conference, Walker stood and admonished Washington, asking him to acknowledge her as a successful, self-made entrepreneur. Walker described how she started out laboring in cotton fields in the South. She went from washing clothes to cooking in kitchens and moved on to establish a successful business manufacturing hair care products.

In 1913, Walker contributed $1,000 to assist in the financing of an African American Young Women's Christian Association (YWCA) in Indianapolis. This was the largest contribution made by an African American donor. Washington accepted Walker's invitation to be a guest in her home during the dedication of the YWCA. He was so impressed that he invited Walker to be a keynote speaker at National Negro Business League's 1913 convention.

The Walkers divorced in 1912. The following year, Madame Walker traveled to Central America and the Caribbean to explore business opportunities, and expanded her company into Jamaica, Cuba, Costa Rica, and Panama. She met Mary McLeod Bethune, the founder of Bethune-Cookman College (now Bethune-Cookman University) in Daytona, Florida, in 1912, at the National Association of Colored Women's annual conference. Walker led a fundraising campaign for the tiny school, starting with her own $5,000 donation. As a result of the campaign's success, the school was able to expand. Walker also contributed thousands of dollars to the Tuskegee Institute (now Tuskegee University) in Alabama. She lobbied for antilynching laws and contributed $5,000, the largest donation ever, to the National Association for the Advancement of Colored People's Antilynching Fund. She also donated $25,000 to other African American organizations.

Walker moved into an elegant townhouse in the Harlem section of New York City in 1916. On August 31, 1917, she convened the first national convention of "beauty culturists" at Philadelphia's Union Baptist Church. More than 200 women from throughout the United States attended the event, where they discussed sales, marketing, and management. By 1919, Walker employed 3,000 people at the Indianapolis facility factory and had more than 20,000 sales representatives.

The construction of Walker's opulent home, Villa Lewaro, in Irvington-on-Hudson, New York, was completed in August 1918. Walker died at Villa Lewaro on May 25, 1919, at the age of fifty-one. Walker's daughter succeeded her as president of the Madame C. J. Walker Manufacturing Company. Lelia, who by then had changed her name to A'Leila, went on to become an important presence in the Harlem Renaissance. In 1927, she converted a floor of her Harlem townhouse into a salon she dubbed the "Dark Tower." It was a place where many of the writers and artists associated with the Harlem Renaissance regularly gathered.

Madam Walker left a legacy that went beyond the beneficiaries named in her will. Beauty salons became important institutions in African American communities. They allowed African American women to develop organizational, leadership, and entrepreneurial skills. The establishments provided a valuable alternative to the menial positions that were otherwise available. Salon owners maintained a level of autonomy that was unavailable to most other African Americans. Madam Walker was a pioneer who led the way for others to follow.—LELAND WARE

WALKER, MARGARET [MARGARET WALKER ALEXANDER]

(July 7, 1915–November 30, 1998) Poet, novelist, essayist, biographer, scholar

Margaret Walker is widely recognized for her 1942 collection of poems *For My People*, and for her epic family history, *Jubilee*, published in 1966; however, her identity as a writer began during the period of the Harlem Renaissance.

Walker was born on July 7, 1915, in Birmingham, Alabama, to Marion Dozier Walker and Sigismond Walker. As the daughter of an educator and a minister, she grew up in an environment in which scholarship was encouraged. During the early 1930s, she enrolled in Dillard University in Louisiana. At Dillard, she met a number of Harlem Renaissance writers, including James Weldon Johnson, W. E. B. Du Bois, and Langston Hughes. Hughes was an encouraging and inspiring influence on her decision to write. After two years at Dillard, Walker transferred to Northwestern University in Chicago.

While in Chicago, she published her first poems in *Crisis* magazine. After graduating from Northwestern University, Walker became part of Chicago's black literary community. From 1935 to 1939, she worked for the Works Progress Administration, initially as a social worker and then as a writer. During this period, she met Richard Wright and became involved in the South Side Writers' Group. Her friendship with Wright encouraged her pursuit of writing and historical research. For Wright, she became a trustworthy friend and supportive colleague, often providing insight into historical and social research that would prove useful for Wright in his own writing.

As the Harlem Renaissance came to a close, Walker made the decision to pursue an advanced degree from the University of Iowa.

In 1942, she completed a version of her collection of poems, *For My People*, which would serve as her master's thesis at the University of Iowa. The publication of this collection brought Walker serious critical recognition as a poet. The collection, like the Harlem Renaissance, is a celebration of the culture and history of African Americans. The poetry reflects the resiliency, creativity, and intellect of an oppressed, yet courageous and determined, people. The title poem, "For My People," is her most frequently anthologized work; this poem represents her as a writer. The poem and the collection are reflective of the folk cultural expression that is characteristic of her work.

Also during this period, she married Firnist James Alexander. After the publication of *For My People*, Walker began intense historical research and received a Rosenwald Fellowship. In 1949, she moved with her husband to Jackson, Mississippi, and taught at Jackson State College (now Jackson State University). She balanced mothering four children, teaching, and her historical research. Her research was rewarded with a Ford Fellowship in 1953.

In the 1960s, Walker returned to the University of Iowa in pursuit of her doctoral degree. In 1965, she earned her Ph.D. Her dissertation is a version of her family history, *Jubilee*; this work was the fruit of her historical research. *Jubilee* was published in 1966, and Walker was once again the focus of considerable critical attention. After completing her degree, she returned to Jackson and teaching.

During the 1970s, Walker published two collections of poetry: *Prophets for a New Day* in 1970 and *October Journey* in 1973. She also published essays, including *A Poetic Equation*, which consists of her conversations with poet Nikki Giovanni, in 1974, and *How I Wrote Jubilee and Other Essays on Life and Literature* in 1980. In 1988, she published one of the most critical and thorough biographies on Richard Wright, *Daemonic Genius*. The biography in some ways addresses the speculation about Walker's relationship with Wright. The book suggests that she harbored remarkable disappointment in her relationship with the writer as a friend. In 1989, she published *This Is My Century*, a collection of new and old poems. This compilation maps the course of her literary career, indicating the influence of different periods and literary movements in the progress of her career as a writer. In 1997, Maryemma Graham edited a collection of essays by Walker entitled *On Being Female, Black, and Free*. The collection includes essays written during a six-year period that are both biographical and critical of social and political issues affecting African Americans.

Walker was diagnosed with breast cancer, which led to her death in 1998. She continues to be recognized as one of the inspiring voices of African American culture of the twentieth century.—REBECCA S. DIXON

WALLACE, BEULAH "SIPPIE"

(November 1, 1898–November 1, 1986) Blues singer

Beulah "Sippie" Wallace, known as the "Texas Nightingale," was a blues singer who had excellent phrasing and rich vocal tones, talents that brought her in contact with such legends as Joe "King" Oliver, Louis Armstrong, and Clarence Williams. Her style of the Chicago shout and moan, with the southwestern honky-tonk, made her among the best blues singers of her time.

Born in Houston, Texas, on November 1, 1898, the fourth of thirteen children, Wallace's involvement in music began at her father's church, where, when old enough, she sang and played the organ. She was given the nickname "Sippie" because her teeth were far apart as a child, and she had the habit of sipping her food. As she got older, Wallace became enamored with the tent-show bands and traveling blues singers, and on several occasions she was allowed to dance in the chorus line. By the mid-1910s, she had begun traveling with a tent show that moved from Houston to Dallas, and she began to sing, act, and do solo ballads.

In 1912, Wallace moved with her younger brother, Hersal Thomas, to the Storyville District of New Orleans so they could work with their older brother, George W. Thomas, who was a pianist, songwriter, and publisher. While in New Orleans, Wallace married Frank Seales in 1914, and they divorced in 1917. She was married to Matt Wallace from 1917 to 1936. Wallace returned home to Houston in 1918, after the death of both parents, but she was still determined to have a career as a blues singer and entertainer. She started out as a maid and stage assistant to a snake dancer, sang with small bands and for other gatherings, and later sang with tent bands throughout Texas. It was during this time that she became known as the "Texas Nightingale."

In 1923, Wallace moved to Chicago with her brother Hersal, and along with their brother George W., they formed a popular trio. Wallace's first recordings, written in collaboration with George W., were "Shorty George," which sold more than 100,000 copies, and "Underworld Blues," both on the Okeh label. Between 1924 and 1927, Wallace recorded more than forty songs, for instance, "Lazy Man Blues" and "Special Delivery Blues," and she worked with such greats as Louis Armstrong, Clarence Williams, and Johnny Dodds. With the deaths of Hersal in 1926 and George W. in the mid-1930s, Wallace lost family and partners. She moved to Detroit and became director of the National Convention of Gospel Choirs and Choruses in the late 1930s.

By the 1940s, Wallace was performing occasionally, but by the 1960s, she had become part of the revival of American folk music and the blues. She performed in Detroit and on tour, and was part of the American Folk-Blues Festival, which took her to Copenhagen, Sweden, in 1966. She introduced the song "Woman Be Wise, Don't Advertise Yo Man," which inspired singer Bonnie Raitt, and appealed to a strong female sensibility. Wallace performed at the Lincoln Center in 1977 and 1980, and recorded a new album, *Sippie*, in 1982, which includes seven new songs and was nominated for a Grammy. Wallace, known as the last of the blues shouters, was considered among the greats, alongside Bessie Smith, Gertrude "Ma" Rainey, and Alberta Hunter, and she was subsequently inducted into the Blues Foundation's Blues Hall of Fame in 2003. She died in Detroit, Michigan, in 1986.—LEAN'TIN L. BRACKS

WARD, AIDA
(February 11, 1903–June 23, 1984) Singer

From the 1920s until the late 1940s, Aida Ward was a popular songstress in the United States, Canada, and Europe. Ward was born in Washington, D.C., on February 11, 1903, and she graduated from M Street High School (later Dunbar High School). She appeared in amateur shows prior to moving to New York.

After performing at the Hollywood Club, Ward appeared in the musical *The Frolics* (1923). She was understudy for Florence Mills in *Dixie to Broadway* (1924–1925) in New York, as well as *Blackbirds of 1926* in New York, London, and Paris. Ward then performed in the predominantly white musical *The Manhatters* (1927). After Mills's death in 1927, Ward costarred in *Blackbirds of 1928*, with Bill "Bojangles" Robinson and Adelaide Hall; the Broadway production featured Ward singing "I Can't Give You Anything but Love." In 1929, Ward recorded the song, and the *Blackbirds* cast performed at the Moulin Rouge in Paris.

Ward toured the United States and Canada, singing with Duke Ellington and Cab Calloway's orchestras, on radio programs, and at the Apollo Theater, as well as the Cotton Club. In 1932, she sang "I've Got the World on a String" in the *Cotton Club Parade* revue. Two years later, she appeared at Broadway's Beacon Theater with comedians George Burns, Gracie Allen, Jack Benny, and Milton Berle.

At least one of Ward's several marriages ended in divorce. She retired as an entertainer in the late 1940s and operated a long-term care facility in Washington until 1969. Jerome Gist, Ward's son from her first marriage, died in 1983. Ward died at Howard University Hospital.—LINDA M. CARTER

WARING, LAURA WHEELER
(May 16, 1887–February 3, 1948) Portrait artist, teacher

Laura Wheeler Waring is best known for her participation in the seminal Harmon Foundation exhibition in the 1920s and 1940s. The exhibition and the African American artists whose works were showcased contributed to the creativity that abounded during the Harlem Renaissance.

Waring was born on May 16, 1887, in Hartford, Connecticut, a world vastly different from the one in which the majority of African Americans lived. Most blacks lived in the South under a system of oppression and racism. Education was limited; opportunities were virtually nonexistent, and discriminatory laws and antiblack violence were pervasive. For blacks, life in the North was less harsh, less constricting.

Waring flourished in her hometown. Her father, Robert Foster Wheeler, was a pastor at Talcott Street Congregational Church, the first black church in the state. Her mother, Mary Freeman Wheeler, was a teacher and an artist. After Waring graduated from Hartford Public High in 1906, she followed in the footsteps of the five generations of her family and attended college. At the Pennsylvania Academy of the Fine Arts, she studied with painters Thomas Anschutz and William Merritt Chase. Among her peers were painter Lenwood Morris and sculptor Mae Howard Jackson. Upon graduation in 1914, Waring received a scholarship to travel in Europe.

Laura Wheeler Waring

Waring's experiences in Europe during this time and in subsequent visits sharpened her artistic skills and broadened her worldview. Her European trips also connected her to some of the leading African American artists, writers, and intellectuals of her day. While abroad, Waring studied at the prestigious Académie de la Grande Chaumière in Paris. For many African American artists and intellectuals, France was a popular destination, providing a reprieve from the confining racial oppressions of the United States and an environment in which they could nurture their artistic, literary, and intellectual development.

Upon her return to the United States after her first trip to Europe, Waring settled into a successful career. Her career, like her childhood and educational experiences, went against the times. Women were expected to marry, bare children, and settle into their roles as wives and mothers. Waring would marry; however, she pursued a career first, becoming a teacher at Pennsylvania's State Normal School. While there, she married Walter E. Waring, a professor at Lincoln University. She went on to accept the position of director of the art department at Cheyney Training School for Teachers (now Cheyney University of Pennsylvania) in 1925.

As Waring's life flourished, so did black life in Harlem, New York. In the 1920s, Harlem throbbed with the excitement and energy of African Americans eager to express their talents, deep love and pride for their culture, and shrewd understanding of the turbulent racial times in which they lived. In 1922, William E. Harmon, a white real estate developer, founded the Harmon Foundation in New York City. The foundation was established to pay tribute to African American artists. In 1928, the foundation hosted the first exhibit of African American artists in history. Waring's refined portraits were included and reflected the pride, accomplishments, and elegance of a people who had transcended a turbulent past and present. In 1944, eight of Waring's portraits were included in the foundation's Portraits of Outstanding Americans of Negro Origin. Her portraits include important African American figures, many of whom played crucial roles during the Harlem Renaissance. Some of her subjects include Jessie Redmon Fauset, a Harlem Renaissance writer; W. E. B. Du Bois and James Weldon Johnson, who heavily supported the Harlem Renaissance movement; and famed opera singer Marian Anderson.

Waring's work, however, did not end with the Harmon Foundation's exhibits. Her work also frequently appeared in *Crisis*, the publication of the National Association for the Advancement of Colored People. (Waring was also a member of this organization.) Her work was exhibited at the Galerie du Luxembourg in Paris; at Howard University in Washington, D.C.; at the Brooklyn Museum in New York; at the Newark Museum in New Jersey; and in the Smithsonian's National Portrait Gallery.

In addition to the exposure she received for her art, Waring received some public tributes following her death in 1948. In 1956, the Laura Wheeler Waring School in Pennsylvania was named in her honor. Her home in Philadelphia was also honored with a historical marker, a visible reminder of the life of a remarkable artist.
—GLADYS L. KNIGHT

WASHINGTON, FREDERICKA "FREDI" CAROLYN
(December 23, 1903–June 28, 1994) Actress, activist

During the 1930s and 1940s, Fredericka "Fredi" Carolyn Washington was one of the first African American women to garner critical acclaim on the Broadway stage and in film as a dramatic actress. She was initially noticed by many because of her beauty and sophistication, yet her legacy extends beyond her early days as an ingenue on Broadway. In addition to her considerable talents as an actress, she is remembered as an activist who obdurately worked to improve Broadway and Hollywood's treatment of subsequent generations of African American actors and actresses.

Washington was born in Savannah, Georgia, on December 23, 1903; she was the second eldest of Robert T. and Harriet Washington's five children. After her mother's death, Fredi and her younger sister Isabel attended Saint Elizabeth's Convent in Cornwell Heights, Pennsylvania, until they were teenagers. Fredi then moved to Harlem; lived with relatives; and continued her education at the Julia Richman High School, the Egri School of Dramatic Writing, and the Christophe School of Languages. She was employed as a bookkeeper at Harry Pace's Black Swan Record Company, where her father worked, until she auditioned for choreographer Elida Webb and was hired for the chorus in Noble Sissle and Eubie Blake's *Shuffle Along* in the early 1920s; Josephine Baker was also a dancer in the Broadway musical, and the two young women became friends. In 1933, Washington married Lawrence Brown, a trombonist in Duke Ellington's orchestra, and the couple divorced in 1951. When Washington married Hugh Anthony Bell, a dentist, in 1952, she moved to Stamford, Connecticut, and retired from show business.

Decades earlier, Washington had debuted as a dramatic actress in the 1926 Broadway play *Black Boy*, which starred Paul Robeson as a prizefighter. Washington was cast as Irene, a beautiful African American woman who passes for white. In 1927 and 1928, she performed in New York and Europe with Charles Moore as the ballroom dancers Moiret and Freddie. In London, Washington taught the Prince of Wales the black bottom, a popular 1920s dance. In 1931, Washington and her sister starred in *Singin' the Blues*, the Broadway melodrama about Harlem life. (Isabel followed in her sister's footsteps as a dancer and actress until she married Reverend Adam Clayton Powell Jr., an assistant minister at his father's church, Abyssinian Baptist Church in Harlem, and ended her career.) Fredi continued to appear in plays in the 1930s and 1940s. These included *Sweet Chariot*; *Run, Little Chillun,* an African American version of *Lysistrata*; *A Long Way from Home*; *How Long Till Summer*; and *Mamba's Daughters*. The latter production starred Ethel Waters as Hagar, the mother of Washington's character, Lissa.

Washington's cinematic credits include the short films *Black and Tan* (with Duke Ellington,1929), *Mills Blue Rhythm Band* (1933), and *Cab Calloway's Hi-De-Ho* (1934), as well as the full-length films *The Emperor Jones* (1933), *Drums of the Jungle* (1936), and *One Mile from Heaven* (1937), which also features Eddie "Rochester" Anderson and Bill "Bojangles" Robinson. In *The Emperor Jones*, Washington once again plays Robeson's romantic interest. Censors, fearful that audiences would assume that the film was depicting an interracial relationship, demanded that Washington's light skin be purposefully camouflaged with darker cosmetics to make the love scenes more tolerable to audiences. Washington's signature role, on the stage or screen, was as Peola Johnson in the 1934 film adaptation of Fannie Hurst's novel *Imitation of Life*. Light-skinned Peola disowns her darker-skinned mother, played by Louise Beavers, and renounces their African American identity, as she passes for white with tragic consequences. Ironically, when the hit movie was remade in 1959, Peola was portrayed by a white actress.

Washington's efforts to sustain an acting career were stymied by the limited number of stage and film roles available for African American women and by individuals on Broadway and in Hollywood who would not cast a black woman who looked white. Frustrated by the lack of acting opportunities, she became a founding member of the Negro Actors' Guild (NAG), located in New York, in 1937. Other founding members included W. C. Handy, Paul Robeson, and Ethel Waters. Noble Sissle was the organization's first president, and Bill "Bojangles" Robinson was honorary president. Washington served as NAG's first executive secretary. The founding members sought to increase African American participation in stage productions, as well as in films; eradicate stereotypical characters and scenes; and press for more realistic images of black life. Washington was also involved with the Committee for the Negro in the Arts, the Cultural Division of the National Negro Congress, and the Joint Actors Equity-Theatre League Committee on Hotel Accommodations for Negro Actors. Her efforts as an activist extended beyond the entertainment industry. For example, she participated in boycotts spearheaded by Adam Clayton Powell Jr. demanding that Harlem businesses hire African Americans.

In addition, Washington found time for other endeavors. She was a casting consultant for various films and plays, including the Broadway productions *Carmen Jones* (1943) and *Porgy and Bess* (1943). Also in the 1940s, she was the theater editor and columnist for Adam Clayton Powell Jr.'s weekly newspaper the *People's Voice*; she wrote "Headlines and Footlights" and a second column, "Fredi Speaks." In the 1950s, Washington acted in radio episodes of *The Goldbergs*, a situation comedy about Jewish life. She was also the registrar for the Howard da Silva School for Acting.

Washington was inducted into the Black Filmmakers Hall of Fame in 1975. She received the CIRCA Award for Lifetime Achievement in the Performing Arts in 1979. She died in St. Joseph's Medical Center in Stamford, Connecticut, in 1994.

Washington was ninety years old and preceded in death by her second husband, who died in 1970. The Papers of Fredi Washington, 1925 to 1975, are housed at the Amistad Research Center at Tulane University.—LINDA M. CARTER

WASHINGTON, ISABEL [MARION MARIE THEODORE ROSEMARIE]
(May 23, 1908–May 1, 2007) Entertainer

Isabel Washington was an attractive, fair-skinned, redheaded actress, singer, and performer in the 1920s who enjoyed many starring roles onstage and in films. She was further inspired by the success of her older sister Fredi Washington, star of the acclaimed film *Imitation of Life* (1934). In spite of her success as an entertainer, Washington chose to shorten her career and became the wife of preacher and civil rights activist Adam Clayton Powell Jr.

Born Marion Marie Theodore Rosemarie on May 23, 1908, in Savannah, Georgia, Isabel's mother died when she was young, and both she and her older sister Fredi attended Saint Elizabeth's Convent in Cornwell Heights, Pennsylvania, before the family moved to Harlem, where Isabel's maternal grandmother lived. In Harlem, Washington worked after school at Harry Pace's Black Swan Record Company, the place where her father, Robert T. Washington, worked. Fletcher Henderson, a premier band leader of the 1920s and house pianist for the company, liked Washington's voice, and in March 1923, at the age of fifteen, Washington made her first recordings.

In 1929, after frequenting theaters where her sister Fredi was rehearsing or working, Washington made her way into show business. She spent time as a chorus girl and worked in the well-known night spots the Cotton Club and Connie's Inn. Washington's performances earned her starring roles in the production *Harlem* (1929), written by Wallace Thurman; *Bombolla* (1929), and *Singin' the Blues* (1931). She also had a key role in the only film blues singer Bessie Smith ever acted in, *Saint Louis Blues* (1929), an important movie documenting the Harlem Renaissance. Washington's performances were reviewed as vivacious, radiant, and ebullient.

Washington decided to give up her career in 1933, after deciding to marry Reverend Adam Clayton Powell Jr., pastor of the Abyssinian Baptist Church in Harlem. Although Powell's father was not supportive of his son marrying a divorced showgirl who had a two-year-old son, Preston, from a previous marriage to Preston Webster, a noted photographer in Washington, D.C., Powell used his determination and charm to gain acceptance for his fiancé, later known as "Belle." The marriage, which lasted for twelve years, was the first of three marriages for Powell. After her divorce, Washington began teaching developmentally challenged children and devoted herself to community activities and causes.—LEAN'TIN L. BRACKS

WASIIINGTON, MARGARET "MACGIE" MURRAY JONES
(March 9, 1861–June 4, 1925) Educator, clubwoman

The years leading up to the Harlem Renaissance, and for a number of years into that time of black cultural reawakening, Margaret Murray Jones Washington worked to improve the lives of people, particularly women, in Alabama. Her

Margaret Murray Washington

work with the black women's club movement in Alabama and throughout the United States was also notable. As leader and holder of other offices within the National Association of Colored Women's Clubs, she helped black women address such issues as health, education, and care of family.

Washington was born in Macon, Mississippi, on March 9, 1861, the daughter of a washerwoman named Lucy and Irish immigrant James Murray. For reasons not specified, her white Quaker brother and sister took her in when she was seven years old. When only fourteen years of age, she taught school for a time and then entered Fisk University in 1881, as a part-time student. Washington worked to sustain herself while at Fisk. Maggie, as she was known by some, engaged in several cultural activities at Fisk. She was associate editor of the students' literary magazine the *Fisk Herald*, president of a literary society, and a member of the debate team. Among her contemporaries at Fisk were W. E. B. Du Bois and Sterling Brown, father of a well-known son by that name.

In June 1889, educator and founder of Tuskegee Institute (now Tuskegee University) Booker T. Washington had dinner with the senior students and also gave the commencement address. Following graduation, Washington hired Maggie to teach English, and the next year she became lady principal and director of the Department of Domestic Service, later to become the Department of Girls' Industries. In October 1892, Maggie became Washington's third wife. She was a member of a fifteen-person executive committee that ran the school during Washington's absence, and she also handled other duties traditionally assigned to a college president's wife. Maggie and twelve other women formed the Tuskegee Women's Club in 1895, and they opened a school near the college, on the Elizabeth Russell Plantation, to train young people and teach wives and mothers the basics of housekeeping, child care, and sewing. Maggie also began a reading club for black men. The clubwomen established Mother's Meetings for blacks in Macon County. When Booker T. Washington addressed ministers and civic leaders at meetings on campus or in the community, he did so in the mornings, followed by Maggie's address to women in the afternoon. The club began a Town Night School in 1910, and offered such technical courses as carpentry, bricklaying, cooking, and sewing to men and women.

The black women's club movement began to reach new heights around this time. Washington organized the Alabama Federation of Colored Women's Clubs in 1899. Joined by local educator and club member Cornelia Bowen, the group undertook a number of much-needed community activities. The women built a nursing home for the elderly and indigent, established a center for troubled youth, and built libraries. Washington's work with the club movement was seen before then, in 1895, when the National Federation of Afro-American Women was organized, and she became its founding president. The next year, the organization merged with the Colored Women's League, headed by community activist and educator Mary Church Terrell, and formed the National Association of Colored Women. When the new group met in Nashville, Tennessee, for its first convention, Washington was elected secretary of the executive board. After holding several positions within the organization, in 1914 she was elected president.

From 1919 until her death, Washington was president of the Alabama Association of Women's Clubs. During her administration, the Rescue Home for Girls was established in Mt. Meigs, Alabama. She worked cautiously but diligently with the white southern clubwomen's Commission on Interracial Cooperation, founded in 1918, to improve educational opportunities for blacks. Her work with black clubwomen in the formation of the short-lived International Council of Women of the Darker Races in 1920 is notable. Washington was a primary mover in its formation and served as its founding president, working to build links between women of color worldwide.—Jessie Carney Smith

WATERS, ETHEL
(October 31, 1896?–September 1, 1977) Singer, actor

Ethel Waters was born to Louise Anderson, a twelve-year old who had been raped by John Waters, a white man. She lived to become one of the most influential blues and gospel singers in recording history. Waters was a central figure in the music recording history of the Harlem Renaissance. While many blues singers were born in the Southern United States and honed their craft on the Chitlin' Circuit, Waters became a pioneer in urban blues, and she worked to erase the color barrier by bringing blues music to as wide an audience as possible.

Waters grew up near Philadelphia, Pennsylvania, and began her career as a singer when she was five years old, singing in church choirs. As a youngster, she was known as "Baby Star" before becoming known as "Sweet Mama Stringbean" while singing on the black vaudeville circuit. Some of her early influences were such white vaudeville singers as Nora Bayes and Fanny Price. Waters had become recognized as a talented blues singer by 1917, based on her singing in Baltimore, particularly the song "St. Louis Blues," and her rise to stardom caused a conflict among some female blues vocalists, most notably Bessie Smith.

Because she was a northern blues singer, Waters had to earn the respect of classic southern blues singers like Smith, who forbade Waters from singing the blues when they shared the same venue at 91 Decatur Street in Atlanta, Georgia. Nonetheless, at the behest of the audience, Smith relented, and Waters sang "St. Louis Blues." Following a 1918 car accident, Waters moved back to Philadelphia, where she washed dishes until 1919, when, at the nudging of supporters, she moved to

New York City at what some call the start of the Harlem Renaissance. The Harlem Renaissance marked the flowering of African American arts, letters, and music, and Waters positioned herself to be part of that movement as she became one of the most popular vocalists of the 1920s.

When she arrived in New York City, Waters sang at the Lincoln Theater before accepting a job for two dollars a night singing at Edmund's Cellar, but she would not remain at Edmund's Cellar for long. By 1921, she was recording with Cardinal Records before switching to the black-owned Black Swan Records, making her one of the first black women to make a recording. Her recordings of "Down Home Blues" and "Oh Daddy" were the first blues recordings for the label.

Willing to make a strong run at living on the sound of her voice, Waters took to the road with Fletcher Henderson to promote her work on the black vaudeville circuit. In 1925, she signed with Columbia Records and began touring on the white vaudeville circuit to promote her new work. As a result of her talent and charisma, Waters broke the color barrier between the black and white vaudeville worlds. On October 20 of that year, her recording of "Dinah" became one of the most important recordings of her career. Not only was "Dinah" the best-selling song of her career, but Waters's recordings with Columbia, along with marking the prelude to the scat singing of Louis Armstrong, helped bring black urban blues to a broader audience. By 1929, the performer was singing at clubs owned by Al Capone for more than $1,200 a week. In 1933, she recorded "Stormy Weather," a work that would later be covered by Frank Sinatra and Billie Holiday.

While she was a talented singer, Waters also emerged as an actress beginning in 1927, with the musical *Africana*. She went on to play significant roles on Broadway and the silver screen of Hollywood, where, in 1949, she earned an Academy Award nomination for Best Supporting Actress in the landmark film *Pinky*. The following year, she received a New York Drama Critics Award for Best Actress, and during her time in film she worked with some of the great artists of her time, most notably Duke Ellington. Along with her voice, Waters was a master of the written word, and in 1951, she published her first autobiography, *His Eye Is on the Sparrow*.

The gospel hymn "His Eye Is on the Sparrow," written during the first decade of the twentieth century, is closely associated with Waters, not only because of the title of her first autobiography, but also because she sang it so soulfully when she toured with evangelist Billy Graham from 1957 until 1976. Waters was a woman of good faith and good hope. In many ways, she could not have chosen a more fitting gospel. Based on the Gospel according to Matthew, the lyrics of "His Eye Is on the Sparrow" exude warmth and comfort, and her clean phrasing highlights her strong faith in a world of uncertainty. In 1977, Waters published *To Me It's Wonderful*, her second autobiography. The book focuses on her life and work with Billy Graham, along with marking a return to the sacred music of her early life.

Waters died in Chatsworth, California, from heart disease in 1977, yet her vocal performances will be remembered for all time. For her lyricism, as well as her contribution to the vocal arts, she was, in 1998, posthumously awarded a Grammy Hall of Fame Award for her recording of "Dinah." "Stormy Weather" won a Hall of Fame Award in 2003, in the genre of jazz, and "Am I Blue?" was given the same recognition in 2007.

Waters was a true renaissance woman. She moved easily from stage to screen, and the blues she sang in clubs early in her life became the gospels she sang for a nation in later life, making her one of the most versatile performers of the Harlem Renaissance. For Waters, music and human experience mattered more than the color of one's skin. Whether it was through print, the screen, the stage, or music, she always bridged the gap between people with her special blend of artistic creativity, deep pathos, and respect for the human spirit.—DELANO GREENIDGE-COPPRUE

WEBB, ELIDA
(August 9, 1895–May 1, 1975) Dancer, choreographer

Elida Webb began her career during the earlier years of the Harlem Renaissance and broke racial and gender barriers in the 1920s. One of Broadway's first African American choreographers, as well as one of the first known African American female choreographers, she helped popularize the Charleston and worked with various entertainers, including Josephine Baker, Florence Mills, Fredi Washington, Lena Horne, and Ruby Keeler.

Webb was born in Alexandria, Virginia, on August 9, 1895. She received dance training from vaudeville singer and choreographer Ada Overton Walker. Webb was married to Garfield Dawson, who was also known as George "The Strutter" Dawson Jr.

Webb was a chorus girl in Eubie Blake and Noble Sissle's *Shuffle Along*, an all-black musical that was staged on Broadway in 1921 and 1922. During the next two years, she choreographed and performed in *Runnin' Wild*, a Broadway musical that featured her rendition of the Charleston. In the late 1920s and early 1930s, Webb appeared in four additional Broadway productions: *Lucky, Singin' the Blues, Show Boat*, and *Flying Colors*. From 1923 to 1934, she was a dancer and choreographer at Harlem's Cotton Club, which featured orchestras led by Duke Ellington and Cab Calloway, as well as such singers as Ethel Waters and Adelaide Hall. The talented and creative performer was also a choreographer for the *Zeigfield Follies*, Apollo Theater, and Lafayette Theater.

Waters died in New York City in 1975. In *The Cotton Club*, the 1984 film starring Richard Gere and Gregory Hines, Norma Jean Darden portrays Webb.—LINDA M. CARTER

WELCH, ELISABETH
(February 19, 1904–July 15, 2003) Singer

Elisabeth Welch is best known as a successful singer and actress who performed in many of the major all-black musical revues in the 1920s, at the height of the Harlem Renaissance. She performed with such artists as Josephine Baker, Adelaide Hall, Bill "Bojangles" Robinson, and Ethel Waters. The singer spent most of her career after the 1930s performing in Europe, while periodically returning to the United States.

Elisabeth Welch

Welch was born on February 19, 1904, in the Manhattan, New York, area known as San Juan Hill. She was of mixed race. Her mother was of Scottish and Irish heritage, and her father of African American and Native American heritage. Her household operated on a strict Baptist perspective promoted by her father, who also worked as a gardener on an estate in Englewood, New Jersey. In spite of her strict upbringing, she made her first stage debut at eight years of age in the classic *HMS Pinafore*. After completing high school, Welch initially wanted to go into social work, but she was cast in the musical *Liza* in 1921, which began a long and successful career. It was during her performance in *Liza* that Welch introduced the Charleston, a dance craze of the Jazz Age, but it would be some time before the dance actually caught on. Because of her father's strict Baptist beliefs, she felt that her decision to become part of the "low" life of show business was partly why her father left the family.

Welch starred in many early all-black Broadway shows, for instance, *Runnin' Wild* (1923) and *Chocolate Dandies* (1924), which also featured Josephine Baker, and in 1928, she performed in the highly successful show *Blackbirds*. She was invited to perform in Paris in 1929, which included performances at the Moulin Rouge. Welch returned to New York City in 1930, to open a new nightclub and fill a singing role in Cole Porter's *The New Yorkers*, which incorporated the controversial song "Love for Sale" (it was considered controversial because of its suggestive lyrics). After the show's run from 1930 to 1931, the singer made her home in London and brought to Europe many showstopping performances. In 1934, Welch shared billing at the London Palladium with Cab Calloway and sang the song *Shanty Town*, written for Welch by Ivan Novello for his musical *Glamorous Nights* in 1935. In addition, Welch appeared in movies with such actors as Paul Robeson in the British films *Show Boat*, *Song of Freedom*, and *Big Fella*, and she performed as one of the first artists on television, all while having a regular spot on the radio series *Soft Lights and Sweet Music*. From the many songs she sang by George Gershwin, Jerome Kern, and Noel Coward, Welch chose "Stormy Weather," written by Harold Arlen and Ted Koehler, as her signature song.

In the late 1930s, Welch continued to sing in various revues while in Europe and performed for the troops during World War II. Her career lasted for nearly thirty years in England, and in the 1980s she performed in New York City, reviving many of the songs she sang for greats the likes of Irving Berlin. She appeared in the show *Black Broadway* in 1980, and in 1986, she performed in the one-woman show *Time to Start Living*, which earned her an Obie Award. Welch died in Northwood, Middlesex, United Kingdom.—LEAN'TIN L. BRACKS

WELLS-BARNETT, IDA B.

(July 16, 1862–March 25, 1931) Journalist, lecturer, social activist, clubwoman, feminist, antilynching crusader

Ida B. Wells-Barnett

Ida B. Wells-Barnett ascended to prominence between 1892 and the decade of the Roaring Twenties, which was an era of unparalleled flourishing of African American culture branded as the Harlem Renaissance or Negro Renaissance. Known for having an activist authority, the Harlem Renaissance era acted as both a commemoration and advancement of the intellectual acumen of American blacks. Expressed as a literary movement and social uprising against structural racism inculcated by the Jim Crow laws, diasporic individuals of African descent from throughout the United States and West Indies used the period to recast the identity of their brothers and sisters through the mediums of music, literature, and the visual and performing arts. This era of black expression also kindled the concept of the "New Negro Woman," especially as it related to female poets, authors, and intellectuals. Wells-Barnett was among the women who used the movement to express their views on race and gender relations.

The oldest of eight children, Wells was born on July 16, 1862, in Holly Springs, Mississippi, to James Wells and Elizabeth Bell Wells. Born into slavery six months before President Abraham Lincoln signed the Emancipation Proclamation and reared during Reconstruction, she came of age during the post–Reconstruction period and spent her adult life fighting the racial inequities wrought by Jim Crow's systemic structural impediments.

Although her parents were slaves, they transitioned from slavery to freedom during Wells's formative years. Her father, a proficient carpenter, launched his own business in 1867, and her mother became noted for her gastronomic talent; however, a little more than a decade after her father established his business and the family seemed poised to become productive participants in the American experiment, they were beset by a dreaded disease that tore it asunder. The yellow fever epidemic of 1878, which was spread by a mosquito-borne viral infection, completely disrupted the lives of Wells and her family. Her father, mother, and nine-month-old brother Stanley succumbed to the epidemic, which swept through not only Mississippi, but raged from the port of New Orleans to Memphis, east to Alabama, and west to the Louisiana Valley.

After the death of her parents and youngest brother, Wells took on the responsibility of rearing her younger siblings. Having attended Shaw University, she taught for a while at a school six miles from her home for a monthly salary of twenty-five dollars. In 1880, she accepted an invitation from her aunt, Fanny Butler Wells, to move to Memphis, Tennessee. In Memphis, she accepted employment with the Shelby County school system as a teacher, a position in which she earned slightly more than she did in Mississippi.

Teaching in Woodstock, Tennessee, which was approximately twelve miles north of Memphis, required her to patronize the Chesapeake, Ohio, and Southwestern Railroad twice a day. Her travels to and from Woodstock catapulted Wells into a career of activism. Having purchased a first-class ticket, when she boarded the train, she took a seat in the "Ladies' Car." After the conductor forcibly removed her, she challenged racially segregated accommodations by filing suit against the railroad in 1884. Although the circuit ruled in her favor and awarded her $500 in damages, the Tennessee Supreme Court reversed the lower court's decision in 1887.

Wells later taught in the Memphis school system, and during summer sessions she matriculated at Fisk University in Nashville. During her stay in Memphis, she became part of an intellectual and politically active African American community. She joined a lyceum, composed primarily of other teachers who enjoyed music, reading, debating political issues of the day, giving recitations, writing, and presenting essays. It was in Tennessee's Bluff City that Wells launched her career as an activist and journalist. Her social and journalistic activities in Memphis would ultimately thrust her into the Harlem Renaissance.

Writing under the pen name Iola, Wells published accounts of her train experience in such African American newspapers as the *New York Freeman* and Detroit's *Plaindealer*. At the National Press Association's conference in Kentucky, she presented a paper, "Women in Journalism, or How I Would Edit." She later became editor of the *Evening Star*. In 1889, the teacher-turned-journalist purchased one-third interest in Memphis's *Free Speech and Headlight*, a militant journal owned by Reverend Taylor Nightingale, pastor of the Beale Street Baptist Church, and J. L. Fleming. Two years later, the "Princess of the Press," as she was called, became a fulltime journalist and editor of the *Free Speech* after the school board fired her for writing a scathing editorial critical of Memphis's substandard racially segregated schools, as well as its unequal distribution of resources allocated to African American schools.

In 1892, events in Memphis changed the course of Wells's life. Law enforcement officials arrested a trio of African American grocers, Thomas Moss, Calvin McDowell, and Henry Stewart, all friends of the fearless journalist. Later, a mob dragged them from the jail and shot them to death in the infamous "Lynching at the Curve." Outraged, Wells bought a pistol for protection, asserting, "One had better die fighting against injustice than to die like a dog or a rat in a trap." In her editorials, the young journalist urged African Americans to leave Memphis. Outraged by this, the most heinous act of brutality perpetrated against African Americans since the Memphis Riots of 1866, where some forty-six African Americans and two whites died during the uprising, she urged African Americans to migrate from Memphis. The African American community listened to the clarion call and emboldened all who could to leave the Bluff City. In addition, there were calls for those staying behind to refrain from patronizing the City Railroad Company. Prodded by angry editorials in the *Free Speech* and calls of "On to Oklahoma," 2,000 African Americans left Memphis and put the streetcar company in dire financial straits. Throughout the spring, Wells's editorials "demanded that the murders of Moss, McDowell, and Stewart be brought to justice." She exposed lynching as a stratagem to eliminate prosperous, politically active African Americans and condemned the "thread-bare lie" of rape used to justify violence against African Americans. Her indictments infuriated white Memphians, principally her intimation that southern white women were sexually attracted to black men. While Wells was in Philadelphia, a committee of "leading citizens" destroyed her newspaper office and warned her not to return to the city.

The "Lynching at the Curve" and her cogent and caustic pen denouncing the atrocity perpetrated by Memphis whites brought Wells national and international attention. Exiled from the South, she persevered in her struggle against racial injustice and the lynching of African Americans as a columnist for the *New York Age*, a newspaper owned and edited by T. Thomas Fortune and Jerome B. Patterson.

Wells moved to New York; bought an interest in the *New York Age*; and intensified her campaign against lynching through lectures, newspaper articles, and pamphlets. Works from this period include *Southern Horrors: Lynch Law in All Its Phases* (1892); *A Red Record: Tabulated Statistics and Alleged Causes of Lynching in the United States, 1892, 1893, and 1894* (1895); and *Mob Rule in New Orleans* (1900). To make her antilynching crusade international, she lectured in Great Britain in 1893 and 1894, and wrote a column entitled "Ida B. Wells Abroad" for the *Chicago Inter-Ocean*. Wells also cowrote *The Reason Why the Colored American Is Not in the World's Columbia Exposition: The Afro-American's Contribution to Columbia Literature*, a pamphlet created to protest the exclusion of blacks from the 1893 Chicago World's Fair. In 1893, she moved to Chicago and worked for Chicago's *Conservator*, the city's first African American newspaper, founded and edited by Ferdinand L. Barnett.

On June 27, 1895, Wells married Barnett, a prominent Chicago attorney and widower with two small sons, and added his name to hers. They later became the parents of four children. She bought an interest in the *Conservator* and continued to write forceful articles and essays, including "Booker T. Washington and His Critics" and "How Enfranchisement Stops Lynching." Her militant views, support of Black Nationalist Marcus A. Garvey, and direct criticism of such race leaders as Booker T. Washington and W. E. B. Du Bois embroiled her in controversies and disagreements with leaders in the African American community. After she applauded the accomplishments of Garvey, the U.S. Secret Service classified Wells-Barnett as a radical.

After a brief retirement from public life following the birth of her second child, Wells-Barnett continued her campaign for racial justice, the political empowerment of blacks, and the enfranchisement of women. In 1898, she met with President William McKinley to protest the lynching of a postal worker and urge the passage of a federal law against lynching. After a burst of violence against African Americans in Springfield, Illinois, she signed the call for a conference, which led to the 1909 formation of the National Association for the Advancement of Colored People (NAACP). She disassociated herself from the NAACP because of differences with Du Bois over strategy and racial politics. In 1910, Wells-Barnett founded the Negro Fellowship League (NFL) to provide housing, employment, and recreational facilities for southern black migrants. Unable to garner sufficient support for the NFL, she donated her salary as an adult probation officer following her appointment to the office in 1913.

An early champion of rights for women, Wells-Barnett was one of the founders of the National Association of Colored Women. In Chicago, she organized the Ida B. Wells Club; as its president, she established a kindergarten in the black community and successfully lobbied, with the help of Jane Addams, against segregated public schools. She also founded the Alpha Suffrage Club, which, in 1913, sent her as a delegate to the National American Woman Suffrage Association's parade in Washington, D.C. Refusing to join black delegates, who were segregated from white suffragists at the back of the procession, she integrated the parade by marching with the Illinois delegation. Through her leadership, the Alpha Suffrage Club became actively involved in the 1928 congressional election of Oscar Stanton DePriest, the first African American alderman of Chicago and first African American congressperson elected from the North. Her interest in politics eventually led to Wells-Barnett's unsuccessful campaign for the Illinois State Senate in 1930.

In 1918, in her unremitting crusade against racial violence, Wells-Barnett covered the race riot in East St. Louis, Illinois, and wrote a series of articles on the uprising for the *Chicago Defender*. Four years later, she returned to the South for the first time in thirty years to investigate the indictment for murder of twelve innocent farmers in Elaine, Arkansas. She raised money to publish and distribute 1,000 copies of *The Arkansas Race Riot* (1922), in which she recorded the results of her investigation.

Wells-Barnett continued to write throughout the final decade of her life. In 1928, she began an autobiography, which was published posthumously, and she recorded the details of her political campaign in a 1930 diary. She died in 1931, after a brief illness.

The women of the Harlem Renaissance were quite diverse. Some characterized themselves as active protesters and were ardent supporters of the struggle against the most vituperative practices of bigotry and racism, while others espoused a reflective position. Notwithstanding, the life of Wells-Barnett epitomizes a lifetime of endless struggle against the societal inhumanity perpetrated against African Americans and women.—LINDA T. WYNN

WEST, DOROTHY
(June 2, 1907–August 16, 1988) Novelist, short story writer, journalist

Considered a minor figure in the Harlem Renaissance tradition, Dorothy West is primarily noted for her novels *The Living Is Easy* (1948) and *The Wedding* (1995), both influential works that attempt to illustrate the lives of the black bourgeoisie and the issues surrounding class in the upward movement of middle-class black Americans.

Born in Boston, Massachusetts, on June 2, 1907, West was the only child of a former slave-turned-businessman and his wife—the first black family to later purchase property in Martha's Vineyard as part of the small and developing black middle class. These experiences perhaps proved the most influential in shaping West's aesthetic and literary approach, her novels foregrounding class as being more important in the United States than issues of color and race.

West's literary career began in 1926, with the publication of her short story "The Typewriter" in *Opportunity* magazine. She later traveled with Langston Hughes and twenty black intellectuals to the Soviet Union to film *Black and White*—a propaganda film about the oppression of the black community. Although the film was never completed, West stayed in the Soviet Union for an additional nine months, only returning to the United States with the death of her father. With her return, West continued her literary pursuits, founding *Challenge* magazine in 1934, with the goal of revitalizing the spirit of the earlier Harlem Renaissance. During her time as editor, she published several notable black authors, from Zora Neale Hurston to Helene Johnson to Claude McKay, before the magazine collapsed due to financial constraints in 1937. West attempted to revive her endeavors with *New Challenge*, publishing works by Margaret Walker, Ralph Ellison, and Richard Wright; however, this magazine also failed following editorial and financial issues, rolling out just a single issue before its demise.

With the collapse of *Challenge* and later *New Challenge* magazine, West worked as a welfare investigator and for the Federal Writers' Project until the 1940s, when she began working for the *New York Daily News*, publishing short stories monthly until the 1960s. In 1947, she moved from New York to her cottage in Martha's Vineyard, where she lived out the rest of her literary career. Shortly thereafter, in 1948, she published *The Living Is Easy*, her semiautobiographical novel. The novel examines the intraracial colorism present in the United States—a thematic approach seldom illustrated in the black fiction of her time, except for such texts as Jessie Redmon Fauset's *Colored American Style*. During this time, West also wrote a column for the *Vineyard Gazette*, never abandoning her journalistic roots, and she eventually wrote her own column on Oak Bluffs from 1973 to 1983.

West's longest and most renowned work is *The Wedding*, which she abandoned in the 1960s due to overwhelming fears that the novel would not be favorably received by the rising Black Panthers and other militant organizations that perceived black people as victims, thus denying the black bourgeoisie. The novel remained unfinished until its publication in 1995, after Jacqueline Kennedy Onassis had encouraged the completion of the project. The book, which illustrates the struggle of interracial relationships to succeed in a racist and classist American society, is arguably the biggest legacy that West has left behind as a notable woman of the Harlem Renaissance tradition. Also published in 1995 was *The Richer, the Poorer*, a collection of thirty short stories and essays that West produced throughout her literary career. Although she never reached fame or recognition until the end of her life, West is truly an underappreciated talent from her time.—CHRISTOPHER ALLEN VARLACK

WHITMAN SISTERS: MABEL [MAY], ESSIE, ALBERTA [BERT], ALICE
(1880–1962), (1882–1963), (1887–1964), (1900–1969) *Vaudevillians, dancers, singers, businesswomen*

The Whitman Sisters

Mabel, Essie, Alberta, and Alice Whitman were the daughters of Albery Allison Whitman (bishop of the African Methodist Episcopal Church, a dean of Morris Brown College, and a noted poet) and Caddie Whitman (who served as their chaperone until her death). Their father taught them to dance as children. They sang and danced in church and on tours, and their brother Caswell performed with them during their youth. He, too, later became a noted musician.

From the late 1800s to the 1930s, the Whitman Sisters had one of the most popular acts in black vaudeville; they were credited with having the biggest, flashiest, fastest, classiest, and most dignified shows, with no bawdy material. The company had between twenty and thirty performers, including dancers, comedians, female singers, a chorus line of twelve women, and a five- or six-piece jazz band led by Lonnie Johnson for nine years. They were credited with providing opportunities and inspiration for numerous performers, most notably Bill "Bojangles" Robinson, Ethel Waters, and Count Basie.

The sisters began their professional career early; their fair skin was an advantage to their acceptance, for they consistently played before white audiences and often with white groups. In 1899, they began their professional career, touring Missouri, Florida, and later the white vaudeville circuit. Alberta joined Essie and Mabel on a European tour, and in 1902, they toured at the Grand Opera House in Atlanta, Georgia. In 1904, the sisters formed the Whitman Sisters' New Orleans Troubadours; each sister had a distinct role. Mabel, the eldest, was the producer, director, and manager; Alberta was considered one of the best male impersonators; Essie was a comedienne and singer (contralto) who worked on costumes and design for the shows; and Alice, who joined in 1909, after their mother's death, was billed as the "Queen of Taps" and a "champion cakewalk dancer" known for such dances as the Shim Sham Shimmy and Ballin' the Jack (she was succeeded by her son Albert, also known as "Little Pops"). Mabel was married to "Uncle" Dave Payton, who tutored the children. Cast members were held to high moral and artistic standards. Their operating base moved from Atlanta to Chicago in 1905.

In 1910, the group became known as the Whitman Sisters' Own Company. Mabel later formed Mabel Whitman and the Dixie Boys, an act that toured Germany and Australia, with her singing and the children dancing. The sisters continued to form road-show companies. Mabel's entrepreneurial talents were evident; she was in charge of the business—organization and bookings—and other members of the family controlled additional aspects of the show. They later toured with the Theater Owners' Booking Association, a black vaudeville traveling circuit, with top billing.

With the death of Mabel in 1943, from pneumonia, the company collapsed. The group's religious and racial grounding are evident in that they provided moral and principled entertainment and a home for traveling African Americans in a racist society. The sisters were integrated and played to an integrated audience, helped further the careers of several performers, and provided racial uplift for countless individuals. Essie founded the Theatrical Cheer Club for performers during the Great Depression. Known as the "royalty of Negro vaudeville," the Whitman Sisters, who had a sense of self and racial pride, presented a broad array of characters and styles, represented high-quality entertainment between 1900 and 1943, and had control of their company. Yet, they have almost been forgotten.—HELEN R. HOUSTON

WIGGINS, BERNICE LOVE
(March 4, 1897–?) Poet

Bernice Love Wiggins left El Paso, Texas, for California in the early 1930s and was never heard from again. The mystery surrounding her life and death make her one of the most enigmatic writers during the waning years of the Harlem Renaissance. Before she left El Paso, Wiggins experienced limited recognition for a brief period of writing. She published poems in the *El Paso Herald*, *Chicago Defender*, and *Houston Informer*, as well as in *Half Center Magazine*. She only produced one book of poems, *Tuneful Tales* (1925), which she self-published, but the poems illustrate an ability to find meaning and convey the complexity of both the black experience and black life on the Mexican border.

Wiggins was born on March 4, 1897, in Austin, Texas, to J. Austin Love. There are no records of her mother, and her identity was never found. Little is known about Wiggins's early childhood, but in 1903, she moved to El Paso with her aunt; it was there that she was given the surname Wiggins. Her first-grade teacher noticed her talent and encouraged her to express herself in rhyme and verse.

Wiggins continued to write at Douglas High School, which was established to train black students to the best of their ability, sensitize them about racial matters, develop a sense pride in their people and community, and spur their leadership. The principal of the school, William Coleman, was a college-educated man who followed W. E. B. Du Bois's ideas on the "Talented Tenth." He believed that Wiggins and her classmates could be trained to join this elite group of leaders. While at Douglas High, Wiggins continued to excel at writing poetry, so much so that Coleman writes in the preface of her book that she was a woman with "poetic visions born of holy passions, high hopes, and a burning enthusiasm."

Nonetheless, much of Wiggins's life remains a mystery. No one knows whether she married, if she had children, whether she had a career, or what happened to her. The literary community is left with questions about her life and "what if" questions about her career. What is left, however, is a few individually published poems and a wonderful book of poetry that demonstrates versatility and brilliance. Those who knew her, like poet J. Mason Brewer, paint a picture of a person who had a "deep knowledge of the psychology of her people." This knowledge is portrayed through the medium of her dialect verse, which at times rises.—MYRON T. STRONG

WILLIAMS, MARIE SELIKA [SELIKA WILLIAMS, MARIE SELIKA SMITH]

(ca. 1849–1937) Opera singer, teacher

Marie Selika Williams was an African American opera singer and teacher whose coloratura soprano voice was known for its brilliance. She was referred to as the "Queen of the Staccato" by both her fans and the press. Her concert career, which lasted more than two decades and embraced the Harlem Renaissance era, took her throughout the United States, Europe, and the West Indies. Despite her acclaim, her tours of the United States were primarily for black audiences.

Marie Selika was born in Natchez, Mississippi, around 1849. Shortly after her birth, she was taken to Cincinnati, Ohio. She began her musical study at an early age under the patronage of a wealthy white family. In the early 1870s, she went to San Francisco, where she studied voice with Signora G. Bianchi and made her concert debut in 1876. It was during this time that she met and married Sampson Williams, with whom she often performed. After two years in San Francisco, she moved to the Eastern United States to begin her concert career. In November 1878, she was invited to perform at the White House for President Rutherford B. Hayes. Williams went to England in 1882, to continue her vocal studies. The following year, she performed for Queen Victoria. By the 1890s, she had settled in Cleveland, Ohio, where, in addition to performing, she opened a music studio.

Following the death of her husband in 1911, Williams retired from performing and spent her time teaching. In 1916, she accepted a teaching position at the
Martin-Smith School of Music in New York. She remained in New York for the rest
of her life.—ANTHONY WILLIAMS

WILSON [GOODALL], EDITH
(September 6, 1896–March 30, 1981) Singer, actress

During the peak of the Harlem Renaissance in the 1920s and 1930s, Edith Wilson enjoyed a successful career recording songs and performing in clubs and other
venues in Harlem and elsewhere, both nationally and internationally. She also
teamed up with some of the biggest names of the era, singing alongside such Harlem luminaries as Cab Calloway and Louis Armstrong. Hers was a prolific career
that continued long after the renaissance had faded, but it still burned brightly in
the memories of those who had witnessed and participated in it.

Wilson was born Edith Goodall on September 6, 1896, in Louisville, Kentucky.
She was one of three children born to Hundley Goodall, a teacher, and Susan Jones
Goodall. Like many African American women, Wilson's mother was a housekeeper
for white families.

Wilson was only two years old when she began singing. The black church she attended offered many opportunities for children to sing and perform in front of a
supportive and encouraging audience. It was at the age of thirteen that Wilson began
working in secret in a show at White City Park. When her parents found out, the
youngster convinced them that she should continue singing despite her age. Her main
argument was that she could make more money singing than she could cleaning and
cooking for white families. At the age of fourteen, Wilson dropped out of school and
plunged into the full-time work of making her dreams of stardom come true.

Wilson would eventually find stardom, as well as marriage. During the early
stages of her career, she performed with Danny Wilson, a talented pianist, and
his sister, Lena Wilson, a blues singer. Danny taught Edith the importance of not
limiting herself to singing blues, and she learned to sing outside the popular blues
genre. Her versatility would help her immensely throughout her spectacular career.
In 1919, she married Danny.

Wilson's career included singing and acting. In the early years, she performed in
African American communities in Chicago, Washington, D.C., and Atlantic City,
New Jersey. By the end of the 1920s, Wilson's resume included forty recordings.
Tragically, in 1928, her husband died from tuberculosis. (She later married a second
time to Millard Wilson in 1949.) Throughout the 1920s and 1930s, Wilson went on
multiple singing and theatrical tours and performed in Harlem in such notable venues as the Cotton Club, Connie's Inn, and Lafayette Theater. Her talent also took
her abroad to England, France, and other countries, where she performed songs in
different languages.

Wilson's career continued into the late twentieth century. She appeared in
films, for instance, *I'm Still Alive* (1940) and *To Have and Have Not* (1944). In the

1950s, she made the controversial move of portraying the Aunt Jemima character on the radio and in special appearances for the Quaker Oats Company. She also provided the voice for another controversial character, Kingfish's wife, on the *Amos 'n' Andy* radio show. Both roles were heavily criticized by African American civil rights leaders, who contended that the characters were based on harmful and derogatory stereotypes.

Following the end of Wilson's stint as the Aunt Jemima character in 1965, she returned to singing. She recorded songs and made popular appearances in nightclubs and at blues and jazz festivals. Her last performance took place in 1980, on Broadway, in the show *Blacks on Broadway*. She died in Chicago.—GLADYS L. KNIGHT

WILSON, LENA
(1898–1939) Entertainer

Lena Wilson, born in Charlotte, North Carolina, in 1898, began her career in the vaudeville circuit traveling in the South between 1918 and 1920, with her brother, Danny Wilson. The two became a trio when Danny married blues singer Edith [Goodall] Wilson, and the group toured the Baltimore and Washington, D.C., area. In 1921, Lena moved to New York, when the Harlem Renaissance was in full bloom, and began singing and recording with different bands, as well as performing in clubs and musical revues. Beginning in 1922, Wilson recorded with the Fletcher Henderson Orchestra, Johnny Dunn's Jazz Hounds, and the Columbia label, and she also appeared in *The Flat Below* at the Lafayette Theater and *Buzzin' Around* at Club Maurice. She went to London in 1926, and performed in *Blackbirds* with Florence Mills. In addition, she sang with her sister-in-law, Edith Wilson, in *Jazzmania*, and with the Duke Ellington Band in *Dance Mania* in 1927. From 1929 to 1931, Wilson performed at the Lenox Club and various other nightclubs in Upstate New York. She married jazz violinist Shrimp Jones and continued to perform in the New York area into the late 1930s. Wilson died of pneumonia in New York City.—LEAN'TIN L. BRACKS

WRIGHT, ZARA
(?–?) Writer

Zara Wright is best known for her novels as published, acknowledged, and reviewed in Chicago during the 1920s. She published two novels during the Harlem Renaissance era, *Black and White Tangled Threads* and its sequel, *Kenneth*. The novels are dedicated to and were inspired by Wright's deceased husband, J. Edward Wright. They follow two generations of African Americans from Emancipation onward and deal with issues of race consciousness, interracial marriage, class, and passing. The characters' experiences are set in Louisville, Kentucky; England; and Italy. Wright's images and accomplishments as a novelist are included in the De Sable Association of Chicago's *The Souvenir of Negro Progress, Chicago, 1779–1925*. Little else is known about her life or other publications she may have produced. Her novels were reprinted in 1975.—LEAN'TIN L. BRACKS

WYNBUSH, OCTAVIA BEATRICE
(1898–1972) Poet, short story writer

Octavia Beatrice Wynbush was born in Washington, Pennsylvania, in 1898, and later pursued higher education at Oberlin College. In 1920, she received a B.A. in German from Oberlin and, in 1934, earned a M.A. from Columbia University. Few details are known about her life growing up and her work experiences. Wynbush's poems and short stories were often published in *Crisis* and *Opportunity* magazines and primarily feature characters from the South who speak in dialect. Her publications, which spanned from 1931 to 1945, placed her among those authors seen as accomplished and successful writers of the Harlem Renaissance era. *Crisis* featured Wynbush on the cover of its March 1936 issue, and in January 1937, her Christmas story "Lady Blanche and The Christ" was also featured on the cover. In 1941, she published her only children's book, *The Wheel That Made Wishes Come True*.

Wynbush taught college in New Orleans, Louisiana, and Pine Bluff, Arkansas, and in 1936, she taught high school in Kansas City, Missouri, where she remained until 1964, when she retired. Although she spent most of her life as a single woman, in 1963, when she was sixty-six years of age, Wynbush married Lewis Strong.
—Lean'tin L. Bracks

Y

YANCEY, BESSIE WOODSON
(1882–January 11, 1958) Poet, activist

Bessie Woodson Yancey, younger sister of historian Carter G. Woodson, published a book of poetry and contributed more than 100 letters to her local newspaper discussing public affairs and racial issues.

Yancey was born near New Canton, Buckingham County, Virginia, in 1882, to James Henry and Anne Eliza Riddle Woodson. In Virginia, she attended a rural school taught by her uncles, John Morton Riddle and James Buchanan Riddle. By 1892, Yancey's family had returned to Huntington, West Virginia, where they had previously lived in the early 1870s. Yancey attended Douglass High School, where she was taught by William T. McKinney, Susie M. James, Leota Moss Claire, Carter Harrison Barnett, as well as her brother, Carter G. Woodson. In 1901, during her brother's tenure as principal, Yancey graduated from high school.

After high school, Yancey became a teacher. She taught at a mining-camp school near Montgomery, West Virginia, and later at Guyandotte before it merged with Huntington. While teaching in Fayette County, Yancey was married and had two daughters, Ursula and Belva. Belva eventually gave Yancey two grandchildren: Nelson and Joan Bickley. Yancey eventually divorced her first husband and was remarried but soon widowed. It was during these years, while she was teaching school and working as a courthouse matron, that she wrote the poetry that would be published in her 1939 book of poetry, *Echoes from the Hills: A Book of Poems*.

While Yancey never published another book, she continued to write poetry and newspaper editorials. Her poem "The Forgotten Boys" was published by the *Pittsburgh Courier*. Between 1946 and 1956, she wrote more than 100 letters to the editor of her local Huntington newspaper, the *Herald-Advertiser*. She wrote so many letters that she took the advice of the editor and began using the pseudonyms

"Bronze" or "The Yank." Yancey would juxtapose international events in the news with African American civil rights and encouraged desegregation. While she had many supporters, she was also threatened for voicing her opinions. The newspaper's recognition of Yancey's talent of writing resulted in one of her letters winning a small monetary prize. As the years passed by, Yancey's health began to decline, until her death in 1958, in the home of her brother Carter, who had provided for her.
—AMANDA J. CARTER

YEISER, IDABELLE
(1897–?) Poet, writer

Idabelle Yeiser was an important part of the literary movement in Philadelphia, Pennsylvania, during the same time as the Harlem Renaissance. Like many of the more accomplished artists in the area, she had her works published in Philadelphia's black literary magazine, *Black Opal*.

Yeiser was born in 1897, and raised in a black middle-class family. She graduated from Montclair State Normal School in New Jersey. She furthered her education by earning an A.B. from the University of Pennsylvania in languages, as well as a D.E. from the Teacher's College at Columbia University and a doctorate in French, also from Columbia. Yeiser traveled in Africa and France between 1925 and 1926, and then returned to Philadelphia to teach. In the May 1943 issue of *Crisis* magazine, she was welcomed to Dillard University in New Orleans, Louisiana, as professor of education, after serving as a curriculum consultant for Philadelphia public schools.

Yeiser's early literary talents won her first prize in *Opportunity* magazine for her submission "Letters," which tells about her travel experiences. The work was also published in *Black Opal* as an example of travel writings. In 1937, Yeiser published her first book of poetry, *Moods: A Book of Verse*. The volume contains sonnets and free verse. Known as the "intellectual poet," her book of poems deals with such issues as her frustration with social and racial hypocrisy, and the status of women in social and political situations. Her second book of poetry, *Lyrics and Legend*, published in 1947, focuses on world peace. Little is known about Yeiser's life after the late 1940s.—LEAN'TIN L. BRACKS

APPENDIX: ENTRANTS BY AREA OF CONTRIBUTION

ACTIVISTS

Andrews, Regina M. Anderson [Ursala or Ursula Trelling, Henry Simons]
Ayer, Gertrude Elise Johnson McDougald
Booze, Mary Cordelia Montgomery
Boozer, Thelma Berlack
Brown, Hallie Quinn
Burrill, Mary P. "Mamie"
Burroughs, Nannie Helen
Butler, Selena Sloan
Carter, Eunice Hunton
Clifford, Carrie Williams
Cooper, Anna Julia Haywood
Cunard, Nancy
Cuthbert, Marion Vera
Du Bois, Shirley Lola Graham [Shirley Graham]
Dunbar-Nelson, Alice Ruth
Eastman, Crystal
Fernandis, Sarah Collins
Fleming, Sarah Lee Brown
Fuller, Meta Warrick
Hampton, Mabel
Henderson, Katherine [Catherine]
Hope, Lugenia Burns
Horne, Lena [Lena Mary Calhoun Horne]
Hunter, Jane Edna Harris
Hunton, Addie D. Waites
Hurst, Fannie

Johnson, Dorothy Vena
Martin, Mrs. George Madden [Mrs. Attwood R. Martin]
Meyer, Annie Nathan
Moryck, Brenda Ray
Ridley, Florida Ruffin [Amelia Yates Ruffin]
Robeson, Eslanda [Cardoza Goode]
Robinson [Roberson], Lizzie Woods
Savage, Augusta
Spencer, Anne [Anne Bethel Bannister]
Talbert, Mary Morris Burnett
Terrell, Mary Church [Mary Eliza Church]
Thomas, Edna Lewis
Thompson, Era Bell [Dakota Dick]
Thompson Patterson, Louise Alone
Washington, Fredericka "Fredi" Carolyn
Wells-Barnett, Ida B.
Yancey, Bessie Woodson

ACTRESSES

Bowman [Bradford], Laura
Brown [Scott], Ada
Brown, Lillyn [Lillian]
Burgoyne, Olga "Ollie"
Bush, Anita
Clough, Inez
Dunn, Blanche
Ellis, Evelyn
George, Maude Roberts
Gilbert, Mercedes
Goodwin, Ruby Berkley
Hall, Adelaide
Hall [Long], Juanita
Harvey, Georgette Mickey
Horne, Lena [Lena Mary Calhoun Horne]
Howard, Gertrude
McBrown, Gertrude Parthenia
McClendon, Rose [Rosalie Virginia Scott]
McKinney, Nina Mae
Mitchell [Cook], Abriea " Abbie" [Abbey Mitchell]
Moses, Ethel
Moten [Barnett], Etta
Peterson, Dorothy Randolph
Preer, Evelyn
Randolph, Amanda [Mandy]
Saunders, Gertrude
Smith, Trixie [Tessie Aimes]

Snow, Valaida
Sul-Te-Wan, Madame [Nellie Conley]
Taylor [Williams], Eva [Irene Gibbons]
Thomas, Edna Lewis
Washington, Fredi
Waters, Ethel
Wilson [Goodall], Edith

ARTISTS

Fuller, Meta Warrick
Jackson, Mae Howard
Jones, Lois Mailou
Prophet, Nancy Elizabeth
Savage, Augusta
Waring, Laura Wheeler

COMMUNITY LEADERS

Andrews, Regina M. Anderson [Ursala or Ursula Trelling, Henry Simons]
Bethune, Mary McLeod
Booze, Mary Cordelia Montgomery
Bowles, Eva del Vakia
Brown, Charlotte Eugenia Hawkins [Lottie Hawkins]
Brown, Hallie Quinn
Burroughs, Nannie Helen
Butler, Selena Sloan
Carter, Eunice Hunton
Clifford, Carrie Williams
Cuthbert, Marion Vera
Haynes, Elizabeth Ross
Hope, Lugenia Burns
Hunter, Jane Edna Harris
Hunton, Addie D. Waites
Nance, Ethel Ray
Robinson, Ida Bell
Robinson [Roberson], Lizzie Woods
Terrell, Mary Church [Mary Eliza Church]
Washington, Margaret "Maggie" Murray Jones
Wells-Barnett, Ida. B.

DANCERS

Baker, Josephine
Burgoyne, Olga " Ollie"

Bush, Anita
Clough, Inez
Forsyne, Ida
Greely, Aurora Borealis
Hampton, Mabel
Hill, Chippie [Bertha]
Mabley, Jackie "Moms" [Loretta Mary Aiken]
McKinney, Nina Mae
Mills, Florence
Moses, Ethel
Snow, Valaida
Webb, Elida
Whitman Sisters, " The Royalty of Negro Vaudeville," Mabel [May], Essie, Alberta [Bert],
    Alice Livingston, Myrtle Athleen Smith

EDUCATORS/TEACHERS

Ayer, Gertrude Elise Johnson McDougald
Bennett, Gwendolyn
Bethune, Mary McLeod
Bowman [Bradford], Laura
Bright, Nellie Rathbone
Brown, Charlotte Eugenia Hawkins [Lottie Hawkins]
Brown, Hallie Quinn
Burrill, Mary P. " Mamie"
Burroughs, Nannie Helen
Bush-Banks, Olivia Ward
Butler, Selena Sloan
Clifford, Carrie Williams
Cole-Talbert, Florence
Cooper, Anna Julia Haywood
Cuthbert, Marion Vera
Day, Caroline Stewart Bond
Dickinson, Blanche Taylor
Du Bois, [Nina] Yolande
Dunbar-Nelson, Alice Ruth
Duncan, Thelma Myrtle [Thelma Brown]
Evanti, Lillian [Annie Lillian Evans]
Fauset, Jessie Redmon
Fleming, Sarah Lee Brown
Grimké, Angelina Weld
Harrison, Hazel Lucile
Holloway, Lucy Ariel Williams [Ariel Williams]
Holt, Nora [Lena Douglas]
Hunton, Addie D. Waites
Jeffrey, Maurine Lawrence

Johnson, Dorothy Vena
Jones, Lois Mailou
Livingston, Myrtle Athleen Smith
McBrown, Gertrude Parthenia
Miller, May [May Miller Sullivan]
Moryck, Brenda Ray
Peterson, Dorothy Randolph
Popel, Esther [Ester Popel Shaw]
Postles, Grace Vera
Reynolds, Evelyn Crawford [Eve Lynn]
Ridley, Florida Ruffin [Amelia Yates Ruffin]
Robinson [Roberson], Lizzie Woods
Savage, Augusta
Shelton, Ruth Ada Gaines [Ruth Gaines Shelton]
Spence, Eulalie
Spencer, Anne [Anne Bethel Bannirer]
Spiller, Isabele Taliaferro
Terrell, Mary Church
Thompson, Clara Ann
Turner, Lucy Mae
Waring, Laura Wheeler
Washington, Margaret "Maggie" Murray Jones
Williams, Marie Selika [Selika Williams, Marie Selika Smith]

ENTERTAINERS/PERFORMERS

Baker, Josephine
Beavers, Louise [Louise Ellen Beavers]
Bentley, Gladys
Blanks, Birleanna
Brown, Ida G.
Burke, Georgia
Cato, Minto [La Minto Cato]
Gee, Lottie
Hawthorne, Susie
Henderson, Katherine [Catherine]
Henderson, Rosa
Jones, Maude
Mabley, Jackie "Moms" [Loretta Mary Aiken]
Martin, Sara [Sara Dunn, Margaret Johnson, Sally Roberts]
Randolph, Amanda [Mandy]
Smith, Ada Beatrice Queen Victoria Louise Virginia [Bricktop]
Smith, Bessie
Washington, Isabel [Marion Marie Theodore Rosemarie]
Wilson, Lena

ENTREPRENEURS

Bethune, Mary McLeod
Bush, Anita
Calloway, Blanche Dorothea Jones
Cuney Hare, Maud
Dean, Lillian Harris ["Pigfoot Mary"]
Gooden, Lauretta Holman
Smith, Ada Beatrice Queen Victoria Louise Virginia [Bricktop]
Spivey, Victoria
Walker, A'Lelia [Lelia McWilliams]
Walker, Madam C. J. [Sarah Breedlove]

JOURNALISTS

Beasley, Delilah Leontium
Bennett, Gwendolyn
Boozer, Thelma Berlack
Butler, Anna Mabel Land
Clifford, Carrie Williams
Cunard, Nancy
Dismond [Hodges], Geraldyn
Fauset, Jessie Redmon
Newsome, Effie Lee [Mary Effie Lee]
Reynolds, Evelyn Crawford [Eve Lynn]
Tarry, Ellen
Thompson, Eloise Alberta Veronica Bibb
West, Dorothy
Wells-Barnett, Ida. B.

MUSICIANS

Anderson, Hallie
Armstrong, Lillian "Lil" Harding
Austin, Lovie [Cora Calhoun]
Burlin, Natalie Curtis [Natalie Curtis]
Calloway, Blanche Dorothea Jones
Cuney Hare, Maud
Du Bois, Shirley Lola Graham [Shirley Graham]
George, Maude Roberts
Gilbert, Mercedes
Green, Cora
Fields, Dorothy
Hagan, Helen E.
Hall [Long], Juanita

Harrison, Hazel Lucile
Holiday, Billie
Holloway, Lucy Ariel Williams [Ariel Williams]
Holt, Nora [Lena Douglas]
Hunter, Alberta
Jessye, Eva Alberta
Johnson, Georgia Douglas [Paul Tremaine]
Lucas, Marie
Price, Florence Smith
Rainey, Gertrude "Ma" [Gertrude Melissa Nix Pridgett]
Shipp, Olivia Sophie L'Ange Porter
Smith, Clara
Snow, Valaida
Spiller, Isabele Taliaferro
Stafford, Mary

PATRONS/PHILANTHROPISTS

Andrews, Regina M. Anderson [Ursala or Ursula Trelling, Henry Simons]
Baldwin, Ruth S.
Boozer, Thelma Berlack
Burlin, Natalie Curtis [Natalie Curtis]
Cunard, Nancy
Draper, Muriel
Dunn, Blanche
Eastman, Crystal
Isaacs, Edith Juliet Rich
Levinger, Elma Ehrlich
Martin, Mrs. George Madden [Mrs. Attwood R. Martin]
Mason, Charlotte Osgood [Charlotte Louise Van der Veer Quick]
Meyer, Annie Nathan
Moten [Barnett], Etta
Ovington, Mary White
Peterkin, Julia Mood
Rose, Ernestine
Walker, A'Lelia

PLAYWRIGHTS

Andrews, Regina M. Anderson [Ursala or Ursula Trelling, Henry Simons]
Bonner, Marita Odette [Marieta Bonner; Marita Occomy]
Burrill, Mary P. "Mamie"
Cuney Hare, Maud
Du Bois, Shirley Lola Graham [Shirley Graham]
Duncan, Thelma Myrtle [Thelma Brown]

Figgs, Carrie Law Morgan
George, Maude Roberts
Gilbert, Mercedes
Graham, Ottie Beatrice
Grimké, Angelina Weld
Heyward, Dorothy Kuhns
Hurston, Zora Neale
Johnson, Georgia Douglas [Paul Tremaine]
Levinger, Elma Ehrlich
Livingston, Myrtle Athleen Smith
McBrown, Gertrude Parthenia
Miller, May [May Miller Sullivan]
Price, Doris D.
Shelton, Ruth Ada Gaines [Ruth Gaines Shelton]
Spence, Eulalie

POETS

Bennett, Gwendolyn
Butler, Anna Mabel Land
Casely-Hayford [Aquah LaLuah], Gladys May
Caution-Davis, Ethel [Ethel M. Caution]
Clark, Mazie Earhart [Fannie B. Steele]
Coleman, Anita Scott
Copeland, Josephine
Cowdery, Mae Virginia
Cunard, Nancy
Delany, Clarissa Mae Scott
Dickinson, Blanche Taylor
Epperson, Aloise Barbour
Fauset, Jessie Redmon
Fernandis, Sarah Collins
Figgs, Carrie Law Morgan
Fleming, Sarah Lee Brown
George, Maude Roberts
Gilbert, Mercedes
Gooden, Lauretta Holman
Gordon, Edythe Mae
Grimke, Angelina Weld
Holloway, Lucy Ariel Williams [Ariel Williams]
Houston, Virginia A.
Jeffrey, Maurine Lawrence
Johnson, Dorothy Vena
Johnson, Georgia Douglas [Paul Tremaine]
Johnson, Helene
Jonas, Rosalie M.

Levinger, Elma Ehrlich
Lewis, Lillian Tucker
McBrown, Gertrude Parthenia
Miller, May [May Miller Sullivan]
Moody, Christina
Newsome, Effie Lee [Mary Effie Lee]
Pitts, Lucia Mae ["Lady Called Lou"]
Popel, Esther [Ester Popel Shaw]
Postles, Grace Vera
Ransom, Birdelle Wycoff
Reynolds, Evelyn Crawford [Eve Lynn]
Rowland, Ida
Spencer, Anne [Anne Bethel Bannister]
Thompson, Clara Ann
Thompson, Priscilla Jane
Turner, Lucy Mae
Walker, Margaret [Margaret Walker Alexander]
Wiggins, Bernice Love
Wynbush, Octavia Beatrice
Yancey, Bessie Woodson
Yeiser, Idabelle

PROFESSIONALS

Andrews, Regina M. Anderson [Ursala or Ursula Trelling, Henry Simons]
Beasley, Delilah Leontium
Bethune, Mary McLeod
Boozer, Thelma Berlack
Brown, Hallie Quinn
Buckingham [Harper], Minnie
Carter, Eunice Hunton
Coleman, Bessie [Elizabeth]
Dean, Lillian Harris ["Pigfoot Mary"]
Haynes, Elizabeth Ross
Hunter, Alberta
Hunter, Jane Edna Harris
Nance, Ethel Ray
Newsome, Effie Lee [Mary Effie Lee]
Porter, Dorothy Louise Burnett [Wesley]
Randolph [Wallace], Richetta G.
Reynolds, Evelyn Crawford [Eve Lynn]
Rose, Ernestine
Ross, Elizabeth
Spencer, Anne [Anne Bethe; Bannister]
Walker, Margaret [Margaret Walker Alexander]

SINGERS/VOCALISTS

Alix, Mae [May, or Liza]
Anderson, Marian
Austin, Lovie [Cora Calhoun]
Baker, Josephine
Blanks, Birleanna
Bowman [Bradford], Laura
Brown [Scott], Ada
Brown, Ida G.
Brown, Lillyn [Lillian]
Calloway, Blanche Dorothea Jones
Chappelle, Juanita Stinnette
Clough, Inez
Cole-Talbert, Florence
Cox, Ida Prather
Evanti, Lillian [Annie Lillian Evans]
Green, Cora
Hall, Adelaide
Hall [Long], Juanita
Harvey, Georgette Mickey
Hawthorne, Susie
Hegamin, Lucille
Henderson, Katherine [Catherine]
Henderson, Rosa
Hill, Chippie [Bertha]
Hite, Mattie [Matie Hite, Nellie Hite]
Holiday, Billie
Holt, Nora [Lena Holt]
Horne, Lena [Lena Mary Calhoun Horne]
Hunter, Alberta
Jarboro, Caterina
Jones, Maggie [Faye Barnes]
Jones, Matilda Sissieretta Joyner [Black Patti]
Mabley, Jackie "Moms" [Loretta Mary Aiken]
Martin, Sara [Sara Dunn, Margaret Johnson, Sally Roberts]
McCoy, Viola [Amanda Brown]
McKinney, Nina Mae
Miles, Lizzie [Elizabeth Mary Landreaux]
Mills, Florence
Minto, Cato [La Minto Cato]
Mitchell [Cook], Abriea " Abbie" [Abbey Mitchell]
Moten [Barnett], Etta
Rainey, Gertrude " Ma" [Gertrude Melissa Nix Pridgett]
Randolph, Amanda [Mandy]
Saunders, Gertrude
Smith, Bessie

Smith, Clara
Smith, Mamie [Mamie Robinson]
Smith, Trixie [Tessie Aimes]
Snow, Valaida
Spivey, Victoria
Stafford, Mary
Sylvester, Hannah [Genevia Scott]
Taylor [Williams], Eva [Irene Gibbons]
Thornton, Willie Mae "Big Mama"
Wallace, Beulah "Sippie"
Ward, Aida
Waters, Ethel
Welch, Elisabeth
Whitman Sisters, " The Royalty of Negro Vaudeville," Mabel [May], Essie, Alberta [Bert],
    Alice Livingston, Myrtle Athleen Smith
Williams, Marie Selika [Selika Williams, Marie Selika Smith]
Wilson, Edith [Edith Goodall]

WRITERS

Adams, Elizabeth Laura
Ayer, Gertrude Elise Johnson McDougald
Bennett, Gwendolyn
Bonner, Marita Odette [Marieta Bonner; Marita Occomy]
Bright, Nellie Rathbone
Brown, Hallie Quinn
Bush-Banks, Olivia Ward
Campbell, Hazel Vivian
Clifford, Carrie Williams
Coleman, Anita Scott
Cooper, Anna Julia Haywood
Cunard, Nancy
Cuney Hare, Maud
Cuthbert, Marion Vera
Day, Caroline Stewart Bond
Delany, Clarissa Mae Scott
Dickinson, Blanche Taylor
Dismond [Hodges], Geraldyn
Draper, Muriel
Du Bois, Shirley Lola Graham [Shirley Graham]
Dunbar-Nelson, Alice Ruth
Duncan, Thelma Myrtle [Thelma Brown]
Fauset, Jessie Redmon
Fernandis, Sarah Collins
Fleming, Sarah Lee Brown
George, Maude Roberts

Gilbert, Mercedes
Goodwin, Ruby Berkley
Gordon, Edythe Mae
Graham, Ottie Beatrice
Harmon, Florence Marion
Harrison, Juanita
Hazzard, Alvira
Heyward, Dorothy Kuhns
Hurst, Fannie
Hurston, Zora Neale
Isaacs, Edith Juliet Rich
Johnson, Georgia Douglas [Paul Tremaine]
Jones, Lois Mailou
Larsen, Nella [Allen Semi]
Love, Rose Leary
Moryck, Brenda Ray
Nance, Ethel Ray
Newsome, Effie Lee [Mary Effie Lee]
Peterkin, Julia Mood
Porter, Dorothy Louise Burnett [Wesley]
Ridley, Florida Ruffin [Amelia Yates Ruffin]
Robeson, Eslanda [Cardoza Goode]
Spence, Eulalie
Tarry, Ellen
Terrell, Mary Church [Mary Eliza Church]
Thompson, Eloise Alberta Veronica Bibb
Thompson, Era Bell [Dakota Dick]
Turner, Lucy Mae
Walker, Margaret [Margaret Walker Alexander]
West, Dorothy
Wright, Zara
Wynbush, Octavia Beatrice
Yeiser, Idabelle

BIBLIOGRAPHY

Abbott, Lynn, and Doug Seroff. *Ragged but Right: Black Traveling Shows, "Coon Songs," and the Dark Pathway to Blues and Jazz*. Jackson: University Press of Mississippi, 2007.

Aberjhani, and Sandra L. West, eds. *Encyclopedia of the Harlem Renaissance*. New York: Facts on File, 2003.

Adams, Katherine H. *A Group of Their Own: College Writing Courses and American Women Writers, 1880–1940*. Albany: State University of New York Press, 2001.

Albertson, Chris. *Bessie*, rev. ed. New Haven, CT: Yale University Press, 2003.

Aldus, Jon. *Dorothy Fields Website*, 2006. Available online at www.dorothyfields.org.

Anderson, Sarah H. "'The Place to Go': The 135th Street Branch Library and the Harlem Renaissance." *Library Quarterly* 73 (October 2003): 383–421.

Andrews, William L., Frances Smith Foster, and Trudier Harris, eds. *Concise Oxford Companion to African American Literature*. New York: Oxford University Press, 2001.

———. *Oxford Companion to African American Literature*. New York: Oxford University Press, 1997.

"Annie Nathan Meyer (1867–1951)." *WebWeaversInk.com*. Available online at www.web weaversink.com/annie.htm.

Anthology of African American Women Writers in Opportunity Magazine (1923–1948). Jefferson, NC: McFarland, 2008.

Appiah, Kwame, and Henry Louis Gates Jr., eds. *Africana: The Encyclopedia of the African and African American Experience*. New York: Oxford University Press, 2005.

Atier, Renée. *Remaking Race and History: The Sculpture of Meta Warrick Fuller*. Berkeley and Los Angeles: University of California Press, 2011.

Bearden, Romare, and Harry Henderson. *A History of African American Artists: From 1792 to the Present*. New York: Pantheon, 1993.

Beasley, Deliah L. *The Negro Trail Blazers of California*. Los Angeles, 1919. Reprint, New York: Negro Universities Press, 1969.

Benjamin, Tribobia Hayes. *The Life and Art of Lois Mailou Jones*. Rohnert Park, CA: Pomegranate Artbooks, 1994.

Bennett, Lerone, Jr. *Before the Mayflower*. Chicago: Johnson Publishing, 2003.

Beyond: Literary Biographies of 100 Black Women Writers, 1900–1945. Cambridge, MA: Harvard University Press, 1990.

"Bishop Ida Robinson, 1891–1946." *Mt. Sinai Holy Church of America*. Available online at http://www.mtsinaichurch.org/history/index.htm.

"Blanche Calloway Jones." *Black Perspective in Music* 7 (Autumn 1979): 281.

Bogle, Donald. *Bright Boulevards, Bold Dreams: The Story of Black Hollywood*. New York: Random House, 2006.

———. *Brown Sugar: Eighty Years of America's Black Female Superstars*. New York: Harmony Books, 1980.

———. *Toms, Coons, Mulattoes, Mammies, and Bucks: An Interpretive History of Blacks in American Films*. New York: Continuum, 2001.

Bolden, Tonya, ed. *The Book of African American Women*. Holbrook, MA: Adams Media, 1996.

Bontemps, Jacqueline F. *Forever Free: Art by African American Women, 1862–1980*. Alexandria, VA: Stephenson, 1980.

Bosman, Erwin. "Whitman Sisters: Why We May Never Silence Them." *No Depression: The Roots Music Authority*, September 3, 2012. Available online at http://www.nodepression.com/profiles/blogs/the-whitman-sisters-why-we-may-never-silence-them.

Bourne, Stephen. *The Black Garbo: Nina Mae McKinney*. Duncan, OK: BearManor Media, 2011.

———. *Elisabeth Welch: Soft Lights and Sweet Music*. Lanham, MD: Scarecrow Press, 2005.

Boyd, Valerie. *Wrapped in Rainbows: The Life of Zora Neale Hurston*. New York: Scribner, 2004.

Boyden, Tonya. "Priscilla Jane Thompson." *Digital Schomburg African American Women Writers of the 19th Century*, 2000. Available online at http://digital.nypl.org/schomburg/writers_aa19/biographies.html.

Bracks, Lean'tin, ed. *African American Almanac: 400 Years of Triumph, Courage and Excellence*. Detroit: Visible Ink, 2012.

Brawley, Benjamin. *The Negro Genius*. New York: Dodd, Mead and Company, 1937.

Brennan, Carol. "Elisabeth Welch Biography." *JRank.org*. Available online at http://biography.jrank.org/pages/2777/Welch-Elisabeth.html.

Brewer, John Mason. *Heralding Dawn: An Anthology of Verse*. Dallas, TX: June Thomason Printing, 1936. Available online at Portal to Texas History, http://texashistory.unt.edu/ark/67531/metapth5146/.

Bricktop (Ada Smith), with James Haskins. *Bricktop*. New York: Atheneum, 1983.

Brown, Lois. *Encyclopedia of the Harlem Literary Renaissance*. New York: Facts on File, 2006.

Brown, Stephanie. "Bourgeois Blackness and Autobiographical Authenticity in Ellen Tarry's *The Third Door*." *African American Review* 41 (Fall 2007): 557–70.

Brown, Sterling. *Collected Poems of Sterling A. Brown*. Sterling A. Brown, ed. New York: HarperCollins, 1960.

Buczkowski, Paul James. "Dorothy Heyward." *Guide to Literary Masters and Their Works 1*. Ipswich, MA: Salem Press, 2007. Available online at EBSCOhost, http://152.12.30.4:2048/login?url=http://search.ebscohost.com/login.aspx?direct=true&db=lkh&AN=103331LM38509790303507&site=lrc-plus.

Bundles, A'Lelia Perry. *Madam C. J. Walker: Entrepreneur*. New York: Chelsea House, 2008.

———. *On Her Own Ground: The Life and Times of Madam C. J. Walker*. New York: Scribner, 2001.

Bunie, Andrew. *Robert L. Vann of the Pittsburgh Courier: Politics and Black Journalism.* Pittsburgh, PA: University of Pittsburgh Press, 1974.

Capshaw Smith, Katherine. "From Bank Street to Harlem: A Conversation with Ellen Tarry." *Lion and the Unicorn* 23 (April 1999): 271–85.

"Caterina Jarboro." *New York Times*, August 16, 1986. Available online at http://www.ny times.com/1986/08/16/obituaries/caterina-jarboro.html.

Cazort, Jean E., and Constance Tibbs Hobson. *Born to Play: The Life and Career of Hazel Harrison.* Westport, CT: Greenwood, 1983.

Champion, Laurie, and Bruce A. Glasrud, eds. *Unfinished Masterpiece: The Harlem Renaissance Fiction of Anita Scott Coleman.* Lubbock: Texas Tech University Press, 2008.

Christian, Robert. "Go Down, Moses: An Introduction." *Michigan Quarterly Review* 37 (Fall 1998): 28–37.

"Claiming Their Citizenship: African American Women from 1624–2009." *National Women's History Museum.* Available online at http://www.nwhm.org/online-exhibits/african american/index.html.

Cohen, Norm. *Long Steel Rail: The Railroad in American Folksong.* David Cohen, ed. Urbana: University of Illinois Press, 2000.

"College and School News." *Crisis* 50 (May 1943): 156.

Composers and Their Music. Urbana: University of Illinois Press, 2007.

Contemporary Black Biography. 99 vols. Detroit, MI: Gale Research.

"Contest Spotlight." *Opportunity* 7 (July 1927): 213.

"Cotton Club Girls." *Ebony* 4 (April 1949): 34–38.

Cripps, Thomas. *Slow Fade to Black: The Negro in American Film, 1900–1942.* New York: Oxford University Press, 1993.

Crochett, Lorraine J. *Delilah Leontium Beasley: Oakland's Crusading Journalist.* El Cerrito, CA: Downey Place Publishing House, 1990.

"Crystal Eastman." *National Women's Hall of Fame.* Available online at www.greatwomen .org/women-of-the-hall/search-the-hall/details/2/55-Eastman.

Cullen, Frank. *Vaudeville, Old and New: An Encyclopedia of Variety Performers in America.* 2 vols. New York: Routledge, 2006.

Cuthbert, Marion. "The Dean of Women at Work." *Journal of the National Association of College Women* 13/14 (April 1928): 39–44.

Davis, Angela Y. *Blues Legacies and Black Feminism.* New York: Vintage, 1999.

Davis, Cynthia J., and Verner D. Mitchell, eds. *Western Echoes of the Harlem Renaissance.* Norman: University of Oklahoma Press, 2008.

Day, Caroline Bond. "University of Michigan Plays, Volume III." *Crisis* 40 (May 1933): 115.

De Luca, Laura, Gerald Horne, and Mary Young, eds. *W. E. B. Du Bois: An Encyclopedia.* Westport, CT: Greenwood, 2001.

Dett, R. Nathaniel. *The R. Nathaniel Dett Reader: Essays on Black Sacred Music.* Jon Michael Spencer, ed. Durham, NC: Duke University Press, 1991.

Dicaire, David. *Blues Singers: Biographies of 50 Legendary Artists of the Early 20th Century.* Jefferson, NC: McFarland, 1999.

Douglas, Winfred. "Natalie Curtis." *Southern Workman* 55 (March 1926): 127–40.

Dreisbach, Tina Spencer. "Willie Mae 'Big Mama' Thornton." *Encyclopedia of Alabama*, 2011. Available online at www.encyclopediaofalamaa.org/face/Article.jsp?id=h-1573.

Egan, Bill. *Florence Mills: Harlem Jazz Queen.* New York: Scarecrow Press, 2004.

"Epperson, Aloise Barbour, West Point Cemetery." *USGENWEB Archives Norfolk Virginia*. Available online at www.usgwarchives.net/va/norfolkcity/cemeteries/westpoint/wpcem-e .html.

"Eslanda Goode Robeson." *Women's History, Gale Free Resources*. Available online at http://www.gale.cengage.com/free_resources/whm.bio/robeson_e.htm.

"Famous Fat Women." *Jet* (May 8, 1952): 56–63.

Fisher, Rudolph. *The Walls of Jericho*. Salem, NH: Ayer, 1992.

"Florabelle Williams Wilson Collection, 1910–1995; Bulk 1980s." *Indiana Historical Society*, 2005. Available online at www.indianahistory.org/our-collections/collection-guides/ florabelle-williams-wilson-collection-1910-1995.pdf.

Floyd, Samuel A., Jr., ed. *International Dictionary of Black Composers*. Chicago: Fitzroy Dearborn Publishers, 1999.

Forbes, Elizabeth. "Obituary: Marian Anderson (CORRECTED)." *Independent*, April 15, 1993. Available online at http://www.independent.co.uk/news/people/obituary-marian -anderson.

Foster, Lillian. "Mabel Hampton." *QualiaFolk.com*, December 8, 2011. Available online at http://www.qualiafolk.com/2011/12/08/mabel-hampton/.

Franklin, John Hope, and Evelyn Brooks Higginbotham. *From Slavery to Freedom*, 9th ed. New York: McGraw-Hill, 2011.

Freedman, Samuel. "Georgia Burke, 107; Acted Character Roles." *New York Times*, December 4, 1985. Available online at http://www.nytimes.com/1985/12/04/theater/georgia -burke-107-acted-character-roles.html.

"Fullerton College: A Pictorial History." *Fullerton College Library*, 2012. Available online at www.libraryfchistory.fullcoll.edu/.

Gable, Craig, ed. *Ebony Rising: Short Fiction of the Greater Harlem Renaissance Era*. Bloomington: Indiana University Press, 2004.

Garber, Eric Garber. "A Spectacle in Color: The Lesbian and Gay Subculture of Jazz Age Harlem." In Martin B. Duberman, Martha Vicinus, and George Chauncey, eds., *Hidden from History: Reclaiming the Gay and Lesbian Past*, 318–31. Markam, Ontario, Canada: New American Library, 1989.

Gates, Henry Lois, Jr., and Evelyn Brooks Higginbotham, eds. *African American National Biography*. New York: Oxford University Press, 2008.

———. *Harlem Renaissance Lives: From the African American National Biography*. Oxford, UK: Oxford University Press, 2009.

Gates, Henry Louis, Jr., and Nellie Y. McKay, eds. *Norton Anthology of African American Literature*. New York: W. W. Norton & Co., 1997.

Gavin, James. *Stormy Weather: The Life of Lena Horne*. New York: Atria, 2009.

"Gerri Major Papers, 1927–1985." *New York Library*. Available online at http://www.nypl .org/scm/20730.

Giddings, Paula. *When and Where I Enter*. New York: Bantam, 1984.

Gikandi, Simon. "Casely Hayford, Gladys May." *Encyclopedia of African Literature*. New York: Routledge, 2002.

Giles, Freda Scott. "Willis Richardson and Eulalie Spence: Dramatic Voices of the Harlem Renaissance." *American Drama* 5, no. 2 (1996): 1–22.

Gilkes, Cheryl Townsend. *If It Wasn't for the Women . . . : Black Women's Experience and Womanist Culture in Church and Community*. New York: Orbis, 2001.

Gill, Tiffany M. *Beauty Shop Politics: African American Women's Activism in the Beauty Industry.* Urbana: University of Illinois Press, 2010.

Gilmore, Lea. "Rosa Henderson (c. 1896–1968)." *Lea Gilmore's It's a Girl Thang!* Available online at http://www.p-dub.com/thang/RosaHenderson.html.

Glasrud, Bruce A., and Cary D. Wintz. *The Harlem Renaissance in the American West.* New York: Routledge, 2012.

Goldenberg, Myrna. "Annie Nathan Meyer, 1967–1951." *Jewish Women's Archive, Jewish Women: A Comprehensive Historical Encyclopedia.* Available online at http://jwa.org/encyclopedia/article/meyer-annie-nathan.

Goodwin Ruby, Berkley. "The Hollywood Mystery: Aurora Greely, Dancer and Leader of Chorus of 30, Has Never Had a Love Affair, Eats One Meal a Day to Keep Her Weight at 105." *Afro American Weekly,* November 7, 1931, p. 16.

Gordon, Linda. *Woman's Body, Woman's Right: Birth Control in America.* New York: Penguin, 1990.

Gordon, Louis. *Nancy Cunard: Heiress, Muse, Political Idealist.* New York: Columbia University Press, 2007.

Gore, Dayo F., Jeanne Theoharis, and Komozi Woodard, eds. *Want to Start A Revolution? Radical Women in the Black Freedom Struggle.* New York: New York University Press, 2009.

Graham, Maryemma, ed. *On Being Female, Black, and Free: Essays by Margaret Walker, 1932–1992.* Knoxville: University of Tennessee Press, 1997.

Greenspan, Charlotte. *Pick Yourself Up: Dorothy Fields and the American Musical.* Oxford, UK: Oxford University Press, 2010.

Gubert, Betty Kaplan, Marian Sawyer, and Caroline M. Fanning. *Distinguished African Americans in Aviation and Space Science.* Westport, CT: Oryx Press, 2002.

"Guide to the Richetta Randolph Wallace Papers 1978.137." *Brooklyn Historical Society.* Available online at http://dlib.nyu.edu/findingaids/html/bhs/arms_1978_137_richetta_randolph_wallace/.

Guillaume, Bernice F. *The Collected Works of Olivia Bush Ward Bush-Banks.* New York: Oxford University Press, 1991.

Guy-Sheftall, Beverly, ed. *Words of Fire: An Anthology of African American Feminist Thought.* New York: New Press, 1995.

Hagood, Taylor. *Secrecry, Magic, and the One-Act Plays of Harlem Renaissance Women Writers.* Columbus: Ohio State University Press, 2010.

Hales, Douglas. *A Southern Family in White and Black: The Cuneys of Texas.* College Station: Texas A&M University Press, 2003.

Hall, Delaney. "Lights and Shadows: Dewey Roscoe Jones and the *Chicago Defender's* Poetry Legacy." *Poetry Foundation.* Available online at http://www.poetryfoundation.org/article/243478.

Handy, D. Antoinette. *Black Women in American Bands and Orchestras.* Metuchen, NJ: Scarecrow Press, 1981.

———. *Black Women in American Bands and Orchestras,* 2nd ed. Lanham, MD: Scarecrow Press, 1998.

Haney, Lynn. *Naked at the Feast.* New York: Dodd, Mead and Company, 1981.

Hanson, Joyce A. *Mary McLeod Bethune and Black Women's Political Activism.* Columbia: University of Missouri Press, 2003.

Harris, Sheldon. *Blues Who's Who: A Biographical Dictionary of Blues Singers*. New Rochelle, NY: Arlington House, 1979.

Harrison, Daphne D. *Black Pearls: Blues Queens of the 1920s*. New Brunswick, NJ: Rutgers University Press, 1988.

Haskins, Jim. *The Cotton Club*. New York: Hippocrene Books, 1994.

Hatch, James Vernon, and Leo Lamalian, eds. *Lost Plays of the Harlem Renaissance, 1920–1940*. Detroit, MI: Wayne State University Press, 1996.

Hatch, James Vernon, and Ted Shine, eds. *Black Theatre USA: Plays by African Americans*. 2 vols. New York: Free Press, 1996.

Hay, Samuel A. *African American Theatre: A Historical and Critical Analysis.* Cambridge, UK: Cambridge University Press, 1994.

Haygood, Will. *King of the Cats: The Life and Times of Adam Clayton Powell Jr*. New York: HarperCollins, 2006.

Haynes, Elizabeth Ross. "Margaret Murray Washington." *Opportunity* 3 (July 1925): 207–9.

Head, James. "Barnes, Faye [Maggie Jones]." *Handbook of Texas Online*, August 30, 2013. Available online at http://www.tshaonline.org/handbook/online/articles/fbaem.

Hemenway, Robert. *Zora Neale Hurston: A Literary Biography*. Chicago: University of Illinois Press, 1980.

Hermann, Janet Sharp. *The Pursuit of a Dream*. New York: Oxford University Press, 1981.

Hill, Errol G., and James V. Hatch. *A History of African American Theatre*. New York: Cambridge University Press, 2003.

Hine, Darlene Clark, ed. *Black Women in America: An Historical Encyclopedia*. 3 vols. Brooklyn, NY: Carlson, 1993.

———, ed. *Black Women in America: An Historical Encyclopedia*, 2nd ed. 3 vols. New York: Oxford University Press, 2005.

Hine, Darlene Clark, and John McCluskey, eds. *The Black Chicago Renaissance*. Urbana: University of Illinois Press, 2012.

Hine, Darlene Clark, William C. Hine, and Stanley Harrold. *The African American Odyssey*, vol. 2. Upper Saddle, NJ: Prentice Hall, 2003.

Hoffmann, Frank W., and Howard Ferstler. "Chappelle and Stinnette (label)." *Encyclopedia of Recorded Sound*, vol. 1. New York: Routledge, 2005.

"Holloway, Lucy Ariel Williams, 1905–1973." *Alabama Authors*. Available online at www.lib.ua.edu/Alabama_Authors=1474.

"Home of Mrs. George Madden Martin." *Annie Fellows Johnston and the Little Colonel Stories*. Available online at http://www.littlecolonel.com/places/PeweeValley/MartinEmmyLou.htm.

Honey, Maureen, ed. *Shadowed Dreams: Women's Poetry of the Harlem Renaissance*. New Brunswick, NJ: Rutgers University Press, 1989.

———. *Shadowed Dreams: Women's Poetry of the Harlem Renaissance*, 2nd ed. New Brunswick, NJ: Rutgers University Press, 2006.

"Hope, Lugenia Burns." *Georgia Women of Achievement*. Available online at www.georgiawomen.org/2010/10/hope-lugenia-burns/.

Horne, Gerald. *Race Woman: The Lives of Shirley Graham Du Bois*. New York: New York University Press, 2000.

Horne, Lena, and Richard Schickel. *Lena*. Garden City, NY: Doubleday, 1965.

Hughes, Langston. *The Ways of White Folk*. New York: Vintage, 1990.

Hull, Gloria. *Color, Sex, and Poetry: Three Women Writers of the Harlem Renaissance*. Bloomington: Indiana University Press, 1987.

Hurston, Zora Neale. *Dust Tracks on a Road: An Autobiography*. Philadelphia, PA: Lippincott, 1942.

Jackson, Buzzy. *A Bad Woman Feeling Good: Blues and the Women Who Sing Them*. New York: W. W. Norton & Co., 2005.

Johnson, Charles S. *Ebony and Topaz: A Collectanea*. New York: National Urban League, 1927.

Johnson, James Weldon. *Black Manhattan*. New York, 1930. Reprint, Salem, NY: Ayer, 1988.

Jonas, Rosalie M. "New York Light and Shade." *Art World* 3, no. 2 (1917): 113–15.

Jones, Adrienne Lash. *Jane Edna Hunter: A Case Study of Black Leadership, 1910–1950*. Brooklyn, NY: Carlson, 1990.

Jones, Beverly Washington. *Quest for Equality: The Life and Writings of Mary Church Terrell*. Brooklyn, NY: Carlson, 1990.

Jones, Eugene Kinckle. "A Dream, a Quarter Century, a Reality! How the Urban League Has Served." *Opportunity* 13, no. 11 (November 1935): 328. Available online at New Deal Network, http://newdeal.feri.org/texts/147.htm.

Jones, Regina V. "How Does a Bulldagger Get Out of the Footnote? Or Gladys Bentley's Blues." *Ninepatch: A Creative Journal for Women and Gender Studies* 1, no. 1 (2012): 1–14.

Jones, Sharon L. *A Critical Companion to Zora Neale Hurston: A Literary Reference to Her Life and Work*. New York: Facts on File, 2009.

Jubilee, Vincent. *Philadelphia's Afro-American Literary Circle and the Harlem Renaissance*. Philadelphia, PA: University of Pennsylvania, 1980.

Kaplan, Carla. *Miss Anne in Harlem: The White Women of the Black Renaissance*. New York: HarperCollins, 2013.

———. *Zora Neale Hurston: A Life in Letters*. New York: Doubleday, 2002.

"Katherine Henderson (1909–?)." *Red Hot Jazz Archive*. Available online at www.redhotjazz.com/khenderson.html.

Kellner, Bruce, ed. *The Harlem Renaissance: Historical Dictionary for the Era*. Westport, CT: Greenwood, 1984.

———, ed. *"Keep A-Inchin' Along": Selected Writings of Carl Van Vechten about Black Arts and Letters*. Westport, CT: Greenwood, 1979.

King, Lovaleri. "*Selected Works of Edythe Mae Gordon*, by Edythe Mae Gordon, Henry Louis Gates, Jennifer Burton, and Lorraine Elena Roses." *African American Review* 32 (Summer 1998): 360–62. Available online at http://www.jstor.org/stable/3042142.

Kort, Carol, ed. *A to Z of American Women Writers*, rev. ed. New York: Facts on File, 2007.

Kroeger, Brooke. *Fannie: The Talent for Success of Writer Fannie Hurst*. New York: Crown, 1999.

Kuhl, Nancy. "Muriel Draper." *Intimate Circles: American Women in the Arts*. New Haven, CT: Yale University Press, 2003.

Laird, Ross, comp. *Moanin' Low: A Discography of Female Popular Vocal Recordings, 1920–1933*. Westport, CT: Greenwood, 1996.

Langley, Jerry, and Sandra Govan. "The Richest Colors on Her Palette, Beauty and Truth." *International Review of African American Art* 23, no.1 (2010): 7–15.

Law, Sylvia A. "Crystal Eastman." *Pace Law Review* 12, no. 3 (September 1992): 529–41.

League of Allied Arts Records (Collection Number 1856). UCLA Library Special Collections, Charles E. Young Research Library, UCLA.

Lewis, David Levering. *W. E. B. Du Bois: Biography of a Race, 1868–1919.* New York: Henry Holt and Company, 1993.

———. *When Harlem Was in Vogue.* New York: Alfred A. Knopf, 1981.

Lewis, Jone Johnson. "African American History and Women Timeline, 1920–1929." *About.com Women's History.* Available online at http://womenshistory.about.com/od/aframwomentimeline/a/aaw1920_time.htm.

Lewis, Samella. *African American Art and Artists.* Berkeley: University of California Press, 2003.

"Lillyn Brown." *All.Music.com.* Available online at http://www.allmusic.com/artist/lillyn -brown-mn0001829772.

Lincoln, C. Eric, and Lawrence H. Mamiya, eds. *The Black Church in the African American Experience.* Durham, NC: Duke University Press, 1990.

Lindsey, Treva B. "Configuring Modernities: New Negro Womanhood in the Nation's Capital, 1890–1940," *Duke University Libraries Electronic Theses and Dissertations*, 2010. Available online at www.dukespace.lib.duke.edu/dspace/handle/10161/2409.

Locke, Alain. "The New Negro." In Henry Louis Gates Jr. and Nellie Y. McKay, eds., *Norton Anthology of African American Literature*, 2nd ed., 984–93. New York: W. W. Norton & Co., 2004.

Logan, Rayford L., and Michael R. Winston, eds. *Dictionary of American Negro Biography.* New York: W. W. Norton & Co., 1982.

Ludwig, Kate. "Brooklyn History Photo of the Week: Richetta Randolph." *Brooklyn Historical Society Blog*, March 2, 2011. Available online at http://brooklynhistory.org/blog/2011/03/02/photo of the week/.

Macki, Adrienne C. "'Talking B(l)ack': Construction of Gender and Race in the Plays of Eulalie Spence." *Theatre History Series* 27 (2007): 86–109.

"Mae Alix, Splits Queen, Divorced." *Chicago Defender (National Edition) (1921–1967)*, January 12, 1935. Available online at http://search.proquest.com/docview/492438732?accountid=14657.

Marcus, Jane. *Hearts of Darkness: White Women Write Race.* New Brunswick, NJ: Rutgers University Press, 2004.

Marian Anderson. Available online at http://marian-anderson.com/.

Marks, Carole, and Diana Edkins. *The Power of Pride: Stylemakers and Rulebreakers of the Harlem Renaissance.* New York: Crown, 1999.

Marteena, Constance Hill. *The Lengthening Shadow of a Woman: A Biography of Charlotte Hawkins Brown.* Hicksville, NY: Exposition Press, 1977.

Martin, Tony, comp. *African Fundamentalism: A Literary and Cultural Anthology of Garvey's Harlem Renaissance.* Dover, MA: Majority Press, 1991.

"Mary Stafford." *All.Music.com.* Available online at http://www.allmusic.com/artist/mary -Stafford-mn0000861160.

"Mary Stafford (1895–1938)." *Red Hot Jazz Archive.* Available online at http://www.redhotjazz.com/marystafford.html.

McBride, Earnest. "Black and Tan Party Rule in Mississippi, 1868–1875." *Making of the United States of America*, 2006. Available online at http://www.bjmjr.net/mcbride/black tan.htm.

McCann, Bob. *Encyclopedia of African American Actresses in Film and Television.* Jefferson, NC: McFarland, 2009.

McDuffie, Erik S. *Sojourning for Freedom: Black Women, American Communism, and the Making of Black Left Feminism.* Durham, NC: Duke University Press, 2011.

"Mission and History." *National Urban League*. Available online at www.nul.org.

Mitchell, Verner D. "A Family Answers the Call: Anita Scott Coleman, Literature, and War." *War, Literature, and the Arts: An International Journal of the Humanities* 20, nos. 1/2 (November 2008): 301–9.

———, ed. *This Waiting for Love: Helene Johnson, Poet of the Harlem Renaissance*. Amherst: University of Massachusetts Press, 2000.

Moryck, Brenda. "Celebrities Gather at Home of James Weldon Johnson." *Afro-American (1893–1988)*, January 10, 1925. Available online at http://search.proquest.com/docview/5 30642950?accountid=14657.

"Mrs. John Dean, Colorful Character, Buried Here Following Death in West." *New Amsterdam News* (New York), July 1929, sec. 4, p. 3.

Mullaney, Janet Palmer, ed. *Truthtellers of the Times: Interviews with Contemporary Women Poets*. Ann Arbor: University of Michigan Press, 1998.

Musser, Judith, ed. *"Tell It to Us Easy" and Other Stories: A Complete Short Fiction Anthology of African American Women*. Jefferson, NC: McFarland, 2011.

"NAACP History: Mary White Ovington." *NAACP.org*, 2013. Available online at http://www/naacp.org.pages/naacp-history-Mary-White-Ovington.

Nance, Ethel Ray. Interview with Ann Allen Shockley, November 18, 1970; December 23, 1970; September 6, 1981. Franklin Library, Special Collections, Black Oral History Collection, Fisk University.

"National Urban League." *Social Welfare History Project*. Available online at http://www.socialwelfarehistory.com/organizations/national-urban-league/.

"Nellie Rathbone Bright (1898–1977) Family Papers" *Historical Society of Pennsylvania*, 2005. Available online at http://www.hsp.org/sites/default/files/legacy_files/migrated/findingaid2057nelliebright.pdf.

Nelson, Emmanuel S., ed. *African American Authors, 1745–1945: A Bio-bibliographical Critical Sourcebook*. Westport, CT: Greenwood, 2000.

Nettles, Darryl Glenn. *African American Concert Singers before 1950*. Jefferson, NC: McFarland, 2003.

Notable American Women: The Modern Period. Cambridge, MA: Harvard University Press, 1980.

Notable American Women, 1607–1950: A Biographical Dictionary. Cambridge, MA: Harvard University Press, 1971.

Notable Kentucky African Americans Database. Available online at http://nkaa.uky.edu/.

Nugent, Bruce. *Gay Rebel of the Harlem Renaissance: Selections from the Work of Richard Bruce Nugent*. Durham, NC: Duke University Press, 2002.

Ogbar, Jeffrey O. "Afterword." In Jeffrey O. Ogbar, ed., *The Harlem Renaissance Revisited: Politics, Arts, and Letters*, 245–47. Baltimore, MD: Johns Hopkins University Press, 2010.

Oliver, Paul. *The Story of the Blues*. Boston: Northwestern University Press, 1997.

Page, Yolanda Williams, ed. *Encyclopedia of African American Women*. Westport, CT: Greenwood, 2007.

Parker, Donna P. "Wallace, Beulah Thomas [Sippie]." *Handbook of Texas Online*, October 29, 2013. Available online at http://www.tshaonline.org/handbook/online/articles/fwaal.

"Past Leaders: Mother Lizzie Robinson." *COGIC*. Available online at http://www.cogic.org/womensdepartment/general-supervisor/past-leaders.

Patterson, Michelle Wick. *Natalie Curtis Burlin*. Lincoln: University of Nebraska Press, 2010.

Patterson, William L. *The Man Who Cried Genocide: An Autobiography*. New York: International Publishers, 1971.

Patton, Venetria K., and Maureen Honey, eds. *Double-Take: A Revisionist Harlem Renaissance Anthology*. New Brunswick, NJ: Rutgers University Press, 2001.

Perkins, Kathy A., and Judith L. Stephens. *Strange Fruit: Plays on Lynching by American Women*. Bloomington: Indiana University Press, 1998.

Peterson, Bernard L., Jr. "Chappelle and Stinnette Revue." *A Century of Musicals in Black and White: An Encyclopedia of Musical Stage Works by, about, or Involving African Americans*. Westport, CT: Greenwood, 1993.

———. *Early Black American Playwrights and Dramatic Writers: A Biographical Directory and Catalog of Plays, Films, and Broadcasting Scripts*. Westport, CT: Greenwood, 1990.

———. *Profiles of African American Stage Performers and Theatre People, 1816–1960*. Westport, CT: Greenwood, 2000.

"'Pigfoot Mary' Leaves $75,000 Estate." *New Amsterdam News* (New York), July 1929, sec. 1, p. 3.

"Pioneers in Professionalism: Ten Who Made a Significant Difference, 1880–1930." *National Association of Social Workers Maryland Chapter*. Available online at http://www.nasw-md.org/?page=12.

Placksin, Sally. *American Women in Jazz, 1900 to the Present*. New York: Seaview Books, 1982.

Poems for Radio. New York: Poetry House, 1945.

"Poetess Honored." *Crisis* 47 (September 1940): 288.

"Powell, Isabel Washington (1908–2007)." *Amistad Research Center*. Available online at http://www.amistadresearchcenter.org/archon/?p=creators/creator&id=471.

"Prominent Journalist, Feminist Thelma Berlack Boozer Passes at 94." *New York Amsterdam News* 92, no. 11 (March 2001): 32.

Rado, Lisa, ed. *Rereading Modernism: New Directions in Feminist Criticism*. New York: Garland, 1994.

Rampersad, Arnold. *The Life of Langston Hughes: Volume I: 1902–1940, I, Too, Sing America*. New York: Oxford University Press, 1986.

———. *The Life of Langston Hughes: Volume II: 1941–1967, I Dream a World*. New York: Oxford University Press, 1998.

Rappaport, Joan Moelis. "Elma Ehrlich Levinger, 1887–1958." *Jewish Women's Archive*. Available online at http://jwa.org/encyclopedia/article/levinger-elma-erlich.

Regester, Charlene B. *African American Actresses: The Struggle for Visibility, 1900–1960*. Bloomington: Indiana University Press, 2010.

Reuben, Paul P. "Chapter 9: Gwendolyn Bennett." *PAL: Perspectives in American Literature—A Research and Reference Guide*. Available online at http://archive.csustan.edu/english/reuben/pal/table.html.

Reynolds, Gary A., and Beryl J. Wright. *Against the Odds: African American Artists and the Harmon Foundation*. Newark, NJ: Newark Museum, 1989.

Rice, Anne P., ed. *Witnessing Lynching: American Writers Respond*. New Brunswick, NJ: Rutgers University Press, 2003.

Robinson, Alice M., Vera Mowry Roberts, and Milly S. Barranger, eds. *Notable Women in the American Theater: A Biographical Dictionary*. New York: Greenwood, 1989.

Robinson, Jontyle Theresa, ed. *Bearing Witness: Contemporary Works by African American Women Artists*. New York: Spelman College and Rizolli International Publications, 1996.

"Rosa Henderson." *Big Road Blues*. Available online at http://sundayblues.org/archives/tag/rosa-henderson.

"Rosa Henderson (1896–1968)." *Red Hot Jazz Archive*. Available online at http://redhotjazz.com/rosahenderson.html.

Rose, Phyllis. *Jazz Cleopatra: Josephine Baker in Her Time*. New York: Doubleday, 1989.

Roses, Lorraine Elena, and Ruth Elizabeth Randolph. *Harlem Renaissance and Beyond: Literary Biographies of 100 Black Women Writers, 1900–1945*. Boston: G. K. Hall & Co., 1990.

———, eds. *Harlem's Glory: Black Women Writing, 1900–1950*. Cambridge, MA: Harvard University Press, 1996.

Ross, Loretta J. "African American Women and Abortion." In Rickie Solinger, ed., *Abortion Wars: A Half-Century of Struggle, 1950–2000*, 161–208. Berkeley: University of California Press, 1998.

Rouse, Jacqueline A. *Lugenia Burns Hope: Black Southern Reformer*. Athens: University of Georgia Press, 1989.

Rush, Theressa Gunnels, Carol Fairbanks Myers, and Esther Spring Arata. *Black American Writers Past and Present*. 2 vols. Metuchen, NJ: Scarecrow Press, 1991.

Rye, Howard. "Liner Notes." *Viola McCoy: Complete Recorded Works in Chronological Order: Volume 1, 1923*. Document Records, 1996.

———. "Viola McCoy." *Oxford Music Online*. Available online at http://www.oxfordmusiconline.com:80/subscriber/article/grove/music/J637000.

Salmon, Nina. "Anne Spencer (1882–1975)." *Encyclopedia Virginia*. Available online at www.encyclopediavirginia.org /Spencer_Anne_1882-1975.

Sampson, Henry T. *Blacks in Blackface: A Source Book on Black Musical Shows*. Metuchen, NJ: Scarecrow Press, 1980.

Sandford, Ann. "Guestwords: Rescuing Ernestine Rose." *East Hampton Star*, March 7, 2012. Available online at http://easthamptonstar.com/Opinion/2012307/GUESTWORDS -Rescuing-Ernestine-Rose.

"Selena Sloan Butler Papers." *Auburn Avenue Research Library on African American Culture and History*. Available online at http://aafa.galileo.usg.edu/aafa/view?docId=ead/ aarl09-002-ead.xml;query=;brand=default.

Shack, William A. *Harlem in Montmartre: A Paris Jazz Story between the Great Wars*. Berkeley: University of California Press, 2001.

Shafer, Yvonne. "Eulalie Spence." *American Women Playwrights, 1900-1950*. New York: Lang, 1997.

Shaheen, Aaron. *Androgynous Democracy: Modern American Literature and the Dual-sexed Body Politic*. Knoxville: University of Tennessee Press, 2010, 124-134.

Shaw, Malcolm. "Ain't Gonna Settle Down: The Pioneering Blues of Mary Stafford and Edith Wilson." *Rustbooks*, July 13, 2010. Available online at http://www.rustbooks.com/ reviews/?p=11.

Sherman, Joan R. *African American Poetry: An Anthology*. Urbana: University of Illinois Press, 1992.

Shirley, Wayne. "Porgy and Bess." *Quarterly Journal of the Library of Congress* 31, no. 2 (April 1974): 97–107. Available online at EBSCOhost, http://152.12.30.4:2048/login?url=http:// search.ebscohost.com/login.aspx?direct=true&db=mzh&AN=1974111031&site=ehost-live.

Simkin, John. "Crystal Eastman." *Spartacus Educational*. Available online at www.spartacus.schoolnet.co.uk/USAWeastman.htm.

Simmons, Martha, and Frank A. Thomas, eds. *Preaching with Sacred Fire: An Anthology of African American Sermons, 1750 to the Present*. New York: W. W. Norton & Co., 2010.

Smethurts, James Edward. *The New Red Negro: The Literary Left and African American Poetry, 1930–1946*. Oxford, UK: Oxford University Press, 1999.

Smith, Jessie Carney. *Black Firsts: 4,000 Ground-Breaking and Pioneering Historical Events*, 3rd ed. Detroit, MI: Visible Ink Press, 2012.

———, ed. *Notable Black American Women*. Detroit, MI: Gale Research, 1992.

———, ed. *Notable Black American Women: Book II*. Detroit, MI: Gale Research, 1996.

———, ed. *Notable Black American Women: Book III*. Detroit, MI: Thomson Gale, 2003.

Smith, Katharine Capshaw. "Bessie Woodson Yancey, African American Poet and Social Critic." *Appalachian Heritage* 36, no. 3 (Summer 2008): 73–77.

———. *Children's Literature of the Harlem Renaissance*. Bloomington: Indiana University Press, 2006.

Smith, Ray. "Notes." *Armand Piron's New Orleans Orchestra*. Azure, 1924.

Southern, Eileen. *The Music of Black Americans: A History*. New York: W. W. Norton & Co., 1997.

———, ed. *Biographical Dictionary of Afro-American and African Musicians*. Westport, CT: Greenwood, 1982.

Spencer, Anne Howard, and Shaun Spencer-Hester. *Anne Spencer House and Garden Museum*. Available online at www.annespencermuseum.com.

Spiering, Julia J. "Waters, Ethel." *Pennsylvania Center for the Book*. Available online at http://pabook.libraries.psu.edu/palitmap/bios/Waters_Ethel.html.

Stephens, Judith L., ed. *The Plays of Georgia Douglas Johnson: From the New Negro Renaissance to the Civil Rights Movement*. Urbana: University of Illinois Press, 2007.

Stewart-Baxter, Derrick. *Ma Rainey and the Classic Blues Singers*. New York: Stein and Day, 1970.

Story, Rosalyn M. *And So I Sing: African American Divas of Opera and Concert*. New York: Warner Books, 1990.

Stratford, Mary E. "Make a 'Racket' of Your Illness." *Afro-American* (Baltimore, MD), July 24, 1954, p. 12.

Sturgill, Erika Quesenbery. "Sarah Collins Fernandis: Pioneering Social Worker from Port Deposit." *Cecildaily.com*, February 10, 2013. Available online at http://www.cecildaily.com/our_cecil/article_46b93b2c-7341-11e2-b1e4-001a4bcf887a.html?mode=jqm.

Taitt, John. *The Souvenir of Negro Progress, Chicago, 1779–1925*. Chicago: De Sable Association, 1925.

Talbott, I. D. "Duke," and Charles M. Murphy. "Minnie Buckingham Harper." *West Virginia Encyclopedia*. Available online at www.wvencyclopedia.orgarticles/259.

Tarry, Ellen, and Nellie McKay. *The Third Door: The Autobiography of an American Negro Woman*. Tuscaloosa: University of Alabama Press, 1992.

Tate, Claudia. "Intro." *The Selected Works of Georgia Douglas Johnson*. New York: G. K. Hall & Co., 1997.

Terrell, Mary Church. *A Colored Woman in a White World*. Foreword by Debra Newman Ham. New York: Humanity Books, 2005.

"Thelma Myrtle Duncan (Brown)." *DCLibrary.org*, 2003. Available online at http://029c28c.netsolhost.com/blkren/bios/duncantm.html.

Thompson, Clara Ann, J. Pauline Smith, and Mazie Earhart Clark. *Voices in the Poetic Tradition*. Boston: G. K. Hall & Co., 1996.

Thompson, Robert Dee. *A Socio-biography of Shirley Graham-Du Bois: A Life in the Struggle*. Santa Cruz: University of California Press, 1997.

Townsend, Chauncey. "Out of the Kitchen." *Crisis* 42 (January 1935): 15, 29.

Turner, Jo A. *Dusky Maidens: The Odyssey of the Early Black Dramatic Actress*. Westport, CT: Greenwood, 1992.

Valade, Roger M., III, ed. *The Schomburg Center Guide to Black Literature: From the Eighteenth Century to the Present*. Detroit, MI: Gale Research, 1996.

Vann, Sonya. "The Early Harlem Musical Scene, from a 100-Year-Old's Perspective." *New York Times*, September 8, 1988. Available online at http://www.nytimes.com/1988/09/08/arts/the-early-harlem-musical-scene-from-a-100-year-old-s-perspective.html.

"Viola McCoy (1900–1956)." *Red Hot Jazz Archive*. Available online at http://www/redhotjazz.com/mccoy.html.

Walker, Margaret. *This Is My Century*. Athens: University of Georgia Press, 1989.

Walker-Hill, Helen. *From Spirituals to Symphonies: African American Women Composers and Their Music*. Westport, CT: Greenwood, 2002.

Wall, Cheryl. *Women of the Harlem Renaissance*. Bloomington: Indiana University Press, 1995.

Wallace-Sanders, Kimberly. *Mammy: A Century of Race, Gender, and Southern Memory*. Ann Arbor: University of Michigan Press, 2009.

Ware, Susan, and Stacy Lorraine, eds. *Notable American Women*, vol. 5. Cambridge, MA: Belknap, 2004.

"Week's Census. Died: Mrs. Aloise B. Epperson." *Jet* 4 (July 1953): 22.

West, Dorothy, Verner D. Mitchell, and Cynthia J. Davis. *Where the Wild Grape Grows: Selected Writings, 1930–1950*. Amherst: University of Massachusetts Press, 2005.

Wheatley, Christopher. *Dictionary of Literary Biography: Twentieth-Century American Dramatists*, 3rd series. Detroit, MI: Thomson Gale, 2001.

Wiggins, Bernice Love. *Tuneful Tales*. Maceo C. Dailey and Ruthe Winegarten, trans. Lubbock: Texas Tech University Press, 2002.

Wilkerson, Isabel. *The Warmth of Other Suns*. New York: Vintage, 2010.

Williams, Susan Millar. *A Devil and a Good Woman, Too: The Lives of Julia Peterkin*. Athens: University of Georgia Press, 1997.

Wilson, James F. *Bulldaggers, Pansies, and Chocolate Babies: Performance, Race, and Sexuality in the Harlem Renaissance*. Ann Arbor: University of Michigan Press, 2010.

Winer, Deborah Grace. *On the Sunny Side of the Street: The Life and Lyrics of Dorothy Fields*. New York: Schirmer Books, 1997.

Wintz, Carl. *Black Culture and the Harlem Renaissance*. Houston, TX: Rice University Press, 1988.

Wintz, Cary D., and Paul Finkelman, eds. *Encyclopedia of the Harlem Renaissance*. 2 vols. New York: Routledge, 2004.

Wirth, Thomas H., ed. *Gay Rebel of the Harlem Renaissance: Selections from the Work of Richard Bruce Nugent*. Durham, NC: Duke University Press, 2002.

"Women Evangelists: Ida Bell Robinson (1891–1946." *Spu.edu*. Available online at http://myhome.spu.edu/popep/profiles/ida_bell_robinson.html.

Women of Change 2009. *Lincolnu.edu*. Available online at http://www.lincolnu.edu/web/library/women-of-change-2009.

"Women of the Harlem Renaissance." *Jim Cullum Riverwalk Jazz Collection*, 1990. Available online at http://riverwalkjazz.stanford.edu/program/women-harlem-renaissance-music-duke-ellington-james-p-johnson.

Women Poets. Ann Arbor, MI: University of Michigan Press, 1998.

Wynbush, Octavia. "Lady Blanche and the Christ." *Crisis* 44 (January 1937): 11.

Yancey, Bessie Woodson. *Echoes from the Hills: A Book of Poems*. Washington, DC: Associated Publishers, 1939.

Yanow, Scott. *Classic Jazz*. San Francisco, CA: Backbeat Books, 2001.

INDEX

Note: Page numbers in *italics* refer to photographs.

ABOUT THE EDITORS AND CONTRIBUTORS

EDITORS

Lean'tin L. Bracks is professor of English and African American literature at Fisk University in Nashville, Tennessee. She is an accomplished academician and currently serves as chair of the Department of Arts and Languages, discipline coordinator for English, and interim director of the W. E. B. Du Bois University Honors Program. Her scholarly interests include slave narratives, biographies, women of the African diaspora, and African American studies, all resulting in publications that reflect her breadth of interests. Dr. Bracks is author of *African American Almanac: 400 Years of Triumph, Courage, and Excellence* (2013) and *Writings on Black Women of the Diaspora: History, Language, and Identity* (1997), as well as editor of the university text *The Black Arts Movement of the 1960s* (2003) and an autobiographical essay in *Children of the Changing South: Accounts of Growing Up During and After Integration* (2012). As editor and contributor to scholarly and cultural resources, her contributions include pieces in the books *Freedom Facts and Firsts: 400 Years of the African American Civil Rights Experience* (2009), *African American National Biography* (2008), *Encyclopedia of African American Popular Culture* (2011), *African American Almanac*, 11th ed. (2010), *Notable Black American Men* (1999), and *Contemporary African American Novelists: A Bio-Bibliographical Critical Sourcebook* (1999), along with writings in the scholarly journals *Black Scholar* and *Nineteenth-Century Prose*. In addition to receiving an honorary degree from her undergraduate institution, Kenyon College, in Gambier, Ohio, Bracks has been recognized by her peers with Outstanding Teaching Awards in the Humanities and the Excellence in Service Award for her many administrative roles.

Jessie Carney Smith is dean of the library and William and Camille Cosby Professor in the Humanities at Fisk University in Nashville, Tennessee. A noted scholar, educator, and librarian, she has written extensively on African American biography, culture, and librarianship, producing several award-winning works. The long list of writings she has produced or edited include *Black Academic Libraries and Research Collections* (1977); *Ethnic Genealogy* (1983); *African American Almanac*, 8th ed. (2000); *Notable Black American Women* (1992); *Notable Black American Women: Book II* (1996); *Notable Black American Women: Book III* (2003); *Notable Black American Men* (1999); *Notable Black American Men: Book II* (2007); *Encyclopedia of African American Business* (2006); *Encyclopedia of African American Popular Culture* (2011); *Black Firsts: 4,000 Ground-Breaking and Pioneering Historical Events*, 3rd ed. (2013); and *The Handy African American History Answer Book* (2014). Dr. Smith is also co-editor (with Linda T. Wynn) of *Freedom Facts and Firsts: 400 Years of the African American Civil Rights Experience* (2009). In addition, she writes the introduction for the Who's Who among African Americans series.

CONTRIBUTORS

Glenda Marie Alvin is assistant director for Collection Management at the Brown-Daniel Library at Tennessee State University in Nashville. In addition to her master's degree in library service, she has a master's degree in U.S. history prior to 1877. Alvin has published biographies in the *Encyclopedia of African American Business* (2006), *Notable Black American Men: Book II* (2007), and the *Encyclopedia of African American Popular Culture* (2011). She has also published articles in library periodicals and currently writes a column, "Collection Management Matters," for the journal *Against the Grain*.

Sharon D. Brooks is a librarian in media services at the Frederick Douglass Library at the University of Maryland Eastern Shore in Princess Anne, Maryland. She has contributed articles to the *Encyclopedia of African American Business* (2006), *Notable Black American Men: Book II* (2007), and the *Encyclopedia of African American Popular Culture* (2011).

Jemima D. Buchanan is a high school English teacher in Baltimore City. She has previously contributed to the *Encyclopedia of African American Popular Culture* (2011) and is currently pursuing her doctoral degree in the Department of English at Morgan State University in Baltimore, Maryland.

Amanda J. Carter is a recent graduate and processing archivist who was awarded an archival assistantship at the Modern Political Archives of the Howard H. Baker Jr. Center for Public Policy in Knoxville, Tennessee, before receiving an IMLS archival fellowship at the John Hope and Aurelia E. Franklin Library at Fisk University in Nashville, Tennessee. Carter is also an avid researcher and writer with a passion for tracing and weaving previously overlooked minority and women's histories into the broader history of our culture.

Linda M. Carter is associate professor of English at Morgan State University in Baltimore, Maryland. She is coeditor of *Humanities in the Ancient and Pre-Modern World: An Africana Emphasis*, 3rd ed. (2009); *Humanities in the Modern World: An Africana Emphasis*, 2nd ed. (2001); *Images of the Black Male in Literature and Film: Essays and Criticism* (1994); and *James Baldwin: In Memoriam* (1992). Dr. Carter has written more than one hundred articles on African American literature and culture that have appeared in various journals and references.

Adenike Marie Davidson is professor of English and gender studies and department chairperson of English and foreign languages at Delaware State University in Dover. She is author of *The Black Novel: Imagining Homeplaces in Early Africa American Literature* (2008) and has written articles about gender in African American literature. Her current research focuses on negritude, the New Negro Movement, and gender.

Rebecca S. Dixon is associate professor of English and women's studies and coordinator of the Women's Studies Program at Tennessee State University in Nashville. Her areas of research are postcolonial studies, African diasporic literature, and gender studies. One of Dr. Dixon's most recent publications is "Slow Your Roll(le), You Ain't Going No Where, Girl: The Conflicted Space of Freedom in African American Women's Literary Tradition" (2012). Her current research is on black British author Caryl Phillips.

De Witt S. Dykes Jr. teaches African American history, American history, history of African American women, history of the Civil Rights Movement, African American urbanization, history of American families, and history of American cities at Oakland University in Rochester, Michigan. He has published numerous biographical articles in reference books and several book chapters. Dr. Dykes has been both an active member and officer in national, state, and local historical and genealogical societies.

Elizabeth Sandidge Evans is reference and government documents librarian at the William R. and Norma B. Harvey Library at Hampton University in Hampton, Virginia. She is a contributor to the *Encyclopedia of African American Business* (2006), *Notable Black American Men: Book II* (2007), and the *Encyclopedia of African American Popular Culture* (2011).

Marie Garrett has served as librarian at Johnson Bible College, Milligan College, and the University of Tennessee. In retirement, she copyedits books for the University of Tennessee Libraries' Newfound Press. In addition to professional articles, Garrett has written biographical essays for *Notable Black American Women, Notable Black*

American Men, the *Encyclopedia of African American Business*, the *Encyclopedia of Appalachia*, and the *Encyclopedia of African American Popular Culture*.

Angela M. Gooden is director of the Community Engagement Center in the Division of Diversity and Community Engagement at the University of Texas at Austin. She has contributed articles to the *Encyclopedia of African American Popular Culture* (2011).

Delano Greenidge-Copprue is professor of humanities at the Manhattan School of Music in New York City. He has written three books and hundreds of scholarly articles and reviews on all aspects of popular culture, the arts, and history. His next book will include a novel on baseball and a critical study of Duke Ellington's Sacred Concerts.

Robert L. Hall served as curator of the Museum at Fisk University in Nashville, Tennessee, before moving to the Smithsonian's Anacostia Community Museum, where he served as associate director of education until his recent retirement. Hall has created museum and city tours on African American art and lectured on art. He was also curator of the Anacostia Community Museum's art exhibitions. These included *A Creative Profile: Artists of the East Bank*; *On Their Own: Selected Works by Self-Taught African American Artists*; *The Art of Charles Smith*; *The Quilt*; *In Celebration of Black Men*; *New Visions: Emerging Trends in African American Art*; and *Anacostia Museum Collects: The Art of James A. Porter*.

Debra Newman Ham is professor of history at Morgan State University in Baltimore, Maryland. She specializes in African Americans, the African diaspora, and public history. Dr. Ham previously worked as an archivist, manuscript historian, and African American history specialist at the National Archives and the Library of Congress. Her publications include *Black History: A Guide to Civilian Records in the National Archives* (1984) and *The African American Mosaic: A Library of Congress Resource Guide for the Study of Black History and Culture* (1993). She is also chief curator of an online Library of Congress exhibit entitled *The African American Odyssey: Quest for Full Citizenship* (1998) and an exhibit catalog of the same name (1998).

Gloria Hamilton is head of Acquisitions and Rapid Cataloging at the University of Chicago Library. She has contributed to the *Encyclopedia of African American Business* (2006), *Notable Black American Men: Book II* (2007), and the *Encyclopedia of African American Popular Culture* (2011).

Helen R. Houston is a retired professor of English at Tennessee State University in Nashville. Her publications include *The Afro-American Novel, 1965–1975: A Descriptive Bibliography of Primary and Secondary Material* (1977) and articles in the *Encyclopedia of African American Business* (2006), *Freedom Facts and Firsts: 400 Years of the African American Civil Rights Experience* (2009), *Notable Black*

American Women (1992), *Notable Black American Women: Book II* (1996), *Notable Black American Men* (1999), the *Encyclopedia of African American Popular Culture* (2011), and the *Oxford Companion to African American Literature*.

Aisha M. Johnson is special collections librarian at the John Hope and Aurelia E. Franklin Library at Fisk University in Nashville, Tennessee. She has investigated diversity needs in the field of library and information science, which sparked her commitment to improving the field's diversity needs and conditions of historically black college and university (HBCU) archives. Johnson is currently a Ph.D. candidate in information studies at Florida State University's School of Information, where she examines southern public library history of African Americans.

Gladys L. Knight is an independent scholar and freelance writer. She is author of *Icons of African American Protest: Trailblazing Activists of the Civil Rights Movement* (2008); *Female Action Heroes: A Guide to Women in Comics, Video Games, Film, and Television* (2010); and the forthcoming *Pop Cult Places: Places in American Popular Culture*.

Sarah-Anne Leverette is a graduate student in special education at Norfolk State University in Virginia. She coached the Hampton University Freddye T. Davy Honors College debate team to first place in 2011, at the National Association of African American Honors Programs' Conference. She also coaches the Hampton University Honda Campus All-Star Challenge team.

Cheryl E. Mango-Ambrose is a doctoral student in history and research assistant at Morgan State University in Baltimore, Maryland. She is also a history instructor at the Community College of Baltimore County. Her major research areas are African American, African diasporan, and twentieth-century U.S. history, with special attention to African American religion and historically black college and university (HBCU) history. Mango-Ambrose's dissertation research focuses on black landownership in antebellum America.

Vivian Martin is a retired assistant professor from Motlow State Community College in Tullahoma, Tennessee; a licensed attorney in New York; and an active layperson in the United Methodist Church. She has studied black church life for more than thirty years and previously published articles about the black church.

Joy A. McDonald is assistant professor in the Scripps Howard School of Journalism and Communications at Hampton University in Hampton, Virginia. She has been a contributor to the *Encyclopedia of African American History, 1896–2006* (2009), the *Encyclopedia of African American Popular Culture* (2011), and *Great Lives from History: Asian Americans and Pacific Islanders* (2011). In 2013, she cowrote an article for *Editor and Publisher* entitled "Daily Newspaper Advertising in the 21st Century." Her current area of interest is media ethics and entrepreneurship in journalism.

Soncerey L. Montgomery is associate professor in the Department of Mass Communications and interim director of the Honors Program at Winston-Salem State University in Winston-Salem, North Carolina. She is also author of *The Heart of a Student: Success Principles for College Students* (2011).

Fletcher F. Moon is associate professor and head reference librarian at Tennessee State University in Nashville. He has previously contributed writings to several reference works, including the *Encyclopedia of African American Business* (2006), *Notable Black American Men: Book II* (2007), *Freedom Facts and Firsts: 400 Years of the African American Civil Rights Experience* (2009), and the *Encyclopedia of African American Popular Culture* (2011), and edited a variety of book projects and online publications. Moon is also an accomplished musician and ordained minister and has worked professionally in music, television production, advertising/public relations, and ministry.

Jewell B. Parham is professor of black arts and literature, children's literature, and freshman composition in the Department of Languages, Literature, and Philosophy in the School of Liberal Arts at Tennessee State University in Nashville. She has written eclectic profiles and topics for publication. Some of these include profiles for *Notable Black American Men* (1999), *Notable Black American Men: Book II* (2007), and the *Encyclopedia of African American Popular Culture* (2011). Other publications include such topics as "National Black Arts Festival," "National Black Theater Festival," and "racial profiling" in the *Encyclopedia of African American Popular Culture*. Parham has also written an electronic publication, "Virtual Learning for Writing the Research Paper" (2007).

Andrea Patterson-Masuka is assistant professor in the Department of Mass Communications at Winston-Salem State University in Winston-Salem, North Carolina. She has coedited two customized communication textbooks and a cultural reader, authored four book chapters, and coauthored a journal article. In addition, Patterson-Masuka has presented at more than sixteen scholarly conferences. Her primary areas of research are the basic communication course, communication education, communication pedagogy, and critical intercultural communication.

Sheila R. Peters is associate professor of psychology at Fisk University in Nashville, Tennessee, and former interim director of the Race Relations Institute at Fisk. She is an author and regional and national presenter on issues of race, ethnicity, and cultural competence. Peters has been a contributor to the *Encyclopedia of African American Popular Culture* and the *Encyclopedia of Race, Ethnicity, and Society*, as well as a coauthor of "Location, Location, Location: Residential Segregation and Wealth Disparity," in *Race and Wealth Disparities: A Multidisciplinary Discourse* (2008). Some of her presentations on cultural issues include "Critical Dialogues: Building and Sustaining Diversity in the Academy," "The Flight of the Black Athlete," and "Building a Covenant Community."

Marsha M. Price is administrative specialist to the director of the Morgan State University Memorial Chapel in Baltimore, Maryland. She is currently pursuing her master's degree in English (creative writing) at Morgan State University in Baltimore, Maryland. She previously served as a proofreader for the university's student newspaper, the *Spokesman*, and as a staff writer for Mount Pleasant Church and Ministries' newsletter, the *Messenger*.

Myron T. Strong is instructor of sociology at the Community College of Baltimore County in Catonsville, Maryland. Dr. Strong's specialties are race, masculinity, social relationships, and ideology. He is author of academic articles and book chapters about masculinity, pop culture, race, ideology, family, and chemistry in numerous journals and texts. These include *Contemporary Perspectives in Family Research*; *Social Problems: A Case Study Approach*, 3rd ed. (2004); the *Encyclopedia of African American Popular Culture* (2011); *Journal of Pyrotechnics*; *Postcolonial Composition Pedagogy: Using Culture of Marginalized Students to Teach English Composition*; and *Letters from Young Activists: Today's Rebels Speak Out* (2005).

Christopher Allen Varlack is lecturer in the Department of English and Language Arts at Morgan State University in Baltimore, Maryland. His research interests include nineteenth- and twentieth-century American literature, with an emphasis on race. He is author of several articles on gender, race, and politics that have appeared in such multiauthored reference works as *Critical Insights: Zora Neale Hurston* (2013), *Defining Documents in American History: Manifest Destiny and the New Nation* (2013), and *Critical Insights: The Slave Narrative* (2014). Varlack's current research is focused on the alternative intellectual strategies of the Harlem Renaissance intelligentsia.

Tanya E. Walker is assistant Professor of English at Winston-Salem State University in Winston-Salem, North Carolina, where she teaches American literature, African American literature, and dramatic studies courses. Dr. Walker's research areas include African American women's drama, black feminist criticism, and black speculative fiction. Her current research project focuses on depictions of sexual violence in contemporary African American women's drama.

Leland Ware holds the title Louis L. Redding Chair and Professor of Law and Public Policy at the University of Delaware. He has also served as a trial attorney with the U.S. Department of Justice in Washington, D.C. Ware is coauthor (with Robert Cottrol and Raymond Diamond) of *Brown v. Board of Education: Caste, Culture, and the Constitution* (2003). His most recent book, *Choosing Equality: Essays and Narratives on the Desegregation Experience* (coedited with Robert L. Hayman, with a foreword by Vice President Joe Biden), was published in 2009.

Faye P. Watkins is dean of University Libraries at Florida Agricultural and Mechanical University in Tallahassee, Florida. She has worked in academic libraries for fourteen years. Her primary areas of interest are the development of information literacy skills and the promotion of lifelong enjoyment of learning and reading.

Anthony Williams is associate professor of music and university organist at Fisk University in Nashville, Tennessee. He previously served as director of the Fisk Jubilee Singers. Dr. Williams's research interests include American music, jazz, and organ music written by black composers. His doctoral dissertation focuses on black composer John W. Work III. Active as a concert organist, he has performed extensively throughout the United States.

Linda T. Wynn is assistant director for State Programs at the Tennessee Historical Commission and a member of the faculty at Fisk University in Nashville, Tennessee, where she teaches in the Department of History and Political Science. She coedited (with Jessie Carney Smith) *Freedom Facts and Firsts: 400 Years of the African American Civil Rights Experience* (2009) and (with Bobby L. Lovett) *Profiles of African Americans in Tennessee* (1996). Wynn also edited *Journey to Our Past: A Guide to African American Markers in Tennessee* (1999). She has contributed to *The History of African Americans in Tennessee: Trials and Triumphs* and *Tennessee Women: Their Lives and Times*, as well as book reviews to *Tennessee Historical Quarterly*.